THE REAL GIANTS
OF SOCCER COACHING

INSIGHTS AND WISDOM FROM THE GAME'S GREATEST COACHES

JOSH FAGA

Meyer & Meyer Sport

British Library Cataloguing in Publication Data
A catalogue record for this book is available from the British Library

The Real Giants of Soccer Coaching
Maidenhead: Meyer & Meyer Sport (UK) Ltd., 2018
ISBN: 978-1-78255-130-0

Aachen, Auckland, Beirut, Cairo, Cape Town, Dubai, Hägendorf, Hong Kong, Indianapolis, Manila, New Delhi, Singapore, Sydney, Tehran, Vienna

 Member of the World Sports Publishers' Association (WSPA)
Printed by Print Consult GmbH, Munich, Germany

ISBN: 978-1-78255-130-0
Email: info@m-m-sports.com
www.m-m-sports.com

CONTENTS

1 Process-Oriented Coaching   20
Jay Martin

Why process beats outcome — Why individual accolades are unimportant — Working hard on you — Never ignore the importance of training the brain — How to be a better coach — What your values tell you about your coaching personality

2 Player-Centered Coaching   28
Rene Meulensteen

You're not a real coach until you get fired — The player jigsaw puzzle as the key to youth development — Letting the players make the decisions — Why you should always add something to your players' game, but never change it — Success doesn't come for free

3 Transitioning From Player to Coach   40
Neil Jones

You might make a better coach than a player — The Canvas Strategy — Why getting to know your players makes it easier to coach them — Soccer always has a winner and a loser — How a clock can influence the realism of your training

4 From Assistant to Head Coach and Back Again   50
Mario Sanchez

The coach that knows why will beat the coach that knows how — Player-centered coaching versus athlete-centered coaching — What comedians can teach us about honing our craft — What Bill Belichick can teach you about being a good assistant coach — Slowly, slowly — The devil is in the details

development — How Brazilians organize tryouts — But coach, we already did this — Dennis Bergkamp coaching 10-year-olds — The spotlight is for the players

11 Coaching the Individual in a Team   136
Michael Beale

Coach someone the way you would like to be coached — Are you a brick wall or a sponge — There are 11 "I"s in a team — Changing the hat of a team — Forward thinking, forward passing, forward running — How to organize a defense — You can go over, around, or through, but you have to choose — Positional small-sided games — Why my best coach was a schoolteacher that knew nothing about soccer

12 Producing Professional Players   156
Darren Sawatzky

You don't get to say "We lost, but we played pretty" — We climb ladders one rung at a time — Get rid of the 9-day coaching courses, coach educators need to have their feet on the ground, in the trenches, helping coaches every day — French training methodology

13 Developing Youth Players   164
Marc Nicholls

The importance of brutally honest feedback — Bio-banding — Playing players down an age group — Where do you prioritize winning — There is more than one way to skin a cat

14 Sports Science and Physical Training   176
Jon Goodman

Why your hardest moments can reveal your true self — The darker side of professional soccer — Soccer psychology — The birth and death of the Nike SPARQ program — The Gold Mine Effect and how the Nike Academy disrupted academy soccer

15 Grassroots Coaching   184
Sam Snow

Coaching coaches how to coach — Where do you want your youth players to be at 15, at 25, at 35 — What's the rush in youth development — Why you shouldn't mistake

21 Applying Characteristics of a Playground to Youth Soccer   270
Jonathan Henderson

A performance playground — What a skate park can teach us about how kids learn — Random practice versus blocked practice — How to get your kids to play more street soccer — What would kids do if a coach wasn't there — We are doing our kids a disservice

22 Soccer Tactics and Training Methodology   278
Albert Rude

The nine soccer structures — The importance of culture in building a game model — To understand the future, we must understand the past — Win one game, get two more — If you want big rewards, they come with big risks

23 Improving Player Communication in Soccer   292
Gerard Jones

Game calls — The biggest communication mistakes that coaches make — We want the knowledge on the field, not the sideline — How to get your players to talk more than you

24 Possession and Scoring Tactics   298
Robin Russell

How data can change the way you train finishing — Why national teams are always worse than club teams — Why scoring the first goal gives your team a 95% chance of not losing — In-swingers, out-swingers, and the reasons why set plays may be more important than you think

25 Youth Development in Soccer   308
Tab Ramos

Stop giving yourself so much credit — You're not a good coach just because you won — Stop talking so much — What your player's faces can tell you about your coaching ability — How to be critical of your own training sessions — Learning every single day — Why you should be optimistic about youth development in the United States

26 Game-Based Decision-Making and Player Development   316
Mike Muñoz

It is non-negotiable to outwork the opponent — Technical training that actually transfers — How to create an environment built on feedback from your peers to improve your coaching — Always have your windows and your doors open

27 The Science of Developing Better Players   324
John Kessel

Why facts don't change people's minds — You don't coach soccer, you coach people — How did you learn to ride a bike — Stop doing drills — Why your players should coach other players — What free-throw shooting can teach you about practicing set pieces more effectively — At the earliest ages of youth soccer, the worst teams win — What Stephen Curry can teach you about producing professional players

28 Game-Like Practice and How Kids Learn   338
Todd Beane

Doing a start-up with Steve Jobs — How to think like Johan Cruyff — If it's not fun, then why are we doing it — Most of the training in the US is crap — Messi doesn't have 50 moves — It wasn't a move, but a solution — Quizas — How a bushel of apples can make you a better coach — What soccer coaches and doctors that used bloodletting have in common — A Montessori school for soccer — The consortium of coaches — How to coach a rondo — Cognition versus competence: missing the boat in youth development

29 Positional Play Training   354
Adin Osmanbasic

The essence of positional play — Finding the free man — Why do teams play a 1-4-3-3 — What happens after we find the free man — How to defend a Pep Guardiola team — The six areas of defensive organization — Why training with goals may be unnecessary — What Pep Guardiola and Antonio Conte have in common, and how they are different from Thomas Tuchel and Jurgen Klopp

30 Coaching Authentically   372
Anson Dorrance

Coaching is a thankless profession — Most people think they are competitive, but I am here to tell them that they aren't — The misapplication of the competitive cauldron — Rules were meant to be broken — Why we are all wrong about substitution

PREFACE

So, why a book? Over 100 podcasts means over 100 hours of recorded insights, practicums, and stories from over 100 coaches. Unfortunately, although our technologically advanced world is quick to pay attention, it is even quicker to forget. The trends of today become the stories of tomorrow. Our world, especially the coaching world, is becoming more and more enthralled with the novel. Our first podcast episode was recorded in 2015 and what Bobby talked about is just as true now as it was then. So, this book will put all of the insights and ideas I have learned in the last three years into one easy-to-access text.

This book is going to draw from the many threads discussed in the 100+ episodes we have done at the *Just Kickin' It* podcast. I am going to serve as the co-author of this book. The other co-authors are the many guests referenced and mentioned in this book. They are the true authors. They are the giants that were courteous enough to allow me to stand atop their shoulders to see just a little bit farther above the clouds. They are the true artists. I am simply supplying them with a canvas.

My hope is that the reader has in his or her hands a tome that is full of practical knowledge from some of the world's best soccer coaches. The tips, insights, stories, and ideas from each of these coaches will equip you, as the reader and a coach, with many "change the environment" moments. No longer will you have to guess or react emotionally to situations because in your hand you have access to the experience and knowledge of coaches like Rene Meulensteen, Anson Dorrance, and Jay Martin. They say that people are more likely to be persuaded by what they hear themselves say; my hope is that, as you read this book, these thoughts, experiences, and ideas become your own.

I should also mention that I didn't write 100 chapters. To do so, would be to write a book that is over 1,000 pages. I don't think coaches are interested in reading the *War and Peace* of soccer, no matter how insightful and interesting it is. I will continue to write behind the scenes and reveal the insights from the many recorded, and non-recorded, conversations that I have. For now, we start with this elite group of coaches that I have compiled after many listens, and re-listens, of every single episode that we have done.

PROLOGUE

Why you should always value ability over success — What Stephen King can teach us about expectations

—How to read this book

In the mid-2000s, a London newspaper conducted a fabulous study to test the role of celebrity in sustaining success. Using plagiarism for the sake of science, the editors of the *Sunday Times* submitted potential manuscripts to book publishers that copied the opening chapters of two books that had recently won the Booker Prize, the most prestigious award an author could hope to achieve, which solidifies a book's place in literary history. Logic would assume that the publishers would have either received the submitted manuscripts with overwhelming enthusiasm and praise, or with extreme skepticism. In other words, the publishing companies would either be thanking their lucky stars for the bestseller that just came across their desk, or they would be calling the authorities and citing the submitted manuscripts for plagiarism. But something else happened entirely. The publishing agents treated the submissions as they would any other submission by an aspiring author—they passed.

One of the books was *In a Free State* by V.S. Naipaul, which—I will reiterate—literally won the Booker Prize. One of the publishing agent's response to the submission read, "It was quite original. In the end though I'm afraid we just weren't quite enthusiastic enough to be able to offer to take things further." This would be akin to professional clubs turning down Lionel Messi on a trial saying, "There is definitely some potential there, but we don't feel that you can impact our club at this specific time." Ludicrous! Why did these publishing agents turn down one of the best-selling books of all time? For the same reason that Stephen King couldn't sell a book under the pseudonym Richard Bachman.

In the 1970s, Stephen King became worried that the public wouldn't accept his books at the same pace that he wanted to write them. He figured that a book a year would be a good enough pace for his fans, but not for his brain. King's solution was to write books under the pseudonym Richard Bachman. This would allow King to continue writing at his preferred frequency, but without bombarding the public with multiple Stephen King books every year. What happened? Well, Stephen King doesn't sell as well when he isn't Stephen King. Obviously, once word got out that Stephen King was writing under a pseudonym, the books became best sellers, but under the name Richard Bachman they were total busts. How could that be? How could the same book meet two entirely different outcomes simply because of the name of the author? The reason is because success and ability are not correlated.

Leonard Mlodinow, author of *The Drunkard's Walk,* explored the role randomness plays in those who become successful and those who don't, allowing him to sum up the relationship between success and ability as a mysterious one.

> *"The cord that tethers ability to success is both loose and elastic. It is easy to see fine qualities in successful books and to see unpublished manuscripts as somehow lacking. It is easy to believe that ideas that worked were great ideas, the plans that succeeded were well designed, and that ideas and plans that did not were ill conceived. It is easy to make heroes out of the most successful and to glance with disdain at the least. But, ability does not guarantee achievement, nor is achievement proportional to ability. And so, it is important to always keep in mind the other term in the equation—the role of chance."*

Ability does not guarantee achievement, nor is achievement proportional to ability. Of course we should all know this to be true. Are we really going to assume that Justin Beiber is the most talented musician of his generation? In the 1960s, social psychologist Melvin Lerner studied the view society takes toward the poor in hopes of better understanding the negative attitude the downtrodden receive in modern society. One of Lerner's greatest findings was that people drastically overestimate the degree to which they can accurately determine someone's ability based on success. Mlodinow interpreted Lerner's research to mean that "we are inclined, that is, to see movie stars as more talented than aspiring movie stars and to think that the richest people in the world must also be the smartest." I am here to inform you that this is nothing more than a fallacy.

It is a common incorrect signaling of the brain that connects somebody's results with their abilities even when it is overwhelmingly incorrect. It is to no fault of our own, however. We cannot see a person's potential, or ability, only their results (e.g., wins and losses, total sales, salary). This leads us down a path of misjudgment where we believe that the results must reflect the ability of the person. Mlodinow again puts it into perspective, saying that "a lot of what happens to us—success in our careers, in our investments, and in our life decisions, both major and minor—is as much the result of random factors as it is from skill, preparedness, and hard work." The harsh truth is that we continuously fall victim to the power of expectations. When Stephen King writes a book, we *expect* it to be good. When Pep Guardiola runs a session, we *expect* it to be good. These expectations; however, delude our critical-thinking skills and keep us from identifying glaring flaws. In fact, an academic study looked at the influence a student's previous grades have on future grades. It turned out that teachers give higher grades to students deemed "excellent" than to students thought of as "weak," even when the homework submissions were identical. We must refrain from correlating success with ability. Just because a coach manages the best club in the country doesn't mean he has some god-like ability. In fact, the truth is that his ability is probably closer to yours and mine than any type of god.

Why did I spend the first few pages of this book talking about manuscripts, Stephen King, and randomness? Because it is important for you to understand that ability and success don't appear in a linear fashion. How many athletes have burst onto the scene as the next Michael Jordan or Leo Messi one season, only to plummet and fall off the face of the planet the very next season? Coaches, general managers, and fitness coaches are all vulnerable to randomness. The truth is that it is very difficult to know if someone is truly talented, or merely the lucky benefactor of being in the right place at the right time. This is important to understand because I have not profiled Pep Guardiola or Jose Mourinho in this book. I have profiled people that have worked with them, talked to them, and competed against them, but it is important that we don't allow the results to paint the pictures in our head about them as coaches. The truth is that we simply don't know if they are truly genius, merely lucky, or a combination of the two. We can venture to guess—and I would lean towards the opinion that they are truly gifted and talented managers—but in this book I have profiled people that I have met, worked with, had conversations with, and learned from. These are people that have ability. But, they are far from perfect. In other words, they are just like you and me. Unfortunately, the only way to know if someone has ability is to look away from the scoreboard. A lot of managers have won big games and trophies due more to the ability of their players, front office, fixture schedule, and other contributing circumstances than their own skill. Therefore, to truly identify someone's ability you have to spend time watching them hone their craft. To know how good a coach is you have to see them and evaluate them in their element Monday through Friday, not just on Saturdays. I have profiled coaches in this book that have won World Cups, Champions Leagues, U20 Championships, and NCAA National Titles, but that is the last reason they are in this book. They are in this book because I have seen them in their element. I have seen them get the most out of their players. I have seen them run a session. These coaches are deserving of the name *giants* because they have true ability. And just as authors should be judged by their writing and not their book sales, so too should coaches be judged more by their abilities than by their success.

I shared a laugh earlier today with a friend of mine over the word *peruse*. Apparently, we had been using the word incorrectly our entire lives. I was under the impression that to peruse was to lightly skim, or gloss over. In actuallity, to peruse is to read carefully, closely, and under extreme inspection. And for the next 300 pages that is exactly what I want you to do—peruse. Please don't read something a coach says in this book and immediately agree with it, adopt it, or sing it as gospel. To read this book correctly would be to read something a coach says and think about it, evaluate it, reflect on it, and then decide if it is useful or not. My hope is that you can peruse this text and determine what is objective and what is subjective. What is fact and what is opinion. This book includes insights from coaches that have won FIFA World Cups, NCAA National Championships, and even the Champions League, but if we know that success and ability are antagonistic toward one another, then we shouldn't let those facts influence our perception of the information included in this book.

Mark Haddon, the English novelist, once said that, "reading is a conversation. All books talk, but a good book listens as well." If you read this book correctly, and if I wrote it properly, that is how it should feel. This isn't a book filled with coaches telling you right from wrong. This is a book filled with coaches that have had some success, probably even more failure, and along the way learned something unique about this great game we all love. This is my attempt to share those unique somethings.

INTRODUCTION

"A single conversation across the table with a wise man is better than ten years mere study of books."

—Henry Wadsworth Longfellow

It all started in the spring of 2015 when Brian Shrum, the women's soccer associate head coach at Duquesne University (where I am the men's soccer assistant coach) said, "Hey, is it hard to start a podcast?" At the time, I thought that was a fairly novel idea, not realizing that a couple years later having a podcast would be as commonplace as having a driver's license. Fortunately for Brian, I had tried to start a podcast a few months earlier, with no success, but at least I had some experience with the matter. Fast forward about a week and we were stumbling, mumbling, and stuttering our way through our first episode with a close friend of ours, Bobby Sepesy, the head strength and conditioning coach at California University in Pennsylvania. And just like that the *Just Kickin' It* podcast was born.

Kaizen is a Japanese philosophy of continuous improvement, and when you are as bad as we were at interviewing people you have no choice but to live by it. Little by little we started to improve and one episode turned into two, which turned into four, and here I am writing this book as we approach 100 episodes. It never really dawned on me that this podcast would result in a book until I was listening to our very first episode with Bobby again. We asked Bobby how he deals with a troublesome athlete; you know, an athlete that talks back or doesn't work as hard as he should—all the things coaches deal with eventually if you coach long enough. Bobby's response was so enlightening that I hit pause and walked around the office until I found someone that I could share what I just heard with. I appreciate our janitor, Roger, lending an ear so that I could share the moment with someone else, although I don't think he found it as enthralling as I did. Here was Bobby's response:

"I was eating dinner the other night and a fly kept flying by my plate. So, I started violently slapping and swinging at the fly hoping to get it to stop. And then I had this epiphany. The more I swung, the more the fly bothered me. And just then, I did the funniest thing. I simply grabbed my plate, sat up, and walked inside the house. And just like that, the fly wasn't a problem anymore. So, I guess, Josh, my answer is that sometimes we just need to change the environment for something—or someone—that was a problem to no longer continue to be one."

I hope that you can grasp how profound that story is. I can't tell you how many coaches I hear every day that complain about their athletes not doing this or not doing that. And every single time I hear Bobby in the back of my mind saying, "Change the environment."

Why did I tell you this story? Because I learned more from that one comment from Bobby than I had from reading the top 15 books on creating a culture, or the latest blog about motivating your athletes. The moment I heard that message from Bobby, I realized the power of conversation. I realized the purpose and mission of our podcast. There is a reason why the book begins with one of my favorite quotes and the mission statement of the podcast.

"A single conversation across the table with a wise man is better than ten years mere study of books."

It is unfortunate that the coaching world is often characterized by isolation and reticence. Many coaches allow the competitiveness of our sport to keep them from sharing their ideas, experiences, and fears with other coaches. How much more advanced would we be as a coaching community if, instead of hiding our fears and concerns about our processes, we celebrated them and shared them with others? That is what the podcast is about. It is about getting other coaches to sit down with us so that we can tell them our fears and ask them our questions and they can tell us theirs. It is a mini-Thanksgiving—absent the turkey and stuffing—full of insights and learning. Every podcast gives us a chance to learn how to be just a little bit better today than we were yesterday.

In a 1676 letter to his rival Robert Hooke, Isaac Newton wrote:

*"What Descartes did was a good step. You have added much in several ways, and especially in taking the colors of thin plates into philosophical consideration. If I have seen a little further, it is by standing **on the shoulders of giants**."*

I love that phrase. A common mistake that people make is assuming that people like Albert Einstein or Galileo were born brilliant and came to their famous findings by themselves. That's just not how it works. Pep Guardiola learned from Johan Cruyff, who learned from Rinus Michels, who learned from Jack Reynolds, ad infinitum. That eureka moment that we have all been told precedes the most famous findings, like electricity or television, doesn't really exist. There is no sudden moment of realization, or inspiration that breeds these massive discoveries. They come from years upon years of study, mentoring, and reading the great works of those that have come before us. And that is what I hope this book can be. I hope that it is an influential step in your pursuit of the eureka moment. Pep Guardiola is not a genius. He wasn't born with some innate ability and he didn't drink some omnipotent soccer coaching alchemy. He is someone that studied the work of Johan Cruyff, Rinus Michels, and those that came before them. Many describe him as a genius, but I would say that he is more of an innovator. He is someone that acknowledged the giants that came before him and, through hard work and arduous study, stands today atop their shoulders as one of soccer's greatest coaches.

My hope, my goal, is to have this book help you stand on the shoulders of over 30 of the best coaches I have had the pleasure of talking to. I have interviewed some of the best youth coaches, college coaches, professional coaches, educators, theorists, and analysts that this game has to offer. Don't be fooled into thinking that you can only learn from someone wearing a Manchester City or Bayern Munich logo on their shirt. This book is a collection of some of the brightest minds this game has to offer working everywhere from grassroots to national teams. No matter where you coach or what you aspire to, I know that by the time you finish reading this book, you will be able to see just a little bit farther than you did before.

CHAPTER 1

PROCESS-ORIENTED COACHING

JAY MARTIN

Jay Martin is the winningest coach in men's college soccer history with a total of 673 wins over 40 seasons at Ohio Wesleyan University. Jay also boasts a career winning percentage of 81%. In addition to being a college soccer coach, Jay is also a professor in Ohio Wesleyan's physical education department and writes for the NSCAA Journal. He has a PhD from The Ohio State University.

Why process beats outcome — Why individual accolades are unimportant — Working hard on you — Never ignore the importance of training the brain — How to be a better coach — What your values tell you about your coaching personality

Jay Martin is arguably the most successful and influential college soccer coach in the United States. However, you would never know it by talking to him. Jay is just as curious, just as driven, and just as humble as he was the day he won his first National Championship. Jay is also living proof that a great jockey doesn't always make a great horse. Jay played three sports growing up and oddly enough chose basketball as his main sport. In fact, Jay was able to turn his college basketball career at Springfield College into a professional career in Germany.

It was in Germany that Jay found his passion for the beautiful game, living in northern Munich where he was able to watch Bayern Munich training every single day. Jay certainly lived in Germany at the right time as I am sure a similar situation would not lend itself to anyone living in northern Munich today. A Bayern Munich session today would have a similar security presence to the Pope at the Vatican. If I tried to sneak into a Bayern Munich session today, Carlo Ancelotti would probably have me thrown out of Europe, let alone Germany. Nevertheless, a young basketball player from northeast Ohio suddenly found himself watching Franz Beckenbauer, Gerd Muller, Sepp Maier, and Georg Schwarzenbeck on a daily basis. Jay attended so many Bayern sessions that he was nearly considered part of the staff.

They say opportunity begets opportunity and Jay eventually met and established a relationship with Helmut Schon, the head coach of the German National Team that won the World Cup in 1974. Jay had completely forgotten about shooting hoops and was fully immersed in the German soccer culture. He transitioned smoothly from a professional basketball player to a student of the game, moving to Dusseldorf shortly after his time in Munich which allowed him to attend Bundesliga games on Saturdays and then make the short drive to Holland to watch Dutch Premier League games on Sundays. Today we can obviously do that with a mere adjustment of our position on the couch, but in the 1970s Jay was a grinder—a true student of the beautiful game in soccer-mad Europe.

Eventually, Jay returned to America where he was eager to put his newfound soccer knowledge to work. Jay began a PhD program at Ohio Wesleyan and soon after was asked to take over as the head coach of the men's soccer team. Forty years later, Jay Martin is still the head men's soccer coach at Ohio Wesleyan.

PROCESS VERSUS OUTCOME

Now that you are well aware of *what* Jay Martin has done, let me tell you about *who* Jay Martin is. When we first met, Jay said, "Josh, I am a dinosaur, my friend." I didn't expect anything less from such a humble man, but let me tell you that Jay is anything but a dinosaur. Jay understands that the game of soccer, much like life, is about relationships. In today's world, we are fascinated by winning and losing. In 2017, for example, we saw FC Barcelona lose to Paris St. Germain 4-0 and everyone in the world was calling for the sacking of Luis Enrique. Well, two weeks later a 6-1 win in the return leg cemented Luis Enrique as one of the Barcelona coaching legends next to Johan Cruyff and Pep Guardiola. Winning and losing are important, but if you measure your self-worth by them then your coaching future is bleak.

In the fall of 1996, Jay Martin found himself at a crossroad. Up to that point Ohio Wesleyan had been to the NCAA tournament 18 straight years. In 1996, Ohio Wesleyan went an impressive 13-2-2, but failed to make the NCAA tournament for the first time in nearly two decades. "At the time, I was obsessed with winning, I felt that if I didn't win a National Championship, my peers wouldn't accept me, but in 1996 it hit me like a ton of bricks and I said to myself, 'Why am I obsessed with winning?' So, I called my two captains together and I said 'Guys, we are changing everything in the program, we are going to focus on the process and we're going to see what happens.'"

What Jay realized was that you cannot control the result or other people's opinions of you. I have noticed that a lot of people in the coaching community are very insecure. Constantly afraid of being found out as a fraud or only hoping to win to avoid the backlash of losing. I see coaches that post 15 times a day on Twitter in the hopes that others will see them as a good coach or someone worth paying attention to.

My favorite author of all time is David Foster Wallace and in his now infamous "This is Water" speech, he says:

> *"If you worship money and things—if they are where you tap real meaning in life—then you will never have enough. Never feel you have enough. It's the truth. Worship your own body and beauty and sexual allure and you will always feel ugly, and when time and age start showing, you will die a million deaths before they finally plant you."*

Take out money and things and insert winning and championships and the message doesn't change. This is why I said that Jay couldn't be further from a dinosaur. Jay realized early on in his coaching career that if you define your success as a coach by how many games you win, then you will never, ever win enough. Jay continued by saying, "In those early days, I would put the result and the outcome on myself. If we lost a game, I wouldn't sleep for like three days, no kidding. And when we won a game, it was right on to the next game, I didn't even take the time to celebrate the small successes and I fell into a very negative rut—a depression of sorts. It took us not getting into the NCAA tournament to really change this program."

Two years later, in 1998, Jay Martin and the Ohio Wesleyan men's soccer team won a National Championship.

Again, Jay is not saying that winning and losing don't matter. It is important not to throw the baby out with the bath water. But if you place your entire self-worth on how many championship trophies you have in your office, then prepare yourself for a very unfulfilling career in coaching.

If we aren't going to focus on the outcomes and only on the process, then how do we do that? Well, it is important to understand that a lot of coaches and teams claim they are process-oriented. However, any time a coach mentions the rankings, standings, the score the last time we played this team, or an accolade for an individual player, these are all just subtle ways of communicating to your players that the outcomes are much more important than the means of achieving them.

A true process-oriented coach is also aware of how they behave on the sidelines. If your team concedes an early goal, how do you react? Arms flailing, clipboard broken over the knee, warming up the first person you see on the bench? Outcome, outcome, outcome. If your team scores to equalize, how do you react? Fist pump, high fives, arms raised like Rocky after he mounts the steps to the Philadelphia Museum of Art? Sorry, but that's outcome. Being process oriented is like being a stoic philosopher. Stoic philosophy is beyond the scope of this text, but its central tenet is that you can only control what you can control (i.e., your actions and your perceptions). That is why Jay advocates against focusing on the outcome, because it is entirely outside the sphere of your control.

Let's say one of your players makes it his goal to become an All-American next season. That's ambitious and lofty, but it is an outcome. Basically, this player has just put the entire success of his season—and the emotions that come with that—on the decisions of other people. That player cannot control whether the coaches on the voting board—the ones that have probably never seen him play—decide in a boardroom meeting one day. He cannot control if they deem him worthy of being an All-American. Obviously, allowing this player to measure his success on such a subjective award outside of his control is careless on our part. So, what should a coach do? What does being process oriented look like? Let's say that same player focuses on getting better each and every day. Perhaps he makes it his goal to give as much effort as he can every single day. That is within his control. That is being process oriented.

During our conversation, Jay opened up a drawer with about 100 NSCAA All-Region, All-America, and All-Ohio certificates from the last five or six seasons. Jay's players never came to pick them up because they simply don't care. When you are process oriented, public perception and laud is out of your control, so you don't put any focus on it. "I don't know who the leading scorer on our team was this past year; we don't talk about it. If one of our players wins the conference player of the week award, we don't talk about it. We have eliminated all discussions and accolades that deal with the outcome."

For Jay, being process oriented is an all-the-time thing. In 2016, Ohio Wesleyan was winning 1-0 against a conference rival, Denison, with 30 seconds left to play. One of Ohio Wesleyan's forwards was taking a throw-in deep in the opponent's half. Game over, right? Well, one poor decision and two passes later Denison had tied the game up. "Of course, I was upset, but I didn't show it. When we score a goal, I don't jump up and down and scream, when the opponent scores, I don't jump up and down and scream. It's hard work, it takes time, but in the end it pays off."

Jay also mentioned how he rarely, if ever, says anything to the referee or reacts to a poor decision. This is truly stoic. The only person that can control the referee is the referee himself. However, coaches around the globe lose their minds over bad calls, and scream and yell hoping that the referee stops the game and reverses his decision which has happened zero times in the history of soccer. Jay's overall message is control what you can control. Focus on your actions and control your perceptions or they will eat you alive.

"I WORK HARD ON ME."

Jay works extremely hard to maintain his process-oriented nature. During our podcast, he mentioned a few times that he works hard on himself. That is why you are reading this book. You are currently working hard on you. The best coaches are lifelong learners. However, Jay goes beyond books and courses to continually challenge himself. Jay has made mindfulness and gratitude a huge part of his life. The infamous Tony Robbins said, "You cannot be angry and grateful at the same time." Jay cited a study out of the University of Chicago which interviewed 10,000 of the most successful people in the world. Although success is quite arbitrary, the study determined that the most successful people in the world all had three things in common. First, they all had some sort of daily meditation practice. Second, they all engaged in various forms of positive self-talk. Last, they all had curated some sort of daily journaling practice.

Jay Martin started journaling in 1980 and hasn't missed a day since. "Journaling is very therapeutic; it helps my efficiency, focus, and effectiveness. I journal every day and I write down the three things I am most thankful for. Today, it was my wife, my children, and the opportunity to make an impact on young men and women." Jay also has a daily meditation practice of 10-12 minutes per day. I asked Jay why he meditates and he responded, "I remember at one point my dad said to me, 'Jay, you are wishing your life away. You are always obsessed with the future, what's going to happen, what the outcome is going to be.' That was the first sign to me that I needed to focus on the now."

If you are reading this, my question to you is: what is wrong with things as they currently are? It is so easy in the coaching profession to worry about the next game, the next season, the next big job, and very easy to forget that coaching is a privilege and a craft. Adding gratitude for the things you have will help you stop worrying about the things you are without. What you will find is that the things you have are actually pretty great. That is not to say that ambition to be a professional coach or a national team coach is bad, but if you are constantly worried about the future, you will certainly miss out on the present.

MENTAL TOUGHNESS

It is no coincidence that Jay's interest in mindfulness has led him to study and teach psychology at Ohio Wesleyan University. He believes that mental toughness is the missing ingredient in the development of athletes in the United States. Instead of the mental toughness that is often thrown around by coaches who make their players do sprints at the end of training and claim that they are training mental toughness, Jay defines mental toughness as "playing at the same level, all the time, both in practice and in competition."

I like this quote and it pairs nicely with a quote that I love by the University of Houston cross country coach, Steve Magness: "People have a misconception on what toughness is. It isn't about gritting your teeth and powering through an obstacle. It's not about mud runs and silly things that look difficult, but aren't. Toughness is about making the right decisions under stress and fatigue. It's about having the ability and wherewithal to slow the world down, make the right decisions, or choose the correct coping strategy."

If you are one of these coaches that thinks wall sits for 20 minutes or walking lunges until your players puke is building mental toughness, then I highly suggest you take a step back and think more about what you want your athletes to do in crucial moments. Do you really want them to grit their teeth and tighten up? Or do you want them to be clear in their thinking, narrow their focus, and execute the game plan?

PRACTICE

Jay doesn't believe we practice well in the United States because of the spotlight media puts on coaches. In fact, professional sports have spoiled youth sports in a lot of ways. Youth coaches see guys like Pep Guardiola screaming from the sidelines and being praised for their tactical adjustments and that becomes their model of success. "What you see is a very coach-centered sporting culture. The players show up and they stand around passing a ball and they wait for the coach to come out and tell them what to do." You won't see that at Ohio Wesleyan.

At the beginning of each week, Jay meets with each player and asks them what they would like to improve in the coming week. Now, during training Jay might go around to each player and ask them what their goals are for the upcoming session and he expects them to have one. Jay gets responses like "improve my passing with my weaker foot," but he will push those players to make their goals even more specific. How many passes will you complete with your weaker foot? How many will you attempt? Jay has created true deliberate practice in this sense. His players are working on a specific weakness of theirs and by making the goal tangible, he has created a self-evaluating feedback loop. The players don't need to go to Jay to ask him how they did, they are tasked with coming up with the skill (improve passing with weaker foot), the objective (attempt 10 passes and complete 8), and the evaluation (did I meet my objective and how can I improve for next time?).

Jay's player-centered approach to practice has resulted in the opposite of the coach-centered approach to practice described earlier. "If you were to come to one of our practices, we usually train at 4:00 pm and you would see every single player on the field by 3:15 pm doing something to make themselves better. The guys have goals, they want to become better players, and while most teams start practice by having their players pass the ball in a circle talking about the NFL game last night, our players are working on themselves."

Jay truly lives and breathes his philosophy on a daily basis. In fact, Jay Martin has never, in 40 years, seen an Ohio Wesleyan soccer player lift weights. "The reason is because when they are in the weight room they are doing it so they become fitter, stronger, and better players. As soon as I walk in the door, it becomes extrinsic motivation and I don't want them lifting weights because of me." Jay has created an environment that promotes intrinsic motivation. I know I have been guilty as a coach of trying to motivate my players with extrinsic methods. For example, I have said things like, "Okay, guys, last sprint and if everyone makes it in 20 seconds, we are done for the day." Well, now they are only going to work hard so that they can go home. Is that what I want? Is that what any coach wants? What coaches want is for their players to be intrinsically motivated, meaning that they are working hard for internal rewards like becoming a better player. "I never want to hear one of my former players tell me that they played *for me*. I hate that. They played for *themselves* and their *teammates* and hopefully there is some sort of intrinsic joy or motivation for playing soccer."

ADVICE TO YOUNG COACHES

By now you are well aware that Jay Martin does not measure himself by wins and losses. However, that doesn't mean he treats games as if they do not exist. You can still win a lot of games and be focused on the process, in fact, I think you will win *more* games by being focused on the process because you are more concerned with what actually matters. Jay mentioned how important it is for coaches to know the difference between attributions and excuses. Excuses live in the outcome-oriented world. They are the reasons we use to explain a loss—blaming the referee, the pitch conditions, or the wind. On the other hand, Jay, as a process-oriented coach, is concerned with attributions. "Attributions are the reasons for your success or failure, not excuses. To what do you attribute success? To what do you attribute failure? Any good coach or business man needs to understand attributions because you need to learn and understand why certain things happened. Not the referee or the rainy conditions, but the legitimate reasons for success and failure. A good coach figures out what those are and gets better." An example of an attribution may be a tactical reason why your team lost the game. For example, if your team plays a 1-4-3-3 formation and the opponent played with a diamond-shaped midfield, perhaps their 4v3 advantage in the center of the field was why your team struggled to defend and maintain possession. That would be an attribution. That is process-oriented because it is something you can control. Now you can go back to the office and improve the way you watch film, plan training, and prepare your team for the next opponent.

Jay Martin is a living, breathing example of a coach that decides on his philosophy and lives it on a daily basis. Jay has an exercise he does with his team every year where he gives them a list of 400 values. He gives the team about an hour to narrow that down to a top 10. Then the team needs to present to him their top 5 values ranked 5 through 1. This is also an exercise that Jay recommends to coaches as well. For example, let's say your top 5 values are honesty, loyalty, accountability, kindness, and responsibility. You would then build your coaching philosophy with those words as your foundation.

I will be the first to admit that, until I talked with Jay, I never clearly defined the values that guide me as a coach. Following the 2016 season, I found myself reflecting over the winter break on how I acted during the season. Let me just say that I was far from living and coaching by the values I want to represent. The question for you now is how have you been acting as a coach? Does that align with the values you hold to be important? Would your players describe you by your values? If you said no to these last two questions, then you need to stop reading and go through Jay's exercise. Come up with a list of values and narrow that list to a top 10 or 15. Take the time to narrow that list to a top 3 or 5. Now, what is your coaching philosophy?

Last, Jay recommends that coaches be true to themselves. "In the end, you have to go to sleep with yourself and you have to be content with the decisions you made and why you made those decisions. I've seen so many coaches try to be Pep Guardiola or somebody else. You can't do that. Only Pep can be Pep. So, if you just stay true to your values and your philosophy, it goes so far in terms of making you a quality coach."

Out of 100 podcast episodes, only one episode has come with tweets praising the guest for the impact they had on *their* lives. That guest was Jay Martin. Former players, former assistants, and current players all commented on our episode about how Jay had changed their lives and impacted them in such a positive way. From sneaking into Bayern Munich sessions in the 1970s to winning a National Championship in the 1990s to continuing to improve in 2017, Jay has proven that in the end it is the relationships that really matter. Winning can be fun. Losing can be hard. "But in the end, it is the relationships with the players that will get you through the tough times."

CHAPTER 2

PLAYER-CENTERED COACHING

RENE MEULENSTEEN

Rene Meulensteen is a Dutch professional soccer manager that last worked for Maccabai Haifa FC. He is probably best known for his work with Manchester United as the first team coach under Sir Alex Ferguson from 2007-2013. He also served as the reserve team manager in 2005 and worked in the youth academy from 2001 to 2006 where he worked with players like Gerard Pique and Danny Welbeck. Rene also managed Fulham F.C. in the English Premier League for a spell during the 2013 season. Rene mentored coach Wiel Coerver and has a company called the Meulensteed Method dedicated to educating coaches on youth development.

You're not a real coach until you get fired — The player jigsaw puzzle as the key to youth development — Letting the players make the decisions — Why you should always add something to your players' game, but never change it — Success doesn't come for free

Rene Meulensteen was fired from Maccabai Haifa FC during the writing of this book. That is the nature of this business. That is the beauty of this book and these giants that we learn from. Everyone in this book has failed many times in their life. Each time they picked themselves back up, learned from their mistakes, and tried again.

The infamous trader and author, Nassim Nicholas Taleb, is currently writing a book called *Skin in the Game*. The basic idea is that if someone doesn't have skin in the game, then you shouldn't listen to them. Why would you invest your money in a stock that your financial advisor wouldn't invest his own in? Every day the soccer world hears from pundits on major television networks who have never coached a day in their life but enjoy criticizing a manager's tactics or training methods. Our world should be celebrating failed managers, not castigating them. They should be celebrated like heroes returning from war and we should all relish in their stories and experiences. Rene Meulensteen failed at Fulham and Maccabai Haifa FC, which means that his chapter and his experiences may be the most useful of them all.

THE PRESSURES OF TOP-FLIGHT PROFESSIONAL SOCCER

Claudio Ranieri won the Barclays Premier League with Leicester City one season after they finished one place above relegation. In August 2015, Leicester City was predicted as 5000 to 1 underdogs to win the premier league. In May 2016, a $100 bet on Leicester to win the Premier League would have resulted in a pay day of $500,000. In February of 2017, Claudio Ranieri was sacked as the manager at Leicester City.

Bob Bradley was hired as the first American coach to ever manage in the Premier League when he took over Swansea City in October of 2016. Less than 3 months later Bradley was fired.

Rene Meulensteen was hired as the manager at Fulham FC in December of 2013. In February of 2014, Rene Meulensteen was fired as the manager of Fulham FC. Rene was hired in August of 2016 to take over Maccabai Haifa FC before being let go in February of 2017.

I could write a 2,000-page novel with more examples of managers that were hired and fired in the most unceremonious of circumstances. The reason I mention these circumstances is to paint a picture of what it is like to manage at the highest level. It is cut-throat. However, even Rene wouldn't want you to feel sorry for him. "Unfortunately, it's the nature of the game. The Premier League has become an uncontrollable monster with the money and TV rights. Every club has their own expectations, but the pressure is the same. The top six are fighting for Champions League places, the middle of the table are fighting for Europe, and there are others just trying to stay in the league and avoid relegation, so there is a constant level of pressure."

Often it seems that coaching at the highest level is a near-impossible situation. Rene said, "For players to buy in and understand the coach's philosophy and to execute it properly, it takes a season to a season and a half, but the harsh truth is that 9 out of 10 coaches don't get that kind of time." However, there are countless examples of the 1 out of 10 clubs that do give their manager time. Tottenham, under Mauricio Pochettino, climbed into the title race in 2017 after finishing outside of Champions League soccer following his first season in charge. "I think clubs that provide time to managers are rewarded if they can stick to their guns during tough times."

It is difficult for Meulensteen not to look back at his time at Fulham and wonder what if. Rene thrived for six seasons as first team coach at Manchester United, helping lead the club to three League Cups, a FIFA Club World Cup, a Champions League title, and four Premier League titles. However, his first spell on his own was a massive failure. The thing that probably most hindered Rene was his time at Manchester United. "I came from Man United, where we did what we wanted with the ball, we played dominating soccer, but I realized that was almost impossible at Fulham." Rene also said, "The harsh reality of top-flight soccer is that there is only one medicine and that is winning."

Premier League coaches like Tony Pulis and Sam Allardyce have made careers out of saving teams from relegation with very pragmatic, defensive soccer that gets results through the use of *via negativa*. Nassim Taleb explains that *via negativa* is the philosophy of winning by not losing. Meulensteen admits that his biggest fault at Fulham was prioritizing *how* he won over purely winning. "I resolved to use a strategy that to this day I felt was the right one because the team had low energy, low enjoyment, so I really wanted to put some life back into the club. At first we saw improvement, but we didn't pick up points where I thought we deserved them." Rene had hoped that by teaching the players and encouraging them to play expansive attacking soccer, he could accomplish the impossible: playing beautiful soccer and getting results. The problem with this strategy is that in order to accomplish the feat of playing beautiful soccer and getting results, a team must have talented players. At the time, Fulham's roster was depleted and their players could not play expansive, attacking soccer like Rene had encouraged at Manchester United. "In hindsight, the one thing I would have done differently is I would have gone to a more tight defensive block to operate from. I realized, too late obviously, that the type of dominating soccer I created at Manchester United was not possible at Fulham in the short term. I switched to that strategy too late and the club pulled the plug."

YOUTH DEVELOPMENT

Meulensteen is arguably one of the greatest youth coaches of all time. Prior to his role as first team manager at Manchester United, Rene was in charge of United's Youth Academy for six years. During that time, Rene worked with future first team players Danny Welbeck, Gerard Pique, and many others.

Rene had his own giant that he used to help him improve as a coach. Rene cited Wiel Coerver as one of the biggest influences on his career. "I still remember to this day walking past the bookstore and catching a glimpse of his book, *The Plan for the Ideal Footballer*, and I went in and started reading it and it was like lightbulbs started going off in my head." Wiel Coerver studied the greatest players of his time such as Di-Stefano, Cruyff, and Beckenbauer. At that time, Rene felt confident in his ability to understand attacking and defending tactics, systems, and schemes, but he had no idea how to produce a player that could beat his opponent in 1v1 situations. That moment was the start of a journey that took Rene from a young coach in a bookstore to the head of one of the most famous academies in world soccer.

THE MEULENSTEEN METHOD

Rene's training sessions always include three steps of progressions: technique, skill, strategy.

Technique drills include a variety of ball manipulations and exercises aimed at getting the players comfortable on the ball while challenging them with something new to practice. Skill, the next progression in the training session, tests the players to see if they can execute the technique in a small game with opposition. Finally, the strategy component of the session puts the players into a small-sided game with various constraints that can emphasize or encourage the use of the technique and skill in a complex game environment.

The first thing that coaches need to do is determine what the purpose of their session is going to be. Rene's favorite saying is "Always the purpose!"

"So, let's say the purpose is to teach attackers how to change the angle of attack using an inside or outside hook move. You then have to ask yourself, 'What are the best games suited to do something like that?' Then what you do is play a small-sided game with four small goals. This way, the player always has another area to attack."

The benefit of this four-goal game is that it allows the player to constantly change the area of attack. The player can then understand when it is appropriate to use the hook move and he can experience the type of results that occur from making that decision. The art of Rene's progressions is that he is really moving along a continuum of simple to complex. He is bridging the gap between awareness and understanding. The players are made aware of the move, or technique, and then they are put in an environment where they can begin to practice the technique in game situations. For a technique to become part of a player's subconscious, Rene believes that they must use the move or technique in four main situations:

1. A defender in front of them
2. A defender to the side of them
3. A defender coming from an angle
4. A defender coming from behind

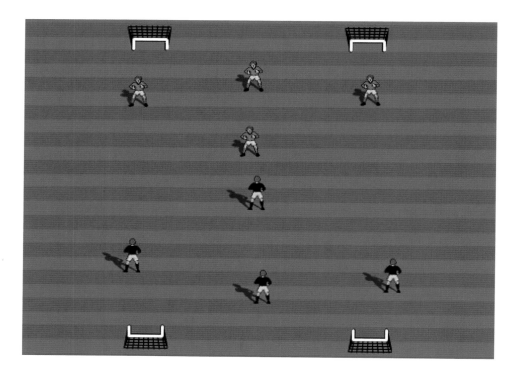

One of the biggest mistakes coaches make in youth development is that their training sessions are neither age nor stage realistic. In other words, the environment created in training is not what the kids need to be exposed to. For example, if you are coaching a 10-year-old recreational team that practices once a week, a training session aimed at pressing out of a 1-4-3-3 is far too advanced for their age and stage of development. On the other hand, if you are coaching a 14-year-old professional development academy team, a training session on using the Cruyff turn is not appropriate for their age or stage of development either.

The key for a youth coach is to be as player-centered as possible. Too many youth coaches are coach-centered, meaning that the entire session is determined by the sound of their voice and their instruction. "We should be trying to create an environment where there is a lot of freedom for expression and play." Too often, the three Ls (lines, laps, and lectures) are violated in youth development. Don't perform drills where your players need to wait their turn to have a chance to touch the ball. Don't start practice by running laps around the pitch. Don't stop practice and give your team a 20-minute explanation of shooting technique. "The goal is to create an environment that is always about two things: repetition and success." The goal is to keep the players constantly on the move in a variety of activities that maximize touches on the ball in a variety of environments.

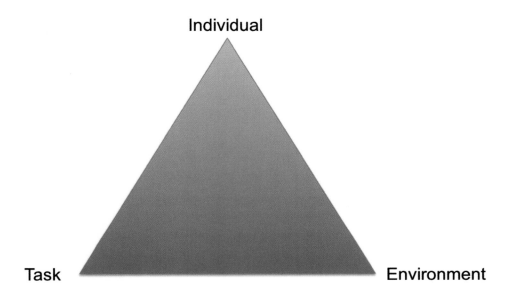

I encourage coaches to consult texts on the constraints-led approach. A constraints-led approach emphasizes the use of games to teach understanding while maximizing the two keys of repetition and success.

Coaches can manipulate any and all of the three variables shown in the image above. Coaches can manipulate the individual through tailoring the activity to address any physical, cognitive, or personality traits of a player or group of players. For example, using small goals for your youth-level goalkeepers to play in because of their small stature may help increase their success and confidence.

Coaches at the youth level can manipulate the environment by playing on a variety of different surfaces while coaches at the professional level can simulate crowd noise during training to influence communication above crowd noise.

Coaches can manipulate the task by introducing rules such as a one-touch restriction, a rule that you can only score on a header, changes in the size of the field, or use of a smaller ball.

"To get it right at the youth level, we need a technical, skillful playground. That is what coaches need to try and create. Give the players a little trick to work with and put them into a small-sided game with different constraints and just let them play." This will create a better development platform for players.

The biggest problem in the United States is the fascination with winning at the youngest ages. Coaches, parents, and clubs at the youth level emphasize winning over development which means that the bigger, faster, and stronger players are always given more playing time or are selected for national teams.

We need to realize that at the youth level winning and success are not mutually exclusive. "Winning does not always come in the form of winning games. Winning is playing the right way. Winning is being down 4-0 in the first half and not conceding in the second half. Winning is something that comes in all shapes and sizes."

Rene made it clear that coaches, youth coaches especially, should not get so carried away with the emotions of winning and losing. They need to constantly ask themselves:

1. Did the kids enjoy the game they just played?
2. Did we try to play the right way?
3. What exciting things have I just seen?
4. Was there a good tackle? Or a great pass over distance?

As a college coach, I have spent numerous summers and winters at US Development Academy Showcases watching the next generation of American players. As a consultant for the Philadelphia Union, Rene spent time at Lakewood Ranch in Florida for the winter USSDA Showcase. For Rene, every game was the same. The game was played in straight lines and he watched as the big defenders kicked the ball to the fast forwards and the aerobic midfielders jogged back and forth between it all, but he didn't see any skill or tactical knowledge. Rene even commented that if he was in an air balloon he would have seen 24 identical games going on simultaneously (24 being the number of fields at Lakewood Ranch). So, to make the time more useful, Rene challenged some coaches standing by to tell him who they thought the best player on the field was. Not one coach could pick the players that Rene saw as the best. Rene was looking for the player that wasn't as physically developed, but was skillful, that did something different, and that didn't just play in straight lines all the time. "Where are the David Silva's, the Xavi's, the Mata's, and the Paul Scholes of America? They are there! I have seen them, but it requires a different way of identifying players. The training comes down to creating a better environment for all kids to enjoy. The more skillful, and the more they get exposed to technique training and skill training, most likely, we will begin to identify players that are better. Players that are comfortable on the ball, that have different solutions, that are comfortable under pressure, that can turn away, and that have unpredictability in forward play."

The key message of the Meulensteen Method comes down to three key areas:

1. Identifying talent—You may not necessarily find the best of the best, but you need to identify the talent that comes through your door.
2. Developing potential—Everyone that comes into a soccer club at a young age has a certain potential and it is the club's responsibility to develop that

potential. What matters most is what are you doing on the pitch with the boys and girls to make them better players.

3. Building successful teams—Success can be defined in various ways; success is not always based on winning or losing.

Around this philosophy, youth clubs need to assess their views on two main concepts:

1. How do they define the qualities of a successful team and what does a top player look like? The answer to this should serve as the guideline for development.
2. How do you transfer that vision into a development model over the different ages and stages?

THE PLAYER JIGSAW PUZZLE

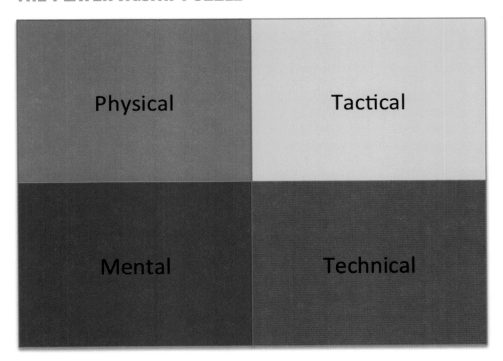

The player jigsaw puzzle was created by Rene to show where our focus should be placed during each age and stage of development.

The emphasis shifts throughout the stages and ages of development. Early on in development a large portion of training is spent in the green corner (technical). But, as players get older and advance through the stages of development, coaches shift their focus into the yellow corner (tactical). This ensures that players begin to develop their awareness, understanding, and decision making in relation to the positions that they play. The later stages of development are defined by bigger spaces of play, larger numbers, and bigger distances to cover.

In the older stages of development, particularly once players have finished their growth spurt, we see a need to emphasize the red corner (physical) as well. Players now begin to work on the strength and conditioning side to better prepare themselves for the larger distances, explosive actions, and dueling, tackling, and jumping required for the adult game.

Throughout development, there is always a focus placed in the blue corner (mental) where we encourage the players to develop their own personalities and identities on the pitch. The mental side also aims to develop and show players how to work hard in training and always push themselves toward improvement.

All areas of the player jigsaw can be emphasized throughout each age and stage of development, but precedence is given to one or two over the others during each age and stage. Coaches should determine what is appropriate for their context, but a simple model is:

- Ages 6-9—Green (technical)
- Ages 10-14—Green and yellow (technical and tactical)
- Ages 15-18—Yellow and red (tactical and physical)
- Ages 18+—Red, yellow, and blue (physical, tactical, mental)

Again, each age and stage should include all pieces of the player jigsaw, but emphasis is given to certain areas over others. This can also be different for each individual. For example, perhaps player A is 17 years old, 6'2" tall, and 185 pounds. Player B is also 17 years old, but is 5'5" and 135 pounds. Player A is physically gifted but underdeveloped in his awareness, game understanding, and decision making. Player B is extremely gifted in terms of his game insight and decision making. Therefore, we may focus more in the red corner for Player B and more in the yellow corner for Player A.

COACHING DECISION MAKING

It is 7:15PM in the United States and a dimly lit turf field is playing host to a local 16-year-old youth soccer team. By 7:17PM the head coach has already stopped practice three times to correct the decision making of his players. By 8:30PM, every single player packs up their bag ready to leave the facility unsure if they did anything right during training and wondering what exactly the coach wants. The next time they return to practice they vow to only make the decisions that the coach wants, rendering them robotic and their decision making slow and ineffective. This isn't hyperbole; this happens every single day across the United States and the world. Decision making defines the game of soccer. Soccer is a continuous game of decision making between 22 players.

Rene Meulensteen refuses to coach the decisions of his players at the youth level. "I totally stay out of the decision! I just provide the tools and the opportunity, awareness, and understanding so that the players can make those decisions for themselves." Does this mean that Rene stands on the sideline during training with his hands in his pockets? Of course not. "The only thing you have to do is guide them at times. To make sure they are aware of what better options there may be. The moment that kids start making the same wrong decision over and over again, you need to make them aware and ask, 'Is this working? No. Okay, why is it not working? What else can you do?' And then they probably come up with the right solution and eventually they get it right."

Rene doesn't see the purpose of telling a young player to pass the ball to a certain player, or to turn when he receives the ball, or to pass it forward instead of backward. Why? Because then the decision no longer belongs to the player. It becomes Rene's decision. A coach that is constantly telling his players what decisions to make is effectively ruining the players' decision making. The players are now reliant on the coach to tell them what to do even though the coach may not see what the players see. "Soccer is a game where you try and help players learn the tools and abilities and then they have to apply them independent of you. To recognize a situation and then make their own decision with the tools that we give them! The more tools they have got, the more creative they will become, the more unpredictable they will become."

When a player receives the ball there are really only three decisions for them to make.

1. Are they going to pass to someone or shoot the ball?
2. Are they going to dribble into available space with the ball?
3. Do they have to create a better situation because a defender is in their way?

The more we put players in environments that create the need to make these decisions the better decision makers players become.

Rene has coached some of the best players to ever play this game. Cristiano Ronaldo has cited Rene as one of the best coaches he has ever had. "The biggest thing I would say in coaching top professional players is to pay attention to how you address them. I would never tell a player like Ruud Van Nistelrooy that I want to *change* something about his game. Instead, I would tell him that I want to *add* something to his game. I would tell him that if we can *add* this to your game, you can become a more complete player." Coaches need to pay attention to how they address their players. If you tell your best player that they need to change something about their game, you will most likely be met with resistance. But, if you tell your best player that you want to add a certain something to their game, which will make them even better, that is how you get Cristiano Ronaldo to call you one of the best coaches he has ever had.

ADVICE TO YOUNG COACHES

A lot of coaches want to climb the ladder as quickly as they can. One day they are coaching their son's recreational youth team, the next they are ready for the Manchester City job. Simon Sinek likes to call that the mountain fallacy. He believes that everyone has to scale a mountain in their career to reach the top. Obviously, people can climb the mountain slowly or quickly, but what is important to keep in mind is that there is still a mountain. And climbing a mountain—no matter how quickly—takes consistency, time, and a lot of hard work.

One of the many brain biases we have as human beings is called *overconfidence.* Obviously, we all know what it means to be overconfident, but do we recognize it when we are the ones being overconfident? The answer is no. We all unconsciously inflate our own abilities at a lot of things whether it is coaching or carrying groceries inside the house. The truth is that "you need to put your hours in as a coach. You only learn to drive, not when you get your license, but when you actually start driving. This is the same with coaching. You need to learn how to adapt, how to innovate, how to be creative as a coach and you only get that by putting your hours in."

A common thread between the 100+ coaches I have interviewed on my podcast is how many of them put in the hard yards. Coaches like Dave Tenney (Seattle Sounders), Erwin van Bennekom (Duke University), and Rene Meulensteen all started off coaching their local youth teams—and not just one team—but, multiple teams, every single day for 40 to 80 hours per week. This is a vital stage in your coaching career because it teaches you, like Rene said, how to innovate, adapt, and create. "If you plan a session for ten players, but only nine show up, what do you do now? Even if you have it all nicely diagrammed on a piece of paper, the fact is that only nine showed up. So, what do you do? How can you make that session not go flat? You have to invest time in yourself to be the best coach that you can become."

Trust me, these situations don't go away when you land that big job with an academy team, college team, or a professional team. I ran a session last week that worked perfectly for the twelve players I anticipated being at training. When I fell asleep that night I couldn't wait for the session to begin. I woke up at 6AM and started getting ready for the 8AM session. A quick glance at my phone informed me that two of my players were sick and one had class. My perfect session that built into a final game of 6v6 was no longer going to work. This is why Rene says coaching—and coaching a lot—early on in your career gives you so much useful experience in adapting to a variety of circumstances. When it comes to training, Murphy's Law is the first law. What can go wrong will go wrong, so you need to be prepared. You are much better off having a session go horribly wrong with your son's under-12 team than you are with the first team of Manchester United. I doubt Ruud Van Nistelrooy or Roy Keane would have been too happy with Rene if he showed up and said, "Sorry boys, but the session I planned doesn't work now because I didn't know Cristiano would be out today. Let's try again tomorrow."

There is nothing wrong with wanting to reach the highest level you can as a coach, but don't sacrifice mastery of the craft to get there because if you are unprepared when you arrive, your stay at the top will be short-lived. "Don't aim for something because it's driven out of ego. Try to be the best coach at whatever level you are at. You have to invest time and do the work. If you want to do something and be successful at it, it doesn't come for free."

CHAPTER 3

TRANSITIONING FROM PLAYER TO COACH

NEIL JONES

Neil Jones is the head men's soccer coach at Loyola-Chicago University in Chicago, Illinois. Neil spent three seasons at Northwestern University under Tim Lenahan before taking over a struggling Loyola-Chicago program. He turned Loyola-Chicago from a 6-win team into a 14-win team in three seasons and has led his team to become one of the top five defensive teams in the country the last two seasons. In 2016, Loyola went 14-4-1, had 12 shutouts, and advanced to the second round of the NCAA tournament. Neil grew up in Auckland, New Zealand before an impressive college soccer career at the University of California at Santa Barbara. Neil began his coaching career at UCSB helping lead them to the 2006 National Championship. Neil is one of the up-and-coming young head coaches in the United States.

You might make a better coach than a player — The Canvas Strategy — Why getting to know your players makes it easier to coach them — Soccer always has a winner and a loser — How a clock can influence the realism of your training

"Two roads diverged in a wood, and I—
I took the one less traveled by,
And that has made all the difference."

—Robert Frost

I am sitting at a local Starbucks in Pittsburgh, PA as I type this chapter, reflecting on my conversation with Neil Jones. His story triggers the Robert Frost poem, "The Road Not Taken," in my head. Neil's story has inspired me to reflect on my own journey. I can't help but wonder what my life would be like if I hadn't decided to stop playing professional soccer. What if I never gave up on that dream? Would I be the man I am today? It's easy to get caught in the daydreams of could-have-been or might-have-done. But, one thing is for sure, there is no going back for Neil Jones.

When two roads diverged in a wood and Neil was tasked with deciding between a career in his home country of New Zealand or the unknown that faced him in a place called California, he soon found himself taking the road to California and and the route of college soccer.

One decade removed from his first National Championship as a coach (at Santa Barbara in 2006), Neil Jones is a veteran NCAA Division 1 head coach at the age of 35. It is four years into his tenure at Loyola-Chicago and he has led the team from a 6-11-2 record in 2013 to a 14-4-1 record in 2016 while also becoming one of the best defensive teams in the country.

Before Neil began his coaching career, however, there was another crossroads that he faced. The decision of whether or not to hang up his boots loomed over the then 24-year-old's head. Trials in Norway, Spain, and even Malaysia all led him to believe that his dream of playing soccer professionally was coming to an end. However, it wasn't until his former college coach and current mentor, Leo Chapel, told him the truth about his ability as a player that he decided to hang up the boots once and for all. "He called me up and said, 'Listen, you are going to make a way better coach than you do a player.' Which was tough to hear at the time, being 24 years old, but it was exactly what I needed to hear."

PLAYER-TO-COACH TRANSITION

If you haven't made it as a striker by the time you're 24 years old, you are probably never going to make it. Neil eventually came to that realization about himself that led to him beginning his coaching career. However, simply making the decision to be a coach doesn't automatically qualify you as the next Pep Guardiola. Coaching can be a lot harder than it looks. "The transition was really hard because my first coaching job was at my alma mater (UCSB) coaching guys that I played with a year or two earlier. All of a sudden, you go from a teammate-to-teammate relationship to a player-coach relationship and it was tough."

I also made the player-to-coach transition at a young age (23 years old). It is extremely difficult to coach players when you are only older than them by a few months. From my experience, which is echoed by Neil, when you are a young coach coaching players around your age, the best thing you can do is to be quiet, listen a lot more than you talk, and put your learning on overdrive. The quote I lived by as a young coach was, "We were born with one mouth and two ears for a reason." Too often the mistake young coaches make is they want to be involved in everything—the planning, the tactics, the training— but it just doesn't work like that. Just because you were a good player doesn't mean you have the first clue how to coach. I know I didn't.

THE CANVAS STRATEGY

One of my favorite authors, and people, is Ryan Holiday, author of *Ego Is the Enemy* and *Obstacle Is the Way*. Ryan was named marketing director of American Apparel at 24 years old. The advice his boss gave him was priceless, "Find canvases for other people to paint on."

If you are reading this book and you are my or Neil's age when we first started coaching, the honest truth is that you most likely have no clue what you're talking about. But let's assume you are the second coming of Jose Mourinho or Pep Guardiola. Even if that is the case, your strategy should still be aimed at being humble while you develop your skills.

Holiday explains, "The Romans had a loose word for the concept, *anteambulo,* and it meant a person who cleared the path in front of their patron. If you can do that successfully, you secure a quick and educational power position." So, what is the role of a young coach applying the Canvas Strategy (i.e., clearing the path)? Simply, it is to make your head coach, other assistants, and your players look good. The way you make them better is by clearing the path in order to free them up to work on their strengths. The key is to find the direction that the head coach is already heading and try to find any inefficiencies that may impede that progress. Find connections or outlets that can be optimized to improve a process.

For example, let's say that the head coach loves to show film to his players every single day. You might observe that they are currently writing down the minutes of the game they want to show to the players and then painstakingly skipping through the full game film to find those moments. Perfect. This is where you shine as a young coach. Your task as the one who clears the path is to improve this inefficiency by purchasing or downloading a video editor, learning how to use it, and then showing the head coach how you can help make the process faster and better; your job is *not* to argue over what clip should be shown or to discuss how you think a 1-4-4-2 is better suited for the upcoming opponent. Not yet. You have to earn that. In fact, Bill Belichick is one of the most noted users of the Canvas Strategy.

Early in his career, Belichick would volunteer for all of the mundane tasks the other coaches didn't want to do. During those early days of the NFL, that was film duty. So, Belichick would grab the film, disappear into a room, and only resurface when the film was cut, edited, and ready to be shown. As Holiday eloquently puts, "The person that clears the path ultimately ends up controlling its destination."

Neil Jones also applied the Canvas Strategy as a young coach. "While I was coaching players that I had played with, I kind of kept my head down and just stayed quiet. It wasn't until those guys had moved on and I had learned more about coaching that I began to develop my coaching voice."

Applying the Canvas Strategy is a must as a young coach and even as an older assistant working for a well-established manager or head coach. The world today has progressed so fast that many people are bypassing the traditional apprenticeship route. An apprentice, by definition, is someone who learns a trade from a skilled employer. Whether you want to admit it or not, if you are a young coach, you are an apprentice. During your apprenticeship you need to learn the craft. Learning the craft means learning how to make rice *before* you make sushi. Neil Jones had a hard time making rice. "The most challenging thing I had to learn in the beginning of my career was simply how to just run a session. From minute one until the end, how do you figure out how to get out of it what you want? I knew a lot of different activities. I knew a lot of good training games, but how did they connect to each other? And how did they connect to each other in a way where at the end of the session the players had actually learned something? These are all questions I had."

This is one of the most difficult things to learn as a coach. In fact, learning how to run a session or coach an activity is truly the art of coaching that no one, not even Pep Guardiola, will ever truly master. Too often young coaches, myself included, get caught up discussing different formations or we pick up books like *Pep Confidential* and think we can apply those same tactics to our own teams. The true secret is that there is no secret. As one of my mentors and legendary strength coach Vern Gambetta always says, "Do you practice the basics every single day as a coach? If not, why not?" Neil revealed in our conversation that as a young coach he spent more time learning *how* to coach than he did reading the latest soccer drill book or tactical article. "I have been to a lot of sessions that are good and challenging and they may make you a better defender, attacker, or possession player, but how does it connect to the bigger game? I struggled with that in my early days."

The best way to learn how to coach is to put yourself around good coaches. I cannot stress this enough. Far too often, coaches short-change the apprentice process in the soccer coaching world. Too many coaches want to climb the ladder as fast as possible, but not enough want to master the craft of coaching. A solid apprenticeship may be anywhere from 8 to 10 years, if not more. But by observing top coaches on a daily basis you can learn the art of when to make coaching points, how to make coaching points, when to make an activity bigger or smaller, and a variety of nuances that you cannot get from a coaching drills book or Jose Mourinho's autobiography. "Coaching courses helped me a little bit, but being around good coaches and watching their sessions is where I really learned how to coach."

Who are you learning from right now? That may be the most important coaching education question of all time. Are you learning from someone? Are you getting feedback on your sessions? How do you know if your session was any good? If you are in your 20s, and coaching your own team, then I urge you to find a respected coach to learn from. Eventually, or rather, inevitably, becoming a head coach too early will come back to haunt you. If that isn't a possibility, then you need to find ways to observe other coaches in order to truly maximize your potential. "Watching other club coaches was huge for my development. Maybe it was showing up early to watch someone else's session, or staying late to see how other coaches ran drills or activities."

Jose Mourinho served as a translator at Barcelona where he observed Louis Van Gaal every day. Behind the scenes he was able to take note of what Louis did well and what he wanted to do differently, but you won't develop that if you aren't learning from anyone. When it comes to an apprenticeship you need to make sure your ladder is against the right wall. In other words, is the coach you are learning from well respected? Is he good at what he does? How do you know? If your ladder is currently against the wrong wall, you need to find a mentor and then flip back a few pages and apply the Canvas Strategy. Only then will you truly be in pursuit of mastery.

PLAYER RELATIONSHIPS

One of the most neglected aspects of coaching is relationship management. You can have the greatest tactics in the world, but if the players don't want to play for that you, then they just won't listen. Players need to know that you care about them as more than just a soccer player and what they can do for you on a pitch. "I didn't know enough about how to motivate individual players or how to coach a group of individuals and make them one team. I remember after my first season at Northwestern, head coach Tim Lenahan pulled me into the office and told me something I will never forget. He said, "You know a lot about soccer, but at the end of the day, the players don't care how much you know, until they know how much you care.'" It is very easy to forget this in coaching. In my experience, I have sometimes forgotten the fact that I don't coach magnets on a tactics board, but human beings. I coach people that have bad days at school, fights with their girlfriends, or restless nights of sleep. Neil learned this lesson early on in his coaching career. Sometimes the best coaching point you can make is simply asking one of your players, "How was your day?" "I realized that Coach Lenahan was totally right. These are smart kids, they are at Northwestern, so if I give them all this great information but they don't think I am really invested in their development as a player and a person, then they aren't really going to be receptive to the information and apply it. I realized that I needed to show more compassion, leadership, and care for these guys in order for the soccer information that I gave them to be applied."

Oddly enough, it seems to be true that the more you get to know your players as people, the more you learn about them as soccer players. Getting to know your players may reveal information about them as people that will be vital to you as a coach and allow you to better understand how to motivate them. Here are three questions you should ask every single one of your players at some point.

1. If I am watching you as a fan for the first time, how do I know that you love to play the game?
2. Who is the most influential coach you have had and why?
3. What do you value the most from playing soccer?

The first question will arm you with information about how the player views himself as an athlete. They may say things like competitiveness or hard work, which will provide you with insight into what they value in teammates and themselves. Their answer to the second question will tell you what they want in a coach and how they like to be coached. If a player says that their most influential coach was like a father to them and always treated them with respect—bingo! Now you know how to coach and treat that player. The last question will cut to the source of why they play the game. Not every player will say winning; some may value relationships with teammates or other benefits of organized team sports. You can use this information to strategically motivate each player. For example, a player that values relationships with teammates can be primed to work really hard in a particular game if you mention to him that you want him to make a sacrifice *for his teammates*.

Neil improved this aspect of his coaching in a simpler fashion. "You've got to spend time with them off the field. You have to know things about their lives. You have to care about things outside of soccer. You have to be able to have some banter about you. Can you take some jokes and give some jokes? Comedy is something that everyone enjoys and it is a great way to connect with a group." This can be hard for coaches because we are so passionate about the game and the craft. However, we have to remind ourselves that sometimes it is okay to talk about something other than soccer with your players, or to have a little fun with them.

CREATING A CULTURE BUILT ON DEFENDING

The first thing most coaches look to improve when taking over a new team is the defensive moment of the game. The goal of the game is to "score one more goal than the opponent." Obviously, this becomes increasingly harder the more goals that you concede. For some reason, it seems to be true that most players don't like defending. Players enjoy the game because they enjoy having the ball, but great players know that the game is about much more than what you do with the ball. In fact, studies have shown that the ball is only at a player's feet for a total of two minutes per game. This means that a player spends 88 minutes of the game without the ball. This includes soccer actions like creating space, pressing, and transitioning.

The quickest way to make a bad team good is to make them more difficult to score on. Teaching a 20-year-old how to have better technique or game insight is nearly impossible. Those behaviors should have been developed already and are much more difficult to learn at age 20. However, anyone can learn how to press their opponent in various coordinated ways. Defending is difficult because it requires hard, hard work. "[In my first meeting] with the players, I told them that hard work was going to be a staple of our team. Something that I consistently said was that 'we were never going to be good enough players to be average defensively."

No team is good enough to be average defensively. In fact, for as good as Barcelona were under Pep Guardiola, their defensive organization was based on intense pressing following a loss of possession in order to hide their weaknesses as a defensive unit. Pep saw that his team wasn't the best defensive team, so he taught them how to press after losing possession in order to quickly regain the ball and maintain possession again. Even in attack, Pep was thinking about defending. "No team that wants to win is good enough to be average defensively. The one thing that you can always control, whether you are at Loyola-Chicago or Manchester United, is the work rate of your players, the attitude of your players, and the defensive stoutness of your program. The willingness to defend is the first thing I look for in a potential recruit."

Loyola-Chicago gave up eight goals in 2015 and eleven in 2016. For the past two seasons, as a mid-major school (comparable to being funded like a bottom-of-the-table EPL team), they have finished in the top five in the country in goals against. "It has become a source of pride for our players and me. We know defending needs to be an important part of who we are."

When Sam Allardyce or Tony Pulis are tasked with being Premier League firefighters and saving a team from relegation, their first tactical move is always defensive. However, Neil doesn't necessarily believe you have to work on defense all the time to be a strong defensive team. "I don't think we work on defending that much. What we do work on every single day is competing. Taking pride in winning. Everything is competitive at our training sessions. We are teaching more than just soccer as a coach, we are teaching life too. There are winners and losers in life. It is important to teach that winning is fun and losing is not." Making your sessions competitive is vital. If you think hard enough when planning a session as a coach, you can make everything competitive. I start every session with mini-band work as part of our warm-up and every day the last person to grab a mini-band owes me 15 push-ups.

John Kessel, director of USA Volleyball, has his own dedicated chapter in this book. But something he always says to me is that it is important for training to be game-like. However, we sometimes ignore the fact that keeping score is part of being game-like. This isn't to say that we only focus on the results—Jay Martin taught us to know better than that. But we cannot ignore the fact that a soccer game involves scoring, and scoring results in a winner and a loser. We still need to focus on the process, those things that our players must do that help increase our chances of winning, but we can't do that without the context of winning and losing. Competitiveness is what gets your team through the tough games when they aren't playing their best. It is something that you can't buy, recruit, or sign; you have to foster it every day in how you structure your environment.

Neil Jones is always looking for ways to make his practices competitive. "We have to commute 15 minutes off-campus every day for training. Every week we create two teams and we play a 30-minute game at the end of the Monday training, the Wednesday training, and the Friday training. We have the teams travel together in two separate vans all week and we keep an aggregate score. For example, if the blue team is up 2-0 on Monday, but they lose 3-0 on Wednesday, then going into Friday it is 3-2. The Fridays are the best training sessions of the week because there is a happy van going home and a sad van going home. The sad van has to go in and see our fitness coach for a little fun after they lose on Friday, but I think teaching those moments of winning and losing and how they feel is important."

Fostering and creating a competitive environment in training is difficult. Sometimes it may mean putting the tactical portions of training to the side and letting players choose their own strategies for how to win. "I am not a huge fan of pattern play, or passing around mannequins because mannequins can't tackle you. They can't beat you. They can't out-compete you. So, everything for us is competitive and that is how we have been able to do so well defensively."

PLANNING SESSIONS

The one thing I love about Neil's approach to planning a training session is that he does so through a process of reverse engineering. Neil starts with what he wants to end with and works backwards from there. "For us, it will always end with some sort of conditioned game to big goals and goalkeepers. It could be four goals or it could be two goals. But the question is: how can we get that game to bring out the topic we want to teach for that day? If we want to work on wide play in the final third, and we want that to come out in a 9v9 game at the end, then what do we need to do leading up to that game to get that topic out of it?" This is a very similar approach to how I plan my training sessions. I always start by looking at where the team is at in our team periodization. Is today going to involve bigger pitches and bigger numbers? Smaller pitches and smaller numbers? My next progression is then looking at what topic we want to address for the day before I begin with the end in mind. How does what we want to train show up in the game? Once this is determined, planning the remainder of the session is usually quite simple and logical. I loved coloring books when I was a kid because the image was already drawn for you, all I had to do was color it in. Planning training should be the same. If you draw the picture first, coloring becomes easy.

One of the coolest things I learned from Neil is that there are no rules to coaching. Coaching can be very enlightening once you realize that no one really knows what they are doing. There are no rules and nothing is off-limits or impossible. For example, I used to think that the session plan was some secret paper that only the coaches could see and have access to. However, Neil thinks it is vital that the players know what the training session is going to be. "We write up every session and post it in our locker room and send it to every player before the session. The players can then start to understand and visualize what we want to focus on for that day."

One thing that is unique about college soccer in the United States is that we use a running clock. In other words, the clock stops when there is a foul, or when there is a yellow card given, or something else of that nature. When the clock hits 0:00 the game is over. There is no stoppage time. There is no injury time. Neil believes that training with a clock is essential to making practice as realistic to the game as possible. "One of the things that I probably do differently than everyone else is I am constantly using the clock at training. I use a visible clock, the one in the stadium that our players are going to be looking at in the game, and the reason I do that is because I want the players to always be aware of the clock during play. As we know in college soccer, the clock is relevant. The clock is running down and once it hits zero the game is over. So, we may play two-minute 3v3 games and I will have the clock running. The players will then have to communicate to one another things like, "Eight seconds left, shoot, shoot, shoot!" If I don't use a clock and I just blow the whistle at the end of two minutes, then the players will have no idea how much time was left." Being game-like means incorporating things in training that also exist in the game. Neil doesn't just make sure his training activities are game-like, but also the environment around the training games. Is there a referee? Is there offside? Is there a clock? Is there a winner and a loser? When you start to ask yourself those questions, you will have a bigger interpretation of what it means to be game-like.

CHAPTER 4

FROM ASSISTANT TO HEAD COACH AND BACK AGAIN

MARIO SANCHEZ

Mario Sanchez is the head men's soccer coach at Southern-Illinois at Edwardsville, an NCAA Division 1 school in Illinois. Prior to his role at SIUE, Mario worked as an assistant coach at the University of Louisville, the University of Akron, and Fresno State. Mario also worked as the head coach at UNLV prior to returning to the University of Louisville as the associate head coach. Mario took over an 8-9-1 SIUE team and has led them to two back-to-back NCAA tournament appearances (2015 and 2016) and double-digit win seasons en route to an NCAA Sweet 16 appearance in 2016.

The coach that knows why will beat the coach that knows how — Player-centered coaching versus athlete-centered coaching — What comedians can teach us about honing our craft — What Bill Belichick can teach you about being a good assistant coach — Slowly, slowly — The devil is in the details

One of my favorite books of all time is Simon Sinek's *Start With Why.* In his book, Sinek examines three aspects of people and companies: the what, the how, and the why. The what is your actual job—coaching, for example. The how is your individual art of coaching or how you choose to coach. But it is the why that is the most important. What purpose does coaching provide you? Why do you care about coaching? These are the questions that, if answered thoroughly, will spring you out of bed each morning. However, if you don't know your why, or have a poor reason for doing what you do, then the only thing that will wake up inspired is your hand as it smacks your alarm clock to pieces. Inspired coaches start with why. As Simon Sinek says, "people don't buy what you do, they buy why you do it."

As a young coach, I have struggled answering the question of why. Mario Sanchez echoed this sentiment when he explained why most coaches get started. "I think as coaches we go through a couple of different phases. Early on, you are like, 'Okay, well, I played soccer and I am not sure what I want to do, so I think I am going to coach.'" Most players that become coaches rationalize this decision by weighing the benefits of being around a pitch all day versus being in an office all day. A lot of players end up becoming coaches because being around the game beats working a 9-to-5 job. Mario understands how that transition feels. "You kind of coach to coach in the beginning, but eventually you transition to a phase where you want to win everything. You don't care who gets in your way, you want to win everything you possibly can. You just want to win and that becomes your reason why." This is another phase that coaches may go through until they find greater perspective.

Eventually, a coach needs something greater than wins and losses to keep coming back to the field each and every morning. "Something I ask myself, now that I have gotten older—and hopefully a lot wiser—is that exact question of why? Ultimately, I have two reasons why. First, the game of soccer has given me so much in life. Everything I have to this day I owe to soccer. My education? I got because of soccer. My career? I have because of soccer. So, I truly want my players to learn to love this game. The reason why I coach is I want to show my passion for the game of soccer and how great it can be, nothing to do with winning, but just how great and fun this sport can be." Mario really opened my eyes to the idea that not everything in life needs a big existential answer as to why we get up in the morning. One of the ideas I am toying with as my why for coaching is because it is fun. As simple as it gets! I think the reason why I coach is because it's fun. Does it need to be anything more than that?

The great thing about sports and being on a team is that it provides everyone on that team with the opportunity to be a part of something bigger than themselves—an essential component of living a fulfilling life. Mario loves that part of the game. He loves that everyone—regardless of their role as a coach, player, or athletic trainer—has the opportunity to improve and reach their fullest potential. "It comes down to the question of, ultimately, how good of a team can we just be? Regardless of the outcome, or the score, can we just absolutely, as people, maximize our ability and our potential?"

It is also important to know why our players play the game. The game of soccer is fun, but it doesn't come without its fair share of scraped knees and hard times. Your players, depending on the level of the game you coach at, will be asked to make sacrifices. They will have to go to bed early on a Friday night to get ready for a game on Saturday. They will have to do a lot of hard work that normal people won't have to do. They will have to get up early for a 6AM practice. They will have to miss three days of school for a road game. If your players don't have a good reason for why they are playing, then they will undoubtedly quit when things get hard. What binds a team together is a common purpose and a common understanding that each individual will contribute their absolute best to a cause bigger than themselves.

It is important to note that your why will change and evolve. The why for a 20-year-old assistant coach may be different than the why for that same coach 30 years later. "I think the why is a natural evolution for people. As a young 20-year-old, I would give that kid a lot of credit if he isn't just thinking about winning. But, I think now that I am getting older, yes, I want to win, but if that is the only reason why I coach then that's shallow. I tell my players all the time that there is only one champion at the end of the season, so just because we don't win doesn't mean we are failures; if that were true then there would be 200 other teams in the country that are failures and I just don't agree with that." Winning plays a role, but to define things like success or purpose based on an uncontrollable result is nothing short of a travesty.

COACHING TYPE

Early on in a coach's career it can be difficult to find your voice. By voice, I mean what you value as a coach and how you exemplify and deliver that value. Generally speaking, there are two types of coaches:

1. Command-style = Direct = Coach-centered
2. Question-led = Guided = Player-centered

Command-style coaches are the ones that take total control of every situation and create an atmosphere where the players have no say. This is a very common approach in professional soccer because of the emphasis on winning and results. The development of individuals will be put on the back burner as the focus shifts toward results at all costs.

Player-centered coaches, on the other hand, welcome input from their players in making decisions. For example, a player-centered coach may show his team the way their upcoming opponent may choose to play and then ask the players how they think they could play to beat the opponent. Lynn Kidman, author of *Athlete-Centered Coaching: Developing Decision Makers* breaks down the philosophy of player-centered coaching very simply, saying that "athletes learn more effectively when they are involved in solving problems and have ownership and responsibility for their learning."

Imagine two scenarios. In the first scenario, you are assigned a book on a particular subject and you are ordered to read it and write a report on what you learned. In the second scenario, you are allowed to pick any book in the library and complete the same writing task. Which book will you learn more from? Which book will you be more excited to read? Which paper will you be more excited to write? This is really the difference between a coach-centered approach and a player-centered approach. "I really think it is important to have a relationship with the players. My method involves forming a relationship with the player off the field to make sure the guys trust me as a person and as someone they can talk to. I want my players to feel comfortable asking me questions, especially about why we are doing something."

Mario is a player-centered coach. While some coaches may take offence to their players asking questions about their tactics, Mario embraces it because "it gives you an opportunity to build trust with the players and have them see you as an approachable human being. I think if the players don't like you, or they only do things because you told them to, at some point they will start to tune you out."

The best coaching advice you will ever receive is to just be yourself. Oscar Wilde famously said, "Be yourself, because everyone else is already taken." This is a thought I will come back to later in this book during Anson Dorrance's chapter. Don't get me wrong, early in your career it is important to mimic other coaches to an extent to see what works for you and what doesn't, but if you find yourself feeling uncomfortable yelling at players, then don't make that your coaching identity just because you saw a video of Diego Simeone losing his mind on a player during training.

Mario values relationships with his players above all else. "You can be the best tactician in the world, but if your players don't like you or accept you as a person, then they won't play for you." There are a number of ways to build relationships and trust with your players. Neil Jones said it best when he said that it is as simple as "getting to know them off the field." Mario Sanchez has a more hands-on approach that he loves. "One thing we do is we literally work out with our guys in the weight room. Not because we want to get ripped or anything, but because it allows us to practice what we preach and also talk with the guys away from the field, and they get to see us as normal people."

It is possible, of course, to be player-centered in some ways and coach-centered in others. Mario proposes that a balanced coaching philosophy is one of the more useful ways. "I am very demanding with the guys and I have expectations of them. I always tell them that if they don't ask a question then I will assume they know what we are doing and so I will have a high demand and expectation from them. But I always tell them that if they don't understand or don't agree with something, then they have to ask. This allows us to talk about their concerns and we both can learn and apply a better, more collaborative approach."

Experienced-based resources, such as Lyn Kidman's book mentioned earlier, highlight some of the benefits Mario is referring to. "It is important to understand that the key to the player-centered approach is to understand a leadership style that caters to the needs and understandings of the athletes. This encourages athletes and enables them to take control of their participation in sport." The evidenced-based research on this approach has shown that athletes subjected to a player-centered approach are more "motivated to learn and they exhibit a greater understanding and retention of both tactics and skills."

I have found myself allowing my emotions get the best of me sometimes when coaching. For example, if a player challenges you in front of the team or questions a specific tactical approach, a common sensation is to feel the hair on the back of your neck stand up. Coaches, for some reason, have an innate desire to appear omnipotent. The problem with that approach is that you will make mistakes. Coaches get things wrong and the quicker you show your players that you are fallible, just like they are, the quicker they will come to respect and appreciate you. When Mario is stopped by one of his players and questioned about a specific aspect of the game during training, instead of getting defensive and telling the player to just do it, he does something that is a lot easier said than done: he listens. This approach, as shown in the evidenced-based research, allows for greater retention of skills and tactics. "I don't want it to be a dictatorship where it's just me telling the players where to go, especially if they don't know why they are going there or if they have questions about what they are doing. I always want guys to ask why we are doing something." It makes for a more productive environment.

In the information age, players have access to the same tactical videos we see as coaches. Players are much more informed and it is quite common for them to wonder why they aren't pressing like Barcelona or sitting in and countering like Chelsea. "This generation likes that and they want to feel like they have a say in the decision-making process. They don't want to be told what to do. Obviously, when I grew up, if you were told to do something you did it without even questioning it, but things have changed."

A bigger take-away from what Mario is saying is that you need to be over-prepared as a coach. There are times where I cannot sleep at night because I am thinking about all the potential objections or questions players may ask about a particular topic or activity. As you are planning your session you need to be your own red team. A red team is a concept developed by the United States military and is a team that is tasked with poking holes in a proposed plan until they can no longer see any holes. Typically, if the group still believes they should move forward with an idea or concept after the red team attacks it, then it is considered a good idea. Create a red team with your training sessions and watch how much better your activities and coaching points become.

COACHES ARE LIFELONG LEARNERS

You are reading this book because you want to get better as a coach. You have questions, but not necessarily all the answers, and that is perfect. What no one is willing to admit is that we all feel that way. Whether you are Pep Guardiola or a first-year coach, you will never stop feeling like there is more to learn. That simply will never stop. And if it does, that means you are falling fast into complacency because we all have things we can get better at, no matter how good we think we already are. Mario was one of the youngest head coaches in NCAA Division 1 at the University of Nevada-Las Vegas (UNLV) in the late 2000s. However, Mario, in a surprising move, left that position to go to the University of Louisville—as an assistant. "People thought I was absolutely crazy. They were like, 'Do you know how hard it is to get a NCAA head coaching job?' But, ultimately, I was in my early 30s and I still didn't know everything I needed to know. I wanted to continue to learn. I wanted to put myself in a position where I was really going to challenge myself as a coach and a person by coaching at one of the biggest programs in the country."

If Mario wanted to be a good coach, then he could have stayed at UNLV and lived happily ever after, but Mario wanted to be a great coach. "In life you always have to challenge yourself. Recruiting on a national level and facing the teams we were playing helped me elevate my tactical understanding of the game. It was all part of my development. That process helped me transition from the head coach I was to the head coach I wanted to be." Coaches that want to go from good to great need to get comfortable with being uncomfortable. During his appearance on the Tim Ferriss podcast, comedian Jerrod Carmichael said, "As a comedian you don't want to go to the same club every night and do the same jokes that you know get laughs. I make it my mission to go to different clubs as much as I can and try to write new jokes every night. I know I will fail, but I am constantly forcing myself to grow, adapt, and improve."

BEING A GOOD ASSISTANT COACH

Being a coach is tough, but being an assistant coach can be one of the most difficult tasks in the world. As an assistant, I will be the first to admit that there are times I disagree with my head coach's evaluation of a situation, opinion of a player, or proposed tactical adjustment. "When I went back to Louisville, some of the other assistant coaches would be like, 'Man, why is Ken (Lolla, the Louisville head coach) doing this?' I had so much more perspective this time around as an assistant having been a head coach. I told them—and I always tell assistant coaches this—that until you sit in that chair, you just won't understand what his mindset is like." It is hard to have the perspective of the head coach as an assistant. I find myself daydreaming sometimes about things I would change or players I would start, but the truth is that it takes experience as a head coach to understand the pressure of being a head coach.

It is easy to talk about different decisions when you are an assistant because the outcome of those decisions falls on someone else. If you refer back to Nassim Taleb and the idea of having skin in the game, being an assistant coach and telling the head coach what to do is similar to a financial advisor telling you where to invest your money. If the financial advisor is wrong, he loses nothing and you lose everything. "It's the head coach's name on the line and that is what assistant coaches don't understand. That is the nature of the business. You win and the players get the credit and when you lose the head coach gets the blame. It's a lot harder than being able to sit back as an assistant and say, 'Yeah, do that, or kick this kid off the team, etc.' but it's not your name on the line." The truth is that nothing prepares you for being a head coach until you are one. That being said, an assistant's job is to paint the other side of the picture. A great assistant knows that when the head coach makes a decision, it is their job to support that decision as if it were their own.

"When I was at UNLV, one of my assistants was Rich Ryerson (who is the head coach there now). I remember we were playing Sacramento State and it was 1-1 and I wanted to play for the tie. Rich was adamant that we went for it and he said to me, 'No way, man! Let's go for it!' We ended up losing 2-1 and I was so mad, but that was an important learning moment for me to trust my gut as a head coach. The funny thing is, Rich called me up last year and said, 'I have to apologize for all those times I told you we should go for it. I was an idiot. Now I know what you were talking about!'" Being a head coach is truly different.

What does it take, then, to be a good assistant coach? If we can't make all the decisions, then what are we meant to do? "I think that one of the biggest traits an assistant coach needs to have is loyalty. That is not even just a soccer thing, but a life thing. I would hope that in life, you want anyone you work with to be a loyal person."

Earlier I mentioned the Canvas Strategy, employed by Bill Belichick as a young NFL assistant coach. Mario believes wholeheartedly in that strategy. "I think building a relationship with the head coach and trying to make the head coach look good are two of the most important traits in a good assistant coach. If the head coach looks good, then everyone looks good. If you don't make the head coach look good, then it will be hard for you to look good as an assistant."

This isn't to say that a head coach is immune to being challenged by their assistants. In fact, that is a very healthy environment. However, many assistants end up going about that in the wrong way. For example, if you want to challenge the head coach because you don't understand a decision he is making, just make sure the challenge occurs in private.

"For me, I always tell my assistants, 'Hey, challenge me, but in private, not in front of the team. I am always open to my assistants asking me why I am doing something and that usually leads to a very honest discussion about it. With that said, once you leave the office you have to all be on the same page." The biggest key to being a good assistant is not blind obedience or being a yes man, but being someone that will challenge and push the head coach in appropriate ways and at appropriate times. But a great assistant also understands that once a decision is made, regardless of whether or not he agrees with the decision, he has to support the decision 100%.

TAKING OVER A PROGRAM

When Mario took over as the head coach at SIUE in 2015, he inherited a team that had been to the NCAA tournament the year before. Mario told me what his thought process was like when taking over the program and I couldn't help but think about a quote that I love: "If you carry around a hammer, everything else becomes a nail." Too often, coaches around the world will take over a new team and immediately look to implement their values, playing style, rules, and expectations. While it is important for coaches to have these things laid out and understood, you need to choose the right tool for the job. "When I came in to UNLV, I came in guns blazing. I came in like I had all the answers and I wanted to change everything and I told the players how we were going to do this, and we were going to be the best team. I told them that we were going to win championships and I look back and I think, 'What an idiot.' I mean, at the time UNLV just wasn't ready for that. If anything, I probably made it harder for the players to succeed because I put unrealistic expectations on them. SIUE was a lot different." Taking over a new team is like eating dinner in a foreign country. How well received would you be if you went to a restaurant in Japan and ordered a spaghetti dinner and asked to eat it with a fork and knife? Countries have customs and cultures that are ignored at your own peril. We often don't see that soccer teams also have customs and cultures. And although we may want to eventually change them to things more prone to winning, we can't eliminate the previous culture in one fell swoop. We will be met with resistance and kicked out of the restaurant even faster than we came in.

Mario's experience speaks to why it is so important for coaches to make mistakes and fail early, with the assumption that they actually learn from their mistakes. "My first experience at SIUE was completely different. I spoke a little about soccer, but mostly I talked about getting to know them and learning about them as people. So, I gave each guy a piece of paper and we set up individual meeting times. On each piece of paper was basic stuff like: their families, their goals for soccer, their goals for college and for life, etc."

I had the opportunity to listen to a presentation from Adam Sadler, the Leicester City opponent scout, and in his presentation he mentioned that Claudio Ranieri's philosophy was "slowly, slowly." Adam mentioned how the first month or so of training it seemed like the team wasn't going to learn anything or be prepared for the Premier League season. "Ranieri told me that he needed to evaluate what he had first before he determined how he was to best utilize each piece. I would panic and say, 'Claudio, we have a game in a week!' and he would always respond, 'Slowly...slowly.'" I love that idea from Claudio. Too often as coaches we try to cram an idea into the last 15 minutes of a session when we might be better served just training it tomorrow. Another example is trying to progress our team too quickly from one topic that they have yet to master. The pressure of results sometimes forces coaches to bypass the process, but what you will find is the best managers and coaches are able to find a perfect balance of patience and progression.

Mario took a very methodical approach to his first spring season in charge of SIUE. "At UNLV, I was freaking in there, man. I was telling them how it was going to be and just totally dictating how we were going to play. But with SIUE, I wanted to see what the players could do, I wanted to see what kind of ideas they had, and then from there I could try to calculate how to implement my ideas and how I preferred things to be done. When I look back, I think I prolonged the development process by at least a year at UNLV because of how naive I was, whereas with SIUE, the slower approach led us to a much better spot and in half the time than at UNLV."

THE DETAILS OF THE GAME

Ryan Holiday, author of *Ego is the Enemy* says, "As our island of knowledge grows, so does the shore of our ignorance." I love this quote because to be a passenger on the coaching journey is to fully live this quote. The more we learn as coaches and the more we come to understand, the less we realize we truly know. In other words, the better you get, the more questions you end up with.

Mario believes that the devil is in the details. Something may seem simple at first, such as coaching soccer, but the more time you spend examining the idea of coaching and all the intricate details, the more you realize how complex it actually is. Mario has become obsessed with the details of the game. "If you are at a team, or a program, that has better players, you can get away with not being very good tactically, but I learned throughout my career that I love making bad players into good players. And the way that you do that is by teaching the game in a very minute, detail-oriented way."

During my conversation with Mario, he gave me an example of a detail he changed during the season and how that influenced the performance of his team. Traditionally, Mario and SIUE like to play a 1-4-2-3-1. However, their upcoming opponent loved to use their outside backs in the buildup, which meant that a one-striker system would allow their opponent's outside backs to get on the ball fairly easily. Mario's approach was to force the opponent to play in a way unfamiliar to them. Mario switched to a 1-4-4-2 diamond midfield and pressed the opponent in a way that forced them into central passes that ended up causing a lot of turnovers during their opponent's build-up play. The result was a 1-0 win against a nationally ranked opponent (whose head coach is also featured in this book).

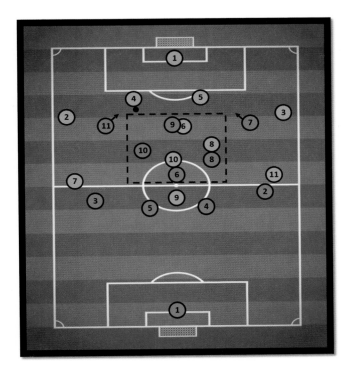

Mario tasked his forwards (SIUE in blue) with starting near the opponent's outside backs and pressing the opposing center backs as soon as they received the ball from the goalkeeper. This forced the opponent's center backs to relieve pressure by playing one of their central midfielders that were outnumbered 4v3 in the central space. This tactical change came through Mario's and his staff's analysis of the opponent and an intense focus on the details of the game.

In a similar fashion to Jay Martin, Mario worked with his team's sports psychologist to create process-oriented goals for each player at SIUE. "We stopped worrying about the final score and instead broke the game down and said, 'Okay, for our left winger our focus is pressing the opposition outside right back every time he receives the ball, or for our forward it is to focus on maintaining possession for us when played in transition. We didn't worry about how many goals we scored or shutouts, but just a pure focus on everyone doing their job. The next day, as a team, we would rate each other on our performance, not the outcome."

Mario's keys to success for his quick turnaround of the SIUE program are an intense focus on the details of the game and coaching the process, not the outcome. "We put a lot of time and effort these last two years into really breaking the game down. We worked tirelessly on improving the communication, tactically, between our players so that our right back knows what our right winger has to do, and so on and so forth. This way, we can approach a game and at halftime we can simply ask, 'Are we all doing what we need to be doing?'"

The more time I spend talking with coaches the more I realize how important process versus outcome is. Unfortunately, in soccer, sometimes your team can do exactly what they need to do and every player can perform their task adequately, but you can still lose the game. But if you yell at your players after a loss in that fashion or allow them to hang their heads, you automatically switch the emphasis of your program from the things within your control to the things outside of your control. Your players cannot control a missed offside call by the referee. They can control pressing the right fullback of the opponent when he receives the ball. If we lose 1-0 because the referee missed a blatant offside, it doesn't mean we blame the referee, but it definitely means we don't blame our players. Mario encourages coaches to always come back to the most important question: did everyone do what needed to be done? If the answer is yes, then getting mad about the result is exactly that—getting mad about something you cannot control.

From the outside looking in, it is hard not to describe Mario Sanchez as successful. He has taken an unheralded SIUE program and turned them into a NCAA top 25 program that is looking to improve on an NCAA Tournament Sweet 16 appearance in 2016. However, success is defined in a unique way for Mario. "How I judge success, ultimately, is did I give my team the best chance to win? I have a checklist that I use at the end of each week and I ask my assistants to rate me and our program on a number of categories: my communication during the week, teaching the game plan, quality of practice, do the players know their roles, do they understand the restarts and set pieces, etc. By doing this at the end of each week I can truthfully manage the only thing I can control, which is myself."

CHAPTER 5

MENTOR–COACH RELATIONSHIPS

ANTHONY PULIS

Anthony Pulis is the head coach of Orlando City B in the USL. Anthony is the son of West Bromwich Albion FC manager, Tony Pulis. Anthony grew up playing for his father and in the lower English leagues before moving to the United States to play for Adrian Heath and Orlando City. Once Anthony retired in 2014, he was offered the opportunity to go straight into coaching with Orlando City's USL side.

Like father, like son — How a red team can help you become a better coach — Giving the players what they need, not what they want — Why the best are obsessed with getting better — Earning your UEFA A by knowing how to defend half-spaces

My dad has worked in sales for over 35 years. Even though I currently coach soccer for a living, something my dad never did, I have adopted traits of his that have influenced the way I am as a coach and person. It always made me wonder if I would be a little bit better tactically as a coach if my father had been a Premier League manager or something like that. When you look at how quickly Anthony Pulis has become a winning coach in the USL, it adds some clout to my theory. Anthony's father, Tony, has managed at Crystal Palace, Stoke City, Portsmouth, Plymouth Argyle, and West Bromwich Albion, his current role. We spoke at length about his father and the influence he has had on Anthony as a coach.

PREMIER LEAGUE DAD

Anthony, in many respects, lived a dream childhood for a kid who loved soccer. For a kid growing up in Wales in the 1990s, telling your friends that your dad is a professional soccer manager was akin to telling them that your dad is Batman. But for Anthony, it was just Dad. "Being around my dad at the different clubs he was at was just the norm for me. During school holidays, when I was a kid, I would literally go into the training ground and be with him all day. It sounds crazy now, but he would literally let me jump into training with the team. I would travel with them, I would sit on the bench during games—which I wouldn't be able to get away with now—but at the time I was so immersed in the everyday of professional soccer that the realities of professional soccer became quite ordinary for me."

It goes without saying that being that involved in the soccer world as a child isn't always about seeing the goals and hearing the songs sung around the stadium. There is a dark side to coaching soccer as well and Anthony certainly witnessed his fair share of those moments too. "I can remember a game when he was managing Bristol City. I was sitting on the bench during the game and we lost 2 or 3-nil, I can't remember. I do remember walking off with my dad and holding on to his shirt standing just behind him, and listening to the fans give my dad some of the worst verbal abuse I ever heard. It was the first time I came face to face with the pressure and abuse that my dad had to deal with on a daily basis. I couldn't help but wonder, 'Why does he put himself through this?'"

I don't know if I will ever manage in the Premier League, but I have a hunch that one of the hardest things to explain to your child is why 15,000 people are calling you a wanker. I mean, for young Anthony, soccer was just a game that he loved to play. He loved being around the professional players. He loved joining in with the fans as they sang his favorite tune. But I can only imagine how confused Anthony was as to why the fans—who had sung his father's name glowingly a week earlier—were now calling for his head.

I can only imagine what that was like to be Tony. Not only does he have to deal with reporters asking him if the rumors are true ("Will you be manager tomorrow morning?"), but, on top of that, he has to figure out a way to explain to his young boy that Batman isn't immortal. It's not an easy conversation, but the way Tony handled those moments sheds light as to why Tony has been a managing staple in England for nearly 20 years. "I remember being in the car with him on the way home and it was honestly like water off a duck's back to him. I remember him telling me very calmly, 'Listen, this is what I signed up for. The pressure and the abuse that people put me through makes no difference to me. I am still going to stick to my beliefs and my way of doing things.'" Obviously, Tony takes a very stoic approach to his managing career. Like Jay Martin said, "If you measure your success on wins and losses, you simply won't last very long as a coach." Tony Pulis knows that results come and go. You will have bad losses and unbelievable wins. However, the coaches that make it long term are the ones that focus on the process, not the outcome, and focus on two things: getting better and controlling what they can control.

I did still wonder if there was ever a time that it all became too much for Tony, but Anthony quelled that idea pretty quickly. "The pressure and things that happened in his professional life, he never brought home. Not once. Whenever he came home from work you would have no idea if anything good or bad had happened that day. He would totally leave work at work and he wouldn't worry about it until the next day." Sage advice for managing the coaching profession.

Anthony clearly learned a lot from his father about how to manage a soccer team, but Anthony's eyes were set on a playing career first. Anthony bounced around multiple clubs in England including Portsmouth, Stoke City, Southampton, and Aldershot Town before finishing out his career with Orlando City.

I remember as a kid I used to fantasize about my dad coaching for Real Madrid so he could sign me to a contract and I would go on to become one of the soccer greats. Far-fetched I know, but that was because it was far from reality. But it was reality for Anthony Pulis. Anthony signed for his father at Stoke City in 2004, but he doesn't look back on that time as cheerily as in my fantasies of playing for my professional soccer managing father. In other words, playing for your father is more a burden than a blessing. "I look back and think that sometimes that wasn't the right decision [to sign for his father]. It was really difficult playing for my father. It got to the stage at Stoke where it was becoming increasingly difficult to be the manager's son and always sort of in his shadows a little bit."

In theory, it sounds like a great idea. A dad coaches a professional soccer team and his son happens to play professional soccer—what could go wrong? "I can remember like it was yesterday walking into that locker room for the first time as the manager's son. Let's just say it wasn't something that I enjoyed. I could almost see everybody stop what they were doing and stare at the manager's son, not Anthony. You could hear a pin drop in the locker room, but I could tell that they were thinking things like: there's the manager's son, we better be careful what we say, I bet he is going to take my spot now, etc. Everyone was walking on eggshells around me. That first week or two was a really, really hard time for me."

The situation improved at Stoke after the other players realized Anthony wasn't receiving any special treatment, he was a normal guy, and it didn't hurt that he could play a little bit. Anthony reflected on his time at Stoke and realized that it wasn't all bad. In addition to creating friendships that still exist to this day, he also met his wife. However, probably the most beneficial thing to come out of the Stoke experience for Anthony was how much he learned about people. "You learn a lot about people in situations like that. Some players were nicer to me than they normally would have been because they know you are the manager's son. Other people were very, very stand-offish because they were probably afraid that anything said to me would somehow make its way back to my dad. The truth was that I was just a normal player, but you can't change people's perceptions." You can't blame the players for acting the way they did. In the US, for example, most parents that coach their kids either treat them with a soccer version of nepotism—or they treat them worse than the average player to compensate for the perception that the coach might be playing favorites. It is a really difficult situation for both the player and the coach. "My dad and I had a very good professional relationship. He knew never to ask me what was being said in the locker room, or what a certain player thinks about the tactics, or anything like that. He knew that would make for a really bad situation for both of us."

Anthony and his father navigated the treacherous waters of nepotism in the Premier League fairly well up to that point. The players had gained respect for their new teammate, who was now known as Anthony, not the manager's son. And Tony was learning how to manage his son like any other player. Eventually, results started to go sideways for Stoke around the same time Anthony was progressing as a potential first team option. The supporters were calling for Tony to be sacked and the assistant coaches were pushing Tony to give his son an opportunity. Tony and Anthony sat down to discuss the situation. "My dad pulled me aside and said 'Listen, I don't want to put you in this situation because I know that if the team carries on losing, and you happen to be playing, the supporters will use you as a scapegoat to get me out.' As soon as he said that, we both kind of looked at each other and realized that I needed to move on and try and navigate the professional game on my own two feet."

Anthony really opened my eyes to how difficult a father-son and coach-player relationship can be. "It's a no-win situation. If you are on the team and you are playing, everyone will say, 'Well, you are only on the team because your father is the manager.' If you are not on the team and you aren't playing, everyone will say, 'What's he doing with his son on the team if he's not going to play him? He must have him on the team just to give him a wage' So, it is a really difficult situation to manage."

COACHING PHILOSOPHY

Anthony learned a lot about management from his dad. Perhaps, soccer management is even genetic. "I think the one trait I inherited from my father is his organizational skills. He is renowned for making sure players know exactly what is expected from them, roles and responsibilities in and out of possession, but 90% of the time he focuses on what they need to do out of possession." Tony is infamous for his attention to detail on the defensive side of the ball. "If you ask any of his current West Brom players where they should be defensively when the ball is on a certain blade of grass on the field, they would probably be able to tell you." Anthony has certainly inherited that attention to detail from his father. "I definitely take a little bit of that from him. I need to make sure that when my players cross that white line they know exactly what is expected of them and what their job is."

Anthony is different from his father in a lot of ways too. "I think on the attacking side of the ball, I would like my teams to play a little more soccer than what my dad's teams do. I want my teams to play out of the back and play quickly through the thirds of the pitch. To be fair, in order to play that way you need to have really good center backs that can take care of the ball and I am not sure if my dad has ever been afforded that." Tony believes that good soccer management is about coaching the players that you have. As much as he would love to have more of the ball, that just isn't reality for the teams that Tony has managed.

Anthony is still young in his coaching journey and admits that he still has a lot to learn. Perhaps his father's pragmatic approach to winning soccer matches will catch up to him at some point. He does acknowledge that his father's approach to each new situation has taught him something important. "The biggest thing he always says to me is you have to play to the strengths of the team that you have. If you have certain players that can't do certain things, don't ask them to do it." That is such an important lesson for any coach to learn. At the youth level, that message is perhaps misguided because the focus is on the player's development, but in elite soccer—where results mean keeping your job—you have to play to the strengths of your team no matter what the perception may be about the style that you play.

I transitioned from a professional playing career into a coaching career in 2013. I am a firm believer that you don't have to play the game at a high level to be a great coach. Arrigo Sacchi put it best, "You don't have to be a horse in order to be a jockey." However, I think that being a former player does provide you with useful experiences and models of what players like in a coach and what players don't like in a coach. Anthony has had a number of coaching influences on his playing career that have helped shape him as a coach. "Everything that we do, whether we're designing a training session, or crafting a presentation for the players, I will always ask myself, 'All right, if I was a player, would I enjoy this? What would my thoughts be on this?'" The thing Anthony valued most in his coaches growing up was one thing: honesty. "One of my biggest policies has been to be as honest as I possibly can. I will never beat around the bush and lead players on; I will always try and be completely honest with them. If they are being left out of the team because of their performance, then I will tell them exactly that. If they are being left out of the team—even when they have been playing well—because the MLS team is sending a player down, then I will tell them that as well. I always respected the coaches that were honest with me."

BEING A YOUNG PRO COACH

They say age is just a number, but try telling that to a 35-year-old pro that is being coached by a 32-year-old. Anthony is a young coach by any metric, but for a professional coach he is very young. Still, there are young managers like TSG 1899 Hoffenheim manager, Julian Nagelsman, that have proven successful despite their age. But for some reason there is still a stigma surrounding young coaches. Earlier in the book, we learned from Neil Jones that as a young coach you should double your listening and decrease your talking, but that is quite hard as the manager.

Anthony didn't instantly earn respect from the players just because he was the head coach; he had to earn it. "In the early days of my time with Orlando City B I also served as an assistant for the first team after Adrian Heath was let go. It was a great opportunity because it gave me experience coaching first-team professional players for the first time. I remember our first game in charge, Bobby Murphy [interim head coach] put me in charge of set pieces: corners, free kicks, throw-ins, etc. So, we are out on the pitch and I am explaining how we want to go about defending corner kicks for the upcoming game and literally straight away, I mean right away, like my first sentence, one of the older and experienced players started to question me about the setup. Really, he was just testing me to see if I knew what I was talking about. He asked what happens if the opponent sends two players out for a short corner and thankfully I had an answer. So, I told him that we will send two players out to match them 2v2 and our back post player will have to move to the six-yard hole, and the player on the six-yard hole will have to move to the near post." Being challenged by your players is a certainty as a coach. If you are a coach that wants to coach at the highest level of the game, then you have to prepare yourself for being challenged. "It was another one of those learning experiences for me that this is a step up and you have to make sure, at that level, that when you are explaining something, or asking the players to do something, you know exactly why they are doing it. And, if something changes, you need to have an answer for them right away." In Mario Sanchez's chapter, I referred to a concept used by the US military called a red team. A red team is essential to be prepared for any question that may come up. If you don't poke holes in your sessions, tactics, or adjustments, then your players certainly will.

My staff and I create a red team on a daily basis during the season. Let's say you have a staff of four coaches and you are preparing to teach your team how you want to press the opponent on the weekend. Split yourselves into two teams of two coaches; assign one team the task of being the defendant and the other team is the red team. Have the defendants give the team talk as you have prepared. During the presentation, the red team will be tasked with asking as many questions as possible, posing as many problems as possible, and trying to find any and all weaknesses in the plan. Sometimes it is helpful to switch roles after a period of five minutes. Once each group of coaches has completed each role (defendants, red team), the coaches should work together to solve any of the problems posed by the red team and incorporate any changes into your team talk.

One of my favorite strategies is to ask my players how they would beat us. For example, if I am teaching my team how I want them to press and our staff has already red teamed it, I will ask my players how they would bypass the press. Fortunately, because the red team already found these potential loopholes and my coaching staff solved them prior to talking to the team, I am able to diffuse any objection until my team knows our press is unstoppable as long as they execute. The point is that when coaching high-level players, whether they are college or professional athletes, you need to be prepared as a coach. At the highest levels, your players will look for problems in everything that you say. They will want to challenge you and prove you wrong. It is your job to over-prepare yourself and your staff, so that you are ready for any potential objection. Like Anthony said, "You need to know exactly why you are doing something and if there is an objection, you need to have an answer ready straight away." If you are unprepared, the players will find that out quickly, and their trust in you—and their desire to play for you—will be tarnished.

Anthony has also put a system in place to monitor his progress as a coach, and to identify areas for improvement. "In the middle of the season and at the end of the season, I gave the players a questionnaire aimed at gathering honest feedback about my coaching. I had a hunch that if I asked all of the players these questions face to face, they probably wouldn't give me the honest feedback I was looking for. The biggest thing, the overriding thing that they all wanted was to just play more. They wanted to have more opportunity to play 5v5 or 6v6 with no rules and just free play. That was hard for me to read because I pride myself on being super organized and every session having a theme and objective. It's not that we didn't play either, we did, we just always had conditions on the game like touch limits or only being able to score from certain areas. But, I thought maybe, yeah, there are some times where we can just play with no restrictions, or conditions that allow the players to express themselves, but it was hard for me to concede." This is one of the hardest parts of coaching older players. You need to train your game model and the way you want your team to play, but sometimes that isn't fun for the players. "My biggest worry was that we would end up having our center back thinking he is a center forward and our left back thinking he is a number 10, and the players basically run around and do what they want. I do think that there is a balance, however, so I began to include some games that allowed or encouraged some free play for the players to express themselves, but I am not sure I liked it." Anthony didn't have to necessarily agree with the feedback his players gave him, but it is important that he went through that process. The best part about receiving feedback from your players is that it opens a dialogue between you and your team. If they want more free play, that challenges you, as a coach, to communicate to them why that won't prepare them for what they need to do in the upcoming match. It creates a conversation between you and your players. Experience has shown me that it isn't necessarily important that the players get what they want, but it is important that their voices are heard.

Anthony did the right thing by getting feedback from his players and then implementing pieces of their feedback. When you ask your players for their opinions or feedback it is vital that you make an effort to recognize that feedback through some sort of acknowledgment like including some free play during training, or speaking with them about their feedback. However, if you disagree with the players on a philosophical level, then you may have to seek some outside opinions. An assistant manager at Southampton gave Anthony his advice which was, "You must give the players what they *need*, not what they *want*. If you give them what they want all the time that isn't going to help their development as players. If they just want to go play five-a-side and small-sided games, tell them to play in the park with their friends. They aren't welcome at a professional soccer club that is trying to help them get better." Needless to say, both pieces of feedback gave Anthony plenty to think about. The art of coaching is knowing which direction will best fit your team and your specific environment.

COACHING MISTAKES

I could write another book—maybe even a couple of volumes—on all of the mistakes I have made as a coach. One of the common themes of all the coaches I have interviewed is failure. They have all tried things, made mistakes, and failed in many ways both small and big. The other trait they all have in common is their resilience. They have certainly made mistakes, but they all have systems and processes set up to reflect on their mistakes, learn from them, and improve their coaching. Anthony is no exception. "A lesson I learned from this year is that I really need to improve my ability to coach in the flow. I am definitely guilty of stopping practice too many times, or too often. At the end of the day, it is important to understand that players want to play. So, I realized I was stopping practice too much, over-coaching, and I have made a conscious effort to find other ways to get my points across." Anthony now waits until a water break or a natural stoppage (e.g., the ball going out of play) to jump in and make his coaching points, but it is still something he is looking to continually improve.

It was refreshing to hear Anthony talk about how much more he has to learn as a coach. One of the processes I have implemented for myself actually comes from the project management world. One of the ideas I implemented is called "Start, Stop, Continue." At the end of every week, I reflect on my coaching over the previous week and I make a list of any new things I learned about my players, my team, and myself. After a thorough brainstorm, I make three lists. One list is all the things that I will *start* doing as a coach. For example, I may start coaching in the flow more. The second list is all the things I will *stop* doing. An example of this could be to stop making coaching points that are 30 seconds or longer. The final list is all of the things I will *continue* doing. An example of something that I will continue doing is asking my players how school is going each day before practice. Notice how I write the word *will*. I don't like the word *try*. For example, I will *try* to stop over-coaching my players. The word *try* gives you a reason not to do something. I will *try* to come to your birthday party means that I am not going to show up. Start. Stop. Continue.

Coaching is a craft that needs to be continually refined. Start, stop, and continue is one process you could implement that may help you on your journey of becoming a better coach. However, before you can do that you need to first admit you have things to learn and improve. Anthony is well aware of his position on the coaching journey. "I am just taking my baby steps to be completely honest. I think the pursuit of mastery is an illusion anyways. I don't think I will ever be completely happy or satisfied with myself as a coach. There is always something you want to improve on or get better at. I am obsessed with improving and getting better. I am constantly watching sessions online, visiting clubs around the world, reading books, taking courses, talking to coaches, and learning from them. I am way off from where I want to be."

This sentiment from Anthony reminds me of something Jay Martin said to me, "I hate to be called coach. For me, I have yet to earn that title. I am not a coach, at least not yet. I have so much to improve before I feel comfortable being called coach." The best are absolutely obsessed with getting better.

UEFA A LICENSE TOPIC: FULLBACKS DEFENDING HALF-SPACES

Anthony's UEFA A license topic was on defending half-spaces against wingers in a 1-4-2-3-1. He was tasked with providing his players with three solutions to the problem posed by the opposition's wingers use of the half-spaces. Half-spaces are an arbitrary description of the spaces in between the widest channel of a soccer field and the center-most channel.

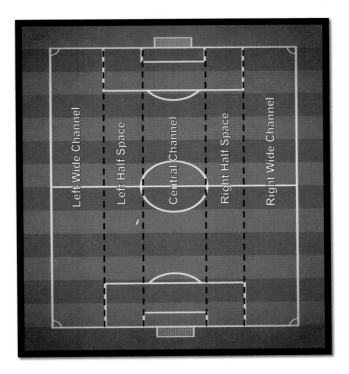

The half-spaces are strategically used by some teams to get their attacking players on the ball with the greatest field of vision and the least amount of pressure. The two images below explain how the half-space allows players to have a greater field of vision with less chance of losing possession.

Here you can see that, from the widest channel, a forward-facing player has three possible passing options. They can either go forward, diagonal, or sideways to the right. Of course, that is a simplification as the player could turn around and go backwards or backwards and diagonally to his left, but you will see why this simplification helps deconstruct these areas of the field and highlight the advantage of the half-spaces.

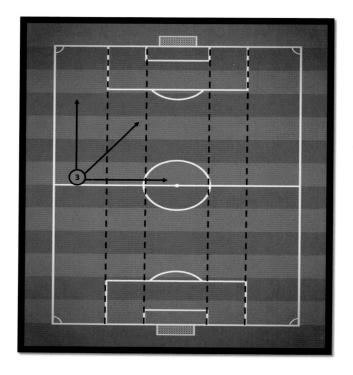

From the central channel, a player has a greater field of vision and five options to pass: forward, two diagonal directions, and two sideways directions. However, the issue with the central channel is that this area of the field is typically the most congested, which increases the chance of losing the ball. So, enter the half-spaces.

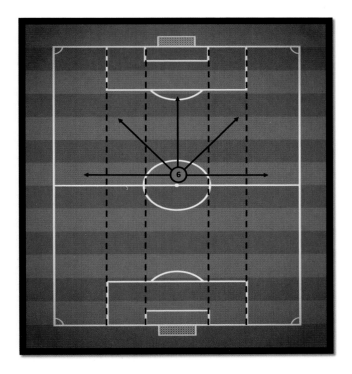

The player here is depicted facing diagonally, which is the true advantage of the half-space. If the player was facing straight on, he would still have the same five options and field of vision as the player who is centrally positioned. However, once the player is facing diagonally in the half-space, they are equipped with an even greater field of vision as opposed to the player who was centrally positioned. Here is a better picture to show the difference in field of vision.

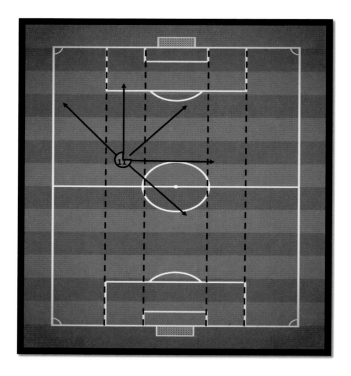

Further explanation of the half-spaces is beyond the scope of this text, but at least we now have context for Anthony's UEFA A topic. Basically, UEFA wanted to see how Anthony would teach his team to combat an opponent's use of the half-spaces. Here were Anthony's three solutions to the problem that earned him his UEFA A.

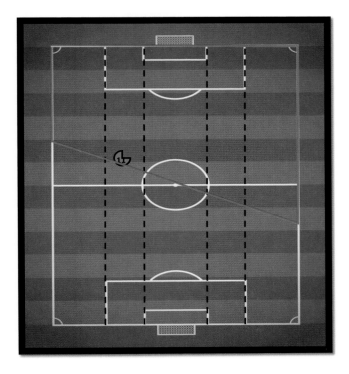

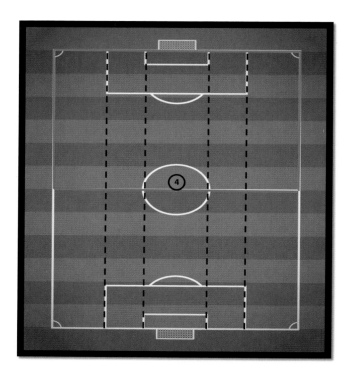

Problem: Winger (#7) is sitting in the half-space unmarked.

Solution: Our ball-side winger (#11) pinches central to mark the available player.

Here you can see #11 on blue (Anthony's team) moving centrally to take away the opponent's #7 as an option. Because of this shift by the winger, the outside back on blue (#3) can now move wider to mark the overlapping fullback.

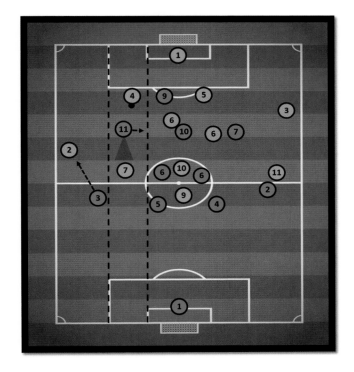

Problem: Winger (#7) is sitting in the half-space unmarked.

Solution: Our ball-side outside back (#3) steps in to cover the available player.

Here you can see the outside back for blue (#3) steps to the unmarked player to stop the winger from receiving the ball in the half-space. This allows #11 on blue to take care of the overlapping fullback (#2) on orange.

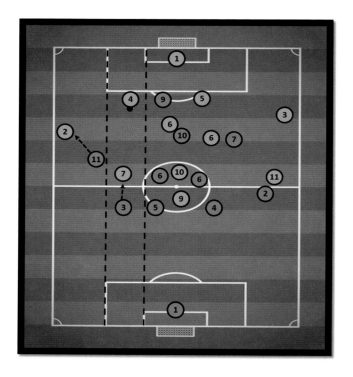

Problem: Winger (#7) is sitting in the half-space unmarked.

Solution: Available holding midfielder slides to pick up the available player.

Here you can see the free holding midfielder for blue (#6) is able to leave his position and pick up the available winger on orange. This allows the winger (#11) and the outside back (#3) to watch for the overlapping run of the outside back on orange. If the outside back for orange (#2) stays deeper to support the player on the ball (#4), then #11 can press him.

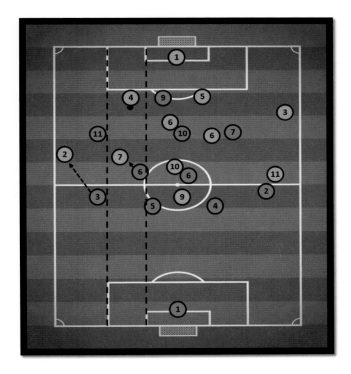

CHAPTER 6

COACHING DIFFERENT AGES, SEXES, AND LEVELS

OMID NAMAZI

Omid Namazi is the head coach of the U18 US Men's National Team and the assistant coach for the US U20 National Team that recently won the first CONCACAF U20 Championship. Prior to his role with the US National Team, Omid worked alongside Carlos Queiroz for four years as the Iran National Team assistant coach. Omid played professionally in the United States for over 15 years before beginning his professional coaching career with the Philadelphia KiXX of the MISL.

The importance of grit — On the other side of fear — Everyone is a son of a gun until they prove to you otherwise — Having your players decide on the strategy — Two different ways to high press out of a 1-4-3-3

YOUTH DEVELOPMENT IN IRAN

Omid was born to Iranian parents in the United States, but moved back to Iran shortly after his birth. I didn't have any idea what the youth development landscape looked like in Iran until I talked with Omid.

Omid Namazi didn't play organized soccer until he was 14 years old and yet he managed to have a 15-year professional playing career. "We played a lot of pick-up games in the neighborhood. Street soccer at the time was huge in Iran. Games of 3v3 or 4v4 were pretty easy to find and we would literally play until my mom or dad would come drag me off the court or street for dinner."

Omid is now fully entrenched in the United States youth development landscape. But that doesn't mean he is blind to some of our development system's obvious weak spots. One thing Omid questions is if our environment breeds the grit needed to make it as a professional in Europe. "The resources available to the kids in the US are comparable to the best countries in the world, if not *the* best. When I compare it to Iran—I mean you can't even compare them to each other. In Iran, it really came down to the individual to push themselves." Omid's last comment is where I want to make a point. Angela Duckworth is a researcher out of the University of Pennsylvania and the best-selling author of the book *Grit: Passion, Perseverance, and the Science of Success*. In her seminal research paper, "Grit: Perserverance and Passion for Long-Term Goals," Angela discovered that a non-tangible human quality, grit, is more influential in determining high achievers than we may think. "We observed that in every studied field, the general qualities possessed by high achievers included a strong interest in the particular field, a desire to reach a high level of attainment in that field, and a willingness to put in great amounts of time and effort." Angela continues by arguing that "creators must be able to persist in the face of difficulty and overcome the many obstacles in the way of creative discovery... Drive and energy in childhood are more predictive of success, if not creativity, than is IQ or some other more domain-specific ability."

Omid Namazi's subjective experience and Angela Duckworth's objective research have driven me to question the development progress we are making in the US and in other parts of the world. I interviewed Adrian Bradbury, a youth coach in Uganda, East Africa, on episode 86 of the podcast. Adrian moved to East Africa from Toronto, Canada in 2015 to start a soccer academy called "Football For Good." The academy is aimed at providing education and opportunities in soccer to young East Africans that otherwise wouldn't have access to such things. In just two years of existence, Adrian has been able to move players on to clubs like Chelsea, Dinamo Zigrab, and Southampton. I asked Adrian how he identifies talent and his response triggered me to think about grit and its role in building future professional soccer players. "The problem you see now among the most elite academies in the world is that they are all competing against each other in the arms race of building: incredible facilities, incredible coaching staffs, the best gear, the best nutrition, and the best setups possible. But when you offer these things to a 13-year-old, it's very difficult to keep them hungry. To keep them determined. To keep them tough. To give them the tools for when it gets hard to be able to internally manage the situation."

Angela Duckworth describes grit as "perseverance in the face of difficulty." Are the best youth academies in the world creating difficulty for their students and players to face? I am afraid the arm's race to garner the attention of the best youth players has completely eroded the development of grit or perseverance. Adrian continues, "The question for my club became how do we keep it a bit spartan, a bit tough, and a bit gritty, and hard, so when they go on trial at a club and there are four other kids fighting for that spot, they won't be looking over their shoulder wondering if they are good enough. They are just going to smash kids and get on with it. You need to create an environment that fosters that, but it's tough to fake or re-create that in an environment where kids are given everything."

Omid is living proof that you don't need to have access to world-class training facilities to become a professional player. I am not making any grand statement just yet, but I will tell you that I think the current trends in academy soccer and youth development in the US, and even abroad, are completely neglecting the development of grit that Angela Duckworth has shown to be significantly more important than any domain-specific ability.

OPPORTUNITY, GOALS, AND NETWORKING

Omid has coached both men and women at the highest level. In 2010, Omid was tasked with coaching the Chicago Red Stars in the Women's Professional Soccer (WPS) league. Unfortunately, the league folded after one season and Omid found himself at a crossroads in his career. He wanted to coach at the highest level he could, but he felt he had maximized his current ability. "I was looking for the next opportunity and that is when a friend of mine that had played in the MLS, Mohammad Khakpour, called me. Mohammed played in the 1998 World Cup for Iran and he was working at a club in Iran at the time called Steel Azin. He called me and asked if I would be interested in coming on board as an assistant."

Omid's story post-Chicago Red Stars reminds me so much of Mario Sanchez's story. If you recall, Mario went from being a head coach at UNLV to an assistant coach at Louisville in order to learn and get better, before eventually stepping back into the role of head coach. Mario's story ended successfully because the decision helped him "become the coach I always wanted to be, but didn't know how to be."

At this point in his career, Omid had been coaching professionally in the United States for over a decade. However, most of that time was spent bouncing around professional indoor teams and some women's professional teams with a short life expectancy. Omid was at a crossroads. He could stay in the US, in his comfort zone, and be a professional coach somewhere in no time. Or, at the age of 44, he could move his entire family to Iran to become an assistant coach again. "To have the opportunity to learn from such great coaches with great experiences was something I just couldn't turn down."

In the end, life becomes a collection of decisions and choices we make. Often, people would rather fantasize about achieving their goal than actually going for it. The reason we have a tendency to do that is because we are never confronted with the truth in our fantasies. However, if we keep our dreams as just that—dreams—then we never have to actually answer the question, "Are we actually good enough?"

American coach Bob Bradley is a perfect example of the importance of testing yourself to find the true limits of your potential and ability. Bob Bradley spent eleven years as the head coach at Princeton University before moving into professional soccer as an assistant. Bob became the US National Team coach from 2006 to 2011 and led the US to some unprecedented success, including a second place finish in the 2009 Confederations Cup. Bob, like Omid, was at a crossroads. The easy road was to find another MLS coaching job where he would probably still be employed today. But Bob wanted to see just how good a coach he actually was. Bob took a job as head coach in politically volatile Egypt where he took the team to within one game of qualification for the 2014 World Cup. That success created an opportunity to become one of the very few American coaches to manage in Europe as the manager of Staebek in Norway.

Initially, Bob had great success with Staebek, saving them from relegation before sustaining success in his second season. However, Bob wasn't done. He wanted to see just how far he could go. Le Havre, a Ligue 2 team in France, became the next opportunity before Bob received the biggest opportunity of his career: managing Swansea FC in the English Premier League. But that story didn't end happily ever after because Bob failed. Bob was fired three months after initially taking charge and, while most pundits, fellow coaches, and society might laugh at Bob Bradley, I applaud him. You see, in soccer, just as in life, we are all clapping for the wrong reasons. We applaud people that win, but ignore those that took a chance and lost. We encourage people's dreams and ambitions, but become unsupportive in their actual pursuit of those dreams. I mention Bob Bradley in this chapter because Omid Namazi also chose to pursue his dream of being a "first-division professional coach."

Jim Collins is the author of the seminal book, *Good to Great*, in which he explains how some of the best companies in the world made the transition from good to great. One of the key principles of every great company is a BFHAG, which stands for a Big Fat Hairy Audacious Goal. We all have—or at least had—one at some point in our lives. Here is the key: we avoid pursuing our goals because we are afraid to be confronted with the truth. Bob Bradley's goal was to be a soccer coach at the Premier League level. That is a BFHAG if I've ever seen one. Goals, if they are big enough, should scare you, but unfortunately for many they scare us so much that we choose inaction over failure.

You see, by not actually pursuing the goal, we can always sit back and wonder "what if?" What if allows us to revel in the daydream of achieving that successful goal because we never had to be confronted with the truth. The scary part about chasing a big dream or goal is that in the pursuit you will be given an answer: either you achieve it or you don't. In other words, you will find out exactly how good you are. Bob Bradley found out how good he was and it wasn't good enough to be a Premier League manager. The aftereffect of that is tabloids and pundits deeming you a failure, but is he? For me, applause should be saved for anybody that pursues their goal with every ounce of effort and energy they have, regardless of the outcome.

Six months after being employed at Steel Azin, Carlos Queiroz, the former first-team manager at Manchester United, was hired by Iran to take over the National Team. In 1996, Omid played one game on loan for Carlos Queiroz, who was the head coach of the New York Metrostars. The connection between the two intrigued Queiroz enough to make contact with Omid to see if he would be interested in helping him as an assistant with the Iranian National Team. "It was a job that I couldn't turn down. I mean, you are talking about an opportunity to work with a guy that has managed Real Madrid and Portugal. Not to mention the opportunity to work for a country that is soccer crazy and help them qualify for the 2014 World Cup."

Put yourself in Omid's shoes for a second. Seven months prior, Omid had been out of a job and looking for work in the professional indoor leagues of the US. Fast forward seven months and he was now on staff with one of the most influential managers of the last 50 years, helping to lead his home country to the 2014 World Cup. That is the other side of fear. That is what staring your goals in the eyes and not being afraid can do.

Omid worked alongside Carlos Queiroz for four years, taking a lot from the experience. "The opportunity to work for Carlos for four years was something that I will never forget. I knew that working for him would give me the experience necessary for me to make the next step in my coaching career." That isn't to say that the opportunity was easy. When you are face to face with the limits of your potential, things can become uncomfortable, but that is where we grow the most as people and as coaches. "It was a very, very challenging environment to work in, but I got so much out of it, and in the end, it made me a much better person and a better coach."

Omid has no hesitation in referring to Carlos as his mentor. He isn't sure he would be the coach he is today without having worked for Carlos. "The biggest thing I learned from Carlos was attention to detail. I have never seen a guy so detailed in my life. Carlos set the expectations for our coaching staff from day one that we were going to do 'everything for the player so that when they step on the field, they have nothing else to worry about but to perform.' Carlos is still in Iran and the players love that about him." Coaches often struggle with knowing how to get their players to play for them. Omid learned from Carlos that if you do everything in your power to help prepare the players for the game, they will return the favor by performing their best. "The guys played hard for him. They loved him because they knew that he would give them everything necessary to perform their best. In return, they would give him everything they had."

Professional soccer is a hard business; agents, prima donna players, dictatorial owners, and fair weather fans all add stress to the job of coaching at the highest level. Carlos knew Omid's goal was to coach at the highest level possible and his advice was simple. "In the game of soccer, everyone is a son of a gun until they prove you differently. He always told me that you have to be guarded. You have to be careful about who you trust and associate with at the highest level."

Carlos also taught Omid that opportunity, especially in the game of soccer, is not always merit based. "I always thought that as long as you were focused on the craft and proved that you can be a successful coach that you would get to the top. Unfortunately, I have come to realize that that isn't always the case. Your network of people that you know is very, very important. Therefore, as a coach, you have to have the ability to network and build relationships with people."

It is perfect that Omid mentioned Carlos' advice about the so-called son of a guns right before he mentioned the importance of your network. I had the opportunity to hear Dick Advocaat, the former Dutch National Team coach, speak, and he provided a piece of wisdom that mirrored Carlos' advice to Omid. "Coaching is a lonely profession. You have to put people around you that you can trust." Dick's advice, Carlos' advice, and Omid's comment led me to a profound realization about job opportunities in the game of soccer. What leads a team or organization to choose one coach over another when they might be equally qualified? Why are coaching jobs more about who you know rather than what you know? You see, coaching really is a lonely profession, especially at the highest level. Carlos isn't being cynical when he talks about the son of a guns in the soccer world. Fans can love you one day and be tweeting about sacking you the next. Staff members can be working behind the scenes to turn the players against you. General managers and owners can be watching your training session while on the phone interviewing your potential replacements. It is extremely hard to trust people in the soccer world because it is a dog-eat-dog world at the top, so managers want to hire people that they have built rapport and trust with. A head coach prioritizes hiring someone he can trust over someone that is a really good coach because when the going gets tough, they have to feel supported. That is why you see coaches like Pep Guardiola, Jose Mourinho, and other top managers bringing their staffs with them from place to place. Trust trumps being the best candidate for the job. Unfortunately, this means that it isn't all about how good of a tactician or trainer you are. Anyone that has ever coached knows that you spend more time with your staff members than your family. Last season, I remember talking about how we should play against our upcoming opponent with my fellow assistant coaches until almost 2AM. Could you imagine having that conversation with a stranger or someone you didn't trust?

Omid, the idealist, believes that coaching jobs should be based on merit and ability. "It bothers me to a point because I think the way people should be selected for jobs is their track record." But Omid, the practitioner, has learned that networking isn't always a bad thing. Networking is your chance to build a relationship with someone that may want you on their staff one day. Networking isn't selling out, it is part of coaching, because in the world of soccer, where you are surrounded by fair-weather people, the last place head coaches want to feel insecure is inside their own staff.

Omid would have never worked for Carlos if they weren't connected by that 1996 New York Metrostars season. "I have learned that networking is important if you want to reach the highest level you can. I used to avoid networking because I wanted to put my head down and focus on the work, but I realized that without having a good network of friends and colleagues, it can leave you looking at the top with no ladder to get there. I have been much more open in creating relationships with other coaches because when it comes to getting a job at the highest level it has less to do with your ability and more to do with the relationship you have with the person hiring."

I used to have a very toxic relationship with the idea of networking because I too believe that the hiring process should be based on merit. However, I am able to tolerate the idea of networking because, instead of looking at networking as sucking up to people that may be able to help you in the future, I use it to help me in the only thing I really care about: improvement. My goal is to maximize my potential as a coach and talking with other coaches outside your network is a useful way to improve, get new ideas, and ask for advice. In fact, you are networking, at least by my definition, just by reading this book. You are learning from coaches outside your network and gaining insights into how they think, make decisions, and view the game. So if you find yourself with an upset stomach thinking about shameless networking, just redefine the relationship and look at it as a way to share ideas and learn something from a fellow coach you would otherwise never learn from.

Omid has been on the wrong end of multiple job opportunities that have provided him experience in dealing with being passed over. "I can tell you numerous times where I was approached to be an assistant coach in the MLS only to be passed over for a former player that had never coached a day in his life. But you have to have the ability to deal with that." Omid uses positive self-talk to rebound from these frustrations. "I say to myself, 'Okay, maybe this wasn't the right opportunity so I have to keep working hard and make sure I do the best job possible with my current team and know that eventually somebody will notice my work and it will be the right opportunity.' You need to have resilience to get through these situations." Jay Martin cited a study out of the University of Chicago that listed positive self-talk as one of the three key traits for highly successful people. Talking to yourself positively following a minor setback is essential to staying in the game. "If you look at it as 'This is stupid, I should be there, I am so much better than that other guy, maybe this isn't for me,' and you have that kind of attitude, you can find yourself out of the game very quickly."

COACHING PROFESSIONAL PLAYERS

Omid has coached players at the highest levels in the world. He mentioned that there is a big difference in coaching his players at the U18 National Team level and the players with the Iran National Team. "At the highest level you are dealing with big personalities and egos and a lot of the players think they know it all. And to be honest, at the highest level, players pretty much know what they need to know so it becomes much more about managing people and their personalities. On the pitch, yes, of course, you need to be tactically sound, but if the players don't want to play for you or don't believe in the tactics, then it doesn't matter how good they are. More than anything, man management and knowing how to manage personalities is the biggest part." Fortunately, Omid's mentor, Carlos Queiroz, had experience working for the greatest man manager of all time, Alex Ferguson. "I have talked to Carlos a lot about this because he was side by side with Sir Alex for six years. Carlos will tell you, Alex Ferguson was not a great tactical coach, but he was the best man manager in the world."

Omid admits that he is a stronger teacher than he is a manager. "My man management is improving, but I am definitely better on the tactical side, which is why I am really focusing on improving my ability to manage relationships because I believe you need to be great at both to be a top coach." Omid believes that the changing personalities of our youth require a necessary evolution in the personality of coaches. "Generations change as we go along, and when I played, the coaches were very old school and it was sort of like a dictatorship. Then, when I played pro, I started to see a shift where some coaches were dictators, but there were newer coaches that communicated more with the players and asked them for their feedback. I believe the trend now is to have a lot of feedback from the players, asking them for their thoughts on the playing style or formation, for example."

Omid is pushing himself to become more of a player-centered coach and he recently allowed the players on his U18 US National Team to decide on the game plan for their match against the US U19 National Team. "I was talking with a Dutch coach about player-centered coaching and he asked, 'Why don't you have your players come up with the game plan instead of you always coming up with the game plan?' So leading up to the game I told my players, 'Look, I always come up with the plan and you guys just listen, and this time, I want you guys to get together in a room, you know who we are playing, and I want you guys to decide on the game plan. You will have to present it to me because I want to know how you want to go about playing, but then it's on you guys. You guys decide.' It was a fun experiment because I employed a high pressing style with the U18s, but because we were playing the U19s, these guys got together and they were a little scared. When they presented the game plan to me they said, 'Coach, we feel that if we go and press, because they are stronger and faster than us, we might get beat, so we want to sit back and see how we do.' I said, 'Okay, great' and we went into the game with their game plan."

Omid enjoyed watching his team implement their game plan, but because they had no experience sitting in and playing a counter-attacking style, they struggled to get out of their end and create chances. However, the U18s were able to stay in the game despite not creating any opportunities. At halftime, Omid wanted to see how they thought it was working. "At halftime, I walked in and asked them how they feel and they said great. Then I said, 'What do you think about us pressing them a little bit?' They responded with a resounding yes because they wanted to get out of our defensive end and we ended up winning 2-1."

Although this experiment put Omid out of his comfort zone as a coach, he learned a lot from the experience. "The whole experience was really positive and it helped me change a little bit as a coach. Even though I feel that I am good with the Xs and Os, the experience brought me closer to my players and proved to me that you get a lot of buy-in from your players when you include them in the decision-making process."

PLAYING PHILOSOPHY

Similar to Neil Jones, Omid always starts with the defensive moment of the game when building his game model and preparing his team. "At the end of the day, if you don't defend well and you concede goals, you are going to lose your players. We need to know how to defend well as a team and then I build the rest of the game model from there." Building a game model is one of the most important aspects of coaching and I will provide details on how to build one later in this book. "Before you choose your system or style of play, you always have to start with the personnel that you have. Based on your personnel, then you can choose how you want to play." Omid provided an example of how he may look at choosing a system of play. "If you want to play a 1-4-3-3, your fullbacks have to be players that can cover a lot of ground and have some pace. If your outside backs don't have those tools or elements, then it's going to be tough to play a 1-4-3-3. Everything is based on what you have. You have to be a coach that is flexible and capable of coaching a lot of different systems of play. Your philosophy can always be the same—you can still play a high pressing game or a counter-attacking game—but your system of play may need to change depending on your personnel."

Omid has built all of his teams to be high-pressing teams. He usually employs a 1-4-3-3 and here are two ways he has organized his team to press that have proven most successful over his coaching career.

The first way Omid employs a high press out of a 1-4-3-3 is by tasking his #9 and ball far winger with applying pressure to the opponent high up the field. In this picture, Omid's team is in blue. The #9 is tasked with pressing the player on the ball (#4 on orange). The ball far winger is tasked with pressing the #5, the left-sided center back, if he receives the ball. The #11 on blue is tasked with standing directly in front of the ball carrier (#4), while keeping the outside back on orange (#2) in his vision. The three central midfielders (#6, #8, and #10) for blue are tasked with a maintaining a specific zone and pressuring any passes centrally.

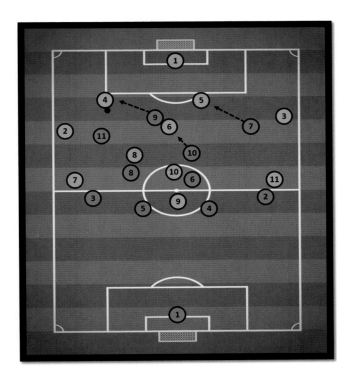

The second way that Omid organizes a high press occurs if the opponent plays in a 1-4-4-2. "That will allow us to release somebody out of the middle, which means that either our #8 or #10 can press the ball-carrying center back." The #9 is responsible for the other center back and the remaining central midfielders have the same zonal responsibilities as before.

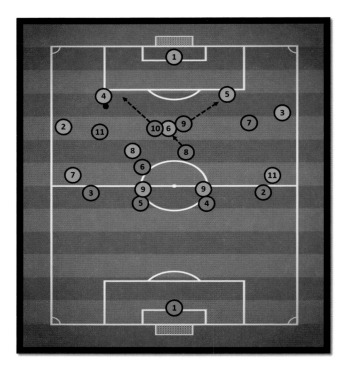

CHAPTER 7

SUCCESSFUL COACHING EDUCATION

IAN BARKER

Ian Barker has been the director of coaching education for the NSCAA since 2012. Prior to his role with the NSCAA, Ian served as the head Men's Soccer Coach at Macalester College in St. Paul, Minnesota. Ian was also an assistant coach for nearly a decade at the University of Wisconsin, helping lead the badgers to a Big Ten Championship and National Championship in 1995. Ian has earned coaching badges through the NSCAA, US Soccer, US Youth Soccer, the English FA, and the German DFB.

Decentralized command — Going from an assistant to the man in charge — When one teaches, two learn — Why 3v1 is harder than 3v2 — Don't just take a job because of a nicer Nike track suit

THE COACHING JOURNEY

Ian will often say, in jest, not to judge him based on his funny accent. The England native received his coaching badges in the UK, while he was just a young aspiring coach still at university and unemployed in the soccer coaching world. Shortly after graduation, Ian moved to the United States and began his coaching career. "What a lot of people don't realize is that all of my experience is in coaching American players." Ian proved to be quite good at it too, helping lead the University of Wisconsin to the 1995 National Championship, beating Bruce Arena's University of Virginia, Clive Charles' University of Portland, and John Rennie's Duke University. "We won the National Title and made our way back to Wisconsin. Three weeks later the athletic director sacked my boss—a controversial move at the time—but we ended up keeping our jobs. At the end of the 1996 season, she sacked him again."

The harsh reality of coaching college soccer in the United States is that there are a lot more things to worry about than wins and losses when it comes to keeping your job. I was a college soccer player for five years and I will eclipse the five-year mark as a college coach in 2018. Ian's experience is not uncommon. Basketball and American football drive revenue at the universities in America. If your program poses any threat to those sports, in any capacity, then they may look to make a change. Wins and losses are still vital to keeping a job, but things like academic progress rates (APR), GPAs, budget expenses, student conduct, and much more all influence an athletic director's decision to keep a coach employed or not.

Ian left the University of Wisconsin in the winter of 1996. His next coaching opportunity was as a coach educator for the Minnesota Soccer Association. "I thought I would last about three months or so before I got back into college coaching, but I really enjoyed the coach education side of the game." Ian, first and foremost, is a practitioner at heart. He loves coaching the game and is very good at it. Luckily for the US, he is also one of the best coach educators in the country, even though he still misses the day-in day-out requirements of a coach. "The problem with my job is not enough contact time with players and not enough time on the field." Ian proposes that this is a natural occurrence in any career involving the game, even coaching. "I think what any head coach in MLS, NWSL, or NCAA will tell you is the more you climb in your career as a coach, the harder it is to stay connected to the field." Ian knows this to be true from his own experience and conversations with many top coaches around the world. "For most coaches, the more they progress through their career, the more they end up with a lot more administrative and management responsibilities. Probably more than they would have thought."

There are countless examples that verify this claim. Alex Ferguson kept plenty busy just trying to manage the personalities of his staff, players, and coaches, which required him to take a step back away from the pitch in order to ensure that the organization itself was running smoothly. In fact, I believe that coaches who retain their up-close-and-personal approach on the pitch often neglect bigger picture items such as: Is my staff happy? Are my players aware of their role on the team? What does the body language of the team tell me right now? Little things that can become big things very quickly.

I know from my own experience that the more you are involved in training, the harder it is to see the little things. For example, I may be leading a session that requires me to be clear and timely in my coaching points and stoppages. While I am waiting for the perfect moment to jump in and make my point, I might miss the fact that John Smith has poor body language during my coaching point. Why does he have poor body language and how is that influencing his behavior and the behavior of his teammates? That is why the most successful coaches choose to delegate responsibility, to cut out these little things before they become big things.

The best leadership book I have ever read is *Extreme Ownership* by Navy SEALs Jocko Willink and Leif Babin. One of their principles of leadership is called decentralized command. The principle of decentralized command states that "good leaders delegate. They trust their teams to execute." Honestly, any assistant coach worth their wage should be able to run a session successfully. But if you feel you have to lead every session because you are the head coach and use your staff to pick up cones, it is probably for one of three reasons:

1. Ego—You need to be the big voice at training in order to feel important and in charge. True leaders put the goal of the mission in front of their personal needs.
2. Trust (or lack thereof)—You have to trust your team of assistant coaches to be able to lead a session and deliver the ideas you want delivered to your players. Don't trust them? Then you either have the wrong people on board, or you need to teach them how to lead a session the way you want.
3. Centralized command—You may want everything done a certain way: your way. It is another manifestation of your ego impeding your ability to lead. You may know *a* way, but to assume your way is the *only* way is foolish and will make your staff feel handcuffed by your approach. Explain to your staff the mission, explain to them what you want accomplished, and then let them execute. This is how you decentralize command. Jocko explains the effectiveness of this approach as allowing "the team enough freedom to determine the best way as to *how* the goal should be accomplished. This gives the team the much-needed freedom to innovate and adapt as the situation changes."

Ian understands that in order to coach at the highest level, you have to prioritize your management duties over your coaching duties. You may deliver the best session in the world, but if your assistant coaches feel like they have no opinion or are being underutilized, do you think you're maximizing the effectiveness of your program? What if a player like John Smith doesn't understand why he is on the reserves? Do you think that may influence the locker room in a negative way? Delegating responsibility and decentralizing command is what leadership is all about. From there, it is your job to make sure everyone stays focused on the mission, understands their role, and executes it.

A perfect example of centralized command leading to the downfall of a manager is Jose Mourinho's second stint with Chelsea. After winning the Premier League in 2015, Mourinho was sacked during the 2016 season. Why did this happen? One theory is centralized command. At the beginning of the 2016 campaign, Mourinho said, "I don't need to buy any new players because I have a team full of champions," referring to his team's recent title-winning season. However, what do you think that communicated to the players that were substitutes or reserves? Kevin de Bruyne opened up on his time with Mourinho saying, "He [Mourinho] never really even talked to me, or any of the substitutes. He only worried about the starting eleven." When injuries struck during the 2016 season, Mourinho needed to rely on the players he neglected for nearly an entire season. Can you imagine what de Bruyne's internal monologue sounded like? Probably something like, "Oh, *now* you notice me." Mourinho is known as a manager that is heavily involved in every training session, but it was his inability to manage the players that weren't involved that led to his demise at Chelsea.

Decentralized command means that Mourinho could have relinquished full control of training on occasion to have conversations with reserve team players about why they weren't playing, what they could do to get into the team, and so on. Mourinho is typically a great man manager, but this example shows how quickly you can lose your players when management duties take a back seat to coaching duties.

Ian feels that coaches need to be educated on the difference between managers and coaches. "When you look at La Liga, the English Premier League, and the Bundesliga, some of these top coaches are actually top managers of people. They are managers of all the things around the game. The actual day-to-day coaching is very often being done by people that are expert trainers, but perhaps don't want to be in front of the camera." Ian does concede that certain levels may allow for a coach to do both; for example, in MLS it may be possible due to the limited media obligations, but he thinks it can create distinct disadvantages. "I see programs, both college and professional, that always defer to the head coach. They aren't empowered to make decisions on their own and I don't think that is valuable. I think if the players know that the assistant coaches are empowered to deliver certain aspects of training and the program, while the head coach saves his or her energy for other important things—including game day management, substitutions, and decisions—I think it can be very powerful." Ian believes that the ability of a head coach to delegate can create a supreme advantage over head coaches that are less willing to relinquish control over everything. "If the delegation is done well, the players really value having the different inputs. On the other hand, if there are a lot of assistant coaches and only one person, the head coach, is pulling the strings, the players will start to wonder what the incentive is to listen to the assistants. If they start to feel that the assistant coaches aren't empowered to make a difference, then they simply will stop listening to them." If the head coach fails to delegate coaching duties, not only will the more important and impactful management duties fall apart, but the assistant coaches will be rendered useless.

Ian taught me that a coach's failure to delegate coaching duties and other responsibilities can lead to management duties being neglected. This means that player relations, motivation, and team culture are often neglected, which can cripple even the most brilliant tactics. Further, failure to delegate responsibilities means a failure to empower your assistant coaches. A failure to empower your assistant coaches means that your players won't see the benefit to listening to the assistant coaches. However, coaches need their assistants. "The assistant coach can be a shoulder to cry on and a system of support for the players. The assistant should be closer to the players and serve as a conduit between the player and head coach." Although the head coach needs to have the serious conversations with the players, the assistant coaches can help assist with the emotional response to certain decisions. Ian explains that "if the head coach gets too close to the players, it can make things really difficult when making decisions regarding competitive success. At the end of the day, the head coach has to make those decisions." Head coaches need to think hard about how to best employ their assistants. Ian confirms that disempowering your assistants is, in effect, a way to disempower yourself.

Ian has experience as both an assistant coach and a head coach. While employed as the assistant coach at Macalester College, Ian was promoted to the head coach upon the departure of his former boss. Ian admitted that moving from the assistant to the head coach with a team is one of the most difficult situations a coach will have to manage. The hardest thing about that transition is that your behaviors may have to change. For example, if you were very close with the players and a shoulder to cry on as an assistant, it can be very hard to transition from that relationship into the more business-like role of the head coach.

Ian developed a couple of strategies to aid that transition. "When I was hiring my assistants, I was looking for guys that were alumni and had played for the program. In my case, I found a guy that was an alum, but didn't play with any of the current players, and the other assistant had played with some of our seniors when they were freshman. That really helped my transition because those guys were able to assume my role as the guy that was closer to the ground, more in the locker room, and able to share a joke with the players. That allowed me to step back gradually into the head coach role."

One question I always ask head coaches on my podcast is "How did you know you were ready to be a head coach?" It is a difficult question to answer because sometimes it is something in our unconscious and something that we cannot verbalize. It would be like asking you to explain why you love your mother—you can't really put it into words, you just know that you do. However, Ian believes that a lot of assistant coaches are far too eager to move into a head coaching role. "There is always this internal discussion of: Do I go and be an assistant coach at a higher level, or do I go and be a head coach at an equal or lower level to progress to the next stage. I think that too often young coaches go and chase a head coaching position when they would have been better served spending more time as an assistant." Mario Sanchez is a perfect example of this mistake. He left Akron as an assistant to become the head coach at UNLV before realizing that he had much more to learn. Mario left UNLV to become an assistant again at Louisville before coming back to the head coaching position at SIUE, where he has built one of the best programs in the country. Ian has mirrored Mario's experience in this regard. "For me, more experience as an assistant was more valuable than going off and making mistakes as a head coach that I may not have been able to dig myself out from."

One of my all-time favorite books is *Although Of Course You End Up Becoming Yourself* by David Lipsky. It chronicles the late author David Foster Wallace's experience during his book tour following the release of *Infinite Jest.* David's main reflection during that book tour was the profound understanding that our entire lives are aimed at finding out who we truly are and continuously making strides to be true to that person.

Ian believes that coaches shouldn't allow outside opinions to tell them what to do next with their career. "You have to know who you are individually. If you have an ego where you really need to be that person making the final decision—and that may be you at the age of 21—then go and get a high school program and be that all-consuming ego. I don't mean that in a negative way either, but if that is the way you are wired and you need to make that final call, then you should probably make the jump when you are younger. By the same token, if you are quite centered, you enjoy the day-to-day interactions with the players, and you don't want the stresses that come with being the head coach for at least a while, then spend a couple more years being an assistant. It's really a question of knowing yourself. Don't compare yourself to another coach that is your age because they are probably not wired the same way as you. The decision is very contextual and only comes through a lot of self-awareness."

COACH EDUCATION

There is no question that coach education is vital. It is easy to criticize some of the required licensing programs in the US and abroad, but at the end of the day, it is a necessary process in the coaching journey. However, do not confuse coaching education with coaching ability. "Coach education doesn't tell you anything about the character of the person or their integrity. There are many people with the highest NSCAA or US Soccer awards that I wouldn't want coaching children." Ian has been involved with coaching education for more than 20 years. Over the last 20 years Ian has identified the qualities that make coaching education a success. "Look, for me, you need three things. You need half-way decent instructors. You need half-way decent content. And then you need candidates with an open mind."

Ian has also developed his eye for candidates that will not have a successful outcome during a course or licensure. "I find that the people who struggle the most in coach education environments are the ones that expect to be given all the information, but don't want to have to contribute to the learning process." Ian's comment came on the heels of an off-air conversation about the coaching world today. The internet has created the information age and that includes information on coaching. Never before in history have coaches had so much access to information about the game. There are hundreds of sessions, activities, and videos put online every single day aimed at improving the ability of coaches. However, that breeds a danger that coaches come to coaching education courses thinking they have it all figured out already. "Everybody, to some extent, feels they are more of an expert than previous generations. So, coaches have to really be honest with themselves and ask themselves the question: Are you really ready to take on new ideas and are you truly open minded?" Although coaches need to have a more open mind, Ian doesn't believe that information overload is a bad thing. In fact, the NSCAA has developed a way to capitalize on our increased access to information. "We have coaches from all over the world attend our courses and some of the candidates may have ideas and information that no one else does. So, instead of sitting that person down in a chair and asking them to listen to us for ten days, we really make an effort to put the coaches together. We have found that most of the learning actually comes from the candidates themselves sharing ideas openly."

PLAYING PHILOSOPHY

A quote that is fitting of Ian Barker and his experience is: "When one teaches, two learn." Ian is a practitioner that has also been one of the best teachers of coaches over the last 20 years. He is, first and foremost, a coach. Having a hand in both coaching and education these last 20 years has given him a very interesting perspective on the game. "Where I am at currently in my own coaching, I would want to play with a back four. I am not really sure about three center backs. I like a back four with one player in front of them to protect them, although we are seeing more and more teams choosing to play with two holding midfield players to protect the back four in the modern game. Now, what we do with the other six, once we got our back four in place, has everything to do with the personnel that you have and what they can do. So, a common thing you will see in the game is a team that says they play a 1-4-3-3, but it really looks like a 1-4-5-1. In similar fashion, you may see a team that says they play a 1-4-5-1, but it really is a 1-4-4-1-1. So, I think we get very obsessed with numbers, formations, and systems, but it has a lot more to do with the personnel. For example, how you employ your holding midfielder (#6), really depends on the ability and personality of your outside backs. If your outside backs can't get forward, then that impacts what the six in front of them can do. However, if your outside backs can get forward and be very aggressive in attacking, then that will impact what your six can do."

The idea that Ian is stressing here is that if your outside backs have the ability to attack and get forward, you may need to task your #6 with holding his position in order to give your team a three-back system to protect against the counter-attack. This will allow your outside backs to join the attack, without your team getting burned on the counter. If you have aggressive outside backs and a #6 that likes to get forward, then a loss of possession could result in a counter-attack against just two defenders.

Here you see that aggressive attacking outside backs will require your #6 to stay back in order to maintain your back line and prevent counter-attacks.

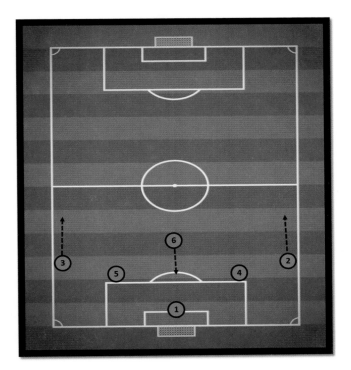

In the opposite scenario, outside backs that cannot provide attacking benefits to your team may be better paired with a #6 that can also get forward and help during the build up.

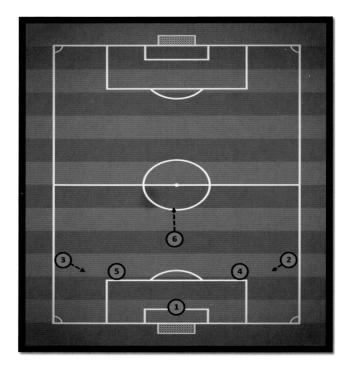

Ian is the type of guy that loves talking about the game and the different tactics employed by teams and managers. During our conversation we discussed the pros and cons of employing a back three against various striker combinations. "I think it's easier for a back three to defend against two strikers than it is against one. The reason is because the lines of responsibility are much, much clearer playing against two strikers than against just one. That is the biggest problem with the 1-3-5-2 in my opinion. I think teams are better served playing with a back four against one striker to give them two center backs to deal with that one striker." Ian explained that because the back three is meant to be engaged, defending against one striker doesn't provide that stimulus. Therefore, teams with a back three, playing against one striker, may struggle to pick up players that drift between lines as they aren't sure if they should step or not. However, against two strikers, it becomes clear that two of the center backs mark the strikers while the other center back provides cover.

Here you can see an example of what Ian is talking about. Because the back three aren't engaged with direct responsibilities, the #10 on orange can find success in the space in front of the center backs because the center backs aren't sure who should step.

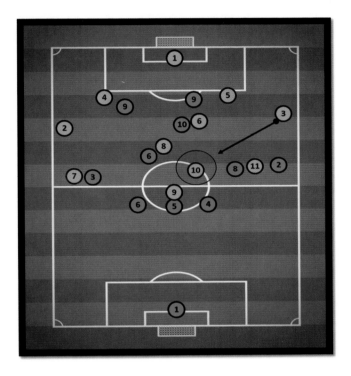

If Ian were to play with a back three, it would be against two strikers and he would employ a libero to deal with any potential ball in behind. "I think you could play with a libero, which is a position that used to be employed back in the day. Basically, you would task two of the center backs (typically the widest ones) with man marking either the two strikers, or the lone striker and the #10. The spare center back would then serve as a libero tasked with either stepping up, or dropping off to cut out any potential dangerous passes in behind the back three."

Here you can see the libero (#5 on blue) playing behind the two man-marking center backs in order to cut out any ball played in behind.

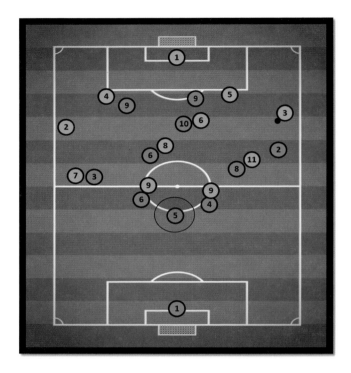

If a player were to check into the six space in front of the center backs, the libero could also be tasked with stepping into that space to mark that player and deny him the ball.

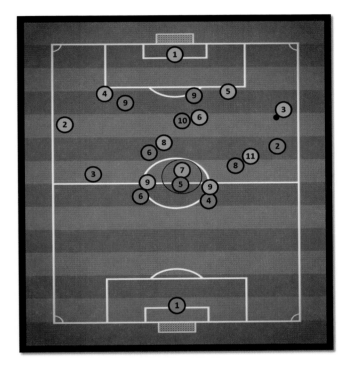

COACHING ADVICE

As a coach educator, Ian is responsible for educating the next generation of coaches. One of the biggest mistakes he sees coaches make is over-coaching. "I think coaches see other sports and they think a coach is someone that stands on the sideline with a clipboard manipulating everything, but other sports are that way because they require specific choreography to execute a specific play. I'm not an expert in basketball, but a lot of it seems choreographed with an end goal in mind. American football is the same. In soccer, we need to stop looking at models of coaches in other sports and let it go a little bit more. I think the way we can do that is by setting up positive environments, creating games with multiple solutions, and turning it over to the players to experience the environment. Now that doesn't mean you just give up as a coach. You still need to provide some insights, you need to ask some probing questions, and you need to stop it and review occasionally, but I do think that we stop the play too often as soccer coaches. When you coach, just make sure that it's relevant and that it is done quickly and concisely."

Ian has served in a variety of coaching roles during his career and he has learned a lot from each. His talent as a coach educator comes from his experience as a coach, which allows him to relate to coaches that have questions regarding the practical nature of coaching. Ian's parting advice to coaches is simple. "Make sure you are good at communicating, whatever that means to you. Have a good sense of perspective; the wins and losses tend to eat the coaches up more than the players, so have some perspective about the outcome. Always try to lead with a smile. The last piece of advice I have is know when to compromise. For example, you may have a family and children that you need to provide for. That may mean taking some jobs and making some decisions that are a reflection of that responsibility. But if that isn't the case and you are a young, single coach, or money isn't a problem, then I think my advice would be to stay loyal to where you are and pay your dues. Don't just bounce around from job to job because there is more money involved or a nicer Nike track suit. I think sometimes in your career, when you are young, a little bit of stickiness is a good thing for your development as a coach."

CHAPTER 8
CREATING A CULTURE
ALLISTAIR MCCAW

Allistair McCaw is an internationally recognized leader in athletic performance enhancement. He is the founder of the McCaw Method and has been coaching world class athletes and coaches with cutting edge training techniques and strategies for over 20 years. He has worked with nearly every sport as an athletic development coach including the Orlando Pirates of the South African Premier League. He is the author of the book, "7 Keys to to Being a Great Coach". Allistair has worked with numerous Olympians, Tennis Grand Slam Winners, and other World Champion athletes.

It all starts with standards — Practicing what you preach — Criticizing privately, but praising publicly — How to choose your team captain — Why the quietest people may have the most important things to say — Blinker coaches — The Finland Phenomenon

Vern Gambetta, one of my mentors and a legend in the field of strength and conditioning, has an awesome quote that defines the mentality required to be a coach long term. "If summer workouts and getting up at 6AM is a grind, then do us all a favor and stop coaching." Vern's comment came out of a conversation about coaches talking about the infamous grind of coaching. It shouldn't be a grind. It should be something you love. Allistair McCaw has been coaching for nearly 20 years and I am not sure he even knows what the word *grind* means. Sure, he knows how to grind, but he would never call it that. "I feel so fortunate because I truly feel like I have never worked a day in my life."

STANDARDS

If you spend enough time around Allistair you will hear the word *standards* so many times that it might as well become your nickname. For Allistair, it all starts with your standards. "Standards for the athlete—and the team—are the foundation for superior results. They are basically a more welcoming way of saying rules." Coaches love to make rules for their teams and players, but Allistair believes that rules were meant to be broken. "If we come in and say, 'Hey, there are rules here,' it automatically puts a negative feel to the environment. We lead by standards. Standards are the guidelines to live by and hold each other accountable."

In James Kerr's *Legacy,* former All Blacks captain Richie McCaw talked about the All Blacks' reflections after a loss. "Typically, after a loss, I will look at the standards we have pinned up in our locker room and the reason why we lost is usually up there somewhere." Allistair has seen standards—or a lack thereof—become the downfall of many teams and athletes. "I see clubs and organizations lose their way due to rules and standards either not being set or not being carried out by all those involved. It is the responsibility of the coach—and the leaders of the team—to make sure those standards are kept in place and adhered to. I have discovered that far too often coaches are quick to sit down and discuss tactics, goals, session structure, and duration of training, but the most important thing, the standards, are typically not addressed or are simply brushed over."

Allistair, like me, is a huge fan of James Kerr's book *Legacy.* For Allistair, culture and standards trump tactics every time. "I love that book because it shows you how important the environment and culture are within a team. I mean, look at rugby. You have fifteen guys on the field and the question becomes what makes them different than the fifteen guys on the field for Ireland, the fifteen guys on the field for England, or the fifteen guys on the field for Australia? Why do the All Blacks have the highest winning record in world sport? It has to go deeper than the Xs and Os. It has to go deeper than the tactics and physicality. So, what is really the difference? I believe it comes down to the standards that are set and the depth of their culture and environment."

We spoke at length about the All Blacks and how to establish a winning culture. The All Blacks have fifteen principles, two of which really stood out to Allistair. "The first one I really like is 'Leave the jersey in a better place than you found it.' When you think about it, that principle itself makes the whole process bigger than any individual. It communicates to the players that their duty is to make sure that they give more than the guy before them did. It's about progression of the All Blacks over time, not one player shining for a brief moment."

I also love that principle because it is a metaphor for life. It is very easy to get consumed with trying to make more money, climbing the ladder of your profession, or being recognized for your abilities. However, those are very fleeting and unsatisfying things. It is easy to get distracted and caught up in the things that don't really matter. It happens in teams too. Players can get consumed by how many goals they score or how many games they start, but what really matters—what stands the test of time—is the team.

That's not just a standard for rugby, but for life. Life is better when you just try to leave the world a better place than you found it. It reduces you to complete humility as well. To realize how small a part you actually play is humbling. Naval Ravikant, CEO of Angelist, has arguably the greatest perspective on life I have heard. During his episode on the Tim Ferriss podcast, Naval explained life this way, "I don't have the quest for immortality anymore. I think I came to this fundamental conclusion. I thought about it a lot. The universe has been around for a long time, and the universe is a very, very large place. If you'll study even the smallest bit of science, for all practical purposes we are nothing. We are amoeba. We are bacteria to the universe. We're basically monkeys on a small rock orbiting a small backwards star in a huge galaxy, which is in an absolutely staggeringly gigantic universe, which itself may be part of a gigantic multiverse. This universe has been around probably for ten billion years or more, and will be around for tens of billions of years afterwards. Your existence and my existence are just infinitesimal. It's like a firefly blinking once in the night."

Now, that doesn't mean we should just give up and not do anything anymore because we are all going to die one day. In fact, that perspective should allow you to realize how profound "leaving the jersey in a better place" is. What makes that so effective for the All Blacks is that they realize they are playing a small part in the history of the All Blacks. It isn't about them. It is about the All Blacks. Can you leave your team a little better than you found them?

The second principle that Allistair loves is called "Sweep the sheds." "Sweeping the sheds goes back to the time when the All Blacks used a farmer's field to train on. There were no locker rooms, but there were sheds. The All Blacks could use the field as long as they left the sheds in a better place than they found it. That was the only rule the farmer gave them. And they have carried that tradition into today. Nobody is exempt from this either. It doesn't matter if you are the best player in the world. Everybody is tasked with that responsibility to leave the locker room in better shape than they found it."

The All Blacks principle of "sweeping the sheds" was kept in-house until a game a few years ago against England made world news. Following a competition between the All Blacks and England, a picture was taken of both teams locker rooms. England's locker room, who lost by the way, was a pig sty. The victor's locker room was swept, mopped, and spotless. "The thing to understand is that this isn't left up to the kit guy or the equipment manager, but the responsibility of every single player to make sure they do their part to tidy the locker room. These little things tell you a lot about why teams are successful and why others are not. It all ends up influencing what eventually happens on the pitch."

Although the All Blacks are a tremendous example of how a team culture can breed success beyond the pitch, standards start with the individual. Allistair talks at length about coaches practicing what they preach. If you are telling your players to eat healthy while eating a slice of pizza—it is hard for your players to respect the honesty of your advice. "The best example is yourself. To demand the respect of your athletes and team you need to be the first one to set that example. If you are the one telling your players to show up on time, work hard, dress appropriately, communicate, always be prepared, and you are not doing it yourself, you cannot expect to win the trust and buy-in from anyone. Your athletes will see your example more than they will hear your words."

Albert Mehrabian is an Iranian Professor Emeritus at UCLA in the Department of Psychology. Professor Mehrabian published a research paper in the *Journal of Consulting Psychology* in 1967 called "Inference of Attitudes from Nonverbal Communication in Two Channels." That paper resulted in the infamous "7%-38%-55% rule" that proclaims that people only hear 7% of the words you use, but pick up 38% of how you say them (tone of voice) and 55% of the body language you manifest. For example, if I cross my arms and scream across the field to one of my players, "Good job!" 93% of my communication is negative. Therefore, chances are that the player won't hear me say "Good job," he will notice that I am screaming and he will notice that my arms are crossed. Both of these things communicate that the coach is probably angry.

If we extrapolate that study and apply it to the notion of "practicing what we preach," we understand that our actions as coaches are much more important than the words we use. If you recall from Mario Sanchez's chapter, he works out in the gym *with* his players. That is the definition of practicing what you preach. If you are going to tell your athletes to work hard in the gym, you better be prepared to do the same, otherwise your words do not match your body language or actions. Funnily enough, Mario doesn't even need to say anything to his players about the gym being important to him, he is showing them just how important he thinks it is. Allistair put it perfectly when he said, "Great coaches are respected for who they are and what they do, not what they say. I recently read Alex Ferguson's book, *Leading*. In the book, Sir Alex mentions that he was at the training facility every morning before the milkman was there." You don't have to constantly remind your players how important showing up on time is when you prioritize it in your own life.

One of the most neglected relationships in a coach's life is the relationship with himself. "Coaches should take care of themselves; they need to eat well and exercise because great coaches have a great energy. How can you expect to have a great energy if you're not taking care of yourself? If you can't take care of yourself and be the example, how do you expect your athletes and teams to follow that example?"

Allistair was at a coaching clinic in Holland in early 2016 when he stumbled on a perfect case of failing to practice what you preach. "There was a coach giving a talk to a group of athletes on the importance of nutrition that included information on bad snacking, bad food choices, and the importance of a proper diet in performance and life. I don't want people to think I am judgmental, but this coach was probably 50-60 pounds overweight. The thing is, the athletes he was speaking to have seen him eating the wrong things on a daily basis, so he wasn't living that life either. I believe that with this new generation, generation iY, they are *watching* you more than *listening* to you." Do your actions support your words? Allistair was in the audience and took note of the pulse of the room. He was watching closely to assess the reaction of the athletes to the information. "I could see these kids just completely zoning out as if to say, 'Really? You're telling us how to eat? And yet you're the one that is eating poorly?' It's just another example of kids watching your example more than hearing your words."

UPHOLDING YOUR STANDARDS

Let's say you take Allistair's advice and you establish standards for your players to follow and abide by. Things are going great. Your players are showing up early, they are dressed appropriately, and they are putting the training gear away after practice like you agreed upon. What happens when a standard is violated? This is one of the most difficult situations for a coach because the reaction is vital to the team moving forward together. "I think the way a coach needs to address it is by citing the importance of responsibility and accountability. Athletes that fail to live up to team standards don't need to be yelled at, they need to be made aware that they are letting their team down. That is being accountable. Their actions don't just affect them but their teammates, coaches, trainers, and parents too." Allistair doesn't necessarily think that something needs to be said in front of the entire group either. "I am a subscriber to the idea of criticizing in private and praising in public. So, I would pull the player aside to deal with it."

Allistair and I talked a lot about espoused values. Often, coaches will hear team rules, or standards that exist in other team environments and want to adopt them as their own. For example, you may want to walk into your locker room tomorrow and tell your players about the importance of sweeping the sheds; unfortunately, your intentions are great, but that isn't how it works. You can't force rules or standards on to your players, they have to be intrinsic.

Allistair and I have similar approaches to creating intrinsic standards with our teams, another way of saying that the players develop their own standards. "I usually meet with every player at the beginning of the season and I ask them to write three things that they are going to bring to the team for that season on an index card. I don't want technical things such as how many goals or assists they will have, I am looking for individual standards. Are they going to promise to work hard, be on time, and bring a positive attitude? This way, when a player violates one of their standards, I can sit down with them, pull out the index card, and say, 'Hey, Johnny, here is what you said at the beginning of the season. You said that you were going to have the right attitude, the right work ethic, and the right effort at every practice. Do you think you are living up to this? Are you living up to the standards you set for yourself?' This will be so much more effective than me just wagging my finger at them because they violated one of *my* standards. If it comes from them, it is much easier to keep the standards high."

IDENTIFYING A LEADER

One of the most overlooked decisions a coach has to make is the choosing of his team's captain. A lot of times, choosing the wrong captain can lead to an awkward locker room environment where the players lose faith in the coaches and team.

A few years ago, my coaching staff and I chose a captain that we thought best exemplified our team and our standards. However, it wasn't until the season was over—a very poor season at that—that our seniors informed us that we lost the team when we chose the captain. The players revealed that we had totally misjudged the situation and the player we chose was a cancer to the team and only seemed like a team player in front of the coaches. It didn't hit me until after the season was over that every time we had the captain say something—whether it was before or after a game, when we needed someone to step up and be vocal on the field, or communicate some belief within the team—the voice delivering those messages was tuned out by every single player.

Choosing your leader is a massive decision, and with over 25 years as a consultant for a lot of different teams and in many different environments, Allistair has established some go-to principles for identifying a team leader. "The leader will usually be the one that is in the center of things. The other players and athletes will be drawn to that particular athlete. They are the ones that usually answer any questions asked by the coaching staff in front of the team. They are not necessarily the best players, but they do have a very dominant personality and figure within the group."

The captain of your team should be viewed as an extension of the coaching staff. They are your ears on the ground that help uphold your standards and drive your team during tough times. "It's so important that you find the right leader within your group. As a coach, your standards are going to be judged and defined by the worst behaviors you accept. Your captain has to be someone that is prepared to uphold those standards but is well respected enough that others will listen. Roy Keane is a great example of a captain that wasn't the best player on the team, but he was the most demanding player. He not only practiced what he preached, but he held every player to the team standards."

The biggest mistake in global soccer today is that coaches give the armband to their best players. Obviously, there may be some bruised egos involved if Cristiano Ronaldo is not the team captain, but the team captain needs to be someone the coach chooses for reasons beyond talent. "Never put talent before character when you are looking for a leader." This idea is probably most violated at the youngest ages. Coaches of youth teams across the world give the armbands to their one or two best players, even if they may not be the best leaders. Allistair believes that at the youngest ages, every player should be given a chance to be in a leadership position. "We need to understand that the quietest kid in the group may have the most important things to say. We forget that. Some of the best leaders are the quietest figures, so how do we know that person isn't a leader when they are never given a chance to lead?"

BLINKER COACHES

Some of the best insights and progressions I have made as a coach have come from resources outside of the domain of soccer. In the summer of 2016, for example, I read seven books and took an online course about project management, agile software development, and scrum. These were all resources written for IT specialists and people working in Silicon Valley, but the parallels between training a team and developing an app are more similar than different. I learned a lot about planning that I was able to apply during our season to much success.

We can learn so much, as coaches, from other industries and even other sports that it would be a shame to relegate your learning to soccer-only resources. American football coaches like Chip Kelly can teach you about maximizing training time, while basketball coaches like Gregg Popovich can teach you about creating a culture of accountability. But coaches from other sports are not the only places we can turn to learn from. Business leaders may be the best teachers of management and leadership skills. Philosophers can teach us about the importance of humility and gratitude in everything that we do.

Allistair warns against coaches that get all of their information from resources specific to their domain. "I always say, 'Don't be a blinker coach', which is like a horse with blinkers. That means that you are only involved in your own sport, you are only looking in your own sport, you only listen to podcasts about your sport, you only associate with other coaches in your own sport, that is a blinker coach. There is so much opportunity to learn from other industries about how the best leaders, managers, and coaches work and why they get the success that they do." Allistair doesn't restrict this to podcasts or book choices either. Even a Saturday spent channel-surfing can result in learning opportunities. "I was watching curling the other day on TV and one of my friends came in the room and said, 'Are you seriously watching this?' and I said, 'Yes!' Have a look at the coaches, have a look at the players. What are their interactions? How do they communicate? Take a look at the focus of the players. Don't just see the sport, but see what's going on around it."

The best coaches are not just students of their sport, but students of sport in general. Allistair cited Pep Guardiola as a coach that makes an effort nearly once a year to fly out and spend time with Argentinian volleyball coach, Julio Velasco, to learn about his training methods and ideas. Eddie Jones, England's rugby coach, is a known follower of Jose Mourinho and was inspired by him to learn more about tactical periodization and its application to rugby. Don't be a blinker coach.

GREAT COACHES

The biggest misconception in the coaching world is the notion that the team you coach for or the position you hold tells others about your ability. I wrote at length about this in the prologue. Ability and outcomes are not correlated. Allistair knows that to be true as well. "We think that the best coaches are the ones we see on TV with the biggest clubs, and that is far from the truth. The way I determine a great coach is not by the level they work with, but what they can do with that level. That is a great coach. For example, it would be really easy for me to work with Roger Federer and sit on the sideline and go, 'Look what I did.' That is so far from the truth; maybe I just got lucky to get to coach a Federer or Ronaldo. The ones that deserve the credit are the ones that developed those athletes."

Allistair believes that one of the most important traits of a great coach is their ability to listen. In fact, Allistair is credited with one of my favorite coaching quotes of all time which is "The number one reason that players don't listen to a coach is probably because the coach doesn't listen to them." The truth is that coaches can get a lot better by just getting a little bit quieter. "As coaches, we have a tendency to think that we should be talking all the time and that is so far from the truth. John Wooden, for example, hardly spoke and when he did speak it was for no more than 20 or 30 seconds at a time. The coaches that are able to listen are better able to tap into their players and find out what makes them tick. That usually means better results. Become a better listener and you will begin to understand more."

Allistair will be the first to admit that he used to talk too much. "I realized that I was speaking 80% of the time and listening 20%. The most radical change in my coaching for the last 20 years is that I want to listen 80% of the time and speak 20% of the time. I can't even explain to you the difference it has made in being able to understand the athlete better. It has made me such a better coach in being able to find the answers to the questions I need to help that team and those athletes."

One thing I learned from Neil Jones and Mario Sanchez is that when you take over a new team you need to override your instinct. Your instinct will be that you want to go in and tell the players how it's going to be and what you're going to change and the things you will accomplish. But that is the last thing you want to do. Allistair has over 20 years of experience working with new teams and athletes on a consistent basis and listening has been the key to success. "One of the biggest mistakes we can make is walking into a situation and trying to fix all the mistakes as quickly as we can. We have all of these ideas in our head and we want to bring them out and impress our athletes, but it's only by stepping back and listening that you will find your answers."

One strategy that Allistair has found useful when working with a new team is to ask the players to come up with two lists. One list will include the top five things they love about the team and program as it currently is. The second list includes the top five things they want changed immediately. This exercise will help you reveal the secrets to success with that program. In one simple exercise, you will know what the players love about being on that team and what they don't enjoy. Eliminate the five things they don't like and include the five things they love and you will be on your way to success with building buy-in with that team. Just by listening to what they have to say, you will find the answers you are looking for.

The truth is that coaches believe that they need to be these omnipotent and infallible human beings that are incapable of a mistake. I have recently gone to the other side of the spectrum to where I love being wrong. If I am wrong that means I am going to learn something and get better. However, some coaches take being wrong as a sign of weakness or ignorance, but the real ignorance is moving through your coaching journey thinking you have it all figured out and you don't need anybody's help. "The insecure coaches will want to find the answers all by themselves." Allistair has made it common practice to invite another coach to watch him train an athlete. Following the session, he will ask the coach for feedback on what he thinks could be improved. "I want them to give me some feedback on how my coaching was, how they felt I interacted with the group. I want to know things like: Was I listening enough? Was I saying the right things?"

Finland's education system has been ranked among the best in the world for the last decade. There is a free documentary, available on YouTube, called "The Finland Phenomenon," that profiles the Finnish approach to education. One of their core methods of improvement is to consistently have other teachers sit in on fellow teacher's lectures in order to provide them with objective feedback on what they can improve.

My co-host, Brian Shrum, is someone that I always go to for objective feedback on my sessions and ability as a coach. I have found that asking Brian to be really harsh in his feedback to me has helped me most dramatically improve my coaching over the last few years. It isn't easy. You will hear things that may hurt your feelings or make you feel embarrassed or bad at coaching, but it is an essential step if you want to improve. Allistair says it best, "The insecure coaches won't feel comfortable asking somebody else." If you want to grow as a coach—and I mean truly grow—take that step out of your comfort zone and ask someone to give you honest feedback on your coaching. Your growth and improvement will be meteoric.

A DAY IN THE LIFE

Allistair is one of the most structured people I know and his unique approach to his daily life is something to learn from. Annie Dillard, in her beautiful book *The Writing Life*, said, "How we spend our days is, of course, how we spend our lives. What we do with this hour and that one is what we are doing." Allistair's daily routine looks like this:

5AM—Wake up
5:05AM—Drink coffee ("The most important thing I can think of!")
5:15AM—Check Twitter (news, articles, etc.)
5:30AM—Check e-mails
5:45AM—Plan top three priorities for the day and things to do
6:00AM—Home gym for 20 minutes to stretch and foam roll
6:30AM—Breakfast (protein shake and a piece of fruit)
7:00AM—Twenty minutes of thoughtfulness (send text messages or e-mails to any athletes competing on that day, students taking exams, a happy birthday wish, or wishing someone well that is ill)
8:00AM-11AM—Train athletes
12:00PM-1:00PM—Lunch
1:00PM-1:20PM—Nap
1:30PM—Preparation for remaining day's training
2:00PM-7:00PM—Training athletes

The most important part of Allistair's day is what he calls the four 20s which is 20 minutes of stretching, 20 minutes of thoughtfulness, 20 minutes of napping, and 20 minutes of reading. "There is no excuse for where I am in the world that I can't make room for those 20 minutes. I cannot express in words what that has given back to me in energy, knowledge, relationships, and gratitude."

CHAPTER 9

RECRUITING

ERICA DAMBACH

Erica Dambach is the head women's soccer coach at Penn State University. Erica has been to nine straight NCAA tournaments and two NCAA Championship Games, has won 8 Big Ten Championships, and helped win the first NCAA Championship in Women's Soccer at Penn State in 2015. Erica was an assistant coach for the 2008 US Women's National Team that won gold in the Beijing Olympics and the 2011 US Women's National Team that played in the World Cup in Germany. She was also the head coach for the US U17 Women's National Team for four years.

Elite people are elite all the time, not just some of the time — Giving 1% more — Identity versus culture — Changing systems — You hired them, now let them work

Like so many coaches featured on our podcast and in this book, Erica Dambach compares her ability as a coach to her ability to learn. At 24 years old, Erica was named the head women's soccer coach at Dartmouth College, a top 25 NCAA Division 1 women's team. During her time in charge, Erica guided the Dartmouth program to back-to-back Ivy League Championships and two NCAA Sweet 16 appearances. What Erica accomplished at Dartmouth is nothing more than miraculous. For a 24-year-old coach, coaching players two years younger, to have the success that she did speaks to her competency and ability as a coach. However, coaching is a true craft to Erica. Although at 26 she had accomplished something many coaches aspire to accomplish in their 40s, she knew she had bigger mountains that she wanted to climb. In similar fashion to Mario Sanchez, Erica left her post as the Dartmouth head coach to become an assistant coach at Florida State under Mark Krikorian, arguably one of the best women's coaches over the last decade.

Erica's time under Mark Krikorian gave her vital experience in dealing with big-time programs. Even though Erica proved she could coach at Dartmouth, her time at Florida State helped her develop her managerial skills in dealing with bigger personalities, bigger budgets, and bigger expectations. The 2015 National Championship was a byproduct of Erica's decision to leave a head coaching position to get better first and ask questions later.

BUILDING A CHAMPIONSHIP TEAM

If you are unfamiliar with Penn State University Athletics, then you are unfamiliar with the expectations thrust upon every sports team that dons the Nittany Lion uniform. Most programs measure success on conference championships or games won, but Penn State measures success on National Championships and Final Fours. Erica mentioned that an Elite Eight appearance would be classified as a good season, but only a Final Four appearance and a National Championship would be considered great.

The biggest priority for college coaches is recruiting. As the saying tends to go, "good players, good coach, but great players, great coach." For Erica and the Nittany Lions, it was about more than just finding a player with talent. "Our team GPA in 2015 was a 3.5. So we look at their behavior off the field sometimes more than their behavior on the field. You could be a very talented player, but if you don't work hard in the classroom that tells me that you have a tendency to choose when and where you will work hard. Elite people want to be elite all the time, not just elite at soccer but sub-par in school."

The most difficult part of recruiting is that it is a two-way street. While Erica is sizing up a potential recruit in terms of their on-field ability and off-field personality, the recruit is sizing up Erica and Penn State to make sure it is a good fit. Erica expects her coaching staff and players to play a big role in recruiting. "When these families come on campus, our entire staff is engaged from start to finish. I expect our team to be involved with almost every single meal. The tours of campus take place with the entire staff, the meals take place with the entire staff and team; we encourage the families to stay for two days if they can, and we really take the time to get to know each and every family member." My chat with Erica really opened my eyes to how ineffective I was as a recruiter during on-campus visits. I tremendously undervalued the importance of having a recruit spend time with the players. The team has a huge influence on whether or not a certain recruit could be a good teammate or a bad fit. After my chat with Erica, I now involve my team with the recruit as much as possible and I always have a follow-up meeting with my players to get their opinion on the recruit. Do you think he will be a good teammate? Will he care about you? Will he work hard? Do you get along with him? Would you want him on the team? These are all questions that, if never asked, may lead to bringing in a potential cancer or bad fit to your team.

Most high school juniors and seniors won't give you much on a visit. A few head nods and some forced smiles is about the best you can ask for in terms of gauging a personality. That is why Erica makes an effort to get to know the family instead. In her experience, that will tell you all you need to know about the values and priorities of the player. "The apple doesn't fall far from the tree, so we want to make sure that the family environment is right to ensure that you get a good egg." If she still isn't sure about a kid after spending two days with the family, Erica will call people off the reference sheet in order to gain insights from high school teachers, guidance counselors, and personal trainers to determine the character of a potential recruit.

Culture is everything when it comes to building a successful team. Unfortunately, many coaches fail to see how ineffectual training and tactics are when you tolerate poor behavior and habits from your players. Erica has set standards for her players and holds them accountable to what she calls the "Three Pillars." "We have three pillars that we live by. The first one is attitude of a champion. To me, this has to do with body language and your approach to training. We talk a lot about training being the best part of your day and on days where maybe you aren't feeling up to it, you may have to exude a little 'fake it 'til you make it.' Our next pillar is blue collar. That means rolling our sleeves up, being humble, remembering that nobody is above the group, and things of that nature. The third pillar is united family, which means that we have a team-first mentality." Of course, anyone can set standards for their team; the difference with Penn State is that Erica not only enforces these pillars, she lives them.

Erica admits that her culture hasn't always been intrinsic. Very often you see coaches force espoused values onto their team in the hopes that all 26 players miraculously have the same exact values. If you recall Jay Martin's approach, he has his *team* pick the values that are the most important to *them*. Similarly, Allistair McCaw will ask his athletes to write down the three things they plan on contributing to the team for the upcoming season. In both cases, the common theme is that they are finding intrinsic values in their players, and then holding the players accountable to their own standards. Your players will not have the same values as you. You need to understand that in order to get the most out of them. Erica admits that she used to post values, sayings, and quotes around the locker room that were completely coach driven. "I doubt the players even saw them or read them because they just didn't care about them. They weren't their values. They were mine." In 2015, Erica implemented the first iteration of what she calls her "2% Talks."

"Once a week we would have a player stand in front of the team and give a presentation to their teammates for five minutes on one of the pillars. The players could present on any pillar or characteristic they felt they embodied, or a pillar that they struggled with." The brilliance of Erica's "2% Talks" is that the players are teaching their teammates about the pillars. There is a ton of research now that shows teaching something is the best way to learn it. Like Ian Barker said, "When one teaches, two learn." "Once they start talking about attitude of a champion and they are the ones showing the YouTube clip, reading the story, or giving the example, and it's coming out of their mouth? It's really hard to be hypocritical and to not live out that value."

Referring back to Allistair McCaw's chapter and his notion of avoiding being a blinker coach, Erica got that idea from the baseball team at Penn State. She had her players present before practice, either once a week or sometimes twice a week. The goal was to create a team that embodied the three pillars of their program. Well, when you have 26 players teaching the subject, it is no wonder that discipline issues, playing-time complaints, and poor effort were completely absent within her 2015 squad.

It is much easier to uphold these standards when you bring in people that embody them to begin with. It is not a coincidence that Erica has a thorough filtering system in recruiting and a great culture. If you get the right people on the bus, it is much easier to get where you want to go. "Managing 26 college-aged females is challenging enough. Bringing on challenging people to the program is just going to make things harder. If the best player in the country wants to come to Penn State but she is known to be a bit of a head case and a problem in the locker room, assuming we have done further homework on her, I will definitely pass on her. Now, she will probably end up at a top program and she may score the game-winning goal against us in the NCAA tournament, but I know that our team will be better off for it. I think our kids will end up having a better experience because of that decision. Yeah, we may have lost that game, but my players won't be chasing around their teammates and dealing with discipline issues for four years."

When Erica talks about the 2015 National Championship team at Penn State it is hard not to hear an inflection change in her voice; that was how special the 2015 team was to her. "One of the things that made them [the 2015 team] so successful is there were zero, and I mean *zero*, distractions in the locker room. There were no social issues. There were no academic issues. They got to bed early, they took care of their bodies; that team wanted to win a National Championship."

Erica is one of the toughest coaches I have talked to. When she speaks, people tend to stop what they are doing and listen. She doesn't buy the idea that people can give everything they have. For her, there is always more that someone can give. In fact, it is that extra 1% or 2% that Erica pushes her players to grab. "A lot of people talk about doing everything they can, right? They say things like 'I am doing everything in my power' or 'I am working as hard as I can,' but there is no such thing. There is always more that you can do and the 2015 team, more than any team I have ever coached, really put themselves out there and extended themselves to as close to the brink as we could get them." Don't misunderstand Erica's notion here, she isn't talking about running an extra mile or pushing themselves through some other militaristic task. "When you talk about 'good to great' at this level, you are talking about getting eight hours of sleep instead of six. You are talking about staying in on Friday and Saturday nights. You are talking about staying laser focused on the task at hand and not letting anything external take you away from that path."

In 2015, Penn State won the Big Ten regular season title and the Big Ten Tournament, two monumental tasks. "Those were just another night for our kids. They went back to work the next day." Penn State was worried about the process, not the outcome. One of the most destructive things for any team is success. You see it all the time: a team wins a big game in the regular season and then loses the next one because they let their focus slip. But when your aim is a national title, you can't let minor successes derail the work necessary to achieve the bigger goal. Erica got her team back on the pitch the next day preparing for the next opponent. It is on to the next one until there isn't a next one to be on to, and at that point, when a season ends, that is the time to reflect on the previous months' work and celebrate.

It is no coincidence that Erica has built Penn State into a National Championship program. If ever there was an anti-blinker coach, it would be Erica Dambach. The women's soccer office is located on the same floor as the men's soccer program, the five-time National Champion women's volleyball program, and the five-time National Champion wrestling program. Erica is constantly asking for advice and strategies from the coaches that surround her. "It is also daunting, to be honest. Being surrounded by multiple National Championship programs really challenges you to improve yourself on a daily basis. Shame on me if I don't pull from the resources that I am surrounded by every day."

The last thing Erica mentioned to me about building successful teams is probably the most important. Erica did not build Penn State into a National Champion in the first year. Not in the first five years. It took Erica eight years to build Penn State into a place where she could start to impose some of the pillars and cultural items that really drove the success of her team in 2015. "In my first few years in charge, I couldn't get my head above water long enough to establish some of the bigger picture items. I was so consumed in the daily work of e-mailing, recruiting, planning training, and scouting opponents that I couldn't find time to see the program from 30,000 feet in the air. I worked hard to start to add staff members and volunteers that could handle things like heart rate data, statistics, leadership training, and other items in order to buy me the time necessary to look at the program from a long-term standpoint."

Here is how Erica delegates responsibility to her staff:

- Associate head coach Ann Cook is "in charge of player development where she makes specific, individual programs for every player. She works directly with our volunteer coach that is tasked with working with our developmental players (those players currently out of the team). Ann works closely with our volunteer to make sure that the players not seeing a lot of time are still focused on their development so that they are ready when their time comes. These individual plans include technical, tactical, nutrition, strength, and sports psychology components. Ann works with our nutritionists, strength coach, and psychologists to determine those specific objectives of the program. Ann is also in charge of our recruitment of committed players. So she is in charge of making sure our committed players are kept up to date on everything related to their process of finishing high school and enrolling at Penn State. Ann's third major responsibility is community relations and involvement that includes community service, and local initiatives to grow the game."
- Goalkeeper coach Tim Wassell is in charge of goalkeeping, set pieces, scouting, and recruiting. "Tim is a genius. Probably one of the smartest people I have ever worked with. I actually convinced him to leave a career in finance to come on board. He should be working for NASA that guy is so smart."
- A new volunteer coach is brought in every year to bring fresh ideas to the program and move the current volunteers on to full-time positions elsewhere in the country. Erica tasks the person in this position with individual development. "This person really is the one that executes the plan that Ann has developed for each player."

Penn State also has a full-time strength coach, full-time nutritionist, full-time sports psychologist, and a full-time academic advisor. Erica understands the importance of delegating responsibility in allowing her to drive the direction of the program as a whole. "The more I talk the more I can't really figure out what I do, but I know I stay busy somehow, I just don't know how." Erica is obviously extremely humble, but she spent the last decade building each role and responsibility of her program to give her the time and headspace necessary to be able to manage her players and focus on the big-picture items of her program.

They say that patience is a virtue. Unfortunately, the mistake that a lot of coaches make is they come in so overzealous that they bite off more than they can chew in the first two years. That overzealousness ends up setting the program back instead of propelling them forward. Erica's message is that you cannot neglect the culture of your program, but you need to put in the work to be able to get the program to the point where you can see it from a different viewpoint. If you try to establish a culture while planning training, teaching the playing style, meeting with players one on one, showing them film, recruiting, and scouting, you will miss important things and probably make cultural mistakes.

Archie Miller, the head men's basketball coach at Indiana University, doesn't even buy the idea that culture is something you start. "I think culture is earned. You don't start talking about culture four weeks down the road. Culture is built over the course of hard wins, hard losses, and overcoming adversity." Erica Dambach shares that sentiment. It has become a cliché that new coaches claim to be building a culture, but that only comes after they have decided on their team's identity. "Identity is different. Identity is something you can start to implement right away, every day. Culture is five or six years down the road when everything they say about you is earned." Erica didn't build a culture in her first year. She created an identity of what Penn State was going to be about. Now, nearly a decade later, she has earned the right to use the word culture.

SYSTEM OF PLAY

In 2012, Erica led Penn State to the National Championship game against the University of North Carolina, coached by Anson Dorrance. During that campaign, Penn State lost both of their starting center backs to injury, which left Erica with a decision to make. Should she play two freshman center backs in the National Tournament, or change to a three-back system? "I learned so much during that season because I had never coached a three-back system before. I took notes throughout that season and it seemed like each week I had an ah-ha moment of 'Oh my gosh, I can't believe I didn't realize that this would be a by-product of playing three in the back.'" One of those ah-ha moments was when Erica learned—the hard way, as you often do—that playing with three in the back caused her team to give up a lot more corner kicks. The opposition will try to attack the spaces your team does not have covered (e.g., the corners of the field). That means there will be a lot more balls played to the corners of the field. That leads to your defenders spending a lot of time running towards the corners, facing their own goal, and kicking the ball out for a throw-in or corner kick. Erica realized that they should be spending more time working on defensive corner kicks and defending deep throw-ins because of this newly discovered fact.

Erica's reflection on that 2012 season made me think a lot about how I approach learning a system of play. A lot of times I will watch Bundesliga, La Liga, or Premier League games to see how different teams and managers implement specific systems of play, but Erica watched her own team. Instead of me learning about the strengths and weaknesses in a

1-4-2-2-2 from watching Red Bull Leipzig, it is much more specific to watch my own team in that formation because the tactical problems will, of course, be different. For example, if Chelsea plays three in the back under Antonio Conte, they might not have to deal with any balls played into the corner because their opponents will raise a completely different tactical issue. For that reason, Erica doesn't subscribe to the idea that you can assume the tactical problems that Chelsea faces in a three-back system will be the same tactical problems your team faces, even if the system is the same.

Erica pays very close attention to what is happening with her team when they make adjustments to their system of play. This allows her to be much more pragmatic in her approach to training her team in a specific way. My conversation with Erica encouraged me to start keeping a journal to make notes about each training session and game. In that journal, I write things that I learned about my players such as: Does our system promote the strengths of my players or take them away? Are our tactics realistic for them to achieve? Is the time and space of our demands possible, or are we asking them to cover too much space in too little time? I don't recommend copying my questions as they are specific to my team and level, but the idea is to start a process, as a coach, where you are reflecting daily in a journal on your team, your players, and yourself. There is no better process for steepening your learning curve as a coach and manager.

Erica's reflection process means that she is continually tinkering her team's system of play to address the problems they face on a weekly basis. In 2015, the year they won the National Title, Penn State played a 1-4-4-2 with a diamond midfield right up until an injury made them deviate from that system. "We lost the player that played as the deepest player in the midfield diamond and we tried to play with a reserve in that position against West Virginia and they just picked us apart. We transitioned into a flat 1-4-4-2 against Stanford and that was probably our best performance of the season. We eventually made the decision to go into the NCAA tournament with five in the midfield (1-4-5-1) because we play against so many 1-4-3-3 formations. Without matching our opponents with three in the midfield, I noticed that we had a higher chance of losing the midfield battle and getting played through more often.

Here you can see the tactical problem that Erica's team faced going into the 2015 NCAA tournament. The 3v2 match-up in the midfield meant that the opponent always had someone free. Although there are a variety of ways to attempt to solve this, Erica chose to match their opponent's 3v3 in the midfield, thus altering their system to a 1-4-5-1.

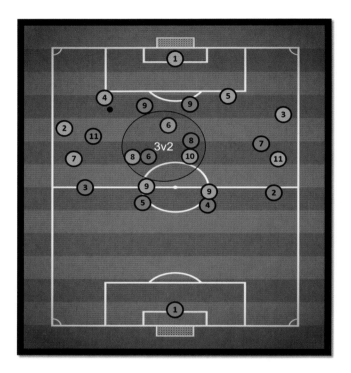

The switch to a 1-4-5-1 gave Penn State a 3v3 situation in the midfield that allowed Erica's team to have much more success heading into the NCAA tournament.

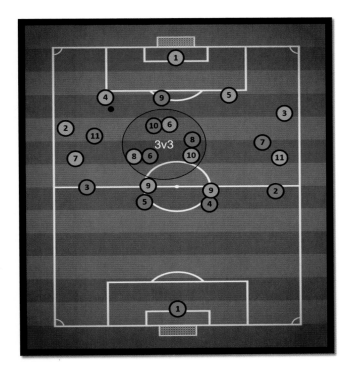

Erica also knows her limitations as a coach. "I am not good enough yet to coach a 1-4-3-3 where the wingers push up high and wide to create space. I just feel that it ends up being too stagnant when I coach it, so I have some work to do in that area. Because of that, our wingers in a 1-4-5-1 ended up getting stuck deep when we had the ball. They just couldn't get high enough, fast enough, unless we sustained our attack. So that's where we spent our time training the 1-4-5-1. We trained sustaining possession long enough so that our wingers had time to get higher up the field."

Erica is one of the smartest and enlightened coaches I have had the pleasure to talk to. Her motto is simple: "Seek first to understand, and then to be understood." She spends the majority of her time trying to understand her players, staff, and systems, which allows her the time to think and reflect on the next strategic move to benefit her program. It has been a long journey transitioning from the exuberant 24-year-old head coach to the wise leader of the National Champions. "When I think about that 24-year-old me, man, she just wanted to micro-manage everything. I look back and I realize that you have to work hard to put people you trust around you and then you have to trust them. I really learned that from Pia Sundhage (former US National Team coach) where she trusted us to execute our roles. Even though she probably would have done something differently, she knew that letting others execute their role gave her the ability to focus on the most important things. By no means did she micro-manage my responsibilities, and in the end we got a lot more done that way. Pia helped me to understand the importance of trusting the people around you. And, you know, if someone isn't doing a good enough job to allow you to trust them, then they simply don't belong there. So I would have told that 24-year-old me to relax a little bit and not micro-manage every last piece. Trust the people around you; you hired them, so let them work."

CHAPTER 10

COACH DEVELOPMENT

TERRY MICHLER

Terry Michler was the 2015 National High School Boy's Soccer Coach of the Year with Christian Brothers College High School in St. Louis, Missouri. He is also the founder of the CBC Dutch Touch website.

The Clockwork Orange — Mistaking theatrics for competence — The coach is a master of observation — What a microwave and a slow cooker can teach you about youth development — How Brazilians organize tryouts — But coach, we already did this — Dennis Bergkamp coaching 10-year-olds — The spotlight is for the players

WHAT IS A COACH?

Terry Michler is the John Wooden of high school soccer in the United States. Terry has been the head coach at Christian Brothers College High School in St. Louis, Missouri for nearly 50 years. He was won over 900 games and is quickly approaching 1000. At 70 years old, Terry is still voracious in his quest to find out the best way to develop soccer players and build winning teams. "I'm a self-learner, I do a lot of reading, and I am constantly looking for resources or ways to improve the things that I do with my teams just a little bit more."

Terry's desire to become a lifelong student of the game was fueled by the biggest influence of his generation, The Clockwork Orange. The Dutch national team of the

1970s, nicknamed The Clockwork Orange, mesmerized the soccer world with the way they played the game, fueled by the pioneer Johan Cruyff. "Way back in the day when I focused on the Dutch, I began to study them because they were offering something that was new, different, and exciting, but most importantly it was challenging. How can you play that way? How can you play at that speed, with that kind of fluidity and skill, and not give up any chances in the process? It was incredible what they did and they were so far ahead of the rest of the world at that time." The Dutch, however—for as talented and paradigm shifting as they were—failed to win a World Cup. Terry believes that the Dutch were far more concerned with the style of their play and not necessarily the outcome of their play, which got us thinking about the problems in the United States.

There is no question that the US prioritizes winning at every single level, and maybe that is our problem. Terry believes that coaches in the US want to win in order to advance their coaching careers, which places the development of the players in the backseat. The coach is more worried about his own development and progression than that of his players.

One of the things that Terry loved so much about the Dutch in the 1970s was that their playing style was relatively easy to explain, but perhaps more difficult to execute. The problem he sees with a lot of coaches in the US is that they tend to overcomplicate everything. "The biggest problem in the US is that the coach still feels he is the most important person. If the coach doesn't say something that sounds really complicated, then he doesn't get to feel like he is above everybody. Coaches like to make it so complicated that no one can understand it, which means that parents and other coaches just assume they know what they are talking about." Albert Einstein is famous for the quote, "If you can't explain it simply, then you don't understand it well enough."

Terry has been fortunate to spend a lot of time in Holland throughout his coaching career and he can say with certainty that, in Holland, it is well understood that the coach is the least important piece of the puzzle. That doesn't mean the role of the coach is not valued or important, but the focus is on the players and their journey. "The coach is seen as the vehicle through which the player develops. Therefore, the Dutch put almost all of their emphasis on coaching education and coaching performance." Perhaps it is cultural. In the United States, you can turn on any sports channel and it is usually the coaches that steal the spotlight. That spotlight is the reason why many coaches get into the profession, regardless of the sport; it is all about them. "In the US, I think it's just our mentality, but if you watch college basketball or college soccer, the coaches are always out in front of everybody; the spotlight is always on the coach. We are obsessed with things like: What kind of shenanigans is he pulling this time? What kind of theatrics does he have on the sidelines? What is he doing to bring attention to himself? So, I wonder whether coaches are even analyzing the game anymore, or are they just actors trying to be theatrical on the sideline so that fans and pundits mistake it for competence?"

THE REAL GIANTS OF SOCCER COACHING

Much like Jay Martin, you will not see Terry Michler running to the corner flag to celebrate a goal, or foam at the mouth because of a bad call by the referee. "I sit during my games. I sit. And I watch. And I observe. And I analyze. And then I process. I never, ever get off the bench, but that just isn't the norm. The norm is to be ranting up and down the sidelines and getting everybody's attention and having everyone think that's coaching, but it's really not." Terry sees it pretty much every game of his high school season. Coaches on the sidelines scream, yell, and wave their arms around trying to get their players to move the way they want. Terry loves having these kinds of coaches in his coaching education courses because his first question always silences the crowd: "What have you done during the week with your kids? What kind of training session have you run during the week if this is the way you have to act during the game?" In other words, if you have to act that way on game day, then you clearly didn't do a good job of preparing them during the week.

It has now become common that the coach is the irrational one during games. This forces the players to be the rational ones. Terry believes that needs to flip 180 degrees. "I always tell coaches that it is their job to be the rational one, the players can be emotional. But you have to be able to tell them after the game what was going on, right, wrong, good, and bad. The coach has to be able to tell them how they can get better from the game they just played." This philosophy is heavily influenced by Terry's time in Holland where they place a premium focus on match analysis. The Dutch will analyze the game rationally and then plan the next week of training based on the things that can be improved from the previous game. "What you see across the US is coaches after the games are totally distraught, ringing their shirts out because they got themselves so worked up that they are full of sweat; they look like a basket case. Then you ask them, 'Hey, coach, what do we have to do to improve?' and he will respond, 'Improve? Hell, I don't know. I was so wrapped up in the game I didn't pay attention to it.'"

Terry has mastered the role of a coach. After 50 years on the sidelines, he has developed a profound understanding of what his purpose is in the entire scheme of things. "What's the role of a coach? A coach has to observe. Observation is critical and you have to observe with a clear mind. You have to know what you are seeing, what you want to see, and how to make up that difference." For Terry, watching and learning from Pep Guardiola, Jose Mourinho, and Antonio Conte is important, but he doesn't believe that we should heed their example of how to behave during a game. "Too many coaches watch the coaches on TV and they see them running up and down the sideline, gyrating up and down, camera focused on them, and that's what coaches think they need to do. That's what they think they should do and for some of them, that's what they want to do. That's not coaching. That's not what it's about. I will say it again: the coach is the vehicle through which the game flows to the players."

Although Terry is critical of the coaching culture in the United States, the trend is not exclusive to just one country. Terry believes that many coaches get it wrong from the start regarding their purpose. "Our coaches need to understand that they are the vehicle through which all of this is possible. They gather the information and deliver it to the player, but it's through the player that everything comes to life. The Dutch emphasize coaching education because they understand that you have to develop the players through the coach."

Terry acknowledges that the US tries to emphasize coaching education, but the intention is completely backwards. For Terry, the order of importance will always be player first, coach second. So, coaching education should be about the coach actually improving and learning something, not receiving a certificate in the mail. That is where the US gets it wrong. It isn't about learning and improving for the sake of players around the country; it is about a coach getting a piece of paper that will help him move up the coaching ladder. "We have the idea that the coach has to have a license, he has to have a letter behind his name, which puts the coach in some kind of stratosphere where he thinks he's something special. I am not convinced as to how all of that relates back to his ability to develop the players."

COACHING

Overconfidence is one of the many brain biases discovered by psychologists Daniel Kahneman and Amos Taversky. Our subjective experience of our ability tends to exceed our actual ability. In other words, we tend to think we are a lot better than we actually are. Terry has been coaching for longer than many people reading this book have been alive and he has curated some thoughts as to what makes a good coach. "The two biggest things for me would be that a coach needs to be able to see the big picture, but with the ability to break the big picture down frame by frame." Terry argues that the second part—the ability to break things down frame by frame—is severely lacking in coaching repertoires. Coaches tend to focus on the outcomes (big picture) when it really has to do with the process (frame-by-frame). "I like to use the metaphor of coaching being a microwave versus a slow cooker mentality. With a microwave, you push the button and it's done. But with a slow cooker, the meal really has to simmer, it has to season, it has to break down, and finally after some time you have the end result, which is always worth it. But it takes time." Terry believes that a good manager needs to know exactly what they want it to look like when it's done, to know the means of getting it there, and to have patience to allow the time for it to develop.

Time is one of the things Terry believes coaches misinterpret the most. "We think that everything has to be done yesterday. That is why we always pick the bigger, faster, stronger kids because then we don't have to worry so much about the time it takes to develop." With that said, Terry doesn't believe that we should cut every kid that has natural athleticism; selecting athletic kids for your team isn't the problem, but failing to teach them how to play the game is.

CULTURE

Everyone talks about it, but what the hell is it? Successful teams like to talk about their winning culture, disciplined culture, or hard-working culture, but *culture* might be the biggest buzzword in sports. Terry describes culture the same way he describes the game: very simply. "Culture is expectations based on what you know about your players, how they behave, what their philosophies are, what their customs are, etc. Culture is the expectations that you have come to expect from a group." Terry has had a lot of success at Christian Brothers, but he will be the first to tell you that he built the culture by focusing on the process. "The process is day by day. We have 100 kids that play soccer at Christian Brothers (varsity, junior varsity, freshman) and they all dress the same at practice. I got that idea from my time in Holland where every kid at the club wears the same training gear as the first team. That lets every kid at our school know how special it is to be on our team and a part of the program."

Culture can extend to playing style as well. Too often, culture is addressed in very non-contextual ways, but all you need to do is look at Barcelona to see how a playing style can define customs and behaviors for a club. "The drills are structured and organized, and everything we do has a purpose. This is how we are going to play, and if we are going to play this way, then we are going to train this way." Terry has very specific expectations for the way his players execute his tactics in training. He thinks one of the biggest mistakes coaches make is progressing drills or activities too quickly. "First, you have to make it right, then you have to make it better. But, first, you have to do it right. Then make it better. Then you can make it faster, or add more opposition. But the starting point is doing it right. So part of my culture is that our players learn to do things right; it is our expectation."

DEVELOPMENT AND MASTERY

Terry isn't one for jargon. If you throw out buzzwords like *culture* and *mastery*, you will probably be met by a shake of his head. "*Development* and *mastery* are words we throw around like they are Halloween candy, but how close do we come to them? We talk about mastery and yet we get nowhere near it." The microwave mentality of soccer coaching in the US is the anti-mastery. Terry loves when coaches memorize 50 or 100 drills. It's even better when they have computer files with thousands of drills in several folders. "I will do similar drills with my players all the time. I have maybe a few for each moment of the game that we do repeatedly in an attempt to master them. What do most kids say when you do something similar? 'Coach, we already did that.' Already did it? What does that matter? Have you done it so many times that you don't even have to think about doing it? Can you do it faster? Can you do it better? Can you do it under this kind of pressure or that kind of pressure? But the mentality is that we already did it."

Terry cannot understand why or how some coaches train for two hours. Time is something that we have the least of and yet misuse the most. When Terry was in Holland, the longest sessions he saw were 70 minutes. "They don't mess around. There are no lines, there are no lectures, and it's go, go, go, go, go. They create a mental drain as well as a physical drain."

YOUTH DEVELOPMENT

Terry believes that we need to get rid of the top-down approach in this country. All of our best coach's coach at the highest level, and all of our money, focus, and energy goes to winning a World Cup. What's wrong with that equation? The problem with that is that the best countries have a bottom-up approach. When Terry was in Holland, he saw Dennis Bergkamp running a session for 10-year-olds. Compare that to some dad that is volunteering to coach his son's team in the US. "If you look at the teams that continually produce good players and good coaches, it is all due to the system in place. Good coaches and good players come and go, but with a bottom-up system, they ensure that good coaches and good players keep coming. In Europe, they put such a huge emphasis on the youngest ages because that is where their future lives. So when you lose a great crop of players at the top, you know there is another group coming in because the system is producing them."

In the mid 1990s, Ajax released a training video called "Dreaming of Ajax" that was followed by similar videos in the 2000s called "Heroes of Ajax." In the first video, coach Patrick Latruex was coaching the U9s and U10s. In the second video, Patrick was still coaching the same age group. Terry had a chance to meet and have coffee with Patrick where he found out that Patrick has coached that same age group for 19 years. Terry believes that we need a similar mentality in the US. "You wouldn't send your kid to first grade and then hope he has the same teacher for second, third, fourth, fifth, sixth, etc. Patrick knows exactly how to deal with 9-, 10-, and 11-year-olds. He is a master of what they need technically, tactically, emotionally, and socially to succeed." Terry thinks that if we had coaches start to specialize and master the coaching abilities required to coach youth levels, we could start to tackle youth-development issues from the bottom up.

THE REAL GIANTS OF SOCCER COACHING

A few years ago, Terry was at the NSCAA banquet watching former FC Dallas coach Schellas Hyndman speak. Schellas' opening remark during his welcome speech was, "I would like to go back to 25 years ago and apologize to every player that played for me because I am such a different coach now than I was then." Terry knows that notion to be true of all coaches. "How much do you learn as you stay in the game? It's unbelievable how much you learn, but the most important thing you learn is that it's not about you. It's about what you can do for your players. As a coach, you need to be open to learn more about the game and how you can better present what you learn to the players. Create an environment that the kids want to come to, that is challenging but fun; kids have to see themselves developing, and they have to see themselves as important and worthwhile." The last thing Terry left me with, after nearly 50 years through the coaching journey, is, "Get off that kick that the coaches need to be the center of attention. Get out of that spotlight and let the spotlight shine on the players."

CHAPTER 11

COACHING THE INDIVIDUAL IN A TEAM

MICHAEL BEALE

Michael Beale is currently an assistant coach with Sao Paulo FC in the Brazilian Serie A. Michael works under Rogerio Ceni, the legendary Sao Paulo club goalkeeper that scored over 131 goals. Michael previously worked as the head coach of the Liverpool U23s where he helped build one of the most successful youth team setups in the world. Michael also worked as the youth development officer and academy coach at Chelsea Football Club for nearly 10 years before moving on to Liverpool FC. Michael is considered one of England's brightest young coaches.

Coach someone the way you would like to be coached — Are you a brick wall or a sponge — There are 11 "I"s in a team — Changing the hat of a team — Forward thinking, forward passing, forward running — How to organize a defense — You can go over, around, or through, but you have to choose — Positional small-sided games — Why my best coach was a schoolteacher that knew nothing about soccer

THE MAKING OF A COACH

It is interesting to examine the steps that lead a coach to develop the philosophy or personality that he has. Typically, a process of reverse engineering can help us determine how and when a coach became the way he is. For example, there is no doubt that Johan Cruyff and Barcelona had a huge influence on Pep Guardiola. That influence has led him to value things like possession and spacing. However, a coach that grows up in the United States, where things like athleticism and pragmatism reign, may view the game totally differently.

Michael Beale is one of the few coaches I have met that has developed a unique perspective all his own. It is all his own because he coaches not to please the players or the fans, but to please the player he used to be. "I always had a feeling of how I thought the game should be played and that was based on what I liked as a player. That has always been at the forefront of my coaching." Now, this isn't to say that Michael hasn't had mentors or influences. He admits that he was fortunate at Chelsea to have a lot of fellow academy coaches to help him see the game through a wider lens. In fact, the biggest influences came from the first-team coaches at Chelsea during Michael's time as the youth development officer; guys like Claudio Ranieri, Jose Mourinho, Luiz Felipe Scolari, Guus Hiddink, Avram Grant, Carlo Ancelotti, Andres Villas-Boas, and Roberto Di Matteo. "There were a lot of fantastic first-team managers during my time at Chelsea and I was able to have access to a lot of their ideas and they sort of percolated through to me. I was able to take a few pieces of information from each and add those to my coaching philosophy and how I viewed the game."

Michael has been open to learning from other coaches since he began coaching. Even though he has been influenced by the likes of Ranieri and Mourinho, he will admit that he is still stubborn in his main belief. "I am very strong willed in my desire to coach players the way I liked to be coached. I know what I liked as a player and that was to be free and to be able to play." Michael has gone deeper than just applying the drills he did as a player, he has tried to apply the way he learned as a player. "I was very much a player that learned by doing things and learning from the experience. I'm a big believer, when training youth players, that we should stick close to the game and include attacking, defending, and transitioning with most things that we do to allow the game to be the teacher. I don't like to move too far away from the game because I think the game is the best teacher."

THE ROLE OF A COACH

Michael began his coaching career as a futsal coach, which is where his love for the individual development side of the game blossomed. As he began his career in the Chelsea FC academy, his focus was on improving every single player as an individual, not necessarily just the team. Influences like Ranieri, Scolari, Mourinho, and Ancelotti gave him an unbelievable education and interest in the tactical side of the game. "As I moved through the ages at Chelsea, I sort of lost sight of the fact that my passion was in developing the individual. I became obsessed with the tactical side of the game because my influences were older, successful managers, but my biggest love has always been the one-to-one relationship with a youth player or a senior-level player, and trying to get the absolute best out of them."

Terry Michler spoke at length about the United States' obsession with coaches. He advised us, as coaches, to step out of the spotlight and let the light shine on our players. Michael agrees that the role of the coach is to be a vehicle through which the player develops and grows. "I spend a lot of time talking to players one on one and I try to plan training *for them*." The important thing to remember when it comes to youth development is that eventually, either at the end of a season or when it is time for a player to move on to the next level, you will hand your players to someone else. Coaches that make youth development about how many games and championships they win are ignoring their purpose. "At the end of each season, as a youth developer, you are handing players on. The length of time you have with them as a team, or as a group, is not very long, so youth development is about individuals not teams."

Keeping that purpose in mind clarifies how we should approach youth training. The sessions need to be made for the *players*, not the coaches. A lot of times, coaches will plan training for their youth team so that their team is tactically prepared for an upcoming game or tournament, but is that what each player needs? Michael believes that, in youth development, "trying to get what the player *needs*, and what the player *wants* together, in every session, is really important."

The relationship between coach and player at the youth level and beyond should not be viewed as hierarchical as it currently is. Terry Michler put it perfectly when he talked about the coach needing to feel superior to his players and peers. The relationship between coach and player should be viewed as, in Michael's words, "the coaches trying to work with the player to get the best out of them."

It is always interesting to find out how people view success. Depending on where you live or coach, success in youth development can be defined as getting a player to sign with his club's first team or getting a player to earn a college scholarship, but Michael defines it in a more abstract way than most. "I think to define success in youth development is to get a young player doing things that he didn't even think he could do himself." We all get caught up in the celebrity of signing first-team contracts or making professional debuts, but isn't coaching really about getting our players doing things they didn't know they could? That could mean developing a player into the next Eden Hazard, but it could also mean teaching a right-footed player how to shoot with his left. It doesn't have to be as grandiose as we sometimes think it needs to be. How much more centered and focused on the individual would coaches be if they continually made their mission "getting players doing things that they didn't think they could do"?

DEVELOPING YOUTH PLAYERS

Kaizen, as mentioned earlier in this book, is the Japanese idea of continuous improvement. At Liverpool, there is no such thing as complacency. Michael and his academy staff are continually talking to the Liverpool youth players about what they have to improve in order to get to the next level. "We are always focused on the next challenge. We don't like letting players fall into a comfort zone." Michael has found that the easiest way to push a player out of his comfort zone is to let him train with the first team. Nearly every day, Jurgen Klopp will have a handful of academy players from Michael Beale's U23s train with the first team. "Some of our most talented players get to train with the first team every day and they realize that Philippe Coutinho, Firminho, Daniel Sturridge, and Adam Lallana are at such a high level that they recognize they need to keep fighting and striving every day."

It is vital that the Liverpool U23 players continue to push and improve every single day to even have a chance at a first-team contract. The Premier League is one of the most competitive and demanding leagues in the world, which means that the U23s need to show that they not only can hold their own in training, but that they can also compete against the likes of David Silva, Theo Walcott, and Zlatan Ibrahimovic. Liverpool continually tries to expose their players to the first-team level as a two-birds-with-one-stone philosophy. They simultaneously acknowledge their most talented U23 players by giving them an opportunity to play for the first team while also showing them just how far off they really are from that level. The players are constantly reminded of how much more they need to improve to be able to compete at a Premier League level. "We always ask the players: is your talent a brick wall now? Or is it a sponge? Are you completely shut off to information and advice, or are you open to learning and improving? These are the questions we continually ask our players, but it's the ones that are like a sponge that have the best chance."

Michael compares youth development at the Premier League level to surfing. "You have to be able to ride the wave a little bit with the players. One minute they think they cracked it because they have a good game, and the first team shows a bit of interest, but the next week they have a poor game and now they are in the dumps about everything. It is really a journey you are going on with the players. You have to be there by their side and help them every step of the way. You need to know what they need, when they need it, and that it is all focused on them achieving their dream of playing professional soccer."

Michael hates the phrase, "There is no 'I' in team." "I think that's terrible for youth development. There are eleven individuals in a team. So, there are eleven 'I's in the team. The stronger you can impact each player in your team, the better your team will be for sure."

IDENTITY

Why do you play the game? Why do you get out of bed in the morning? What is you at your best? These are just some of the questions Michael asks each and every Liverpool player in order to give them the best chance at playing for the first team. "We talk a lot about identity, you know, what player do you want to become? We sit down with the player and we try to get them to tell us what their identity is as a player. What is you at your absolute best?" Michael and his staff are trying to find out what is going to give each player the best chance of playing in the first team. "It really comes back to whether you are a goal scorer, a goal creator, or a goal stopper? If you are a goal scorer, then what type of goals do you score? What type of chances do you miss? Okay, then how can we improve the chances that you are missing? How can we continue to score the chances that you do score? What sort of small games can we make in training to accomplish this? Are there other areas or departments we can utilize, whether it's the analyst department, the sports science department, etc. We don't leave any stone unturned when it comes to helping a player to be a first-team player."

Liverpool looks at four things in developing the identity of their players:

1. Self-awareness—"What is your awareness of yourself and your identity?"
   a. Example: I am a big, physical, goal scorer that can finish in and around the box. I want to be like Zlatan Ibrahimovic.
2. Self-management—"Now you know yourself and where you want to go, but what are your daily rituals? How are we going to plan your training for you? Not for the team, but for you? It's about your journey of getting to the first team."
3. Awareness of others—"How do you fit with the rest of the team? How do you take your playing style and your identity and fit that into a team?"
4. Relationship management—"A lot of young players struggle with communicating because the world has changed. Young people would rather text you than have a conversation, but it is important to be able to stand in front of a senior person—whether it's a veteran first-team player or the owner of the club—and be able to speak. The way you dress, the way you carry yourself, the way your agent represents you, the car you drive—there are so many things that you can improve in the way young players carry themselves to be able to make an impressive human being."

Once he gathers that information, Michael's job is simple—at least, it is to him. "My job is to fine tune their identity, which is the skills they already have, and manage their pathway to the first team." Michael takes a bottom-up approach to development. He takes a player's natural identity and brings it to its maximum potential. Jed Davies, current assistant coach for the Ottawa Fury in USL, says that, "a player's identity is the collection of their technical, tactical, physical, and psycho-social traits. For example, Zlatan Ibrahimovic is Zlatan because no one told him he couldn't be the enigmatic—at times, arrogant—player that he was and still is. That is what made Zlatan, well, Zlatan."

Michael Beale doesn't coach the Zlatan out of his players. He determines what traits make them great and he makes sure he is providing an environment that brings those traits to a first-team level. A common development in academies throughout the US is to force every age group to play the same exact system as the first team in exactly the same way. In fact, that is an idea that is often applauded by coaches around the globe, but what are the consequences of that approach? Are we fostering the identity of our players, or are we fitting everyone into a box? For example, if the first team play a three-back system, but the academy has an unbelievable left back that likes to overlap and cross balls in, is he out of the system? If the first team plays with inverted wingers (i.e., wingers that play on the opposite side of their dominant foot so they can cut inside and create), are wingers that can serve the ball cut from the program?

Michael Beale has created a system that can change based on the identity of the players that he has. He will still set up his team in a 1-4-3-3 for most games, but the identity of the players he has available for selection will determine the tactics employed by the team. Michael refers to this concept as "changing the hat" of the team. Here is an example of various changes he can make to the team's hat depending on the type of players he has available for selection.

This is what Michael refers to as the core of the team. These eight players—which includes the goalkeeper, back four, and midfield three—are developed in the same way in order to provide the team with defensive balance and to build their attacks in creative and unique ways. This allows Michael to employ a much more flexible hat of the team. Here are the variety of hats that Michael has used with the Liverpool U23s.

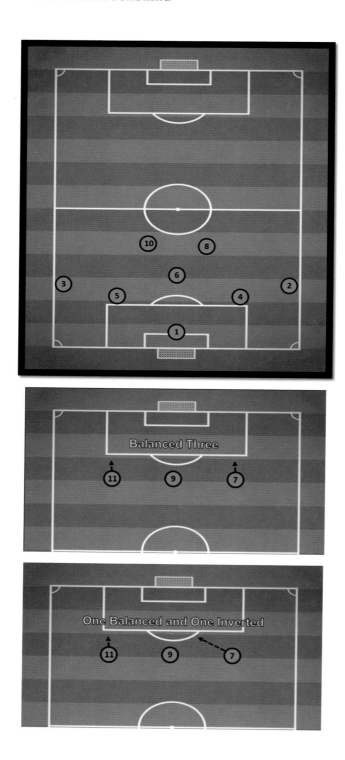

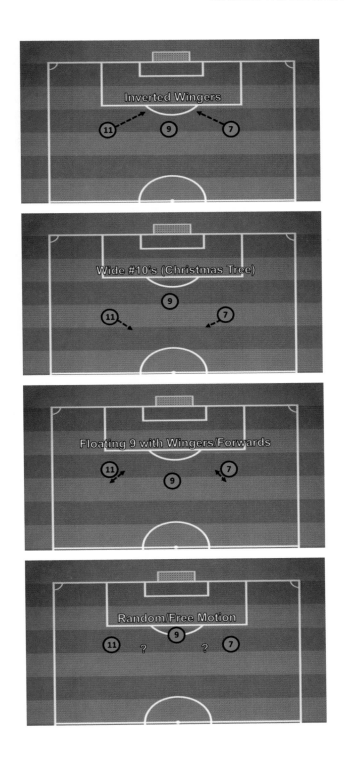

The benefits of this approach are many. This allows the Liverpool U23s to be unpredictable in the way that they attack, but most importantly, it maximizes the strengths of his individual players. Instead of asking a creative winger that prefers to cut inside and go 1v1 to sit on the touchline and whip in services, the game model adapts to the identity of the players he has. Changing the hat also allows Michael to move in and out of styles and tailor tactics accordingly. Pressing schemes and key passing areas can all change based on these identities. There are a variety of different combinations that can be employed, but the message for coaches is that your tactics and approach should be tailored to the identity of the players that you have, not the other way around.

SOCCER IS A GAME OF 1V1S

Michael has taken his early futsal influence and developed an eleven-a-side philosophy based on the dominance of one individual player over his opponent. He believes that if he provided you with eleven technically excellent players, then you, as a coach, could mold them and teach them any playing style that you wish. However, if the players are not technically excellent, now you may have to adapt your idealistic playing style to suit their needs. "I think what we see in modern soccer is that coaches are limited by the technique of their players and their ability to outplay their opponent in 1v1 situations." Anytime you mention 1v1 to coaches, we immediately picture players lined up facing each other practicing step-overs and feints. But, as Michael says, "it most certainly isn't that."

Along with Pepijn Lijnders and Alex Inglethorpe (also academy managers at Liverpool FC), Michael emphasized the ability of Liverpool players to outplay 1v1 upon their arrival to Melwood in early 2010. The perception of what 1v1 training is and what Liverpool have actually trained are very different things. "We wanted players that could handle 1v1 situations. We aren't talking about circus skills. It comes back to a player's identity—what kind of player are you? What sort of opponents do you do well against? Which ones do you not do well against? How can you outplay your direct opponent in each game? In possession or out of possession, we are asking our players if they can receive the ball, if they know how to mark someone or track runs. A lot of our training comes back to that."

Michael is a firm believer that having technically excellent players makes anything the manager wants to do easier. "The biggest message I would give to any youth-development coach is that everything becomes easier if your players are technically very good. Tactics become a lot easier. For example, if you want to work on playing out from the back and you have players that can handle the ball, playing out from the back becomes easier."

Soccer isn't just a game of 1v1s to Michael, but also a game of 2v1s. In other words, how does a player connect and combine with one other player? Liverpool's academy managers are constantly observing their players' interactions with their teammates. It could be a pair of central midfielders or a right fullback and a right winger, but the question is how do they connect with other players?

Liverpool has made the ability to outplay 1v1 one of their most important training focuses because "if you can outplay your opponent 1v1, soccer becomes so much easier." Michael isn't saying that we need to develop every player to be able to beat four guys off the dribble—again, don't misunderstand what he means by outplaying 1v1. "It comes down to knowing what a person's playing personality is. The beauty of soccer is you can go to any game in the world—no matter what the level—and you will have different personalities within each team. You will have good attacking players, fast players, slow players, tall players, short players, good defenders, good passers, so in each team, there are a lot of different personalities. Andrea Pirlo outplays 1v1 in a completely different way than Paul Pogba, and yet they are both outstanding central midfielders. So when we talk about outplaying, it's not dribbling. Outplaying can mean you have brilliant receiving skills to be able to twist and turn to play forward. You could outplay by making more passes and moving the opponent. It may be a central defender that uses his physical strength to overpower his opponent. It might be a defender that reads the game really well so that he can intercept passes. We talk to our players about which one fits them and their playing identity."

Michael will often ask players what their 9 out of 10 is. In other words, what is a player's best quality? It is vital that players figure out what makes them great. What makes them really special? By focusing on that quality, they can be players that can outplay their direct opponent. That is truly what outplaying 1v1 means. It means that a defender that can read the game and intercept passes executes his identity better than an opposing winger that likes to receive in front of him and get on the turn. Which player will utilize their best quality—their identity—to outplay the other 1v1? That is where Liverpool focuses their youth-development efforts. Put even more simply, outplaying 1v1 means being a better you than your direct opponent is a better him.

Focusing on a player's identity and strengths doesn't mean that Liverpool neglects areas of weakness. But, in a way, they actually do. They won't work on skill moves with a big physical center back. Instead, the Liverpool academy coaches try to "'round their game off behind their strengths.'" For example, let's say we have a player that we would characterize as a dribbler. To round their game off behind their strengths we could develop the following skills in training:

- The ability to beat players on both sides
- The ability to cross the ball off both feet
- The ability to shoot off both feet
- The ability to not always dribble, but pass and overlap or pass and underlap

The Liverpool philosophy is focused on what their players CAN do, not what they CAN'T do. "We are always looking at what players can bring to the game. I think it's really tough when coaches are always telling you what you can't do and what you need to improve. What we say to a player is, 'What makes you an elite young player? Why are you at Liverpool? Why are the coaches investing in you? It's really, really important that the players know what they bring. They have to have a real strong identity as a player on the pitch. That is how we design their training."

THE TRAINING

Michael and the U23s are extremely structured in how they plan their training. With such an individual focus, it is essential that everyone is on the same page and that the staff understands which players they are working with and what they are working on. Typically, a lot of individual work is done at the end of training that is either opposed or unopposed, but the session itself will always be contextual to the player's individual needs. "We are very skilled in how we manage a session. If we are playing an 11v11 game, certain staff will speak to certain players to make sure they get the most out of the session." Michael makes sure that—whether they are playing 4v4, 7v7, or 11v11—the theme they started the session with remains throughout the session. If a player is focusing on improving a specific aspect of his game, that focus will be the focus of every single activity for that player. "If you are working with a young fullback and you want to improve his 1v1 defending then you need to cut all the fluff away from the session and get him into 1v1 defending from the moment he arrives in the morning. So maybe it's something where he goes into the gym in the morning and works on some specific footwork patterns, then maybe he goes out 10 minutes early before training and has someone move his feet by dribbling at him, and then maybe when the session starts you get straight to that point."

Michael does not like to waste a lot of time in training. They spend a lot of time discussing each and every player and what each player needs, specifically, to make it to the first team. Spending 20 minutes a session working on passing patterns with the whole team is a waste of at least a few players' time, if not everybody's. "If it's an area that is crucial, then it might be the difference between a player making it as a professional player or not. The role of the staff is to put that player in that position as much as possible."

Liverpool doesn't just identify areas for improvement, work on those, and call it a day. Michael really opened my eyes to how specific a coach needs to be in order to truly improve a player. Saying that a player needs to improve his dribbling is nonspecific and vague. "When coaches say things like, 'He can't defend 1v1' to me that's such a broad statement. What type of players can't he defend against 1v1? You need to ask that question because there are lots and lots of types of players that can beat people 1v1." Michael and his staff are continuously dissecting their players in order to ensure they are giving them the best chance possible at making the first team. "If you are a wide player, we might say, 'Okay, what kind of fullback are you very good at beating? Are you good at beating someone that is bigger and stronger because you are quick? Well, how do you get on against quick defenders? It's a real self-journey, and that is why we have to have such skilled staff because it takes a lot of work."

When Michael gets into the office to plan a session he always starts with the same two questions:

1. How many players do I have today?
2. What do they need to get to the next level?

From there, Michael splits the players up and assigns specific players to specific staff members. Generally, the Liverpool U23s will have 15-18 players, so Michael will take a group of 5-6 players and his two assistant coaches will also take a group of 5-6 players. Michael couldn't verbalize a way to understand his training sessions. "You would have to come and watch us train for at least 4-5 days to really get it." But he did tell me that you wouldn't show up and be able to ask him what he is working on that day. "I don't look at it like 'Oh, today we are working on playing out of the back or playing through midfield, we are working on the players that we have in front of us and what they need."

PLAYING STYLE

Michael prefers attacking soccer. He likes players that can beat their opponent off the dribble, get the fans off their backside and on to their feet. "I think it's the most exciting thing in the world." Although his love for attacking soccer will not change, Michael has learned that coaching youth soccer means sometimes working with the players that you have. "The formation that we use is dictated, most of the time, in youth development, by the players that we have. One year you may have two fantastic wide players and one center forward, so it makes sense to play 4-3-3. The next year you may have two outstanding center forwards." Michael asked me what I would do if I were the coach of the Liverpool youth team that had a young Michael Owen and Robbie Fowler. "How could you only play one up top if you had a young Michael Owen and Robbie Fowler? You would certainly play two up front." Although formations are important to an extent, Michael believes that how you play the game and the principles you have for your team are far more important.

Michael worked in youth development for nearly 16 years before accepting an assistant position at Sao Paulo in 2017. In those 16 years, he learned that the playing style applied to the youth team has a lot to do with the first team manager's non-negotiables and playing principles, but not necessarily with what the youth coach prefers. "You need to find out what the manager's non-negotiables are. What are his principles of play? Then, you emphasize those every single day."

Forward thinking. Forward passing. Forward running. That is the Liverpool way. "I love that saying because it gives your team an intent when they have possession. It's not just possession for possession's sake. It's possession to score goals. We want to be exciting to watch. We also tell our team to 'own the ball and own the pitch.' You own the pitch by dictating the area you are going to allow the other team to play in. Owning the ball comes down to how technically excellent your players are."

Michael sees a lot of teams that make building out of the back a priority. He wonders why some teams emphasize playing to their center backs if they can't handle the ball? "Tactics are one thing, but you have to know who your best players are and figure out ways to get them on the ball. In a lot of the academy soccer I watch, the defenders are having all the touches, and sometimes the goalkeeper is having more touches than the forward players or the wide players, and that's a shame. At Liverpool, the reason we say 'Forward thinking. Forward passing. Forward running' is because we want our players to play the ball into the final third. We want players to be able to take the ball into the final third, and we want our attacking players on the ball."

The information age has equipped a lot of coaches with a lot of information regarding tactics, styles of play, and systems of play. Opponent scouting has become one of the most important parts of a modern soccer coach's day. Knowing how your opponent is going to set up and play is vital to crafting a game plan to beat them. Michael has had experience scouting youth teams from all over the world, which has provided him insight into the most common ways teams try to set up and play. The most common defensive organizations he has seen are below:

Medium block—"You could play against a team that set up in a medium block to keep you from playing through the middle. That means they give up a little bit of space in front and a little bit of space in behind, and they typically allow you to build to a certain area before coming after you."

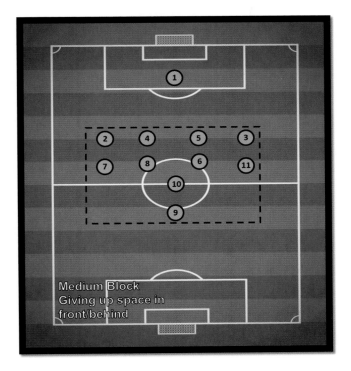

High press—"They might be a high-press team, which means they come right after you and leave a lot of space in behind."

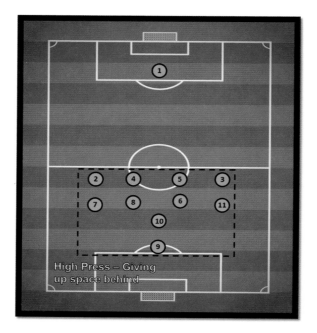

Low block—"They could also set up in a low block. A low block means that they leave all the space in front of them, but nothing in behind them. This is often the most difficult to break down."

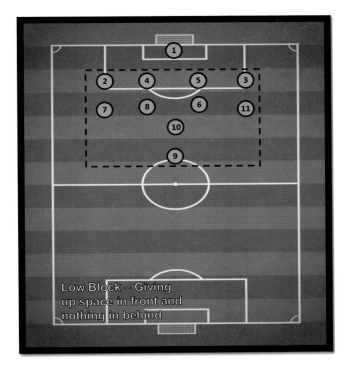

Low Block – Giving up space in front and nothing in behind

Each of these strategies—low block, medium block, or high press—are intended to dictate where your opponent can play on the pitch. More specifically, they are determining where the opponent can play by shortening the length of the pitch in various ways. Michael has noticed that it isn't possible to shorten the width of the pitch. "A team cannot be on the left at the same time that they are on the right." Because an opponent cannot shorten the width of the pitch, Michael wants his Liverpool team to always play with width. However, Michael believes that, at the U23 level, the players need to be able to problem solve. He doesn't like to solve every potential problem for his players before the game even kicks off. "In U23 soccer, you never how the team is going to come out, so my job is to see if the players can problem solve during the game. For example, we could be playing a team that is in a medium block, but they could score first and decide to sit back in a low block and play us on the counter. Now the spaces on the pitch change. Therefore, what's needed to be successful in the game changes." Michael believes that there are three ways to penetrate the opponent:

1. Go around them
2. Go through them
3. Go over them

How the opponent chooses to organize themselves defensively will determine which option or options are available. For example, if the opponent sets up in a low block, there will be no space to go over them. Therefore, you will have to try to go around them or through them to score. Michael tries to allow his players the opportunity to problem solve during games, but he doesn't let them go into a game without any information. "We know how we want to play. We know who our most dangerous players are for that particular game. Then we may train or talk about ways in which we can get them on the ball, and how they can be effective. From there, we have to problem solve in the game."

Michael doesn't believe that you can teach players a playing style in one or two sessions. In fact, beyond little bits of information he believes that "players are the product of their last 200 or 300 training sessions. It's never going to be what you did the day before the game, but what your players know as their beliefs and your club's beliefs about soccer over the last 200 or 300 training sessions."

Michael talks with the Liverpool U23s a lot about "winning their positional small sided games. It's 11v11 when you walk out of the tunnel, but from there it is just a collection of 1v1s, 2v1s, 3v2s, etc. So you need to teach your players how to play out from the back against two forwards. Does it change when they have a #9 and two wingers? How do your two center backs play out now? If it's man to man in a midfield 3v3, could a center back step into midfield and a winger pinch in to make it a 5v3? These are all the things that you can get better at in training. A lot of coaches say that their team can't get better at 11v11 because they only have twelve players in training, but I still think you can train the fundamentals of the game in the small-sided games." Michael usually keeps his game-day chats—either pregame or at half-time—pertaining to these positional small-sided games. He feels that one area coaches neglect is talking about what may happen next in the match. "If we are winning at half-time, we may ask the question 'Will our opponent be the same team in the second half that they were in the first half?'"

One of Michael's biggest pet peeves is when a coach recaps the first half to the players at half-time. "It's very important at half-time that you don't just give the players a recap of what just happened in the first half. They know what just happened; they lived it themselves. They just played that half. It's more like, 'Come on now, what's next? How are we going to improve in the second half?'" Another half-time mistake, particularly at the youth level, is when coaches sub a player that is struggling. Michael sees that as a tremendous opportunity for the growth of that player. "Sometimes a player is having a tough go of it and a lot of coaches default to taking him out, but maybe this is a great time to challenge him to win the second half. Can he win his little battle in the second half?" That is just another example of Michael always thinking about what the individual player's needs are, not the team's. The team might need a substitution, but that player needs to stay on to try and bounce back in the second half.

Michael sees training as a chance for the coach to get everything right regarding the individual player's development. But the game is about problem solving. We can get everything right in training to prepare our team for the match, but Michael considers the match to be a Pandora's box, where the potentialities of what could transpire are unpredictable. "Too many coaches get frustrated during the game because they don't respect the restrictions that the other team is putting on your team. Games are all about problem solving and trying to find a way to be effective and to try and win."

Michael doesn't subscribe to the notion that possession is the most important statistic in soccer. In fact, he doesn't see how you can even call it possession if the opponent wants you to have the ball. Sometimes, it's not such a good thing to have 70% or 80% possession because the opponent is in a low block and that's what they want. They want you to have the ball, so you have to ask yourself how effective your team is being with the ball. "Sometimes the best thing in a game like that is to have 50-50 possession, or maybe even less, because it brings the other team away from their goal a little bit. If you give the ball to a team sitting in a low block, they almost let their guard down. Sometimes you have to allow a little bit to get what you want."

Michael does know that his team's possession should be purposeful and sustained in the opponent's half. "We want 70% of our possession to be in the opponent's half. So we don't want 70% possession total, we want 70% of whatever possession we do have to be in the opponent's half." Michael's philosophy is about getting his attacking players on the ball. In order for them to truly be effective, they need to have the ball near the opponent's goal. "We don't want our center backs to be hitting the ball back and forth and side to side, we want to get the ball into the opponent's half. We want to excite people and our players. We want people to be excited when they watch Liverpool soccer. So 70% of our personal possession is up near your goal, not on the edge of our box."

Michael's biggest piece of advice to coaches working in youth development comes from nearly two decades of work at the highest level of youth development in the world. "I hope a lot of coaches can start to understand this because I certainly can now: it's not a beauty contest. Sometimes I watch youth-development games and coaches are like, 'Oh, yeah, we play out from the back and we play into midfield,' but I sometimes watch and think, 'Okay, great, but that brilliant center forward you have—or that fantastic number 10 or those wide players you have—they never touch the ball. Soccer is about creating and scoring goals, and when the opponent has the ball, it's about stopping them from scoring on your goal. In other words, defending as far away from your goal as possible. You don't want the opponent to have any possession in your half if you can help it."

Michael has learned that a great personality is essential for a coach, especially the higher he climbs up the coaching ladder. "When you work with young players it is a little bit easier because it isn't their job. They are just kids playing for fun, but when you start working with full-time professional players, you have to be willing to give up a little bit of ownership of the training and games to the players." Like other coaches in this book, Michael believes that you have to use your staff as well. "If you have a staff, use them. If you have a session of ten players, a ratio of 1 to 10 is much worse than 2 to 5."

Michael left our conversation with sage advice for someone as young as he is. Nearly 20 years at the top level of youth development has left Michael with more wisdom about life than perhaps even soccer. Michael made it to the U23 level of a Premier League club before he was denied his dream of playing professional soccer. He had a lot of great coaches along the journey, but his best coach was a schoolteacher named Michael Rollington. "The reason he was my best coach was not because he was a fantastic soccer coach. It was because he believed in me as a person. He had a fantastic personality. He could interact with me. So that is a massive piece of advice that I give to coaches is that you have to have a personality to interact with people. First, you should inspire them with who you are. Second, you should inspire them with the game. The game is also very simple: attack and defend goals. It's very competitive, it's fast paced, that is the essence of why people love soccer. Don't go too far away from that. Don't try to reinvent or recreate the game. I think that is another big one."

There is no question that for Michael, it all comes down to personality. "I think personality is huge. I think without it, you are working with someone else's son or daughter and trying to inspire a love for the game. If you are unable to do that, then there are other areas of soccer you can work in. If you are on the pitch working with young players, then you have to make sure that you can interact and inspire."

CHAPTER 12
PRODUCING PROFESSIONAL PLAYERS
DARREN SAWATZKY

Darren Sawatzky is the head coach of the Seattle Sounders U23 PDL team and the Tacoma Stars of the Major Arena Soccer League. Darren played professionally in Major League Soccer for the New England Revolution, Dallas Burn, Colorado Rapids, Seattle Sounders, and Portland Timbers. He was also one of the first coaches to finish and pass the French Formation License administered by the French Football Federation.

You don't get to say "We lost, but we played pretty" — We climb ladders one rung at a time — Get rid of the 9-day coaching courses, coach educators need to have their feet on the ground, in the trenches, helping coaches every day — French training methodology

Darren Sawatzky's name may not be as recognizable as Sigi Schmidt's or Bruce Arena's, but the impact he has had on US soccer is unquestioned. Darren played in the very early days of Major League Soccer following his playing career at the University of Portland under legendary coach, Clive Charles. He finished his USSF A license while finishing out his playing career for the Seattle Sounders, a club he would come to call home for quite some time. Darren joined up with current Sounders head coach, Brian Schmetzer, following a collegiate coaching career at the University of Washington. Brian and Darren led Seattle to the USL championship in 2007 before Seattle was given a Major League Soccer expansion bid. Adrian Hanauer, the Seattle Sounders' general manager, asked

Darren to become the first academy manager in club history. Darren built the Seattle Sounders Academy into one of the most prolific in the country, producing players such as Deandre Yedlin (Newcastle United, US National Team) and Jordan Morris (Seattle Sounders, US National Team). Since laying the foundation for one of the most successful academies in our country, Darren has transitioned to become the head coach for the Seattle Sounders U23s and the Tacoma Stars in the Major Arena Soccer League. Since that transition, the Seattle Sounders U23s have produced 54 professional players in the last four years.

DON'T CALL ME COACH

Darren, like many former players (myself included), found the transition from player to coach difficult. You think you know it all as a player, but the first time you are the one with the whistle and the clipboard, you realize how much you don't know about the game. Darren found more of a physical discomfort in the transition as his body quickly became confused by the lack of high-intensity running and slide tackles it had become accustomed to.

Darren learned very quickly that the word *coach* doesn't really paint the correct picture of what that job entails. "Everybody thinks you are coaching soccer and, up to the age of 17, you're not. You're educating players on how to play the game; you're an educator, not a coach." Being one of the first academy managers in the United States meant that he qualified to take the French Formation License very early on in his career. The course is a 2.5-year mammoth that challenges coaches on all aspects of the game. "It was extremely difficult; it made getting a Master's degree look like pre-school. The course was fundamentally a Master's degree on how you educate, teach, and develop players around the world. I learned a whole lot about what I don't know, and I learned even more about what people believe they know that they actually don't know."

One of the things that Darren learned is that people around the United States think they know how to produce professional players. "It's actually comical listening to half the people that say that because they need to go and look at how it's been done around the world. We don't do it like everybody else does and that's why we haven't produced world-class players." Darren isn't saying that the United States needs to become Spain or Italy, but we need to look at how other countries have done it. We need to look at how they modeled their system, but not copy their model. Americans are known for winning games they probably shouldn't, and exhibiting world-class work rates, and never-say-die attitudes. Darren believes that if we can marry that personality with the developmental structure that is happening around the world, we can have something that is pretty special.

Darren's biggest problem with the development system in the US is some of the advice that gets thrown around and adopted throughout the country: namely, the idea that winning isn't important. "Whoever said winning isn't important doesn't ever win. I agree that we are educating players, and sometimes a loss can be better for the development of a player than a win. But at the end of the day, American kids on a playground know exactly how many goals they've scored, how many baskets they've made, how many races they've won, so they don't need you to keep score." They are always keeping score. It's good that American kids are competitive because soccer is a game, and you play games to win. "You don't play games to lose and say 'Oh, but I played pretty.' It doesn't work like that."

The French Formation course taught Darren a lot about our approach as a country to competing on the world stage and just how far off we are. Darren pointed out that there has yet to be a foreign-based coach to win a World Cup. "We need American coaches—white, black, hispanic, doesn't matter—but American coaches that understand the American mentality. Living in a country is its own thing and you have to understand that. If you are Brazilian and you coach Brazilians, you understand how Brazilians think, how they grew up, why they are the way they are. That's such an important thing." Darren believes that coaching education is vital to ensure that our coaches continue to develop in order to push the United States over the hump from a developmental standpoint. "It comes down to the environment you create to help maximize the potential of each individual player. When you work with kids, you have to make sure that the way you deliver your message and the way the training sessions are set up help each individual player maximize their ability." However, this is ignored far too often across our country. "We do not do a good job in this country. We still have tons of coaches that put down 7,000 cones and run drills. Some of these drills they've seen from Barcelona or Bayern Munich, but they don't understand how to deliver the message. They don't understand how to bring out someone's potential and help each kid educate themselves. That is an art, my friend. And that is what we have to get better at."

Darren cites the French Formation License course as the most influential course he has ever taken. Oddly enough, the message the instructors gave him at the end of the course was, "When you leave this course, you will have more information than any coach you know, but it will already be outdated." The message between the lines was that the minute you think you have it figured out as a coach, things change. The game is constantly progressing, so you have to continually learn, grow, and adapt as a coach.

The US soccer-coaching schools are moving in the right direction because they are now evaluating coaches over a period of time. Darren learned that there is pretty much no benefit to the way things used to be done. Coach education done over a week or ten days fails in truly evaluating a coach's ability to implement theory. "Now you have a 3-, 6-, or 8-month course where you learn theoretically, and then you go back and put it to practice. During your practical application, you are evaluated and helped by a mentor before you go back and do it again." The reason Darren believes this is one of the best ways to evaluate coaches is because it actually allows coaches to change their behaviors as a coach. Instead of sitting in a conference room taking notes for 10 days and then filing them away for the rest of your life, coaches must take those notes and implement them over a period of 6-12 months. Now, instead of coaches earning a license simply because they attended, coaches need to demonstrate that they have successfully changed their coaching behavior to reflect the information provided by the instructors.

THE LADDER OF DEVELOPMENT

Darren believes that too often coaches shortchange the stages of development. If we are teaching the game, we need to teach our players how to climb the first rung of the ladder before moving on to rung two, three, four, and so on. "When I coach, I teach through phases of the game, and within those phases, I teach principles. I start with the simple principles of the game within a phase, but until those are in place, you cannot move on to the next piece. The mistake I see is that we skip phases of development, which means we don't make sure things are in place before moving on to a larger game, or drill where things are much more complex." When Darren first started the Sounders academy, their coaching staff were spending a majority of their time in teaching players aged 12-16 principles of play that should have already been addressed at younger ages. He had a continuous feeling that their entire system was behind because the kids hadn't been taught how to climb the first rung of the ladder.

Let's say you had a U14 team for an elite academy. Today, you want to train building out of the back. That means you will need to have your players in realistic space with realistic numbers and positions to make it specific and worthwhile. Darren argues that when they went to train this in the early days of the Sounders academy, many of their players didn't understand when and how to move to create space. For Darren, that is the first rung of the ladder that should have been addressed at age 8. "We're talking about the creation and use of space. So even in a 2v1, when should a player move to create the appropriate angle and passing line to receive the ball? If the player not on the ball is being marked by the defender, when should he move to receive the ball? Let's say he moves away from the defender as his teammate puts his head down or takes a touch. Now, by the time his teammate on the ball picks his head up and sees he is an option, that pass will either be intercepted or met with a ton of pressure. Therefore, the player being marked has to read when his teammate is prepared to play before moving to create space. So in the beginning of the academy, we had a lot of players that didn't understand simple movement (i.e., when to move and why to move). The goal of movement is to create the most amount of space and time for yourself, but we had a lot of players that simply reacted." Darren's point is that if those players had been taught how to move off the ball prior to arriving at the Sounders academy, the players would already know how to create space and time for themselves, which would allow the building-out-of-the-back session to be much more productive. Instead, when stages of development are missed or rungs of the ladder are skipped, sessions on various phases of the game, such as building out of the back, suffer immensely due to a lack of understanding of basic principles of the game.

There are two main contributors to this problem in the US and around the world. First, coaches at the grassroots level are typically volunteer dads getting their information from random websites. This isn't the fault of the volunteer dad; it is more a systematic problem that our country doesn't make grassroots a priority, which means the higher-level coaches navigate towards the higher levels where they can make a living. The second contributor is coaches yelling out generic things such as "pass and move." "Sometimes movement is a half-step forward or two half-steps back. All you are doing is looking to create space from your opponent. To do that requires you to adapt to the environment, not just run around like a chicken with your head cut off because coach said to pass and move. It comes back to the education of our coaches in this country. We have to help our players to understand *why.*" John Kessel, the director of USA Volleyball, has an awesome quote that I love, "The player that knows why beats the player that knows how." We might be coaching our players how to move, but do they know why they are moving? "Because if they know why they are moving, then sometimes they will pass the ball and know *not* to move. If they know movement is about creating space, then they may pass the ball and notice the defender marking them dropped off and left them unmarked. The hope would be, in this case, that they would know to not move at all because the defender's movement created space for them. But if the coach just yells at everyone to pass and move, then, yeah, he will probably just run himself into being marked again."

A wise man once said that anyone can point out a problem, but that the real art lies in providing a solution. Darren thinks that we are misusing coach educators in this country. "They don't need to be teaching 9-day courses; they need to be down there on the grassroots level mentoring coaches. They need to be down there every day standing next to a young coach or a new coach, talking to them about why they are doing some of the drills and activities they are doing. For me, I think it's the only way. The only way that I think coaching education can work is if the mentor—the expert, the person that really understands—is right there with you, working things through, critiquing you, and really breaking you down. Otherwise, you don't get better at what you do."

YOUTH DEVELOPMENT

The Seattle Sounders U23s have won multiple Western Conference Championships in the Premier Development League, but Darren Sawatzky is more proud of the 54 players from their program that have signed professional contracts in the last four years. "My job is to take 18-22-year-old guys and give them the finishing pieces they need to turn professional, whether that means signing with the Sounders or being drafted by another team." Darren would be lying if he said there aren't times where he forgets that purpose. "There are moments where if we were a professional team, I would either sub a player off, change personnel, or change formations, but I never do. Because when that happens, I have a player in an environment that he is struggling with. I need that player to push through that challenging environment for his own personal development—win or lose for us. If that player is able to overcome that hard environment and adapt to it, that is going to prepare him to be a professional player a year later." This is a very similar sentiment to the way Michael Beale approached the Liverpool U23s. One of Michael's questions at the beginning of every day that he asks himself is "what do these players need to get to the next level?"

Darren considers himself more of an ecological coach. He sees the value in being very clear with your tactical objectives as a pro coach, but as a youth-development coach he wants to create players that can adapt to different environments. "I want players to adapt to the environment. I want *them* to look at it, and I want *them* to figure out what's going on."

Darren's experience has shown him that the players that end up making it as successful professional players had coaches growing up that created environments for them to figure out. "I learn very quickly from players—without even asking what their coaches were like in club or college—what kind of environment their coach provided. The guys that can adapt to changing environments in the game had coaches that challenged them mentally. The ones that don't and that need you to tell them what to do all the time had joystick coaches that yelled at them and told them what to do the whole game."

Darren is getting players at the end of their development cycle. In similar fashion to Michael Beale at Liverpool, the Sounders U23s is the last stop before signing a professional contract or finding a job. Because of that, Darren includes specific variables in his training environment to prepare each player for life as a professional.

1. The environment has to always be competitive—"I try to bring in a minimum of two very good players at each position. I brought in two #10s that were the kings of their college teams, but only one of them can play. So they are forced to compete with each other to get into the game."
2. The environment has to be pedagogical—The French Formation License taught Darren that going from small to big in training is not necessarily the only way—or even the best way—for players to learn and improve. "In the French way of developing players—and the Spanish do this too—they start with a game. You start with a game that brings out the principle that you

want to work on. You need to make sure you are very good because the game at the beginning has to bring out the principle or the whole session is screwed. Then during that game you ask rhetorical questions without coaching. I ask questions like, "How would you create space there?" "How can you help him?" The goal of these questions and the game is to turn their brain on and get them thinking." Once the beginning game has completed, the French Formation License teaches the coach to take a situation from that game—ideally, one that the team is not performing well—and train it. The French methodology teaches coaches to move from the situational training into a technical application of the situation. Finally, the session ends with the same game that was played in the beginning, but with a clear improvement in the principle that was being trained. "The whole idea is that the environment has to turn on their brain. How do they adapt and fix whatever issue it is that you are working on? How can you, as a coach, set that game up so that when they play on Saturday, it comes out."

I always go back to my office after training and try to reflect on whether the session was successful or not. Each coach will have a different version or definition of a successful session, but I tend to side with Darren's interpretation. "You look for the pattern of play that you were looking for. If I am working on breaking down a low-block defense using combination play but every single time they go through and get a shot on goal, then you've set up your activity wrong. I mean, yes, you are having success, but you set up your activity wrong. The environment is wrong. I define success by comparing how little success my players have at the beginning of the session with the amount of success they have at the end of that session. The cool part is that it translates to the game. If they can solve a problem in a difficult constraint that you created in a training activity and they adapt, your team is going to play some pretty good soccer on Saturday."

CHAPTER 13

DEVELOPING YOUTH PLAYERS

MARC NICHOLLS

Marc Nicholls is the academy technical director with the Seattle Sounders. Marc has twice been named the USSDA Academy Coach of the Year. Prior to his role in youth development, Marc was the head coach of the Carolina Dynamo of the USL PDL, where he led the team to the division title in all three seasons, including a PDL National Final appearance in 2012 and US Soccer National Championship in 2013. Marc holds his USSF National A license, the FIFA Futuro III program, as well as the prestigious French Formation License. He is currently a national staff member for US Soccer.

The importance of brutally honest feedback — Bio-banding — Playing players down an age group — Where do you prioritize winning — There is more than one way to skin a cat

Pretty much every person you ever meet will have some sort of philosophy, some type of subjective way of making sense of the world around them. In soccer, particularly youth soccer, that is even more true, but Marc Nicholls is wise enough to admit that having a philosophy is difficult. "My philosophy is still evolving. I think before you can have a philosophy, you need to have experience. Not just any experience, but varied experience." Marc likes the term *current thinking* rather than philosophy. Philosophy implies that he is stuck in his ways while current thinking opens the door to the possibility of being wrong and changing his views. "If I were to sum up my current thinking, I don't think you can ever go wrong by focusing on the human qualities of the players. I feel that being the best teammate, having the right outlook on life (in terms of social skills, behaviors, work rate), and having fun are the things I look for in my players at the Sounders. For me, these are the type of players that have the biggest chance." Marc's starting point then isn't the game, but the person. You can have all the skills in the world, but being a professional is much more than being skillful or talented. Marc likes to make sure the right person is in front of him first, before deciding if he can play the game.

Marc, like a number of the coaches interviewed for this book, also completed the French Formation License. During the intensive course, he had the opportunity to do site visits with Leon and Real Sociedad. "The course and the site visits have really shaped me as a coach." The course included a heavy focus on the psychological element of coaching that Marc described as an intense focus on knowing yourself and embracing who you are. The starting point for the course was finding out who you are on a deep, human level, and then building coaching skills on top of that foundation. That is something Anson Dorrance talks about at length in his chapter.

Marc and I connected on that sentiment as I often see coaches flip a switch when they go into coach mode. There is nothing that will drive you out of coaching quicker—or make you appear more inauthentic to your players—than being someone you're not. As Jay Martin likes to say, "Stop trying to be Pep Guardiola, only Pep can be Pep. Just be yourself."

The course also deeply challenged Marc with feedback on his coaching. The French course filmed every session that Marc ran, and each session ended with a review of the film and criticism from his peers on what he could improve. They critiqued everything from his coaching points, body language, inflection, and more. Marc feels that we are missing very direct and objective feedback in all facets of our lives. For example, a week before our conversation, Marc's daughter came home with a grade in one of her classes of 105%. Although Marc was a proud father in the moment, he wondered how in the world someone could achieve a 105%. "Where can you go from there?" In coaching, there is always something you can improve. The instructors on the French course were extremely honest with him. If they didn't think he performed well, it was made very clear that he wasn't at the acceptable standard and that he needed to do better.

Marc has created a culture within the Sounders academy that welcomes peer review and feedback. He likes to strike a balance and not be too overbearing, but if it were completely up to him, he would film more training and hold more meetings. Nevertheless, Marc admits that the culture within the academy coaching staff is one of non-stop feedback and review. It didn't happen overnight because a culture built upon feedback— particularly harsh feedback—can take a while to get used to. Marc benefited from having his fellow staff members also go through the grueling French course where they learned the value of continual feedback on sessions and strategies. Even for the coaches that have not taken the course, Marc admits that the glow of the course can speak volumes. "I had one of our staff coaches tell me that he wants more critical feedback because he can see how the course has affected me and a few other coaches on our staff. It has made us more hungry to learn and a bit more thick skinned and welcome to criticism. Coaches that really want to get better and be the best they can, deep down, want to be told how they can improve no matter how difficult it may be to hear."

YOUTH DEVELOPMENT

Marc is fearful that there is a youth soccer epidemic happening around the globe. The victims? Late bloomers. An emphasis on winning is all it takes to sway a coach into choosing a more physically capable player with no soccer talent over a smaller player with potentially great talent. The latter won't win the battle, but he may win the war.

The Seattle Sounders have some objective items that they look for when scouting players for their youth team that go beyond the typical eye test used in the US. "We look at a player's capacity to compete and to work. We also pay attention to the way the player moves in terms of his engagement in the game. Does he know where to move and why to move there? We also look at more easily recognizable things such as his first touch and vision. But the human qualities still matter for me because that is often the biggest predictor of future success in this game. Does he love the game? Does he have an infectious personality? Does he want to compete in every moment of the game and every day of the week?"

The Sounders have one of the simplest, yet most accurate, descriptions of their youth development vision: "To maximize each player's potential." The reason why I love this is because it is not realistic for every player to play in the English Premier League. For some, Major League Soccer will be their maximum potential, but for others, maximizing their potential may mean playing college soccer at some level. The ambition of the academy is obviously to produce players for their first team, but they also understand that the percentage of academy players that will achieve that is very small. That is why Marc emphasizes the human qualities in addition to the soccer qualities. "My goal is to ignite a lifelong passion for the game. Maybe he won't be a future player, but a coach, or a sports scientist, or even work in ticket sales. A passion for the club and the game is important."

The Seattle Sounders, like most Major League Soccer teams, have a USL team now that wasn't an option even three years ago. Players like Deandre Yedlin and Jordan Morris—both fixtures with the US National Team—went to college and left early to sign with the Sounders. But with Seattle Sounders 2 as an option, youth development has become much more interesting in the United States. "We have to look at our young players now and we have to predict their potential because now we are able to give them professional experiences at an earlier age." Marc doesn't discount the college route all together. In fact, he is realistic to the fact that, for 80-90% of his players, college is the most realistic option for their abilities. The most important thing for Marc is that they keep kids playing the game. You never know who will go to college and blossom into a potential professional for the first team. The more kids from their academy that they can keep playing—whether it be for a college team or their USL team—the better chance they have of producing players for their first team.

Marc would be lying if he said he was fully comfortable with the idea of sending his players to college. Educationally, college is something that is highly valued in American culture, but Marc gets nervous sending promising first team players to various college programs across the country. "I always worry that the college coach won't see the player the way I do. So I may have a player that I feel has big potential, but when he goes to college, for whatever reason, he may not play very much. This could be because of a different playing style or what the college coach needs to do to win, but I think the college setup hurts the players more than anything."

For those that are unfamiliar, the college system in the US plays a 25-game competitive season over the course of three months. Teams play two or three games every single week for twelve weeks. In fact, some college tournaments are played in a Thursday, Friday, Sunday fashion—three games in four days. The college season is then followed by a nine-month off-season where the teams are restricted in how many hours they can train per week and are only allowed six exhibition matches. It is a detriment to the youth-development process for players entering the last stage of their developmental window. "It's survival. It's crammed into a short space of time. The academy players are coming into college having played FIFA rules in the academy—you know, three substitutions, stoppage time, etc.—but in college, there are basically unlimited substitutions that change the game so dramatically that sometimes it doesn't even look like soccer." There is no question that the college soccer setup needs to change, or it will be simply bypassed. Academy managers like Marc are already having second thoughts about sending their kids to play in the college system and it won't be long before academies bypass the college system completely. "I really am not sure if it is the right pathway for some of our elite performers. I think the college system's current setup is something that is holding us back as a country from a development standpoint, especially for players at the formative years of 18-22."

With all that said, the Sounders philosophy is still to "maximize each player's potential." That is something that is so important in youth development because every player is different. As Marc told me, "each player is different. They have different needs, they are from different places, different economic backgrounds, they have different ambitions, and, as a result, different opportunities." The Sounders understand that college is an important option for a lot of their players regardless of the potential setbacks to their development as a potential professional player.

BIO-BANDING

A 12-year-old at your club is dribbling through his teammates at practice without being touched. His vision and awareness resemble that of a player much older. The question a lot of youth development coaches in this country are asking in this situation is how to best challenge this player to continue his development. Do you play him up with the U14s, or even the U16s, and risk potential injury? Or do you keep him at his current age to ensure he can physically compete, risking the negative impact the training environment is having on the growth of that player?

The Seattle Sounders academy has a lot of players in their program that you would describe as late bloomers: undersized and pre-pubescent, but technically and tactically gifted for their age. In fact, it is not uncommon for some of the local youth clubs in Seattle to second guess their decisions about a player that they cut from their team when the Sounders sign him to their academy. While a lot of clubs in the Seattle area are looking for the bigger, faster, and stronger players to help them win tournaments, Marc Nicholls is looking for the player that has the biggest potential to be a future pro, rendering size and stature irrelevant. "We have to make sure that we don't ever condemn a player because he is too small. We have to observe the player in a different way. We look at things like the way they move and their capacity to play the game, not their sprint speed or size."

The Sounders look for technically gifted soccer players and not physically gifted athletes. Marc is looking to win the war, while fellow youth coaches want to win the battle. Nevertheless, Marc is often tasked with deciding how to approach the debate involving biological age versus chronological age. "I am not sure if I agree with the idea that playing with bigger or more physically gifted players is a bad thing for these late bloomers. I think that living in that hostile world allows those players to develop other qualities in the way that they think. They have to think faster due to their lack of speed and power." Marc is also not advocating that coaches carelessly play gifted players up several age groups without some sort of objective plan.

The Sounders use science to help them make these decisions. They gather the peak height velocity (PHV) for every single player in their academy. PHV is used to determine the time when a player will experience their fastest rate of growth during their growth spurt. That data has supplied Marc with interesting information. "We know that with our U14s, we have some players in the bodies of 17-year-olds, but other players in the bodies of 12-year-olds." The Sounders tend to err on the side of caution with young biological players by keeping them with players around their age for the most part. They will still give them opportunities to train up an age group, but Marc thinks the next evolution of their bio-banding program is to play certain players down an age group. For example, a U14 that is in the body of a 12-year-old may play games with the U12s once in a while in order to "aid biologically, but also to give the player some confidence by having a slightly different game experience instead of always being the smaller, weaker player on the pitch."

Marc also disagrees with Sir Matt Busby, respectfully of course. The notion that if a player is good enough, then they are old enough isn't necessarily best practice. Marc's experiences in youth development have shown him that with more creative players, coaches need to be careful about playing those players up an age group. "You want to make sure that they are getting as much of the ball as they can and that they are in realistic situations." However, he has seen that defenders are a better option when deciding which players should play up an age. "I think defenders can be pushed up, depending on the individual, but it is easier to push defenders up because they have more of a destructive game and you can learn a lot about them by making the job harder for them." Creative players need to have a game experience where they are on the ball to allow them the capacity to show their skill. Defenders can play up an age due to the nature of their position being more destructive in nature.

There is a distinction among the teenage years as well. Marc believes that we have to be very careful with 13- and 14-year-old players, but players aged 16 and 17 could—and should—be used against older competition. "That is the age that I think the saying 'if you're good enough, you're old enough' applies. At that age, there are players overseas making first-team professional debuts so I think that if players are at that level, they need experience playing against professionals that are much older and much more physical."

YOUTH PLAYERS POSITIONS

No coach will disagree that eventually players need to specialize in one position, but at what age is typically the more difficult question to answer. "For the most part, we like the players to experience at least two positions up until the age of 15, but it's not a hard and fast rule that we have. For example, I think one of our current players in the academy came out of the womb as a left back. It's all he ever wants to do, but occasionally we will play him as a left winger." It is a little chicken and egg sometimes, but Marc believes that all players have a propensity to choose one position over another. For example, occasionally he will put the players into random teams and tell them to go play where they like and naturally certain players move to the back, while others move to the midfield, and still others move up top. "We don't instill rigid positional play with the players until about age 16. Even then there is some movement between positions."

Deandre Yedlin, the club's most successful player now playing for Newcastle United, is a great example of why the Sounders don't like to typecast their players until the later stages of development. "Deandre played mostly as a central midfielder for the Sounders academy, but now plays Premier League soccer as an outside defender." It is important that players understand a variety of positions because typically as they go up a level and as the demands of the game increase, they may need to play somewhere else to succeed and be effective.

CLUB PHILOSOPHY

There are many ways that academies and clubs around the world choose to skin a cat, so to speak, but Marc Nicholls thinks it is very important for a club to have *a* way. That could refer to the playing style and training environment, but it could also extend to things such as how the locker room is kept and when players show up to training. Within the Sounders system, from the first team down to the U12s, they are having more and more discussions about the Sounders way and what that actually looks like. "We have a starting point of a 4-3-3, but we call it a flexible 4-3-3. The triangle in midfield can change which can make it a 4-2-3-1 very quickly, so we are developing players that are capable of adjusting to the various demands of the game. We provide a framework for the players and the coaches that extends from the first team and down, but we can never take away the natural role of each coach and the group they put on the field." Marc Nicholls and Michael Beale are very similar from this standpoint. In fact, last season, Marc's Sounders team had two terrific #9s. Michael Beale asked, "If you had Robbie Fowler and Michael Owen, how could you put one of those guys on the bench?" Well, neither could Marc. "They were both in the top five of goal scorers in the country so we played with two strikers. You can't be so idealistic about the way you want to play that you neglect the importance of pragmatic thinking."

The Sounders are flexible with their system, as one should be, but not with their style and approach to the way their teams play. "We want to be proactive and exciting. This is something that we are still developing, but you can already see that philosophy starting to establish itself with some of the players our first team is signing. Nicolas Lodeiro was signed last year to be a creative and exciting #10 to fit our intended playing style, and he catapulted the team to the MLS Cup in his first season." The impact Lodeiro has had on the Sounders academy is massive. Lodeiro has provided a windshield that every #10 in the Sounders youth academy can strive for. As author Daniel Coyle says, "You need to fill your windshield with people you want to be." The Sounders aren't educating their academy players about the Sounders way because their academy players are seeing it live every Saturday.

WINNING AND LOSING IN YOUTH DEVELOPMENT

Ask five coaches about winning and losing in youth development and you will probably get five different answers, ranging from "winning at the youth level is absolutely meaningless" to "winning at the youth level is the only thing that matters." Two-time US Soccer Academy Coach of the Year Marc Nicholls believes that "it is easier to theorize about winning when you aren't doing much of it." Marc doesn't think wanting to win is the problem because that is something that human beings, even young ones, tend to naturally strive to do. Like Darren Sawatzky said, "Go to your local park and tell me that the kids playing basketball aren't keeping score." They most certainly are.

Marc believes that the real question lies in where coaches and academies prioritize winning. It isn't as black and white as many academies and coaches like to think—in fact, it is extremely grey. When your team isn't winning, it is easy to sit back and say, "Well, it's not about winning it's about development," but Marc knows that the repercussions of not winning go beyond just the score. "There are a lot of times as an academy coach that my team found themselves on a bad run and I thought to myself, "You know what—we need a win here! When you win a game, the players get more confidence; they have more faith in you as their coach, and that allows you to accelerate development in many ways." When you are coaching 12s and 13s, winning means very little, but by the ages of 16 and 17 or 18 and 19, winning becomes a much bigger priority. Winning still isn't *the* priority—developing players for the first team is—but as your players get older they have to understand that in a first-team environment, when you don't win a match a lot of bad things can happen. Losing at the first-team level means that coaches can get fired, players can get released, and wages can be reduced, so they have to understand the consequences of winning and losing. "We prioritize the result and winning at different levels throughout the program."

The graph below explains the appropriate prioritization of winning at the various ages and stages of development that the Sounders have adopted.

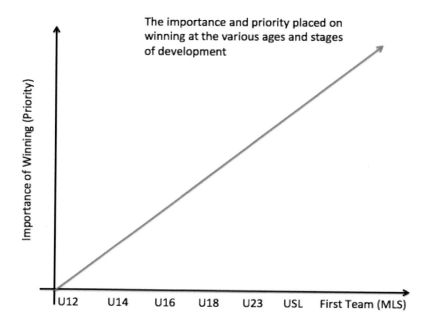

The importance and priority placed on winning at the various ages and stages of development

Importance of Winning (Priority)

U12 U14 U16 U18 U23 USL First Team (MLS)

The priority that an academy places on winning is extremely important in deciding whether or not they are successful. Marc has seen some U14 academy teams that don't win very often, but that has to do with the size of the players they choose to play and the style of play they may exhibit. For example, a U14 team may have players that are biologically smaller than the 14-year-olds they are playing against. If you compound that with the risky playing style they are using, the team may lose. However, it all comes back to the intent and the priority placed on winning. That particular team is prioritizing the style of play and development of their players over winning whereas their opponent is prioritizing winning over the style of play and the development of their players. "For me, that is the model. That is the way you are going to have the most success in developing players. But at the U16 and U18 level, we may need to turn those performances into results because the players need to understand that. Eventually, when they are with our USL team playing professional matches—I mean, players get win bonuses for a reason—it is important."

TRAINING

The influence of the French Formation License is heavy in the Seattle Sounders Academy. Similar to how Darren Sawatzky approaches training with the U23s, Marc tends to start training with a game as a part of their game-based approach. "We feel that starting with a game allows us to create players that can adjust and adapt. The result is that we develop players that are independent decision makers. So when a situation occurs in a match, the problem can be solved by a decision, as opposed to something that the player doesn't own, such as a coach's decision." Marc is not a fan of unopposed training. When a coach tells players to play the ball to cone A and then run to cone B, the coach has taken away the decision from the player. Training then becomes a series of predetermined repetitions instead of a series of decisions within the uncertainty that the game provides. The focus during an exercise where players are provided with the decision becomes purely execution. "Those exercises become about executing technique. I am not saying that we won't use things like that or use other models, but I would say that we are mostly game-based." The Sounders will do Coerver-type drills with their younger players a couple times a week to give the players some confidence. Marc has found that it gives players comfort and confidence with the ball.

It is important to remember that the Sounders academy started in 2008 with Darren Sawatzky. Youth soccer in Seattle is still, in many cases, in its infancy. When Marc compares their younger players to younger players in southern California, he wonders how he can catch up to the technical excellence of those players. Therefore, Marc has implemented some technique training with their younger ages with the intent of producing more technically competent players so that they are able, at the age of 14, to introduce their game-based model. "There needs to be some sort of technical foundation in order to play in a game-based model. Yes, you need to make decisions, but those decisions are very much based on what you can do with the ball. You will never see the pass that you can't make."

The Sounders academy will also end sessions with technique training rather than at the beginning. This is an iteration that Marc learned from the French Formation Course. The instructors of the course consulted with Tony Parker, the San Antonio Spurs star, and were given an ah-ha moment when Tony mentioned that the most important time to be able to execute a free throw is at the end of the game. Therefore, the French course taught their candidates the importance of ending the occasional session with the technical component of a topic. "Executing the technique at the end of the game is hugely important given the emotions involved, the mental fatigue, and the physical fatigue. Having gone through the course and experimented with this model, I have to admit that I am sold. We don't end every session with technique training—in fact, more often than not, we end with a bigger game looking for the topic that we trained—but during our foundational blocks, we will end with some technical execution."

Marc wanted to leave coaches with a simple piece of advice. What you have been told about coaching isn't necessarily the only way to do things. It is okay to train in a way that is, at times, countercultural. The technical execution at the end of training is one idea that shows things don't always have to be trained from simple to complex; we shouldn't always believe that there is only one way to do things. This book is proof that there are many, many ways to coach this game. The more open we can be to the fact that we are wrong about most things, the more open we can be to learning and the better coaches we will become. There are a lot of things that we simply accept as fact in the coaching world and the more we can challenge these traditions, the more we can advance the art—and science—of coaching.

CHAPTER 14

SPORTS SCIENCE AND PHYSICAL TRAINING

JON GOODMAN

Jon Goodman is the academy manager at Notts County Football Club having previously served that same role for the Nike Football Academy. The Nike Academy is a full-time academy program that discovers and develops the world's most talented 16- to 20-year-olds. Jon and the Nike Academy are based at the FA's National Football Center where they train 24 of the top adolescent players from around the world using some world-leading coaching and development programs aimed at improving each individual player. The goal of the program is to get as many of their players signed to professional contracts as they can. David Accam and Tom Rogic are some of the most notable players to come out of the program, having represented their countries, Ghana and Australia, respectively.

Why your hardest moments can reveal your true self — The darker side of professional soccer — Soccer psychology — The birth and death of the Nike SPARQ program — The Gold Mine Effect and how the Nike Academy disrupted academy soccer

One of my all-time favorite movies is *Moneyball*, the 2011 film starring Brad Pitt, which chronicles the rise of analytics inside Major League Baseball. Michael Lewis has since re-written a lot of what he claimed in his book *Moneyball,* which led to a lot of myths regarding data and sports, but it is still an interesting look at a pivotal time in sports history. One of my favorite lines from that movie is when a young Billy Beane is cut from his Major League contract. The scout tells him, "We're all told at some point in time that we can no longer play the children's game; we just don't know when that's going to be. Some of us are told at eighteen, some of us are told at forty, but we're all told." That is how I got into coaching. An accumulation of injuries in a short period of time early on in my professional career was the game's way of communicating to me that my time as a player was done. I got into coaching because I still loved the game and if I couldn't accomplish what I wanted as a player, then maybe I could help others achieve their aims.

Jon was an aspiring young professional for Wimbledon Football Club and the Ireland National team before tearing his ACL at age 26. Jon started a sports science degree to fill the boredom of rehab and by 29 he had been told that he could no longer play the children's game either. It is actually quite normal for players that struggle with injury-riddled careers to get into sports science and the physical preparation side of the game. My own personal history of injury is what led me to become enthralled with the physical development of soccer players. There is no question that Jon's injury-plagued career influenced his interest in a part of soccer he never knew existed. "It's amazing because it was only 14 or 15 years ago, but in those days there was no such thing as sports science. There were no dedicated physical trainers. During my rehab, I actually trained with Olympic decathlon gold medalist Daley Thompson and I just fell in love with the physical conditioning elements of soccer. I also thought to myself that maybe sports science could be a nice little niche that I could build into a secondary career in soccer. It was like getting a second chance at making a career out of soccer." It was during the rehab process that Jon Goodman began his coaching journey.

Jon began his career working in the sports science departments of Wimbledon, Watford, Reading, and West Ham during the 2000s where he began to develop his own ideas on how to best prepare soccer players from a physical standpoint. That bred a feeling of expertise, but also frustration with how sports science and physical training were being administered to players across the Premier League. In 2007, Jon started Think Fitness, which was like a UK version of EXOS in the US. The idea was to provide a team of consultants that could work with professional teams across the globe to help them in their approach to conditioning and training their players. Think Fitness began working with clubs like Tottenham, Southampton, Norwich, and Reading, and associations like the FA, but one of the more interesting partnerships that came across Jon's desk was a little company called Nike.

The nice little niche that Jon wanted to fill had finally manifested itself into a full-blown opportunity. Nike wanted to start a soccer academy and they wanted Jon's services to help aid in the physical development of their players. "Nike were looking to set up an academy for unsigned young soccer players looking for a professional training experience as free agents. We started six years ago and we helped build a support team around the coaching staff. It started as part-time work for everyone involved, but the objective was clear: to get young soccer players professional contracts."

Just like that, the Nike Academy was born. The first year of the program only included a couple of training days per month, but Jon and his team of part-time coaches were able to get one player a professional contract. "That really made it all seem worthwhile." Jon, who had his promising career cut short by injury, was finally able to make things right by helping another promising young player make his dream come true. The surprising success of the academy got Nike thinking. If Jon and his team could produce a full-time professional soccer training a couple times a month with a bunch of part-time coaches, imagine what they could do with a full-time staff and Nike-backed resources. "Very quickly after that we went full time. That meant that we now had a full schedule of games on a weekly basis, we started a global competition called 'The Chance,' where players competed to gain entrance to our academy, and it really just took off." In just six seasons of existence, the Nike Academy have signed over 50 players to professional contracts. In fact, a couple of their players have even gone on to make their international debut for the senior national teams of their respective countries.

THE NIKE ACADEMY

Signing 50 players to professional contracts in six years is nothing short of remarkable. Jon is not afraid to admit that they are starting with a very elite player pool from the start. The Chance program, which has since been renamed Most Wanted, creates 25 competitions in 25 countries including Brazil, Norway, Sweden, Japan, Australia, Korea, USA, Peru, and all of Europe. "It is amazing to have the global reach that we do to get players into the academy. Each country has thousands and thousands of players try out, and from each country's competition, we choose two players for a total of 50 players. From that group of 50, we will take around eight players. Straight away, we are picking from an extremely strong group of players."

Jon was almost apologetic regarding the recruitment process used by the Nike Academy, almost as if he feels Nike is using some sort of unfair advantage or secret alchemy. But, when you think about it, they are using the same means of identifying players that every academy in the world can use. Let's not forget that a large majority of their player pool comes from other European academy teams' *rejects*. A lot of the players are cut from their academies and left without a club. The Most Wanted competition is aimed at identifying which rejects are actually future professionals in disguise.

All of it got me thinking and asking the question: do the majority of clubs need to rethink their approach to identifying and developing talent? Well, in 2017, Brentford FC—one of the most forward-thinking clubs in the world—closed their academy. From the U8 to U21 level, Brentford no longer funds an academy program. One of the backers and owners of the Brentford team is author and strategist, Rasmus Ankerson. Ankerson wrote a book in 2012 called *The Gold Mine Effect* that studied why some of the best athletes in sports such as soccer, golf, and athletics tend to come from similar regions of the world. Despite having some of the worst training facilities in the world, why does Jamaica continually produce some of the fastest people in track and field? I recommend reading Ankerson's book for further analysis, but my point is that we need to examine Brentford's decision to cut their academy.

Instead of having academy teams from U8 to U21—like almost every other team in the world—Brentford is going to fund an elite squad of 18 players between the ages of 17 and 21. Hmm, where have we heard that before? Brentford FC's elite team will play against category one academy teams and international teams just like the Nike Academy does. This is why I found it funny that Jon was apologetic regarding Nike's process, because I think it is groundbreaking. I think the Nike Academy, whether they knew it or not, were disrupters that flipped academy soccer—and youth development—on its head. Ankerson is a specialist in finding little-known places that can produce amazing athletes with unconventional methods. I wouldn't be surprised if the decision to revamp Brentford's academy came through studying the model employed by the Nike Academy. Nike's Most Wanted competition and their academy can be viewed as a marketing ploy, but maybe, just maybe, they are showing us the future of academy soccer.

Rasmus Ankerson and Brentford FC certainly think so. Brentford's club released the following statement along with their announcement to close their academy: "The development of young players must make sense from a business perspective. The review has highlighted that, in a soccer environment where the biggest Premier League clubs seek to sign the best young players before they can graduate through an academy system, the challenge of developing value through that system is extremely difficult." In other words, why would Brentford continue to sink money into youth development when any player they produce will be snatched up by bigger clubs? Of course, that means money into the club's pocket, but does the money from selling a handful of players now and again off-set the money being spent to fund a full-fledged academy? Brentford doesn't think so. Additionally, a lot of clubs want a first team capable of climbing to the Premier League or the top division in their country. But if the best players in your academy are consistently getting signed by bigger and better clubs—clubs that you compete directly against—then what are the chances of accomplishing that feat? If your club isn't climbing the pyramid, then they are missing out on the huge revenues granted to Premier League clubs. If a club is missing out on these revenues, then how can they fund an elite academy capable of producing top players?

This dilemma has led the Nike Academy—and now Brentford FC—to the decision of playing a different game. They are letting other clubs spend time and money developing players so that they can hedge their bets on the idea that, through the development process, there will be players let go, unsigned, or discarded that they can bring into an elite training environment and sell directly to first teams—or their first team—for little to no cost. Whatever the future holds, there is no question that the Nike Academy and Jon Goodman have shown clubs around the world a different way to produce professional players. Now the question is who is going to pay attention?

PLAYING MODEL

Nike has been very successful in their recruitment, but the training is another big part of their success in moving players on to professional clubs. "We have a very defined playing style and structure of playing." The Nike Academy does not play in a league, but they have a very strong program that features matches against U21 clubs from FC Barcelona, Inter Milan, and Arsenal.

Jon emphasizes having a simple game model to allow the players to best understand their roles and showcase their talent. "We generally play a 4-3-3. We really nail down the positions and get every single player to know what they are doing within our system."

Additionally, Jon has established a strong sense of reflection on the process and not the outcomes. They focus on what each player is tasked with and hold them to that standard during each match. "If we reflect solely on the outcome, then we may miss out on the potential to gain knowledge, learn, and get better and better." Last season the Nike Academy beat Barcelona's U21s 3-0 and Inter Milan 4-0, and lost to Liverpool 5-3. "The goal of the program isn't to win games, which is why we don't focus on the outcomes. Our goal is to focus on the process of each of our players getting better and performing their individual role in the team better so that we can cause top clubs problems. If we can cause well-established academies like Barcelona, Inter Milan, and Liverpool difficulties, then our players are going to get recognized and noticed."

The players also take ownership over their own development. Jon has the players cut their own clips from each match and send them to clubs in order to earn trials. Jon will help when he is needed, of course, but for him it is important that the players take control over their own destiny. Jon believes that if he made every single phone call it would be akin to having your mommy and daddy call someone for you. The Nike Academy doesn't receive any compensation for players signing with professional clubs. This communicates to the players involved that belonging to the academy is a privilege, not a right. "We do cut players. If they aren't improving or they aren't getting to the level we expect, we will release them. We don't want to waste their time and block the opportunity for the next person to come into the academy."

The Nike Academy is residential. The fact that they aren't tied to a particular league affords them the opportunity to play any team in the world. Being residential also means that the Nike Academy can train as often as they like. Jon is the first to admit that the success of the program has more to do with the structure than the execution. But that structure has led to a lot of academies around England asking more questions regarding their own development structures.

In fact, for a guy that has produced 50 professional players in the last six years, Jon was one of the most humble coaches I have had the opportunity to talk to. Jon fully believes that the success of the Nike program isn't some secret training philosophy or method that he is hiding from the world; it is the structure of the program itself. "Most good coaches would have similar success to what I have had. It's not down to the coach. It's not down to any particular aspect. It's the whole entirety of the program."

WHAT DOES IT TAKE?

The Nike Academy has had managers like Pep Guardiola, Arsene Wenger, and Jose Mourinho attend their Most Wanted trials to assess and pick the players that eventually go on to join the Nike Academy. After producing 50 professional players in six years and having sideline chats with some of the world's greatest managers, Jon has established some knowledge on what professional coaches are looking for. "We had a player named Callum Harris that signed for the Wolverhampton Wolves last year. After speaking with their coach, it was quite simple really. Callum offered something, as a central midfielder, that their current players in that position didn't. For Callum specifically, that was his 1v1 ability, his ability to play forward and bypass opponents with forward passes, and his ability to score goals." Jon believes that the attributes of each player are secondary to the circumstances that they are in. Quite simply, if a player on trial is better than the player at the club currently in his position, then the club will be ready to sign a contract. "Their thinking, typically, is that if this player is already better than what we have and he hasn't been in a professional training environment yet, then just imagine how good he can be." The academy sets up 45 games a year between the Nike Academy and professional U21 clubs or first teams. That means that their players have 45 opportunities to prove they are better than the players at the clubs they are playing against. Again, the structure of the academy is what allows for such a big success rate.

It is also interesting to note that of the seven Nike Academy players that signed professional contracts in 2016, six were attacking players. "My experience has shown me that it is much more difficult as a defender or goalkeeper to sign a professional contract. Teams and managers are always looking for the player that can change a game or score a goal, which is why we have had mostly wingers, strikers, and attacking midfield players sign deals." Due to that fact, Jon has employed his team in a very expansive and open attacking game. "We don't focus on the result, but we always play to win. I want us to play in a very attack-minded way. We go at teams, and when you go at teams, it gives all your players the freedom to express themselves and show their personalities." Jon believes that sometimes, like in a traditional academy, players are a little bit oppressed and tasked with specific responsibilities that may handicap their ability to get noticed. The Nike Academy provides a platform where the players really have nothing to lose. "They can really go after it because they are all there to prove people wrong." Jon summed up how coaches and managers identify talent very simply by saying, "At the end of the day it comes down to can you score? Can you create? Or do you stop? And then from there it's all about how well you do it."

CHAPTER 15

GRASSROOTS COACHING
SAM SNOW

Sam Snow is the coaching director for US Youth Soccer. Prior to his role in the US Youth Soccer Technical Department, Sam was a US Soccer national staff instructor and the director of coaching for the Louisiana Soccer Association. Additionally, Sam has coached at Florida Southern College, University of South Florida, and Virginia Wesleyan College. Sam is at the forefront of coaching education in the US, and is charged with directing the largest youth sports organization in America, the US Youth Soccer Association.

Coaching coaches how to coach — Where do you want your youth players to be at 15, at 25, at 35 — What's the rush in youth development — Why you shouldn't mistake advanced motor control, due to puberty, for advanced technical ability — Have your kids play a lot of sports if you want them to be better at their sport of choice

Michael Beale talked to me a lot about the importance of people choosing the right career for their personality, especially in the soccer world. Some coaches don't have the personality or the skill to be a coach, but maybe they could be a great general manager, scout, or athletic trainer. Sometimes the decision should be based on where you find your passion. Sam Snow was on his own coaching journey, working his way up the college soccer ladder in the US, when he started to teach coaching-education courses on the weekends. It was then that he realized what he wanted to do for the rest of his life. "I fell in love with coaching coaches how to coach."

GRASSROOTS SOCCER

As the director of coach education for US Youth Soccer, Sam is charged with leading the largest youth sports organization in the US. US Youth Soccer is a subsidiary of US Soccer that aimed at grassroots coaching. The first thing that I wanted to discuss with Sam is the prevalence of tryouts in the youngest age groups in our country. Sam believes that tryouts hold no place at that age, particularly at the grassroots level, and is just an ego stroke for the coaches and parents. The coaches like it because they feel empowered to make decisions on who they think the best players are and the parents get to feel proud that their child has been selected.

I wasn't sure where I sat on this discussion, so Sam framed the question a different way. He said, "Josh, if I asked you to rank your college players from 1 to 26, 1 being the best and 26 being the worst, that ranking would not only be subjective, it would vary week to week and month to month, depending on current performance." For Sam, we should be focusing on putting the kids in the right environment and developing each and every player. Truth be told, we cannot predict the 10-year-olds that are going to be future pros. Anyone that tells you they can also has a bridge for sale in Brooklyn.

John Kessel, who has a chapter in this book, is the director of USA Volleyball, and the quote that he lives by as a coach is, "I never want to be a kid's last coach." It may sound gushy and cliché, but the truth is we don't know which players will end up becoming professionals, or National Team-level players. There are so many late developers in a variety of sports, not just soccer, and the more players we can keep playing the sport, the better chance we have of producing top players. If you disagree with that, then flip to John's chapter now for his objective reasons as to why we can't predict future pros at a young age.

Sam, along with several US state associations, have developed a plan to combat the tryout mentality in youth sports. Sam proposes that clubs establish an academy model for their U6, U8, U10, U12, and any age group they see fit. By using the academy model, Sam wants clubs to develop pools in order to provide proper training environments to more players. "In a youth academy approach, the players are not assigned to teams. They train in pools. For example, maybe on Field 1 is Pool A, on Field 2 is Pool B, and on Field 3 is Pool C. The players are then allowed to move, in their training progressions and regressions, from pool to pool. That decision is obviously made by the coaching staff. The coaches may decide that Johnny needs to move from Pool C to Pool B, or Brian needs to be moved from Pool A to Pool B. The coaches can do that on a regular basis, so that the kids are consistently put in the most appropriate training environment for them. This model will more accurately challenge how a player is performing at that particular moment and time."

This is not only important from a performance and ability standpoint, but also from a biological standpoint. A player that is progressing nicely should be moved from Pool C to Pool B in order to be involved in a more challenging training environment to aid in his or her development. But what about a player that has just gone through puberty? Or a player that is suffering from a common youth sports injury? Well, Sam proposes that a player in this situation could be moved from Pool A to Pool B, or even to Pool C, to help them catch up with the growth of their body. Once the player has finished their growth spurt and their coordination abilities return to normal, then they can be progressed back to Pool A, or B.

The youth academy setup also helps clubs on game days. "We can have a player play on game day with Pool A and then move them back to Pool B or Pool C. If a club has players missing for a variety of reasons, they can move players up or down, or they can make the decision to move players in order to find the right fit for each player from a competition standpoint."

Sam has been on the ground floor in the rollout of the youth academy setup in states such as Minnesota and North Carolina. "In the end, this really serves the players in the club in a much more significant way."

Youth Sports Issues

Not only is Sam working to improve the delivery of soccer sessions at the grassroots level, he is also at the forefront of addressing issues plaguing all youth sports. Sam was invited to attend the Project Play summit in Washington, DC to strategize how to address some of the most common issues across youth sports. "Project Play brings in leaders in politics, sports, and sport manufacturing, and we were talking about a number of things regarding youth sport in America. The overriding question was: how we can put things in a healthier direction for all participants in youth sports?"

One of the issues discussed at the summit was the concern of what happens to athletes as they progress in their sporting careers. "The adults in charge, more often than not, only look at the short term, or are even unaware of the long term. They don't even think in the long term. They don't ask themselves questions like: where do I want this player to be when he or she is 20? Or 27? A lot of the parents don't think that way. Coaches don't think that way. Players don't think that way." This short-term approach has led to youth sport coaches selecting the more physically imposing players for their teams to help them win games and tournaments now. "Coaches select the players that are the most athletic in that moment, or are just ahead of their peers from a biological standpoint."

People think that coaches select the players that are the most athletic but the least technical. In fact, the players that are the most athletic—or physically developed—at the youth ages are actually *more* technical than their teammates. "If a player is ahead by a couple of years in physical growth than their peers, not only are they bigger, stronger, and faster, but they also have better technical ability due to finer motor control and limb control. Better motor control shows up in better ball skills." This shows just how difficult it is to not pick the athletes.

Coaches may say, "Well, he is athletic, but look at his technical ability!" It is important that we don't mistake fine motor control due to an early growth spurt for advanced technical ability. "It's easy to pick athleticism over other skills, such as ball skills or tactical skills. Tactical awareness is much harder for a lot of coaches to see. The first piece of advice I give coaches that don't know how to evaluate a player's tactical awareness is to watch what they do when they don't have the ball. If they make good decisions when they don't have the ball—in terms of their positioning, awareness, etc.—that tells me that the player is reading the game, and has a tactical clue. Other players come alive when they are on the ball, but then they fall asleep the rest of the time. That's probably not going to be a future player. In fact, that is a player that will eventually level off in their performance and fail to make the higher-level teams at a certain point. Whether it's at age 15, 20, or even 25, eventually they will level off and other players will pass them by."

Sam believes that the true talent identifiers are the ones that can spot the late bloomer. Which player has incredible technique despite being biologically underdeveloped? Is there a player that lacks motor control, but positions themselves extremely well defensively? These are the things to look for to spot the best 20-year-old, but not necessarily the best 10-year-old.

Sam is often asked about his opinion on players playing up an age group. Sam usually tells coaches to let two key principles be their guiding light in deciding if a player should move up—or down—an age group. "If a player is 9 years old or younger, their existence on this planet is still measured in single digits; what's the rush? Keep the kid where he is and teach him how to be a leader, teach him to become a more well-rounded and complete player. If a player is 10 or older, then we could potentially look to move him or her up. I'm not against moving a kid up if the moment is right. But I don't think that is an appropriate question to ask until we get to be 10 or older."

There still needs to be some thorough work done by the club in order to make the best decision for the long-term development of the player. "I think the issue becomes that the coaches, parents, and administrators involved don't do a thorough enough review of the player. There really needs to be a full 360-degree evaluation and review of that particular player. That doesn't happen to the depths that I feel it needs to, which means that most of the time the decision is being made based on athleticism. Whether the coaches say that is why or not, it ends up that the kid is a little bigger, stronger, faster, and perhaps more skillful. But whether or not the kid is more tactical is a completely different question. Coaches are making the decision based on athleticism and skill, but they aren't looking closely enough at the psychological and tactical traits of the player, and they aren't looking at the social impact on that player's current team and his next team."

Sam believes that the social impact is one of the most neglected regarding the decision to move a player up an age group. For example, if you move a kid up an age group, who is he going to displace on the other team? Assuming the older team has a full roster, who is going to be kicked off of that team to make room for this younger player? Sam also mentioned that if a player is good enough to be moved up an age group, then that should mean that he is good enough to be in the starting line-up. If that's not the case, then there is no need to move him up. "If the kid is good enough to move up, then that should mean he or she is good enough to be in the starting line-up. There is no point in moving a kid up if they are only good enough to be on the bench at the older age group. In fact, you do more harm than good that way." Therefore, if he is going to be in the starting line-up, not only will the coach have to kick a player off of his team, he will also have to remove a player from the starting line-up to make room for the younger player. Before a decision regarding players playing up an age group can be made, coaches need to perform a thorough review of the player. "It's a 360-degree review of the player within all four components of the game: fitness, technique, tactics, and psychology. You need to look at the social impacts on both teams involved. Finally, you need to look at the logistics of the family involved. All of these aspects need to be considered before making a final decision."

A few years ago, Sam took charge of a U17 girls club team in Tennessee. On that team was a 14-year-old girl that was on the U14 US National Team. "She was easily the best technical and tactical player in the group, and athletically she could more than hold her own. But it took a full year for that team to accept her because she was completely outside of the soccer team. I mean, she was in a completely different stage of life and social life from the rest of the kids. She didn't go to the same school as everyone else and even if she did, they were in completely different grades taking completely different classes." Sam's experience coaching that team showed him the importance of the decision to move a kid up an age group. There needs to be a thorough review done and a lot of questions asked before making the decision.

EARLY SPECIALIZATION

As recently as 20 years ago, kids growing up played nearly every sport. Kids were playing three sports a year and changed their sports with the seasons. Soccer season became basketball season and basketball season became baseball season. In my youth, I played soccer in the fall, wrestled in the winter, and resumed soccer in the spring. Today, kids are playing one sport every day for an entire year. If they do anything outside of their sport, it is usually some sort of isolated training to improve their ability to play their one sport.

Early specialization is one of the hottest debates in youth sport and the director of US Youth Soccer feels that people, particularly parents, need to be aware of the current research. "There is a good deal of research that shows early specialization, particularly in team sports, hurts you more than it helps you in the long run. We have kids now that develop physical injuries that become chronic much earlier in life. Injuries that used to happen to athletes in their 30s are now happening to teenagers and even pre-teens." You can also have too much of a good thing. I remember coming back to my club team after the culmination of my high school wrestling season feeling re-invigorated and ready to play soccer again. "We are seeing a lot more psychological burnout. Even if the kid really loves the sport, it is really helpful to take time away from that sport to play another sport, spend time with your family doing something outside sports, whatever it might be. You will probably come back to soccer more passionate and more diligent than before. Even professional players take breaks."

Sam has also seen the link between early specialization and dropout rates. "I have yet to come across a club that has as many 18-year-olds playing as they do 8-year-olds. They always have attrition as the players get older." Unfortunately, research has shown that early specialization has a positive effect on the short term. Parents, coaches, and even technical directors see the short-term benefit of early specialization and assume that the trajectory of a particular player is going to skyrocket now, just as long as they can keep their training volume up. On the flip side, players that take a break from soccer to play another sport may suffer in the short term in their sport of choice. "You can see an immediate growth and improvement in a player over a three-month period when a player has devoted themselves to a whole lot more training. But in the long term, that ends up leading to a massive drop-off. It might be one year from now, five years from now, or ten years from now, but it will lead to a sharp drop-off in growth and improvement among other things." Due to this fact, a lot of college coaches across a variety of team sports—soccer, baseball, basketball, lacrosse—are looking for athletes that underwent a multi-lateral development, or, in other words, they played a lot of sports. "They know that by the time those players get to be college players, they end up being better players. They end up becoming a better athlete and more tactically savvy. Early diversity in the pre-teen years is essential."

CHAPTER 16

ASSISTANT COACHING

ERWIN VAN BENNEKOM

Erwin van Bennekom is the associate women's soccer head coach at Duke University. Erwin joined Duke in 2015 and helped lead the Blue Devils to the NCAA Championship game where they lost to Penn State University, coached by Erica Dambach. Prior to his role at Duke, Erwin coached at the University of Alabama (NCAA-D1) and at Sky Blue FC of the NWSL. Erwin holds his UEFA A, USSF A, and a variety of other coaching licenses.

Coaching 50 hours a week on the field — Thinking like one on game day — It's okay to have a bit of fun — It's all about the next opponent — Keeping the ball for the sake of keeping the ball

Any quality or strength that you overuse can become a liability. Tony Schwartz, CEO of The Energy Project, explains that "if you overuse honesty too much, it becomes cruelty. So what was a strength in one circumstance, becomes a liability in another." It is human nature to respond to difficult situations by doubling down on our strengths. For example, if I am an extremely honest person, when put in a tough situation like evaluating an assistant coach of mine, I may become even more honest to the point that it becomes cruel. As Tony Schwartz explains, "Our instinctive response to stress is to invariably respond with more of our strengths. When we have a feeling that our strengths aren't serving us well, we actually try to use more of them! But the opposite of honesty is compassion. Honesty overused is cruelty and the antidote is compassion. It's not that you have to choose between being honest or being compassionate, it's that you want to be able to move flexibly between honesty and compassion to better address a complex problem."

Erwin van Bennekom exemplifies the ability to move flexibly between competing emotions—most notably confidence and humility—in the same sentence. Erwin opened up our podcast exemplifying his emotional intelligence. "I was the youngest coach ever to receive my UEFA B license through the KNVB, but if I look back at the quality of my final session, I don't think I should have ever passed." Although it may seem innocuous, Erwin's ability to move flexibly between confidence and humility, as well as other emotions, is the foundation of his success as a coach—and even he may not even realize it.

THE COACHING JOURNEY

Erwin joined Soccercenters five days after his college graduation. Soccercenters is a Dutch company that trains American players in America using Dutch methodologies. "You pretty much got a set wage and started working 40-50 hours a week on the field. I coached all ages and sexes from U6 boys and girls to U18 boys and girls." We can argue about Malcolm Gladwell's interpretation of the 10,000-hour rule, but there is no question that Erwin accumulated many hours of deliberate practice while working with Soccercenters. "Coming over to the States and coaching 40-50 hours a week gave me an advantage over other coaches. It really helped me develop as a teacher and a coach, but if you ask most people over here that are coaching in college, nobody has ever coached 40-50 hours a week. At least most people haven't. Just having those hours of coaching, training, and trying different things really helped me a lot."

A lot of people would look at Erwin now and think, "Wow, how lucky he is to be coaching at Duke University," but Erwin wouldn't describe it that way. After a few years of coaching upwards of 2,500 hours a year, Erwin volunteered at the New Jersey Institute of Technology. Not many people would volunteer their time to learn and grow as a coach. In nearly every industry, recent college graduates with no work experience want to make a six-figure salary, leave work at 5PM, and make all the important decisions. Young coaches are just as overzealous. Let me tell you that putting in the hard yards is one of the absolutes of coaching that will stand the test of time. You can't expect to be treated like Pep Guardiola when you have not earned that respect or put in the time that he has. Everyone wants to be a top coach, but no one wants to do the work that it takes. Erwin wanted to do the work.

Erwin spent three years working an unpaid position at NJIT before a conversation with Jim Gabarra, then the head coach of Sky Blue FC of the NWSL, opened the door for Erwin into women's professional soccer. From there, Erwin moved through a few college soccer coaching jobs before landing the associate head coach position at one of the best programs in the US, Duke University. The take-away from Erwin's journey is that the hard yards are essential. Don't be above volunteering. Recall the Canvas Strategy from Neil Jones' chapter. When you are a young coach you need to create the path for others to succeed. Do the jobs no one wants to do, set down cones, keep track of time. It isn't sexy, but it is essential.

Recently, Erwin was catching up with some of his friends that took the UEFA B course with him. Some of those conversations made him realize that, of that elite group, he is the only one still coaching full time. Most of the guys that Erwin went through the course with had to transition into 9-to-5 jobs, while others have been relegated to coaching on the weekends. For Erwin, some of his European friends criticize the college system in the US, but he is the one laughing because he gets to do what he loves every single day. The college system has its flaws, but it provides opportunities for coaches and players to continue their journey in the game. Erwin isn't sure if he has ever worked a day in his life.

One thing that Erwin does know is that he hates the word *coach*. Sticking with his flexibility to move between emotions, Erwin drew upon a little cockiness to say, "Trust me, this will be the only time I say this, but the word *coach* is such an American thing." Obviously, Erwin was a little tongue in cheek, but he does think the word *coach* comes from other American sports. "I think it comes from sports like American football where *coach* implies the idea of 'I'm going to tell you what to do, you do it, and we are going to win the game.'" Erwin doesn't like the word *coach*, but he loves the word *teacher*. For Erwin, a teacher is someone that helps his or her players discover their own unique love for the game. A coach, on the other hand, forces their love and passion for the game onto their players.

Erwin will admit that he has a long way to go to achieve teacher status. "A few years ago, I thought I was all that, that I knew everything and had it all figured out, but recently I have realized just how much more there is to know and understand." Erwin cited listening to our podcast episode with Jay Martin as one of the things that showed him how much more there is to know. "I had never heard of him, but once I started listening I was so impressed. Coming over from Europe, you know, we think we know it all and we say, 'American coaches this and American coaches that,' but then I started listening to people like him, and you realize how much more there is to learn. Listening to stuff like that shows me just how much more I have to go."

ASSISTANT COACHES

The trickiest role to navigate in soccer is that of the assistant coach. Tasked with a lot of responsibility but never the final word, being a good assistant coach can be more art than it is science. If you never question or challenge the head coach, then the performance of your team may suffer, but challenge too much and you could find yourself out of a job.

Remember the importance of moving between states flexibly? A great assistant coach knows when to challenge, but also knows when to balance that with agreement. "I'm very straight up with my head coach here. If I think a player should be playing, for example, I will tell him that multiple times—always behind closed doors—so he knows exactly what my perspective is. I think it is dangerous to keep your opinions to yourself because it can negatively impact the team. But once a decision is made, I support it 100%. On match day, I side with the head coach without question."

Jose Mourinho expressed a similar sentiment in an interview with *Get Football News.* "I do not need yes men. I want people who have their own opinions and people who contest my decisions, questioning them. But, on game day, we need to think as one."

THE PROCESS OF WINNING AND LOSING

Although Erwin is a fan of Jay Martin, he isn't quite as Zen as the wise old coach at Ohio Wesleyan. Erwin will sometimes find himself riding the roller coaster of emotions that comes with wins and losses. However, Erwin is more concerned with the process of how they lose and the process of how they win. "I am okay losing sometimes if it is something we can build on. For example, if the opponent breaks our press consistently or something like that, now we have something to build on for the next game. We had a few games last year where we won and I thought to myself, 'Okay, we will get nothing out of that' because there was nothing to build on. So, I wouldn't say I care about the result, but more the process that leads to the result. If there is nothing to the game and you can't use what you learned from the last game toward the next game, then there is nothing in that for me."

Erwin doesn't believe that the outcome tells the whole story either. For example, in 2015, Duke made it to the National Championship game where they lost to Penn State. Duke moved into 2016 with the same starting eleven that made it to the National Championship in 2015, but they lost in the Elite 8. "You can't look at the result and say you were or weren't successful. I mean, there are other teams, too, you know. They are also getting better. It's not just us." Although making it to the National Championship game was enjoyable, Erwin knows that Duke played better soccer in 2016. "The year that we got to the final, we were so pragmatic in the way we played: very defensive, with a counter-attacking style. But in 2016, I think we felt a little prouder of the way we played."

STYLE OF PLAY

If you asked ten coaches about the playing style of their team, you would probably get ten coaches that tell you they are possession based. "Everybody in college soccer will say that they like to keep the ball, they like to possess the ball, and it's funny to me because nobody really does. I know so many teams that tell people they build out of the back, and then every time they have a goal kick, they kick it as far as they can." Erwin admits that every coach, including himself, probably views their team in a brighter light than perhaps reality would elicit, but he still believes in a possession-based philosophy. "I do believe in having possession so the other team can't score. I think that is pretty straightforward. But I think a lot of coaches now view possession as this cool thing that if you aren't possession based, then you aren't cool anymore. For me, it's as simple as 'We want to go forward as quickly as we can, but with possession of the ball.' I don't make possession an objective in itself."

Duke's star center back in 2015 was Olympic medalist Rebecca Quinn, a Canadian National Team member that is capable of 70-yard long balls on a dime. "We had Rebecca Quinn this year, and the way we would play is, when she had the ball, she would try to hit it 70 yards to our left forward. For me, that's still possession."

Erwin, again, is capable of being flexible between two extremes. On the continuum of pragmatic and idealistic, Erwin is capable of sliding between both depending on the context. In 2015, Duke lacked the player personalities required to press high up the field, so they sat in a low block. Erwin ideally doesn't see the game that way or like to play that way, but he understands it. And he knows that "you have to use what you have in a way that can help you win games, because that's the business we are in."

TEACHING A GAME MODEL IN COLLEGE SOCCER

Due to the lack of time available for training, Erwin spends the majority of the short preseason teaching his team the fundamentals of how he wants them to play. "We spend a lot of time in the off season coming up with how we want to play, and then we teach that in preseason. From there, we kind of just let it go and try to build on it throughout the season. But I do know that there isn't time during the season to teach the way you want to play; you just don't have time for it." In season, Duke plays games on Thursdays and Sundays. Monday is a day off, Tuesday is a recovery day, and Wednesday is the day before the next game. Friday and Saturday are also recovery days, which leaves pretty much no opportunities to train and improve the playing style of the team, at least not during the season. Therefore, Erwin uses a lot of video sessions in season to help bridge the gap not provided by training. "The way we decide to play in the beginning of the season looks a lot different than how we are playing by the end of the season because we will learn things every game. Those things will have us make small changes now and again to the game model, so it evolves throughout the season into something pretty different."

Due to the limited amount of training that can be done in season, Erwin teaches these changes through video. "Most of our sessions are based on what we are going to do in the next game. How are we going to attack the next opponent? How are we going to defend the next opponent? It's not really about how we want to play, it's more about, 'Okay, how are we going to win the next game?'"

IT'S OKAY TO DO SOMETHING FUN, BUT IF GIVEN A CHOICE, ALWAYS GO OPPOSED

Erwin grew up in Holland where training always resembles the game. If you come up with a training session in Holland, it better resemble the game to some capacity. Unopposed passing patterns are unacceptable in Dutch culture, but Erwin doesn't see it that way. At Sky Blue FC, Erwin started developing ten-minute unopposed passing patterns as a way to challenge the players after the warm up. "Yes, it was unopposed, but it at least made them think. It wasn't something they had already done 100 times and could do in their sleep; it was different every single day."

Erwin has continued that tradition at Duke University, and he feels it is something fun between him and the players. "It is my way of challenging them by seeing how difficult I can make it, and I challenge them to see if they can keep up with it and execute the pattern." Erwin has become quite infamous on Twitter for posting these daily passing exercises, despite the criticism he has received from some of his Dutch friends. "A lot of my Dutch friends will reach out to me and ask me what the heck I'm doing, but I really am not that idealistic that I won't do something the players enjoy." The reality is that Erwin does often create a passing pattern that resembles a pattern of play that will be effective against an upcoming opponent. "West Virginia press in a 4-3-3 with their wide forwards really, really narrow, so leading up to that game we basically worked in a pattern of our holding midfielder dropping between the center backs and our holding midfielder finding our right or left fullback. I then made a passing exercise that was like a smaller version of that."

Erwin strongly believes that it's the players that matter, not what some coach on Twitter may think of your unopposed passing warm-up. "How I grew up, everything has to relate to the game and I don't always agree with that. The players like it, there is a technical component to it, there is some rhythm to it, it makes the players feel good, it's a fun environment, it's quick and aggressive, and I do my best to relate it to the game." With that said, Erwin feels that when given the choice between opposed and unopposed, "always go opposed. If you can do something with pressure, then choose pressure all the time." What Erwin has found is that when they go straight into opposed work following the general warm-up, the players always take a few minutes to get a feel for the ball and work themselves into the activity. "We cannot go straight into 4v2s right after warm-up without having touched the balls and expect our players to be able to respond appropriately to defenders. We go into decision making as quick as we can, but we definitely do some unopposed stuff before. I have seen that help give our players an even better warm-up and it gets them to feel good at the start of a session. I have noticed any time we go straight into opposed work the players end up having someone steal the ball away from them 100 times in a row as they get a feel for the ball." That's not exactly how you want to start a session.

One of Erwin's close friends is the Liverpool first-team assistant coach, Pepeijn Linders. Even with Liverpool, Linders will build up a topic starting unopposed. For example, when working on building from the back, Liverpool may start with an unopposed version focusing on the execution of the technique. Linders will then build upon that with different variations of pressure. Pressure doesn't always mean opposition; pressure can also mean reduced time to complete a certain number of passes or reduced space. "Technique is the execution of a decision, but the decision can be built up with different means of pressure. Even at the highest level with Liverpool, it's not just, 'Oh, this is what you want to do? Okay, let's go straight to the game and now there are three forwards running at you." Again, Erwin understands how to move between hot and cold, pragmatic and flexible.

The time constraints in college soccer force Erwin to forego traditional ways of building a session. "If the topic was, let's say, building out of the back, we may start with a smaller version of that topic in an unopposed passing pattern. Then we would progress to a more realistic space, but it would still be unopposed. Finally—and I might fail my UEFA A license because of this—we usually go straight into a bigger game like 11v11. If it was the spring season and we had more time to train, then our sessions would be completely different. In season, our sessions are about an hour max. We just don't have the time to go through all sorts of progressions. It pretty much becomes, 'Okay, we play this and this team this weekend, this is how we want to build out of the back." Erwin comically suggested that if he had to teach his team how to build from the back midway through the season, they would have much bigger problems anyway. "Everything is related to the next opponent. We would say to the players, 'Okay, this is how the opponent is going to press, and this is how we want to build against them." Erwin predominately uses video to show his players where the spaces will be and what their movements should be. In season, the sessions are pretty much getting the players to understand the spaces, constraints, and tactics for the upcoming game using video, then having the players experience those briefly in training, and that's it.

When soccer becomes results oriented—meaning that there are important stakeholders concerned with the wins and losses of your team—everything becomes about the next opponent. Erwin says there isn't time to train your philosophy in the middle of a competitive season. "If you read *Pep Confidential* and *The Evolution,* which are about Pep Guardiola, even he says that everything they do in training has to do with the next opponent. Their whole entire season is dedicated to each opponent. There is no isolation of, 'Okay, this is our philosophy,' it's little tweaks along the way to explain to your team, 'Okay, this is what the next team is going to do, so we are going to do things this way.'"

Opponent scouting is an integral part of results-level soccer. In order for your team to have success, the coach needs to know exactly what the opponent is going to do to disrupt the way his team intends to play. For example, if you like your team to progress from the back using your wide players or outside backs, for example, but you notice that the opponent likes to set pressing traps in wide areas, that is fairly important information to know. If you want your players to be successful in that game, then you need to help them find other ways of progressing from the back, which is where Erwin puts a lot of his focus. "The first thing I look for when scouting—and I mean this with all due respect to our opponents—is whether they have an actual clue of what they are trying to do? We play some teams and I will watch three or four games and think, 'With all due respect, I don't think they know how they want to press, I don't think they know how they want to build up, there is just no structure to it." Erwin says that a lot of coaches will argue that their players aren't talented enough to press or build up, but Erwin thinks that is completely incorrect. "It doesn't matter what the level is because a team that is well coached will have a consistent way of doing things. You don't need elite players to teach them how to perform consistent actions together."

Most of the time, Erwin focuses his attention on two aspects of the game that determine the information he wants to give his team.

1. How do we build up against these teams? In other words, how do they intend to press us? Do they sit in a low block?
2. How do they build out of the back? How do they want to play? Do we need to prepare ourselves for long balls, or can we effectively press them to turn the ball over?

One thing about college soccer that Erwin has noticed is that most teams will end up playing the ball long anyways. They may play short from the goalkeeper, but then the center back will end up hitting a hopeful ball as far up the pitch as they can. Erwin has learned that his team is better off sitting in a mid-block in order to prepare for the long ball, rather than have his players work their butts off to press only to have to recover 30 or 40 yards. Another key aspect that Erwin focuses on is avoiding a lot of transitions. He has noticed that the more transition moments there are in a game, the more his team fatigues. This creates a game that becomes less about soccer and more about chaos. "We're trying to avoid too much transition. We try to avoid losing possession of the ball too much or too repeatedly, and then we try to avoid too many long balls from the other team because then the game becomes all about second balls."

Erwin has found a lot of success by sitting in against teams that only hit long balls. "If you give space and time to teams that aren't used to having it, it tricks their players into thinking they are better than they are. So, instead of hitting long balls, which they are very good at, they might actually try to play the ball on the ground because we sit off them. The lack of pressure takes away the urgency to hit the ball long, so they try to play on the ground, and they end up giving us the ball."

RECRUITING

It doesn't matter what level you coach at—be it professional, college, men, or women—player recruitment is a big part of the job. How does Guardiola decide who to buy from another club? How do NCAA college teams put together their recruiting classes? No matter the context, the question remains the same: do you go after the best individual players possible, or do you go after players that fit a specific identity within your playing style? Erwin has had a lot of discussions with coaches around the country, and he finally feels that he has found an answer. "I strongly feel that we should be recruiting players based on what we are trying to do. We should really have a profile for each position of what type of player we are trying to recruit, instead of going out and trying to get the best players." Erwin's reasoning is simple, "The best individual players are not going to win you a National Championship, the best team will."

Erwin has seen a lot of programs that take the opposite approach and it never works out for them. "There are teams that will sign ten center midfielders, but it's going to be hard to create a team out of ten center midfielders that all have the same qualities."

The most important attribute that Erwin tries to uncover about a player is their willingness to win. For him, competitiveness can make up for lack of skill, athleticism, or game insight. "Yes, everybody wants to win, but I want to find out how much. How competitive are they? How much do they want to put on the line to win a game? That can be hard to figure out, but I know that if you can spot that in a player, you can teach them your tactics; you can't teach an internal motivation to want to win at all costs."

FROM YOUTH TO COLLEGE

Erwin feels that there are a lot of good youth coaches out there, but the biggest thing still missing from the youth game in the States is a tactical objective to training sessions. "The players get developed technically and physically because sessions are intense, but in terms of a tactical side being developed? I still don't think that exists in most cases. If you see the possession activities that are being run, it's just possession for possession's sake. There is no real thought to it. The session isn't being progressed in a way where the players have to think. The coaches might have the team play 6v6+4 neutrals and it looks great, but are we just trying to keep the ball? Are we just making passes? Or are we actually trying to accomplish something?"

Erwin wants players that can come to Duke and understand how to prepare for an opponent, players that know how to execute different strategies to accomplish a tactical objective. He doesn't want players that have learned how to keep the ball for the sake of keeping the ball. "We all need to develop better thinking players and players that are capable of solving more issues within the game. Everything we do needs to be related to some sort of tactical decision. We're not just playing out of the back, we are playing out of the back against somebody that is pressing in a coordinated way. This creates players that come to understand and recognize which spaces are available. I would love to see more thought process-based sessions."

CHAPTER 17

POSITIONAL PLAY

KIERAN SMITH

Kieran Smith is a UEFA A licensed coach that has coached for clubs in the English Premier League, Scottish Premier League, and the Spanish Leagues. Before moving back home to England after some intense work in Spain, Kieran was the head coach for the U19 CE Europa Juvenil C team. Kieran moved to Spain without a job and without speaking the language to learn about juego de posición, the playing style that has come to define FC Barcelona and Pep Guardiola. Kieran Smith has become a go-to reference on positional play, and he has given a variety of presentations across the globe on the subject. In addition, Kieran has published a book on rondos called Rondos and Positional Games: How to Use Spain's Secret Weapon.

I was scared out of my mind — Playing a goal kick to your center back is suicide — I just want to talk to anyone smarter than me — The esoteric nature of positional play — Your team is just keeping possession, stop calling it positional play — A formation doesn't dictate how you play, but how you play dictates the formation

At 26 years old, Kieran felt that he had reached a glass ceiling on his progression as a coach. He had bounced around a couple of clubs in England including Manchester

City and Tottenham, before returning to Scotland to continue coaching. Growing up, Kieran had two dreams. One was to play professional soccer in Spain. If that didn't work out, the second dream was to coach in Spain. His playing days long behind him, Kieran found himself in a now-or-never moment to make his second dream come true. "I had a conversation with my fiancée and we decided to move to Spain. I didn't speak the language. I didn't know anyone. I had zero contacts. I was scared out of my mind."

Once Kieran made the move to Spain, the work had just begun. No job. No contacts. No ability to speak the language. But what Kieran did have was the intent that he wasn't going to take no for an answer. "That first year, I think I went to almost every team in Madrid. I watched anywhere from about 300 to 500 sessions, because most clubs have their own training facility. I would just hang out at each facility until about 5PM and I would watch the U8s, and stay until about 11PM when the older groups would finish training." Kieran may have been unemployed, but he was getting the education of a lifetime.

On Saturdays, Kieran would show up to a facility at 11AM and watch matches until about 7PM. Eight straight hours of watching soccer allowed Kieran to watch five matches every weekend that varied in age group, but personified the Spanish style he had come to love.

Kieran spent most of his first couple of weeks learning the language, and watching a ton of sessions. His hope was that he would eventually meet the right people to get his foot in the door. "I eventually got my chance with a B team that played in Madrid in the Preferente League called Parla. It was the fifth tier of Spanish soccer." Kieran's dream was to coach in Spain, but his first training session was more like a nightmare. "My first session in charge, I was asked to run the whole session with 42 players. I had never coached in Spanish before and I had never spoken Spanish for that long before, so it was quite intimidating. I was thrown right into the deep end." Kieran was a far cry from the glory of Guardiola at the Camp Nou.

In order to get his foot in the door, Kieran had to work for free at Parla. Their training time was from 8PM to 10PM, and when you add in the commute time, Kieran was getting home at 1AM every night. He found this first period in Spain not only the most difficult in his coaching career, but also in his life. "I was getting home at 1AM every night and I wasn't getting paid a dime for it, but I had to do it in order to get some sort of traction in Spain."

Even though the circumstances seemed dire, Kieran managed to impress. A few months later, he found himself coaching the Juvenil A team at AD Alcorcon, which plays in the Segunda Division in Spain (the league under La Liga). To date, Kieran is the only British coach to have worked at that level of youth soccer in Spain. Kieran was eventually offered the job as the head coach of the CE Europa Juvenil C team where he was employed at the time of our conversation. Kieran has since moved back to England, but the lesson to be learned is that you have to chase your dreams, they will not chase you. "I was in London one day, and I basically looked myself in the mirror and said, 'Listen, you don't speak Spanish. No Spanish club is just going to call you in London, say come to Spain, teach you Spanish, and let you work there.' I was delusional if I believed that. So, it was a case of if I wanted it, then I had to go and get it."

POSITIONAL PLAY

Kieran was first introduced to positional play by a Spanish coach that had spent a lot of time in Mexico. Ironically, Guardiola learned most of his current methodology and application of positional play concepts while playing in Mexico for a club called Dorados Sinaloa coached by Juanma Lillo.

In 2008, a 22-year-old Kieran Smith was eager to watch the new manager of FC Barcelona transition into his coaching career. A young Spaniard that played at the club named Pep Guardiola was tasked with taking over the Catalonian club. It was that same year that Kieran began his fascination with and intense study of positional play. Guardiola's appointment at Barcelona allowed Kieran to check his theoretical understanding of positional play with what Guardiola's Barcelona were doing on the pitch. In fact, Barcelona's pre-season tour in 2008 took place in Scotland, where Kieran happened to be working at the time. "He was training at St. Andrews and he had some friendlies in Dundee and Edinburgh. My friend was living in Edinburgh at the time, so I was able to crash at his place so that I could see some of those early sessions." Watching some of Pep's early work with a Barcelona team full of stars like Iniesta, Henry, and a little Argentinian named Lionel Messi opened Kieran's eyes to how difficult the concepts were, even to players of that caliber. "I saw how difficult it was for guys like Henry and Iniesta to pick up the concepts and I thought to myself, "If it's hard for them, then I am really screwed." It was then and there that Kieran realized nothing short of intense study would be acceptable in being able to understand positional play.

As a young coach, splitting time between England and Scotland, Kieran's passion for possession soccer wasn't well received. "I mean, this was right on the cusp of possession soccer becoming commonplace. Today? Everyone wants to play like Barcelona, but back then a lot of people looked at me as if to say 'Why do you want to play that way?' They thought playing a goal kick to your center back was suicide." Luckily, a coach educator in England named Ray Lee gave Kieran some sound advice. "Don't let anyone tell you how to coach. If this is what you believe in, and this is how you think the game should be played, then you have to become the absolute best at it." That doesn't mean Ray was easily convinced by Kieran's ideas. "Every drill I came up with or idea I had, he would just look at me and say, 'Why? Why do you want to do that when you could just do this?' If I was able to give him a good enough reason, then he would just laugh and smile because he was trying to test me. It's one thing to have strong beliefs, but you have to have some objective reasons behind your beliefs, so that you can answer that question. If you can't answer the question, "Why do you want the players to do that?" then you need to take a step back and solve that first."

Kieran wanted to become the absolute best he could at positional play. Stephen Covey, author of *7 Habits of Highly Effective People*, says, "Seek first to understand. Then to be understood." That was the mission Kieran was on. He began translating Spanish texts, watching old games, and, of course, moved to Spain. Once he moved to Spain, he visited Rayo Vallecano—a club famous for its positional play under Paco Jemez—for a month every summer. "I would spend a month at the club every summer, and although I never got to talk to the manager, I just wanted to talk to anyone smarter than me. It may have been someone that works with the first team, an academy coach, or even a kit manager, but the more questions I asked, the more I learned, but also, the more I realized I didn't know. I had to keep learning and keep learning and keep learning."

Kieran has been studying positional play for nearly a decade. He still believes it to be one of the most misunderstood types of soccer there is in the world. "Positional play is massively misunderstood."

Ask any coach in the world how they want their team to play and they will usually answer, "Like Barcelona." The problem—as Kieran strongly believes—is that no one really knows how Barcelona plays. How can you teach what you don't know? It comes back to Stephen Covey, "Seek first to understand. Then to be understood." Too many coaches have failed to do the work necessary to truly understand possession soccer. As a result, teams around the world, at all levels of the game, believe that the objective of the game is to keep the ball as long as possible. But the objective of the game is to score one more goal than the opponent. Passing the ball in a U shape on top of your 18 for 95% of the match is not possession soccer. "I think the biggest misconception is that possession is good. You ask a lot of coaches what their philosophy is and they say possession, but that doesn't make an awful lot of sense. Possession is the tool that we use to carry out the model of positional play. But don't just say we want possession of the ball because that doesn't make a lot of sense."

Every weekend we watch teams like Barcelona, Manchester City, and Bayern Munich and yet we misunderstand a fundamental concept of the game. In and of itself, we believe that just having the ball is good, but that isn't correct. "Teams that think just having the ball is good also think that because they build out from the back, that means they are using a possession based model. But, what you see is usually one of two things. First, a team will play in a 4-3-3 and the goalkeeper will play to the center back. The center back plays to the holding midfielder, who plays out to the fullback. The fullback is pressed, and he kicks it long. Second, the same sequence occurs, except maybe they pass the ball around in a horseshoe shape for a few times until it makes its way back to the goalkeeper, and then the goalkeeper kicks it long. The funny thing is that everyone thinks the team is playing good possession soccer because they play out from the back." Playing the ball from your goalkeeper to your center back, but having your center back kick it long is not possession soccer. In fact, you may as well just have your goalkeeper kick it long from the goal kick; it will save you time.

Kieran believes that the crux of positional play lies in what happens in the middle of the field. "What I find with the vast majority of teams is that they work on playing out from the back; they work on lovely combinations in and around the opposition 18-yard box, but they forget about the middle. And the middle is the most important part." Put simply, you can't progress through the thirds without going through the middle. Kieran doesn't believe that there is anything wrong with skipping the middle third and going long with the ball; in fact, positional play includes moments like that, but Kieran can't stand the coaches who think they use positional play just because they play short goal kicks.

There are a lot of videos on the internet that are intended to highlight the use of positional play by various teams, but Kieran will make it about 30 seconds into those videos before realizing it is just possession. "There is nothing wrong with just having possession. You can use possession to progress and move up the pitch, but just because you are using possession doesn't mean you are using positional play, and vice-versa."

Kieran believes that in order to understand the difference between possession and positional play, a coach needs to have the ability to look at the game below the surface. Kieran will often watch Barcelona games with coaches that will say, "Oh look at them keeping possession, that's fantastic." But coaches need to look three or four levels deeper than that. "If I have possession, what is happening three or four moves down the line? If I pass to him what else happens? If I make a vertical pass, what is the chain reaction to that? You need to know what you are looking for. I think the biggest problem that people have is that they are just looking at the possession."

During the 2016-2017 Barcelona campaign, Marc-Andre Ter Stegen, the Barcelona goalkeeper, often had better passing statistics than the other 21 players on the pitch. Kieran found a lot of coaches simply impressed with the fact that Barcelona plays their goalkeeper, but to understand why is the real art. "One of the biggest reasons to go back to the goalkeeper is to separate the space between units of the opponent. That's one of the most basic things across any type of possession soccer." We see it all the time with teams like Barcelona and Bayern Munich. The center backs will have the ball at the bottom of the center circle and they will pass 50 yards back to their goalkeeper, and a lot of people will ask, "Why did they do that?" In fact, that was one of the earliest "why"s that Ray Lee challenged Kieran with.

Kieran's answer then is the same as his answer now: "because there is no space to play forward. If we go back to the goalkeeper, and we all drop, the opposition will have to step up the field, which gives us space to play." For Kieran, it is the little things like that—which people don't see—that fuels the misconceptions about possession. It's not just about keeping the ball. It is much, much more than that. "There is an element of keeping the ball. You have to have patience, but there is no point in having patience and keeping the ball if you don't know what you are looking for when you get it."

At this point, Kieran has made a clear distinction between possession and positional play. So what then is positional play? Kieran tends to defer to Juanma Lillo, the coach that has had the greatest influence on Guardiola, to define positional play in its simplest terms. "It is simply a way or style of understanding the game."

I was fortunate enough to watch Kieran give a presentation on positional play in 2016 and his opening line put the depth and breadth of understanding this style into perspective. "I am going to talk for over 90 minutes today, and I may only uncover or reveal,10% of what there is to know about positional play." If someone tells you that they understand positional play, or that it is simple, then they probably don't understand even the first thing about it. To understand the complexity of positional play is to understand, as Kieran did, how much there is that we don't know. But how do you begin a marathon? By taking the first step.

The number one concept of positional play is creating superiority behind the next line of opposition pressure. That can be done on the first pass or it can be done by keeping possession and circulating the ball. The key "is that you are trying to manipulate the opposition's position until you can make what you want to happen happen." There are many nuances to this, but one example is circulating the ball and moving the opponent until you can play behind their line of pressure.

There are three types of superiority that can be achieved in a soccer match: qualitative, numerical, and positional. Numerical superiority is simply achieving a numerical advantage in a certain area of the field or behind the opposition line of pressure—a 5v3 for example.

Positional superiority is something that can influence the opposition in a way that you want to. Kieran likes to say, "You can have numerical inferiority, but positional superiority." An example of this is a situation where the opponent has two center backs, but they are playing against one forward. If one of the center backs is known to not be very good at passing out from the back, then you can employ your striker closer to the center back that is better on the ball. This will give the striker positional superiority which will influence the play of the opponent, even though it is a 1v2 situation.

Another example of positional superiority is exemplified by Sergio Aguero. Aguero will often find himself in a 1v3 situation where he is up against three center backs. However, he is able to position himself toward the back post when the ball is wide and then sprint toward the near post area. The center backs are static because they are already positioned where they are supposed to be when a cross is coming in, but Aguero is just now sprinting to his final position. The center backs cannot see Aguero coming and thus he has created positional superiority.

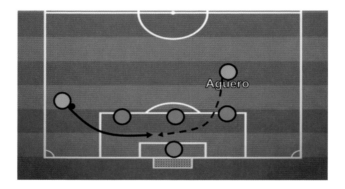

A final example of positional superiority is the 15-pass rule established by Pep Guardiola. If you are unfamiliar with that rule, Pep encourages his players to complete 15 passes upon winning possession from the opponent to allow his team time to transition into their attacking organization and to place the opposition in a defensive organization, which makes it harder for them to counterattack. "Positional superiority also comes from the order. The 15 passes refers to the moment when the team is traveling together and the importance of maintaining the order. What happens is they keep the ball, and move the opposition out of the way in order to camp the central defenders on the halfway line. Now, there might be the same amount of players in the half, but positionally, there is superiority because there are triangles, which allow the team to play in and out of lines, to circulate possession, and to play wide, and that is when they become positionally superior."

Kieran describes the positional setup of the team in this instance as three center backs across the halfway line, the wingbacks all the way up to the opposition fullbacks, the striker between the two center backs, and the two wingers or #10s, pushed on to the highest line so that there are five players on the highest line. In addition, you will have superiority in between lines. Most teams may set up in a 4-1-4-1, but if you have two #10s on either side of the opposition holding midfielder then you are positionally superior.

"For me, it's position over possession every single time. If you are not positioned well, you cannot play forward as effectively, you can't keep the ball as effectively, and you cannot put your plan into motion as effectively. That is when it becomes possession for possession sake." This is another example of why teams may play all the way back to the goalkeeper from the halfway line. If the positioning isn't as good as it needs to be, then the ball needs to be restarted with the goalkeeper to create a better position higher up the field. "They need to make sure that, positionally, everyone is where they need to be."

Pep Guardiola revealed his frustration with people's perception of his playing style as being all about possession in the 2016 book, *The Evolution*. "Possession is rubbish! It's a game of position, not possession! It's about how you place yourself in relation to the others on the field when you have the ball. It's all about where you should be, so that you can continue pressing when you lose it."

Kieran echoes Guardiola's point by stressing position over possession, but it's people's fascination with possession in rondos that drives Kieran to say "Rubbish! Everyone knows what numerical superiority is, which is why we work on 5v2, 5v3, and 6v2 rondos—that's numerical superiority—but the real genius is in knowing what that looks like positionally. That is where the concept of traveling together, as a team, with the ball is so important. Traveling with the team means that we are positionally superior." For Kieran, understanding positional superiority comes back to understanding triangulation. "If I always have two passing options, then I am positionally superior. The question is: every time someone on your team has the ball, do they have two or three passing options?"

Guardiola is able to orchestrate a counter-press with his teams because of their positioning with the ball. As a coach, I have been guilty of implementing a counter-press with my team without acknowledging the positions I was demanding them to be in while we were in possession of the ball. The reason Barcelona is able to counter-press their opponent so successfully is because of their positioning while in possession. As Johan Cruyff said, "Do you want to know how Barcelona win the ball back so quickly? It's because they don't have to run back more than ten meters as they never pass the ball more than ten meters." If you look at the image below, you can see the triangles and diamonds that Barcelona create based on their positioning. This positioning allowed Pep to iterate the infamous six-second pressing rule, but it was only possible if their positioning was correct. The mistake coaches make is they have their players 25 yards from one another and then they want them to press to win the ball back, but it's just not possible. Position over possession, yes, but also position before pressing. "That spacing between players, which is usually 8-10 meters—if you lose the ball in the middle of that, then the three or four players closest can press aggressively, while the rest of the team gets back into their defensive positions." Another misconception is that Barcelona immediately counter-attack once they win the ball back during a counter-press. "They actually start again.

They win the ball within those six seconds and then they pass the ball until they find a center back at the halfway line, and everyone gets back into their positions. That's really what positional superiority is."

This diagram as an example of how the 15-pass rule employed by Pep Guardiola can help establish the correct positions in the attacking half to be able to circulate possession, play between lines, and manipulate the opposition to be able to create scoring chances.

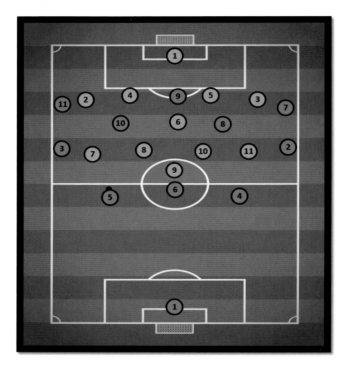

Finally, qualitative superiority is about finding situations on the pitch that are equal in number, but unequal in quality. For example, a 1v1 between Messi and an opposing defender is really not a 1v1 because the quality of Messi is superior to the quality of his direct opponent.

Another important concept of positional play—now that we understand the importance of superiority—is the concept of playing between lines or behind lines. One of the concepts that is vital to accomplishing this is the concept of provoking a press. Provoking a press from the opponent is key to being able to play behind the opposition line of pressure. In the image below, the backwards pass from the orange left back to the orange left-sided center back, provokes the blue attacking midfielder to press. As the blue attacking midfielder presses, he leaves space behind him for the highlighted player on orange to receive behind the opposition line of pressure.

There are a variety of ways to provoke a press, but Kieran likes to think of all the possibilities in reverse. "You almost have to think of it backwards and ask what some of the main pressing triggers are. It could be a horizontal or square pass, passing to a player with his back to goal, a backwards pass, or many others." One pressing trigger that isn't used enough in soccer is the ability of the center back to draw a press on the dribble. "What you see too often is a center back gets on the ball and he has 15 or 20 yards of space in front of him, but he passes to the defensive midfielder—who has someone on his back—rather than dribble forward. If he dribbles forward, especially into midfield, he creates a superiority on his own. Eventually, he will attract a press of some kind, and if he doesn't, then he just runs all the way up and scores." As the center back dribbles into midfield, his teammates have to work on moving a couple yards to the left or right of their opponent, so that they can receive behind the opposition line of pressure.

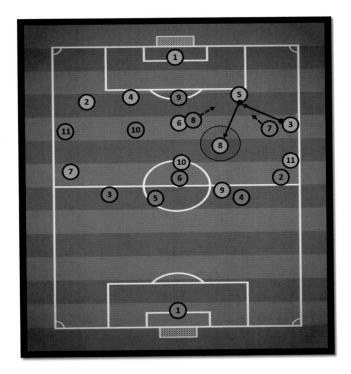

Here is an example of the orange right-sided center back dribbling into midfield to draw a press while the advanced midfielder moves to his left to receive behind the opposition's line of pressure.

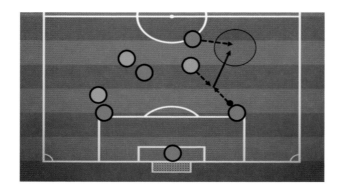

Kieran also loves the horizontal pass in drawing a press. One of his favorite examples came from Barcelona against Real Madrid at the Santiago Bernabeu. "Xavi and Iniesta were literally standing on the halfway line just passing the ball back and forth for what seemed like 5 minutes. The fans started whistling and jeering the Real Madrid players and so they responded by pressing, and Xavi just played right through their press."

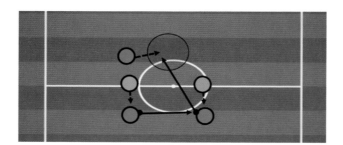

Another one of Kieran's favorite methods to draw a press is using a player receiving back to goal. Playing the ball to a player facing his own goal triggers a press from the opponent that creates available space behind the player that presses. "If you imagine three players in a vertical line—let's say it's the holding midfielder, a #10, and the striker—the holding midfielder would play to the #10 with his back to goal. This would draw a press. The #10 would play it straight back to the holding midfielder, and then move to his left. At the same time, the striker would move to his right to create a passing line. In this scenario, we have attracted the press, created the space, and now we can play deeper."

Here you can see the holding midfielder play the #10 which draws a press from the blue defender. The #10 moves to his left and drags the pressing defender with him while the striker moves to the right, creating space and a passing line for the holding midfielder to play directly to the striker.

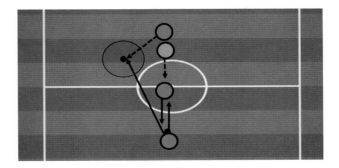

There are a number of ways to attract a press, but the most important thing is that your players know what they are doing. "The players have to know the purpose of receiving a pass back to goal. If they just receive back to goal because they want to get on the ball, then the pressing opponent is going to win it. However, if they know how to attract a press, and why that it is important, then you can make Real Madrid look as silly as Xavi and Iniesta did at the Bernabeu."

Another means of manipulating the opponent is to keep the ball on one side of the pitch until you can switch it to the other side where there is a 1v1 or a 1v0. As Guardiola likes to say, "we keep the ball on one side of the pitch so that we can score from the other."

This is an example of a team that may overload one side of the field with players, keep possession there on that side, and wait for the opponent to move their position. The opponent will usually move a lot of their players to that side to be able to defend that side effectively. When this happens, orange will know to move the ball to the other side where they have a 1v0 or 1v1.

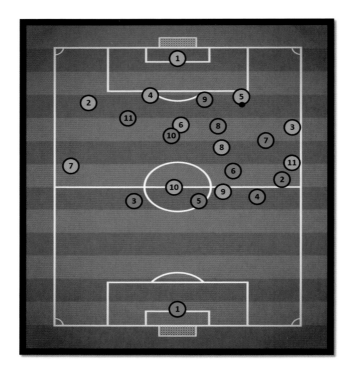

There are many concepts to understanding positional play, but the most recognizable is certainly the concept of creating superiority. A sub-concept of superiority is the idea that the superiority has to come during the initial phase of the game. In other words, a team needs to establish superiority right from the start, playing out from the goalkeeper, or they won't be able to bring the ball out effectively. "We need to play out from the goalkeeper cleanly because that sets up the rest of what we want to do."

It isn't hard to see how possession became confused with positional play. To recognize positional play, a coach or viewer has to be really adept at the concepts of positional play. Possession is easy to recognize because of its binary nature: either a team has the ball or they don't. Anyone can recognize that, which is probably why possession has been misused across the world since 2008. But Kieran can finally clear it up. "Possession is the tool that allows us to manipulate the opponent."

The next positional play concept is the concept of having players on different receiving lines. The goal here is to always create width and depth, but with players receiving on different levels. "If you are in a 4-3-3, let's say you have your goalkeeper, the two center backs, the holding midfielder, and then the fullbacks wide on both sides of him to create three receiving lines."

The figure shows an example of the three receiving lines created by the goalkeeper, center backs, holding midfielder, and outside backs.

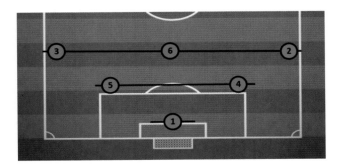

In addition to having players on different receiving lines, another concept is to have players on different widths and heights. "That allows us to stretch the opposition as much as possible." An example of players on different heights would be the outside back in the picture above moving higher up the pitch as the holding midfielder moves lower.

Perhaps the most difficult positional play concepts to understand are the concepts of the free man and the third man. "That is where the triangulation comes from. So when people say things like, "Create triangles" or "Create diamonds," that is the concept they are referring to. In fact, there is a good bit of objective research coming out now that the more triangles and diamonds you can create on the pitch, the better your ball circulation will be. The reason these are important is because these feed into the ability to create positional superiority, qualitative superiority, numerical superiority, or whatever it may be."

The concept of the third man is really understanding the idea that we always need to have two or three passing options available at all times. This ensures that we have a free man available. Adin Osmanbasic, another student of positional play, has a chapter in this book as well. He defines the free man as a player that is unmarked, with allotted time and space to be able to turn and play forward. However, there is a difference between the free man and the third man. "The free man is sometimes the third man, but he is not always the third man. This is where things can get difficult. You can honestly spend two hours talking about the difference between creating the third man and creating the free man."

Here we see Busquets, Xavi, and Iniesta form a triangulation between them. Busquets plays to Xavi who then plays across to Iniesta. In this instance, Iniesta is receiving behind opposition pressure so he is the free man, but also the third man.

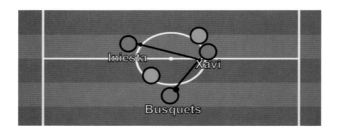

In this example, we can see that Barcelona has three in the back. Busquets is dropping in between the center backs, but they are being pressed 3v3. In this instance, Iniesta drops down behind the line of opposition pressure. "He has created superiority behind the opposition line of pressure; he's not necessarily the third man, but he is the free man." A third man is typically the third player in a triangulation. So because Iniesta is not the third part of the triangle between Pique, Mascherano, and Busquets, he is just a free man, someone behind opposition pressure that has available time and space to play forward.

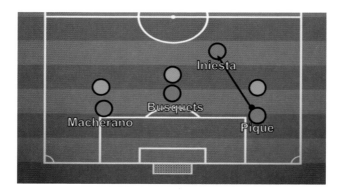

Another concept of positional play is movement. Movement can come in a variety of different forms. For example, a player could move with the ball (i.e., dribbling) to force the opponent to press, or to make an opponent move out of their zone. David Alaba is one of the best in the world at moving with the ball to create different aspects of positional play.

Another form of movement is movement without the ball. "We see this a lot with Pep Guardiola teams. Let's say that their right back has the ball—Dani Alves, for example—and the left winger will sprint in between the opposition fullback and center back, not so that he can get the ball, but so that the left fullback can get on the ball as the free man in a 1v0. This would ask questions of the opponent. Can they get over quick enough? Do they leave a gap? Can we exploit that?"

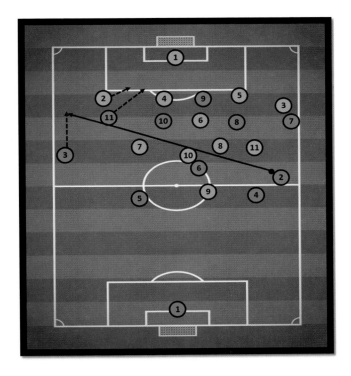

It is common for Kieran to finish a presentation or a chat with a coach, and for them to only say one thing, "Wow, I didn't realize there was this much to possession soccer." For Kieran, he always has a follow-up comment to that. His goal is to really drive the point home that positional play isn't something every club in the world is doing. "The problem is that if you are trying to implement positional play, and you miss out on one or two concepts, it just doesn't work. That is where you end up having possession for possession's sake." For example, if you don't have a free man you can pass to, then that means you can only pass to someone that is marked, and if he passes it backwards, then you don't progress. If a center back is on the ball, everyone is man-marked, and he keeps passing it back to the goalkeeper or plays it long, then that means the team cannot progress. If that center back doesn't know that he must dribble forward to make something happen—create space, draw a press from the opponent, or create a 2v1—then

215

what happens is nothing. "If you miss out on one or two of the concepts, then you end up in that roundabout of constant possession. But maybe the next thing is you play it forward, you get a corner, and you score from the corner, and now you think you are the best possession team in the world. If you truly want to implement a possession style of play, then you have to look deeper."

Everything is great in theory, but in practice it can be an entirely different beast. Kieran has coached in the UK, Scotland, Spain, US, and Canada. It isn't always easy to implement a possession philosophy in cultures that aren't traditionally possession based. "You have to sell players on making runs and not getting the ball. You have to sell players on moving the opposition, so your teammate can get on the ball." Kieran has been able to achieve buy-in with players by being honest with them while appealing to their strengths. For example, on the first day of training with a new team, Kieran likes to prepare the players for what they should expect. "I always say, 'Listen, I am new to you, and you are new to me. We need to understand each other. Initially, I may have to stop and talk, and explain things more. But every single session that we come to, I will speak less, and less, and less.'"

Players may not want to make hard sprints without the ball to get someone else on the ball, so Kieran will often pick a strength of theirs, and relate the positional play concepts to that. He may talk to a winger that is fantastic at 1v1 and say, "If I can get you the ball with space and time to take on the opposition fullback 1v1, would you like that?" The player will of course say yes, and then Kieran will explain the movements and concepts that need to happen in order for that 1v1 to occur. Some of those movements and actions require the winger to not be involved with the play, but by Kieran appealing to their strengths first, he is able to help the players understand why they are doing what they are doing.

Spain is a very command-style country. Command-style coaching is characterized by very direct and explicit coaching points. If you compare that with guided discovery, which is asking questions to help players solve answers, Kieran is somewhere in the middle. "I am more in the middle now because of my experience in Spain. There is still some guided discovery, but it is much more on the command (e.g., 'I want you to do this because...' or 'I want you to do this and understand why'"). Kieran has adopted pieces of the command-style approach because he knows the kind of soccer he wants. Positional play isn't something that can be taught through guided discovery at 18 or 19 years old. Therefore, Kieran has to be a little bit more direct in how he teaches the concepts—but that doesn't mean it's all about him. "I want my players to leave the session thinking, 'How intelligent am I?' rather than 'How intelligent is my coach?'" In order to accomplish this, Kieran puts his players in situations where they have to problem solve for themselves.

Kieran creates situations for players to repeat similar activities on a consistent basis, but with small changes in the outcomes or stimulus. For example, Kieran may spend the first week of training working on building out from the back. One of his favorite ways to train the concepts that he wants is by playing a double-area game (i.e., a pitch that is the width of the 18-yard box, but the length of two 18-yard boxes stacked on top of one another). "My focus as a coach is going to be on the goalkeeper, the defensive line, and the midfielders. I am going to talk about positioning, selection of passes, movement, etc. Now, two weeks later, I might do the exact same setup, in terms of organization, and the back line, goalkeeper, and midfielders should know exactly what's expected of them. Now my focus may be on the press, working with the strikers, and maybe even an advanced midfielder of the team. The setup is the same, the structure is the same, the intensity is the same, but now I have switched my focus a little bit as a coach."

Kieran has developed a specific way that he likes to build his sessions that he developed during his time in Spain. He never separates the tactical from the technical, the technical from the physical, or the tactical from the physical. "They are all one." Therefore, his session may begin with a rondo, before moving into a technical activity that mimics the tactical element of the day. He might combine those with the physical requirements involved with executing the tactical and technical actions.

The following is an example of a potential session run by Kieran Smith:

Sample of a simple session

 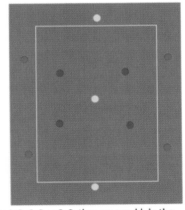

We could start the session with rondos normally 4v2, 6v2 or 8v2. then we would do the technical/physical circuit shown in picture one. Player 1 does the ladder/hurdles then passes the ball to the player in the middle who bounces it back & player 1 plays long to 3. 3 receives, turns & dribbles through the cones & finishes in the goal. Players move to next position and goes both ways. We then move onto the 4v4+3 and look for the up back through shown in previous slide. Then onto PoP & look for the same pattern with our key players(#4, #8/10 & #9)

Source: justkickinitpod.com/2016/08/04/guardiolas-4v43-by-kieran-smith/.

"Even though the technical and physical circuit is more of a passing sequence, later on when I get into my more positional- and tactical-type games—let's say we are working on finding the third man—that seed has already been planted. Even before I get to the point where I have to talk about the tactical concepts, they are already familiar with it."

Kieran is not afraid to talk during his sessions. In fact, he feels that it is a requirement to coach at the highest levels. "At the younger ages I think, yeah, you can maybe put them in rondos or 4v4 games where they have to work on creating width and depth, and maybe you don't have to say much; you can let the game be the teacher. But, with the older age groups, there certainly has to be a lot of talking." There is a famous video of Pep Guardiola in Doha, the capital of Qatar, during his first year in charge of Bayern Munich. The video is on YouTube and is about eight minutes long. About seven and a half minutes of that video feature Pep gesticulating and instructing, as his Bayern players stare and listen. At the youth levels, it is common to warn coaches about violating the three Ls: laps, lines, and lectures, but Kieran—and I guess Pep Guardiola—agree that at the higher levels, a more command-style approach is essential to having your team ready for the next opponent. However, that doesn't mean that being more direct gives the coach license to be complicated. There is a fine line between being direct and being complicated. "It doesn't have to be super complex in how you communicate to players; I'm actually totally against that unless you know that a player likes information in that sort of way."

However, having a more command-style approach does not mean that you have license to scream at your players to run faster or pass quicker. That's being a dictator. Kieran will still use questions at times, but he does so in a way that leads the player to the answer he wants. For example, a common mistake players make, even at the highest levels, is they will do anything to get on the ball. "One of the coaching points might be when a center back gets on the ball. Let's say that the holding midfielder is behind the opposition line of pressure, but then he moves toward the center back and receives in front of the opposition line of pressure."

The holding midfielder is behind the opposition line of pressure.

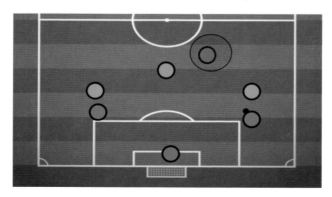

The holding midfielder moves toward the center back and receives in front of the opposition line of pressure.

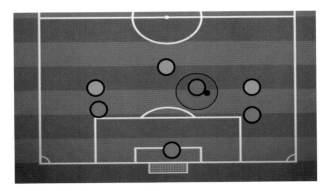

Kieran cites this as one of the most common errors players make when first learning positional play, as they have a bad habit of chasing the ball in order to receive a pass, without taking notice of their position or the position of the opponent. "I might stop it and say, 'Well done, you got the ball; however, where is it better to receive the ball? Here?' And I will show them their current position in relation to the opposition. 'Or here?' And then I will step back a few yards and show them receiving behind the opposition line of pressure. Then I may ask the player, 'Is it better for you to receive here?' And the player will always say yes. Then I might ask, 'What can you do if you receive here?' The answer is usually something along the lines of 'Turn' or 'Turn and play forward.'" Kieran will be more direct than that sometimes, depending on the complexity of the concept he is teaching, but guided discovery has its place in his coaching repertoire.

One of the drawbacks of adopting a possession-based philosophy or positional play concepts within your team is that players, owners, and fans may question the philosophy if results are not in favor of the team. Pep Guardiola received a lot of criticism from English journalists during the 2016-2017 campaign with Manchester City; they questioned his team's decision to play short on goal kicks, something atypical in the English Premier League. Kieran believes it is important not to blame the philosophy because results are negative. Instead, a deeper analysis is required by the coaching staff to diagnose exactly where things have gone wrong. "A lot of people may look at the surface and say, 'This isn't working!', but we need to understand why it's not working. Which are the concepts that we are losing? Which are the concepts that we're not using? Because this works! Positional play works. The greatest team in history—Barcelona under Pep Guardiola—used this style of play and they used it well. They used it so well that it was used by Spain, Germany, Bayern Munich, etc. It's not the philosophy." Coaches cannot demonize positional play or possession because they aren't working for them. They need to understand where their execution of the concepts is going wrong. "Maybe we are getting caught in that trap of coming too close to the ball, or we're not finding space, or we're not being patient enough. It could also be the other way too. Maybe we are getting caught in the counter-attack all the time. What are my distances between players? Are we pressing hard enough? Have I showed them how to press? What is my system of play against the opponent? Am I playing two at the back and they are leaving three up high because they know we are going nowhere with our possession? It's about looking deeper."

It is important to keep in mind that positional play is not an easy concept to implement. At Kieran's last club, CE Europa, the first team manager used positional play. From the start of the season in August until the end of October, CE Europa didn't win a match. But in mid-October it clicked. From November until the end of that season CE Europa didn't lose a single match until they lost in the playoffs. "It takes time. It's a difficult thing to put into place, but if you stick with it, analyze your own matches, and take note of where the mistakes are occurring, you will be able to solve it."

Kieran advises coaches not to get caught up in trends when deciding their intended playing style for an upcoming season. Following the 2014 World Cup, where Louis Van Gaal's Dutch team had success playing a three-back system, it seemed as if every team in the world suddenly decided that the three-back system was superior.

Kieran will watch anywhere from 25 to 30 matches of a particular system he is interested in before deciding if it is useful or not. "In order to look at every single variation possible, I watch 25 to 30 matches of teams using the system across nearly every continent. Some are from Latin America, some are from South America, England, Europe, etc." Kieran isn't watching for the formation. Formations don't tell you anything about how a team intends to play. Guardiola famously refers to formations as phone numbers. In fact, during his three-year spell at Bayern Munich, Guardiola used a total of 23 different formations, which is only six shy of Marcelo Bielsa's statement that there exists a total of 29 possible formations in soccer. However, Pep's employment of 23 different formations just goes to show how useless they are. Formations are a starting point. A formation should be chosen because it gives your players the best chance to execute your intended playing style or tactics, but that is the extent of their use. From there, once a formation is chosen, success comes down to the intent of your team, and the way that you want to play. Kieran sums it up best, "A formation doesn't dictate how you play, but how you play dictates the formation."

Kieran won't go as far as Pep did and call formations just phone numbers, but he doesn't see them as the end all be all that many make them out to be. "I am somewhere in the middle because for me, if I want to implement my model of play, the system is quite important. The system informs how I want to train, the system informs the patterns, the system informs how I am going to construct attacks, what happens when I lose the ball; so the system is part of it, but I use the system to carry out my plan, not the other way around."

CHAPTER 18

THE PHILOSOPHY OF SOCCER

JED DAVIES

Jed Davies is an assistant coach with Ottawa Fury FC of the United Soccer League (USL). Jed has published two books: *Coaching the Tiki Taka Style of Play* and *The Philosophy of Football: In Shadows of Marcelo Bielsa*. Jed is one of the smartest soccer brains I have ever met and he is also one of the most curious and humble people too. The first time I met Jed he spent more time asking me questions than I asked him. He is a true student of the game and his knowledge about tactics and the history of soccer is astounding.

In streetlights and shadows — The philosophy of soccer — Objectivity — Penetration over possession — Freedom versus structure and the importance of action scripts — How to scout your opponent most effectively

Jed Davies lives his life by the streetlight effect. The streetlight effect is a story about a man looking for his keys that goes like this:

> *A police officer sees a drunken man intently searching the ground near a lamppost and asks him the goal of his quest. The inebriate replies that he is looking for his car keys, and the officer helps for a few minutes without success, then he asks whether the man is certain that he dropped the keys near the lamppost.*

*"No," is the reply, "I lost the keys somewhere across the street." "Why look here?"
asks the surprised and irritated officer. The drunken man responds, "The light is
much better here."*

This short anecdote inspired Jed during the writing of both of his books. "The more I
began to dig into the unknown, the vaster it became." Jed had no idea how Barcelona
dominated world soccer for four years under Pep Guardiola. He could have looked in an
area under the streetlight, like most people did, and say things like, "It's simple—they are
keeping possession!" But Jed wasn't satisfied with that. That is how Jed approaches every
waking moment of his life. He thrives in the darkness, the unknown, and the undiscovered.
Having spent time with him in person, I know firsthand that his goal will be to try and
take you there with him. He isn't one for conversations that confirm each of our biases. He
wants to be wrong. He wants to find something new. He wants to increase the scope of
the streetlight. "If I ever lose that curiosity, I think that would be the day I stop coaching."

TIKI-TAKA

Tiki-taka is a phrase that became synonymous with Guardiola and Barcelona soccer from
2008 to 2012. Spanish commentator Andres Montes compared the way Barcelona move
the ball to that of a Spanish toy called the tiki-taka. "Estamos tocando tiki-taka tiki-taka."
The short distance passes made an audible tick that Montes found eerily similar to the
tick of the juggling toy called the tiki-taka.

From 2008 to 2012 the world began to obsess over possession. Coaches were posting
videos of their teams passing the ball 50 to 100 times in a row. Akron University, then
coached by current Portland Timbers manager Caleb Porter, posted several videos
entitled: Akron Soccer: Death by 1000 Passes. Possession was in and direct soccer
was out. Keeping possession became more important than scoring goals and winning
matches. Coaches around the globe would lose 3-0, but claim to have played better
soccer. Everyone claimed that dominating the ball meant dominating the match.
Everyone except Jed Davies. "I had this firm belief in 2008 that the only way to play
was by dominating the ball. But I had this drive inside of me to research it because deep
down, I knew it wasn't right." Thus, Jed began his odyssey to get to the bottom of the
ins and outs of possession soccer. Was it as simple as keeping the ball? Or was the whole
world missing something bigger?

About a year before Jed published his first book, a seed began to grow in his mind
regarding the purpose of possession. "I was already asking myself, 'What's the purpose of
possession?' Because so often I would see games where one team would dominate the
ball, but not necessarily dominate the game." It was this fascination over the purpose of
possession that led Jed into the world of Marcelo Bielsa.

THE REAL GIANTS OF SOCCER COACHING

Marcelo Bielsa is an enigmatic soccer figure whose genius is only exceeded by his mystery. The one thing that isn't mysterious anymore is that Bielsa favors penetration over possession. Marcelo Bielsa was the first figure that really drove Jed away from this idea that you could only dominate a game by dominating the ball. In fact, Jed realized the possession-based heretics began their arguments with preferences, but not necessarily objectives. Jed didn't want some subjective reason as to why possession was better; he was looking for an objective philosophy of the game.

Raymond Verheijen, the famous Dutch coach and coach educator, classifies the orders of soccer as follows:

1. Communication (team tactics)
2. Decision making (game insight)
3. Execution of decision (technique)
4. Soccer fitness (communication, decision making, execution of decision as frequently as possible and for as long as possible)

Jed realized that most youth coaches he was surrounded by argued that possession was better for developing the technique of youth players. Again, we begin to see that there is no objective thought here, but subjective preferences. "The problem with that comment is that you are prioritizing technique over communication, the real philosophy of the game."

Verheijen likes to compare the soccer world to the world of commercial flight. Airplane pilots know exactly what they are to do when flying a Boeing 757. Could you imagine if a pilot grabbed control of the plane and said, "I don't think we should land at JFK, I think I'm going to go to land in Tampa"? The result would be subjective chaos, where people's preferences take precedence over facts. We do the same thing in the soccer world. Coaches say things like, "Our players need to work on technique," and we all nod our heads in agreement, but what are we agreeing with? Is what's being said even correct? Jed has transitioned into the world of the objective. "The question shouldn't be what's *your* philosophy, it should be what is *the* philosophy."

If you look at the game objectively, then the order of preferential soccer actions becomes the following. The best thing that you can do with the ball is:

1. Score a goal
2. Assist a goal
3. Assist the assist

Up to this point, most coaches would agree with that order of preference. If a player can score, then he should score. If a player can't score, then he should try to pass it to someone that can. If a player can't pass it to someone that can score, then he should pass it to someone that can pass it to someone that can score. However, it is at this point that subjectivity rules the soccer world. Some coaches believe that the ball should be played wide for crosses, while others believe that we should try and create 1v1 situations to create shots.

Jed has made it his mission to transform the subjective nature of what happens after a player can no longer assist the assist to an objective philosophy of the game. First, Jed needed to determine what follows the three highest priorities of the game (scoring, assisting, assisting the assist). After much analysis and thought, the objective to consider next is the concept of breaking lines. To understand how to break lines of the opponent, we need to understand what spaces we are trying to get the ball into. Jed prioritized these spaces as follows:

1. Behind the opposition central defenders
2. Behind the opposition full backs
3. In front of the opposition central defenders
4. In front of the opposition full backs
5. Behind the opposition central midfielders
6. Behind the opposition wide midfielders

Getting the ball into each of these spaces will result in a varying response from each opponent. Therefore, the philosophy of soccer now becomes as follows:

1. Score
2. Assist
3. Assist the assist
4. Get the ball into key spaces

Then, the goal of possession would be to create the conditions to achieve the objectives above. There are objective reasons as to why achieving the priorities of the game can become difficult. Understanding these reasons will help us understand our team's behavior on the ball. We may not be able to achieve the top four priorities of soccer because:

1. The opposition are compact horizontally
2. The opposition are compact vertically
3. The opposition are layered in between their midfield and defense (or beyond)

Therefore, the responses required from the team in possession are as follows:

1. To spread the opposition out vertically
2. To spread the opposition out horizontally
3. To remove the layers of the opposition.

Jed believes that these three processes are where coaches should be putting most of their efforts. "Most of the training content on the ball should center on achieving these three responses, so that the highest priorities of the game can be achieved." For Jed, every pass has a purpose. That purpose revolves around the priorities of the game. Here is an example of a team removing the layers of the opposition to penetrate between lines and achieve the higher priorities.

The opponent is in a 1-4-4-1-1. We need to be able to reduce the layers in their midfield by moving the ball to pull them into a flatter position. Removing layers is similar to taking an iron to the shape of the opponent and trying to pull them into flat lines that are easier to penetrate with vertical passes. The center back plays to the holding midfielder, who plays out to the opposite center back. Following the pass from the holding midfielder to the left center back, the holding midfielder drops centrally in order to pull the opposition into a flat 1-4-4-2.

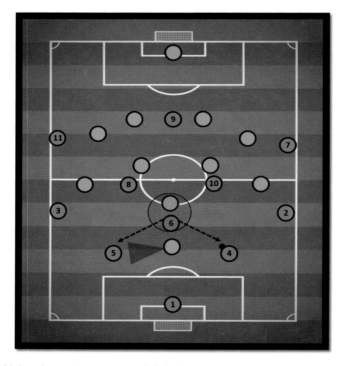

Source: justkickinitpod.com/2016/07/08/jed-davies-using-the-6-to-facilitate-higher-priorities-from -episode-54-of-the-podcast/#more-564.

Here you see the movements that occur to allow the higher priorities to be achieved.

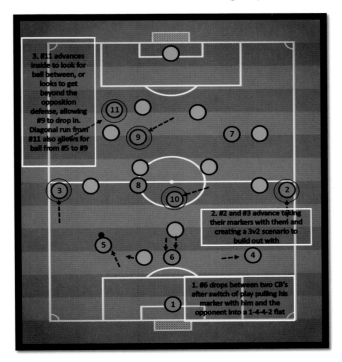

3. #11 advances inside to look for ball between, or looks to get beyond the opposition defense, allowing #9 to drop in. Diagonal run from #11 also allows for ball from #5 to #9

2. #2 and #3 advance taking their markers with them and creating a 3v2 scenario to build out with

1. #6 drops between two CB's after switch of play pulling his marker with him and the opponent into a 1-4-4-2 flat

Source: justkickinitpod.com/2016/07/08/jed-davies-using-the-6-to-facilitate-higher-priorities-from -episode-54-of-the-podcast/#more-564.

Jed's philosophical reference is not complete. If we are unable to create the conditions for the above, then the next step is be to find new areas to attack the opponent's block. This can be achieved by playing a pass greater than 15 yards to create new angles for attack. For example, that may mean switching the ball to the other side of the field, or quickly playing around the back to create a new angle to attack from the other side. Finally, the last step is to retain possession, and, with every new pass, to return to the highest priority available. Jed Davies' philosophical reference is complete as below:

1. Score
2. Assist
3. Assist the assist
4. Play beyond and between the opposition's defensive lines
5. Create conditions for above
   ○ Spread the opposition out horizontally
   ○ Spread the opposition out vertically
   ○ Pull the opposition into a flat line or find spaces behind where they are flat

6. Switch into new angles (15+ yards) direct or indirect through others
7. Retain possession and, with every new pass, return to highest priority available

I love philosophy and I recently listened to a debate between Daniel Dennett and several other philosophers discussing the existence of consciousness. While seeing true intelligence and linguistic capabilities in action was entertaining, I didn't leave the debate with any practical relevance to my everyday life. So what is the biggest takeaway from Jed's philosophy of soccer?

Jed's friend, Joey Lombardi of the Canadian Soccer Federation, recently developed something called advanced platforms. An advanced platform essentially means a player receives the ball between lines facing forward (thanks to Kieran Smith, we know that to be a free man). With advanced platforms, the player that made the pass and the player that received the pass would both get a point in this system created in Canada.

Pepeijn Linders, Liverpool's first-team coach, has developed something called initiatives. In a sense, initiatives are the same idea—you get a point every time you play or receive between lines. There is a company in Germany that has developed something called IMPECT that measures the amount of players that are bypassed by a particular pass. These are a variety of methods and measures that are intended to explain one thing: playing in-between and behind lines is a priority. The coolest thing about the Canadian FA is that in all of their studies, they have never seen a team lose that has achieved more advanced platforms than their opponent. Jed thinks that is pretty important. "If a team is making more passes between lines, getting more players to receive between lines facing forward, and they are always winning? I think that is something really significant in terms of how we should be thinking about the game."

The game is about penetration, not possession. Jed knows that every pass must have a purpose, and that purpose is to try and achieve the priorities of the game. "Every pass has a purpose. If you want to start building a game model around possession, then all the priorities—and how you plan to teach or organize your players to achieve them—need to be considered. In terms of your preparation and thinking, anything less will catapult you into the grey areas of wondering why you have the ball.

The thought process that surrounds the possession-based subjective philosophy is also extremely flawed. "The traditional thinking goes: you have the ball, therefore, you are in control. That's the thought process and it's not correct. The thought process should be constantly asking the question, 'Are we controlling the game?' If you refer to the objective framework of priorities, are we controlling the key spaces? Are we moving the opposition out of position to be able to exploit? Those are the control elements. If you are just thinking about the ball because it's such an easy thing to see, you are using a get-out-of-jail-free card." What Jed means by that is that the ball is such an easy thing to track. Anyone with eyes can see who has the ball and who doesn't. It is one of the most binary things in soccer, but to correlate having the ball to controlling the game is a fallacy. "The get-out-of-jail-free card allows you to make easy attributions that may or may not be true. You can say things like, 'Well, we had 70% possession, therefore, we are better.'" But to truly understand control asks a lot more of you as a coach, and too many coaches don't want to put in the work or the study required to be able to objectively analyze the game from that standpoint.

For Jed, there are two extremes in the current landscape of global soccer. There are coaches that don't believe possession is useful at all, and would rather play the ball long, direct, and go chase it. Then there are the coaches that view possession as the sole objective of the game—more important than winning, more important than scoring—and that want to achieve 100 passes in a row, but could not care less if they go nowhere with it. Then there is Jed. "Possession with penetration, and a purpose for every pass. That is where I sit on the spectrum."

I subscribe to the notion that you can't call it possession if the other team wants you to have the ball. When I train the defensive organization of my team, there are always passes that we will allows because they don't hurt us. Typically, these are passes that occur in front of our midfield—which are usually visualized by the infamous U-shaped passing structure that many teams use to circulate the ball from one outside back to the other—and don't penetrate our defensive organization at all. Therefore, Jed believes that teams and companies that are using things like initiatives, advanced platforms, and IMPECT are trying to send the message that the passes that matter are the ones that bypass the opposition and their lines of defense. Your team may have 70% possession, but what are they doing with that possession?

STRUCTURE VERSUS FREEDOM

Jed is one of the most well-traveled students of the game that I have come across. He has worked in Canada, the US, England, Wales, and Estonia, and he has talked with top coaches around the globe. Sometimes coaches criticize his objective approach by saying that it takes the decision making away from the players, but Jed knows that is not the case. In fact, Jed sees a spectrum of coaches. There are coaches that advocate giving the players complete freedom, and then there are the coaches that dictate every single move their players make. "I think where you sit on that fence can be dangerous depending upon if you are too far to one side or the other. Do you believe in freedom, or do you believe in structure? That is really the spectrum."

Jed believes that the answer lies in understanding decision making. There are really two orders of decision making: well-ordered scenarios and complex scenarios. "Well-ordered scenarios can have structures and clear maps as to what to do. However, a more complex scenario may favor the intuition of the players, rather than structure."

Jed's best resource on understanding decision making is Gary Klein's book *Streetlights and Shadows: Searching for the Keys to Adaptive Decision Making.* In that book, Klein introduces the recognition primed decision (RPD) model. A study aimed at testing the model showed that nearly 80-90% of all actions from fire fighters and other professions follow the RPD model to make decisions during complex situations. The RPD model basically shows that people in complex situations combine intuition with analysis. An example of action scripts in soccer would be something like the techniques required to pass or shoot the ball.

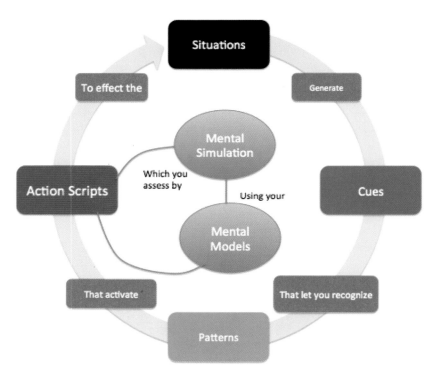

Data from *Philosophy of Football: In the Shadows of Marcelo Bielsa* by Jed Davies.

One of Jed's favorite Marcelo Bielsa quote is, "Totally mechanized teams are useless, because they get lost when they lose their script. But I also don't like ones that only rely on the inspiration of their soloists, because when God doesn't turn them on, they are left totally at the mercy of their opponents." This perfectly illustrates the dangers of giving your players too much freedom or too much structure.

For Bielsa, a coach must help players develop certain action scripts in order to respond to specific situations. "It is about recreating the situations that players will be in over and over again, with each situation revealing various cues—and therefore action scripts—that can be employed." Jed believes that these action scripts are where coaches come into play. "Action scripts are where you make mental simulations and mental models in your players. Mental models are things that feel familiar to you." An example may be training how you want your team to build out of the back against various pressing structures. If you put your players in that situation enough in training, they will start to develop mental models that allow them to recognize the familiarity of the situation, which will lead to improved decision making. "For me, that is where coaching becomes great—when you fully understand the balance between freedom, structure, and decision making."

OPPOSITION SCOUTING

Prior to his role with the Ottawa Fury, Jed worked for Magnus Pehrsson, the former Estonian National Team manager and current Malmo FC coach. Jed was tasked with scouting some of the best national teams in the world. Through that experience, Jed developed fascinating insights and tactics about effective ways to scout an opponent. Jed scouted teams like England, Portugal, Sweden, and Australia, and was charged with creating strategies to stop players like Cristiano Ronaldo and Zlatan Ibrahimovich.

The first thing Jed does prior to watching even one minute of video is to write down his vision of how the game is going to go. Jed uses information that he already has about the abilities of his players, and the abilities of the players they are playing against. In addition, he gathers information from Magnus regarding how he intends to set up the team. "For example, if we are playing England, I already know that we are going to be defending in a low block and counter-attacking. That helps anchor my decision making, and it helps me remain focused on key aspects of the opponent. I know that my target while watching the opponent play is to look for areas we can exploit on the counter." Jed also makes sure that he watches England play against opponents similar to Estonia. Although it may be entertaining, watching England against Spain isn't going to help him determine which areas Estonia can exploit on the counter-attack. Spain will have 75% possession and almost no instances to counter-attack. Therefore, Jed finds it important to choose games where England's opponent is set up in a similar fashion to how Estonia plans to play. He selects games where the opponent is playing England in a low block, so that he can assess how England has approached games like that in the past. How do they try and break down a low block? What areas have been successfully exploited on the counter in the past? This is vital information to provide Magnus, so that training can be as specific as possible.

For the England match, Jed determined that one of the most successful counter-attacking strategies was to draw England's fullbacks forward so that, upon winning possession, Estonia could play immediately behind the English fullbacks. Jed determined that

England really struggle when opponents are able to get in behind their fullbacks because Gary Cahill will always sprint out of his position to press the player that received in behind. That means that one of England's best players would be out of the box. Therefore, crossing the ball from those positions became important for Estonia to train in the lead up to the match.

The key for Jed is to start with the overall theme of the game. Playing against San Marino has a different theme than playing against England. Once the theme is well understood, the process is then about finding solutions to potential problems that may occur. Next, specific matches are chosen for viewing based on themes and strategies similar to the game that you are about to play. As Jed watches the games, he is looking for how a team responds to those specific moments that define the theme of their match. "How does a team defending in a low block respond to big switches? How about short passes? How about negative passes? The whole time I am just seeing how they respond to the situations that will define the match."

Jed's position with Estonia was very specific, so he does believe in a more general framework to scouting effectively. The following framework would be more applicable to situations where the opponent is of equal ability to your team. However, if you are playing a team much better than yours, then following a framework that is similar to the one used by Estonia would be more effective.

The framework is as follows:

1. *Opponent formation and system of movement*—This is the reference for everything that is going to happen. For example, it may be that the opponent plays in a 1-4-2-3-1. They may position their outside backs higher up the pitch. In addition, they may also push their wingers into central areas.
2. *Style and intent*—What are they trying to accomplish with the way they play? Are they trying to create crosses from wide areas? Are they trying to use combinations to get in behind your back line? Are they trying to isolate dribblers?
3. *Levels of communication*
   a. Collective—How does the team operate as a whole?
   b. Sectional—How do the individual lines behave in various moments? (ex. How does the back four organize in a low block?)
   c. Group—How do the right fullback and right winger work together? Do they have a consistent relationship?
   d. Individual—What are the individual identities that may cause problems? Do they have a player that is very good at beating players on the dribble?

4. *How does the team behave in the six moments of the game?*
   a. Attacking organization
   b. Defensive organization
   c. Attack-to-defend transition
   d. Defend-to-attack transition
   e. Set pieces
   f. Transition to transition (e.g., when no one clearly has the ball, moments of 50-50)
5. *Sub-moments*—These are the themes of the game that Jed discussed earlier. If you plan to play in a low-block defense and attack on the counter, then how does the opponent play and respond to low-block systems? What areas can you exploit on the counter?

CHAPTER 19

THE PHILOSOPHY OF DEFENDING

JED DAVIES, PART 2

The following is my attempt to expand upon Jed Davies' Philosophy of soccer and the work he did in his book *The Philosophy of Football: In Shadows of Marcelo Bielsa.*

I *think*, I *feel*, I *believe*... A pronoun and a verb that can only mean one thing: the person speaking is about to give you their *opinion*. I wish I had better news for all of us, but a belief is just something we *wish to be true*. We hope that it is true. But, the truth is that it is based on our experiences and our opinions that have filled our brain with biases and inaccuracies. Unfortunately, the soccer world is full of *opinions*, but scarce on *facts*. When someone issues a statement that is based on their judgment, their point of view, or their opinion, that is called being *subjective*. When someone says something that is based on facts, that is called being *objective*.

> *"In my opinion..."*
> *"From my perspective..."*
> *"It has been my experience that..."*

Subjectivity means that someone is just giving you *their* outlook or *their* expression of opinion. But, these statements are incredibly biased and based on assumptions and beliefs that are completely unverified. In soccer, people develop concepts based on subjectivity, assumptions, experiences, and opinions. Coaches that develop concepts, or ideas, based on subjectivity are creating nothing more than the *flavor of the month*.

One week you are playing a 1-3-4-3 because Chelsea used it, but next week you are inverting your fullbacks because Pep Guardiola did it. In 2010, you were diving into the Spanish methodology, but in 2014 it was all about Germany. And, in 2018, when another country wins, we will all drop our German books and start studying that team. Imagine yourself driving. You get in the car and pull out of your driveway, but you have no clue where you are going. Maybe you take a left, and then a right, and then you heard that going straight on a certain road is supposed to be really good. Before you know it, you are lost and have no clue how to get home. Lewis Carroll, author of *Alice's Adventures in Wonderland,* says it best, "If you don't know where you're going, any road will get you there."

So, how do we avoid this as soccer coaches? We must take a philosophical starting point. We need to start with *objectivity.* We don't start with somebody's opinion because why would one opinion be any better than the other?

Objectivity completely eliminates any subjective perspective by following a process that is purely based on the hard *facts.* Objectives are concepts that are based on principles and rules and without bias. They are universal concepts that apply to soccer coaches everywhere. They aren't influenced by where you are from, what league you coach in, or what courses you have done. They apply to all of us because we all coach and play the same game.

Now, does this mean that our experiences and opinions are useless? Well, yes and no. They are when we try to force our opinions on others as if they were double-blind, research-backed facts. But, if we use objectivity as our starting point first, then our opinions, experiences, and perspectives have meaning. It is only when we have developed an objective starting point and reference that we can begin to subjectively apply the philosophy. The goal is to *subjectively apply an objective reference.*

The goal of this chapter is to add to the objective reference created by Jed Davies most recent book, *The Philosophy of Football: In the Shadows of Marcelo Bielsa.* After having gone through the book for, I think, maybe the fourth time, I am ready to expand on his work. We are two men in search of something very similar: *objectivity.* I don't care much for subjective conversations about how *you think* the game should be played. I try to avoid subjective conversations about what *you prefer* as the best training methods. Subjectivity is *your* personal application of *something,* and what I'm interested in is what that *something* is. What guides your application? Too often, people are subjectively applying from *nothing.* They follow no manual, no model, no objective philosophy to guide their thought processes—they just simply apply.

Jed has tried to make the attacking moment of the game objective. Instead of writing articles about subjective zones on the pitch and arbitrary "channels" that we should all use, he has sought to understand exactly what the purpose of having the ball is. I am not saying that those channels, zones, and other arbitrary terminology like "half-spaces" are useless. In fact, I use some of those very things, but, I use them based on an objective philosophy of soccer. They are at the level of application, not philosophy. Those things *are not* objective. Too many theorists claim those things to be at the level of philosophy, or objectivity. But in reality, those things are subjective, which means they are useful at the level of application, but not at the level of a philosophical approach to soccer.

The objective philosophy of the attacking moment of the game goes as follows: When your team has the ball, the highest order of objectives is to score a goal. When we have the ball, the first thing we should be looking to do is score. If our players cannot score, then they should be looking to make an assist. What if they can't make an assist? Then, they should pass to someone that can make an assist. It is at this point that we can start to build an objective philosophy of the attacking moment of the game.

When a soccer team has possession of the ball, they should be looking to achieve the following three objectives in order of priority:

1. Score
2. Assist
3. Assist the assist

But, what happens when our team cannot achieve the three highest priorities of the game? The action required to score is shooting. The action required to assist is passing. The action required to assist the assist is also passing. Therefore, we know that passing actions precede shooting actions and the eventual objective of the game—to score.

When we break down the passing action, we understand that the best pass is an assist, the second best pass is to assist the assist, and from that point things can get very subjective. So, let's take a step back. These are the football actions required to achieve the highest priorities of the game.

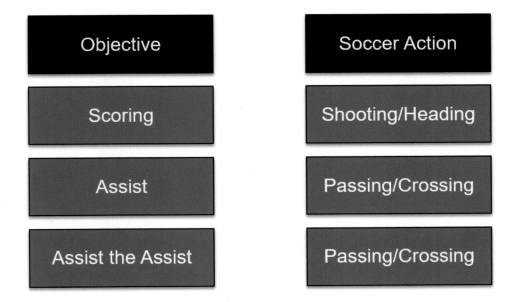

Objective	Soccer Action
Scoring	Shooting/Heading
Assist	Passing/Crossing
Assist the Assist	Passing/Crossing

Based on this, we can now start to determine where to go from here. If we cannot achieve any of these three objectives of the game, then what actions do our players have to make to be able to create the scenarios where we can achieve them? Well, we know that it is easier to achieve a shot on goal when there is only one defender than it is when there are 11 defenders. So, if we cannot achieve those three objectives of the game, then we need to pass the ball, or move the ball, past as many opponents as possible. If we can pass it by 10 players, then we have a much greater chance of achieving the highest order of the game, which is scoring. However, if we only pass the ball by one player on the other team, then it will be much more difficult to achieve the highest order of the game.

Consequently, Jed looked at the concept of breaking lines, or bypassing the opponent's lines, as the next logical objective of the game. In other words, the objective of the game, if we cannot achieve the three highest 3 orders of priority, is to pass the ball into key spaces on the field by eliminating as many players on the opposition as possible. Jed has determined that the key spaces are as follows:

1. Behind the opposition central defenders
2. Behind the opposition fullbacks
3. In front of the opposition central defenders
4. In front of the opposition fullbacks
5. Behind the opposition central midfielders
6. Behind the opposition wide midfielders

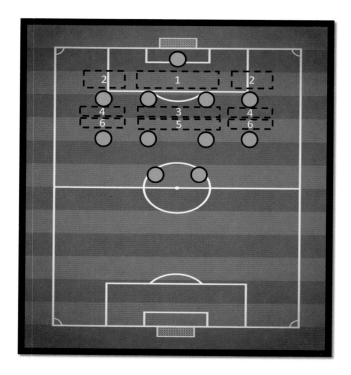

The key spaces of the game that we need to move the ball into in order to achieve the highest priorities of the game. Listed by numerical superiority from 1-6.

The reason why these spaces are prioritized the way they are is because of the number of defenders eliminated when the ball moves into each space. For example, space #1, behind the opposition center backs, eliminates 10 players on the opponent's team and only leaves the goalkeeper to beat. At this point, it is much easier to score. Wait a minute, doesn't space #2 also eliminate 10 players on the opponent's team? Yes, of course. But, the space behind the fullbacks of the opponent is farther from the goal than the space behind the center backs of the opponent. For this reason, it is marginally more difficult to achieve the highest priority of the game, to score, from this space as compared to the space #1. In other words, space #1 is better than space #2, and space #3 is better than space #4 because even though they eliminate the same number of players respectively, the goal is in the middle of the field, not on the sides. Therefore, those central spaces (#1 and #3) are easier to score from than the spaces in the wide areas of the field (#2 and #4).

This is objective. It is easier to achieve the highest priorities of the game (scoring, assisting, and assisting the assisting) by moving the ball into space #1 with possession than it is in space #2, than space #3, and so on. Well, what happens if we cannot play into any of these spaces? What then? Jed believes that the next logical priority is to make soccer actions to create the conditions to achieve the objectives listed previously. If for any reason we find it difficult to move the ball into these key spaces, it is for one, or more, of the following three reasons:

1. The opposition are compact vertically.
2. The opposition are compact horizontally.
3. The opposition is layered in between their midfield and defense, or beyond.

Based on these facts, we can determine the necessary objectives to create the conditions to resume achieving the priorities of the game. If we cannot score, assist, or assist the assist, then we need to look to move the ball into the key spaces of the game that allow us to achieve the highest priorities of the game. If we cannot move the ball into those key spaces, then it is for one, or more of those three reasons. If that is the case, then the priorities become:

1. To spread the opposition out vertically
2. To spread the opposition out horizontally
3. To remove the layers in the defensive shape of the opponent

Finally, Jed completes the objective philosophy of the game by saying that if we cannot achieve those three priorities, we must look to play the ball into a new area of the field, retain possession, and with each new pass in the sequence of possession, try to return to the highest orders of the objectives.

Based on this objective philosophy, coaches around the world can apply based on their preferred style, methods, and organizations. But, now they will be applying based on *something*, not *nothing*. Every coach will have their own preferences as to *how* they wish to achieve these objectives, but this chapter is focused on *what* those objectives are.

At this point you may be saying, especially if you read Jed's book, "OK great, but we already know this. Weren't you supposed to be adding something?" Yes. Everything you just read is thoroughly explained in over 250 pages in Jed's book. What I want to add is the philosophy of defending.

Objectively, when you have the ball you are attacking, when you don't have the ball you are defending, and the moments between those phases, called transitions.

To this point, we have adequately theorized the objectives of the attacking moment of the game. But, what about defending? Well, there are two phases in attacking: building up and scoring. We build up in order to create chances to score. Thus far, we have attempted to objectify the building-up phase of the attacking moment. When we are building up we are trying to achieve the objectives of the game by moving the ball, and us, to achieve the highest priorities of the game: scoring, assisting, and assisting the assisting, and so on.

When we don't have the ball, we are defending. Defending is the counter to attacking. So, when we don't have the ball we are *disrupting the build-up* of the opponent and *preventing scoring.* Those are the two phases that make up defending.

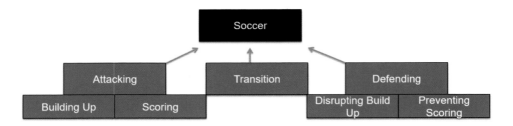

So, we know that in soccer, when we have the ball we are attacking. When we attack we are building up and scoring. We know that when we are building up, we are trying to achieve the priorities of the game detailed earlier. Scoring is the highest priority and main objective of building-up.

We also know that when we don't have the ball we are defending. When we defend we are disrupting the build-up and preventing scoring. But, the question is what is the *objective* way to do that? Every coach has a subjective application of defending, a preference as to how they would like to defend, but what is the objective philosophy of defending?

Let's take a look at the objective organization of soccer again.

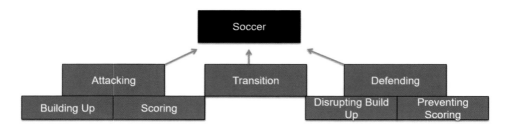

This allows us to see something fairly important. Attacking and defending are polar opposites of one another. Like multiplication and division, or addition and subtraction, one is the counter to the other.

Attacking	Defending
Building Up	Disrupting Building Up
Scoring	Preventing Scoring

Fortunately, Jed objectified building-up and scoring for us. This leads us to the next logical objective of the game—the objective philosophy of disrupting the build-up and preventing scoring.

We can see clearly that the objective philosophy of defending (disrupting the build-up) exists as the counter to the objective philosophy of attacking (building up).

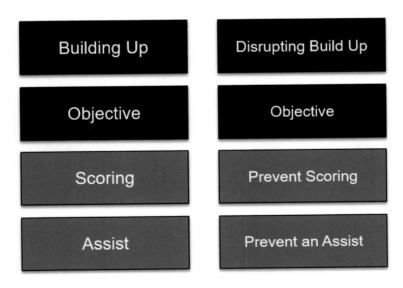

Building Up	Disrupting Build Up
Objective	Objective
Scoring	Prevent Scoring
Assist	Prevent an Assist

We achieve these objectives and priorities through soccer actions just like we do in the attacking moment of the game.

Here you can see the objective soccer actions that allow us to achieve the priorities of defending. I have listed a few examples of soccer actions, but note that this list is not exhaustive. There are other soccer actions that can prevent scoring and prevent an assist.

If a team cannot achieve the three highest priorities of building-up, then they will look to move the ball into the key spaces. Therefore, the objective philosophy of defending and disrupting build-up is to make soccer actions that counter those of the team in possession. When the attacking team cannot score, assist, or assist the assist, then we want to deny the ball from moving into the following spaces.

1. Deny the ball into the space behind your central defenders.
2. Deny the ball into the space behind your fullbacks.
3. Deny the ball from moving in front of your central defenders.

4. Deny the ball from moving in front of your fullbacks.
5. Deny the ball from moving in behind your central midfielders.
6. Deny the ball from moving in behind your wide midfielders.

Fortunately, Jed has already told us how we can achieve these objectives as the defending team. We achieve the above priorities by

1. being compact vertically,
2. being compact horizontally, and
3. creating layers between our midfield and defense (or beyond).

The objective reference of disrupting the build-up is complete. It is at this point that coaches should begin dipping into the level of application. In other words, *how* do they want to go about achieving the objective priorities of defending? For some of you, these objectives may seem unnecessary. Why do we need all of this theory? I know that I want my team to be compact, so what? And that is exactly the point. Earlier in this chapter I explained how most coaches simply just apply. I want my team to press! But, why? I want to use positional play! But, why? Most of the time, the reasons are either subjective or nonsensical. Coaches may say things like, "I don't want the opponent to be able to breathe!" OK, great, but what the hell does that mean, and why do you want that? Or, "I want to have possession of the ball." Yes, of course. But, what do you want to do with that possession? The coaches that know *why* and *what* will beat the coaches that know *how*.

A lot of coaches know *how* to teach a pressing coordination, but do they know *why* they are pressing. Do their players know *why* they are pressing? Do they know *which* priority of disrupting the opponent's build-up pressing helps them achieve it? Maybe they do. And if so, that's great! But, many coaches don't. Many coaches subjectively apply the organization of their team based on the newest trends, latest articles and books, or most popular managers. I hope by this point that you understand that those things are completely subjective. They are all at the level of application.

Reading *Pep Confidential* is great, but I hope you understand it is entirely subjective. It is *his* application of something. Without understanding what that something is that he is applying from, you end up applying someone else's subjectivity. Applying someone else's subjectivity results in *chaos*. Pep, Mourinho, Bielsa are all subjectively applying from objectivity, or at least I would hope that they are. They understand the objective characteristics of soccer. So, if we take their subjective application as objective, we are going to severely miscalculate.

You see, objective philosophy helps coaches become better at the level of application. In that sense, it may be the most important part of soccer. With objective characteristics of the game spelled out and understood, we can now read articles, books, and watch interviews through a whole new light. How does what Thomas Tuchel just said relate to the objective of attacking and building-up? Why is he organizing his team that way? Oh, he wants to try and move the ball into the space in front of the opposition center backs to create chances. And, he is doing that because the opponent is spread out vertically. Now, you can theorize whether or not that applies to you, your team, your competition, and your league.

What would happen if you subjectively applied someone else's subjectivity? Well, what if every team in your league is vertically compact, and you show up to the field one day and start preparing your team to play into the spaces in front of the center backs. "Hey guys, Thomas Tuchel plays this way! It must be good!" And then the result is an absolute trainwreck. But, if you objectify Tuchel's subjectivity, you can learn a lot more about soccer. You will know *why* he is doing what he is doing. You will understand *what* he is trying to accomplish from an objective standpoint. And from that standpoint, you will have a better understanding of *how* you may, or may not, apply it.

OK, now that we understand the importance of objectivity, let's see the objective reference in its entirety.

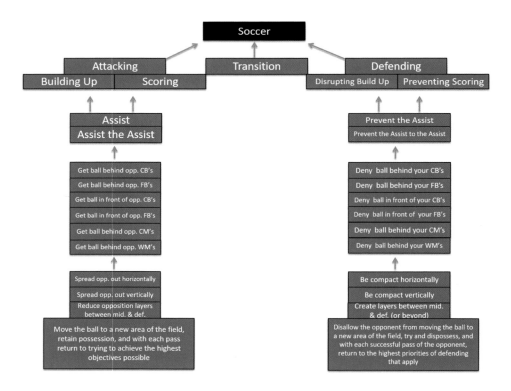

You will probably note that I made one change to Jed's objective model. While I acknowledge that the purpose and highest priority of building-up is to score, by definition, if you are scoring you are no longer building-up. Therefore, I didn't include scoring underneath building-up. The final moment of the build-up is the assist. Similarly, the final moment of disrupting the build-up is preventing the assist. Once the assist is being made, the phase of defending switches to preventing scoring by making soccer actions that achieve that (tackling, intercepting, blocking, saving [GK], punching the ball [GK], tipping the ball [GK], etc.).

In addition, the final objective of defending is quite interesting. When your team is attacking, the last objective is to move the ball into a new area of the field, often called "switching the play," in order to create a new angle at which the team can achieve the higher priorities of attacking. The attacking team will also want to retain possession during this moment. Therefore, the last objective of defending is to disallow the opponent from moving the ball to a new area of the field, or switch the play, and subsequently try and dispossess the opponent of the ball. Finally, if the opponent is successful in retaining possession, with each successful pass the opponent makes, the defending team returns to the highest priorities of defending applicable.

It is important to note that these priorities are not *sequential*. They are, in fact, *consequential*. In other words, they don't follow a logical order. By that, I mean that we don't have to move the ball behind the opposition center backs to be able to score a goal. That is why with each new pass, the players should return to the highest priorities of the game and move down from there to find what they can, or need to, execute in the moment to be able to achieve the higher priorities. For example, the first thing you may have to do defensively is get compact horizontally and vertically to deny the opponent from achieving the highest priorities of attacking. Although those priorities of defending are lower down the objective list, your team may need to "jump" to those priorities based on where the ball and the opponent is. However, that is all at the level of application. That is for you, as the coach, to determine.

Another example to aid in the understanding of the consequential nature of these objectives was when David Beckham scored from the half-way line against Wimbledon. Beckham was in the space in front of the opposition fullback and 60 meters from the goal. However, his cognitive process immediately asked if he could score from where he was, and he made the decision to do so. Therefore, it was a *consequential* decision. It was a result of perceiving the environment, seeing the goalkeeper off of his line, and jumping to the highest priority of the game—scoring. In other words, these objective priorities of attacking and defending are not logical progressions from one to the other. You don't need to reduce the opposition layers, then spread them out vertically, and then horizontally. No, the purpose is to always be seeking the highest priority possible. If it is not possible, then we want to achieve the next best priority available, and so on.

This objective philosophy is to be used by you to apply based on the logical structure and characteristics of the game. But, these are *objective*. You cannot deny that it is easier to score against one defender (ball in behind the opposition center backs) than it is to score against 11 defenders (ball in front of the opposition forwards). You also cannot deny that the purpose of attacking and building-up is to score. The purpose of defending and disrupting the build-up is to prevent scoring. From there, the remaining priorities are the logical consequence of the previous priority. But, soccer is not logical or sequential. So, these priorities will help you, as a coach, use your knowledge and experience to determine *how* you want to go about achieving the highest priorities and *how* you want your team to behave when they can't achieve the highest priorities.

Using this objective reference, coaches can now successfully move to the level of application and determine *how* they think their team should organize themselves in order to achieve the priorities and objectives of building-up and disrupting the build-up. With a philosophical starting point, it is now possible to subjectively apply objectivity.

CHAPTER 20

TACTICAL PERIODIZATION

NICK COWELL

Nick Cowell is the head women's soccer coach at St. Edwards University in Austin, Texas. Nick is in the top three winningest head coaches of all time in NCAA Division 2 soccer. Nick is an expert in tactical periodization and has successfully applied it to the collegiate setting. Nick taught himself Portuguese to be able to translate Vitor Frade's original texts (Vitor Frade is the creator of tactical periodization and developed the methodology out of the University of Porto).

Are you willing to learn a language to hear the truth about tactical periodization — How to create a game model — Principles, sub-principles, and sub-sub-principles — The morphocycle — How to handle multiple game weeks — A team that thinks with one brain

Raymond Verheijen, the Dutch coach educator and former Wales assistant coach, has a unique way of putting motivation into perspective. If you were to tell him you can't do something—for example, maybe you tell him that you can't run a mile in under 6 minutes—his response would be something along the lines of, "What if I put a lion behind you?" There is nothing like necessity when it comes to motivation.

Nick Cowell found himself with a lion behind him when trying to solve a problem specific to college soccer. Nick was confounded by the brevity of the college soccer season.

Nearly a decade into his college coaching career, Nick started to become frustrated with the inevitable peak and decline of his team's performance that ultimately defined each college season. "The college season is so short and every game is so important that I didn't want my team to have performance peaks and valleys. No game is more important than any other; I mean, you could lose a game at the beginning of the season that could cost you a postseason bid. I was looking for a way to create stability of our performance, and that is when I came across the work of Vitor Frade and tactical periodization."

Vitor Frade's work on the methodology of tactical periodization is written solely in Portuguese. Although a lot of coaches have been able to learn through translations of the work, the translations aren't necessarily a true representation of the theories. In fact, Frederico Morais—a former student of Vitor Frade—told me in an interview that, "Everything published in English is totally wrong. There are so many misrepresentations."

Fortunately for us, Nick Cowell—a former language major in college—taught himself Portuguese to be able to understand the theories of tactical periodization more accurately. "I basically taught myself with books, CDs, and some different things. It wasn't too uncommon to see me at a red light speaking Portuguese to myself. I probably looked a little crazy, but I made it my goal to learn the language. Once I learned the language, it just opened up a whole new world of books, articles, and papers that were coming out of Portugal at the time."

Nick became enthralled with tactical periodization after reading a Portuguese biography about Jose Mourinho. Being able to speak and read Portuguese meant that Nick could locate those source texts and get to the heart of Mourinho's methodology. Eventually, all of that reading and researching led Nick to the research being done by a professor out of the University of Porto named Vitor Frade.

Vitor Frade is the father of tactical periodization. Unfortunately, similar to the way *possession* and *positional play* have become buzzwords, so too has *tactical periodization*. In fact, I don't think there is a coach alive that doesn't consider himself a tactical expert and because most coaches think they are tactical experts, they all think they are using tactical periodization, which couldn't be further from the truth. Tactical periodization is not training with tactics. It is a methodology about much, much more than that.

WHAT IS TACTICAL PERIODIZATION?

Nick's journey led him to a fairly simple definition of a very complex methodology. "The basic belief of tactical periodization is that the most important factor in a team's success is the way the team plays together. The team needs to understand a central game model or way of playing." Tactical periodization knows that the sum of the whole is greater than the sum of its parts.

THE REAL GIANTS OF SOCCER COACHING

Tactical periodization is aimed at bringing about a specific style of game through collective and individual intentions. What does this mean? It means that you train and teach your game model every single day in a variety of ways so that the product you see on each match day reflects the game model (i.e., playing style) you want. Instead of drilling technique or things in isolation, we train the game model so that our players can practice their collective interactions to reveal a collective intention on game day.

Traditional training methodology calls for the isolation of fitness, technique, psychology, strength training, and other trainable characteristics of soccer players. Traditionally, soccer players do fitness with the fitness coach, technique work with the technical coach, strength training with the strength coach, and so on, and only after every player has developed competencies in all of these areas are they brought together to work on tactics. The technical prose needed to fully refute the traditional mechanistic approach to training is well beyond the scope of this book, but, in their 1997 text, *The Art of Systems Thinking*, Joseph O'Connor and Ian McDermott paint a perfect picture that illustrates the inadequacy of the traditional mechanistic and isolated approach to training. "Nobody would take apart a piano to look for its sound." In other words, the sound is created through the interactions of many things. Soccer is not something that is a result of fitness, technique, tactics, and psychology. It is a constant flow of all those things interwoven together for 90 minutes. They do not exist separate from one another in soccer. "Tactics are the central part of the philosophy and they are what coordinate all of the physical, technical, and psychological; they all come from the tactical work that you do on the field."

Soccer is a complex system which can be looked at as a series of elements interacting between themselves in order to reach a specific outcome. These elements must have a similar intention and understanding between them to successfully navigate the moments of order and disorder that characterize soccer. A soccer team is a complex system, which means so too is the opponent. "A game—where you have one complex system competing with another complex system—is another level of complexity. Therefore, there always exists this tension of the order you want within your team and the disorder that is created by two complex systems interacting." This is where the role of tactics enter into the discussion of tactical periodization.

The complexity of soccer creates many unbalanced situations that require both teams to seek out a specific model of self-organization. Therefore, a complex system (e.g., a soccer team) is always in a dynamic state moving between and within phases of order and disorder.

I will try not to make this section too wordy and esoteric, although the topic is complex. It just further proves the point that soccer is not simple, and not only is soccer coaching an art, it is very much a science, too. In an effort to make it simple, let's refer back to the idea of a team moving in and out of phases of order and disorder. A simple way to think about it is as follows: Imagine the opponent has a goal kick and they are going to build out of the back. You, as a coach, have trained your team how to press a team that is building from the goal kick. In other words, you have taught them how to self-organize in that moment of the game to establish *order*. Now, if the opponent is able to play out of your pressure and find a player that turns and starts dribbling towards your goal, there now exists a moment of *disorder* in the game. The organization of your team's press is now disorganized. Therefore, the key to any match lies in seeing which team can self-organize faster and more efficiently. For example, if the opponent is able to set up and organize their attacking organization with width and depth before your team can get behind the ball and set up in a low defensive block, then chances are your team will lose the match if that trend continues. Therefore, extreme importance is paid to the self-organization of complex systems in tactical periodization.

Self-organization is something that should be trained. Pre-determined self-organization strategies are developed in something called the game model. The game model can be looked at as your team's organization strategies for the four moments of the game: attacking, defending, transitioning from defense to attack, and transitioning from attack to defense.

The game model is essential in order to implement tactical periodization successfully. You need to know what you want the collective, group, and individual intentions of your team to be in order to train it. The game model is the interaction between the coach's ideas about the game, the players, the club, the game principles, and much more. It is best summarized in the image below:

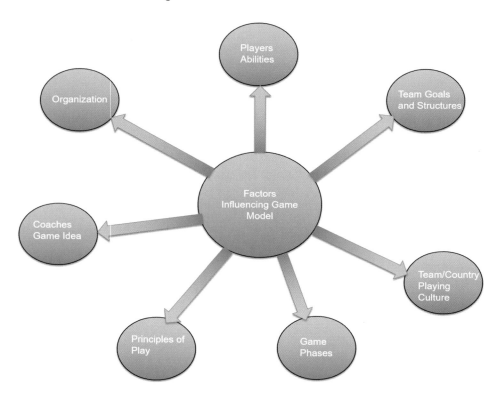

The coach needs to consider all these things when deciding how he wants his team to play. What technical, tactical, and physical attributes do your players have or need to have? What are the human, financial, and time constraints of your staff? How do you want your team to attack, defend, and transition? What is your background, preference, and philosophy as a coach? What principles of the game are important to the way you want to play? Basically, a game model is the creation of your team's identity.

PRINCIPLES OF TACTICAL PERIODIZATION

Tactical periodization also involves very specific principles that make it a methodology. These principles are what make the difference between a team that uses tactical periodization and a team that just says they are using it. Again, it is *not* simply training with tactics. Violating any of these principles is to go against the entire methodology.

Principle of Specificity

Training must be a simulation of various situations that occur in the game or are influenced by the game model. As Nick puts it, "every exercise that you design in a practice has to exacerbate your principles of play. Everything that you do should have a relation to how you want your team to play." The principle of specificity also describes training exercises as *fractal* in nature. A fractal is a geometric figure in which similar patterns occur at progressively smaller scales. In other words, your training exercises should be viewed as mini versions of the game. "Every session should allow the players to learn the principles that you are trying to teach them."

Nick never starts a training exercise without explaining to his team why they are doing what they are doing. "I think if you can tell your players why you are doing an exercise, you will get much more out of the activity." Too often, Nick sees coaches using drills or training exercises that they get from other coaches or teams but that usually have nothing to do with how they want their team to play. "Sometimes we fall into this trap of thinking a certain exercise would be good for our team, but if it has no relation to the game model, then the effects of that exercise might take your team backwards. It might lead to confusion and have adverse effects on your team."

Specificity does not necessarily mean that training should be deterministic. In other words, we have to make sure that we include the randomness and complexity of the game. For example, if you are working on building from the back and every repetition is set up to start from the goalie so the attacking team can get the ball to a specific player before starting over again, that is deterministic. To maintain the randomness and complexity of the game, every activity needs to have attacking, defending, and transitioning; otherwise, training becomes deterministic and unrealistic. Would you ever build from the back to a certain player and then have to start all the way back from the goalkeeper again? Repetition is important, but not at the expense of realism and randomness.

Another aspect of the principle of specificity is that any training outside of the game model is irrelevant. "The training exercises that don't relate to the game are not necessary. Even though it might be good to go to the gym and hit on a punching bag for 30 minutes, that is totally unrelated to the game. It is fitness that doesn't relate to the game."

Principle of Propensities

This principle basically states that it is necessary to create training exercises that make it possible for certain behaviors to be repeated with great frequency. In other words, if you are training the ability of your team to counter-press, the exercise you create should be constructed in a way that allows for a lot of counter-pressing opportunities to occur.

Principle of Hierarchy

The principle of hierarchy states that a coach should create the game model by starting with the principles. Before coming up with the sub-principles and sub-sub-principles for each moment of the game, the coach needs to determine the essential behaviors he wants his team to exhibit during the four moments of the game. These are discussed later in this chapter in more detail.

Principle of Horizontal Variation

This principle breaks up the playing style of a team into various phases throughout the week. The week should follow the progression of regeneration from the previous game into an acquisition phase to build up the playing ability of the team before tapering off prior to the next game. This principle uses a variety of methods to create two types of variation throughout the week.

1. The level of complexity of the principles are varied throughout the week. Some days, principles are trained, while on other days, sub-principles and sub-sub-principles are trained.
2. The dominant muscle contraction regimen will vary the muscular contraction used between tension, duration, and velocity.

Overall, this principle calls for a day-to-day variation between levels of training intensity and volume.

Principle of Performance Stabilization

The week-to-week cycle is similar in structure so the players can consistently perform on the weekends. Nick Cowell set out on his journey to learn about tactical periodization because of this principle. There is a daily variation that exists in tactical periodization, but not a weekly variation. Each week follows a similar daily variation called the morphocycle. There is no annual plan, mesocycle, or microcycle. Each weekly morphocycle is the same throughout the entirety of a season.

Principle of Conditioned Exercise

Players should execute similar actions in training that they execute—or need to execute—in the game. This is achieved through position-specific training. This is similar to the principle of specificity, but goes one level deeper. Specificity argues that every training exercise should include the four moments of the game and the principles of the game model. But conditioned exercise argues that each player needs to be training in their specific position or space on the field. In other words, a left back should be played as a left back in training. Playing as a striker will not help that player improve his ability to influence the game model from his specific position.

Principle of Complex Progression

This principle argues that there needs to be a planned progression of tactical ideas throughout a given period. That is why the morphocycle, developed by Vitor Frade, specifies which days are dedicated to training the principles, which are dedicated to training the sub-principles, and which are dedicated to training the sub-sub-principles.

Principles of Tactical Fatigue and Concentration

This principle introduces the psychological and cognitive aspect of soccer. The focus required from the players must be managed and periodized as well. The word *intensity*, which is often thrown around carelessly in soccer, is not useful as a measure of some sort of physical intensity. Instead, Vitor Frade uses *intensity* to refer to the intensity of concentration. In other words, a player having to focus and concentrate on his role during the four moments of the game, as specified by the coach's game model, is very intense. This intensity of concentration should be varied so that some days require great focus, while other days require less focus. Nick Cowell likes to think of it in an even simpler way. "If I had a player run 40 meters, that would be somewhat physically intense. However, if I had that same player run 40 meters while carrying a tray full of glasses, that would be cognitively intense as well. So when I think about the word *intensity*, I think about the concentration required for the duration of the session. Are you asking your players to think a lot about their responsibilities? Then regardless of how much running they are doing, it is intense."

MOMENTS OF THE GAME

It is essential that a coach knows how he wants his team to behave during the four moments of the game. "The game is looked at in the four major moments and that is the starting point when coming up with your main principles." The four moments of the game are:

- Offensive organization
- Transition from attack to defense
- Defensive organization
- Transition from defense to attack

PRINCIPLES, SUB-PRINCIPLES, AND SUB-SUB-PRINCIPLES

As you begin to work through your game model as a coach, you will need to establish principles, sub-principles, and sub-sub-principles that will help you determine what you train each and every day. The field size, dimensions, duration, number of players, and so on are all dependent on whether we are training the principles, sub-principles, or sub-sub-principles.

Principles are the tactical patterns of action that you want your team to express during the various moments of the game. For example, "your main offensive principle might be to play vertical passes as quickly as possible. In transition from offense to defense, it might be to apply pressure to the ball as quickly as possible." I like to think of principles as your team-level tactics, the general patterns which characterize your team and give it its identity. Principles are the behaviors that are exhibited by the collective group, defined in the picture to the left.

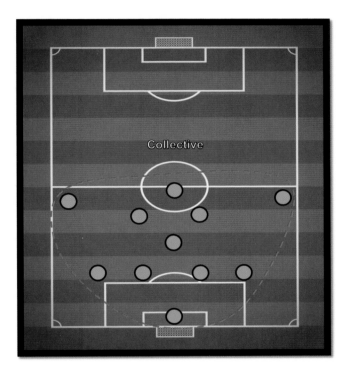

"Eventually you will need to flush out your principles into sub-principles, which are more detailed behaviors of your principles. For example, a sub-principle may specify a certain area of the field in which the principles are to occur. Sub-principles are the intermediate patterns of the game that support the general patterns. In his book *What Is Tactical Periodization?*, Xavier Tamarit defines sub-principles as "specific behaviors that occur inside the previous levels." In other words, the sub-principles focus on the specific behaviors of inter-sectorial relationships, sectorial relationships, and group relationships that aid in achieving the principles of the team. The sub-principles focus more on specific lines and groups of players in specific moments, but they should never be taught in a way that loses the wholeness of the game.

Inter-sectorial relationships deal with players from different lines of the team and how they interact. For example, how do three attackers and three defenders work together in a high press?

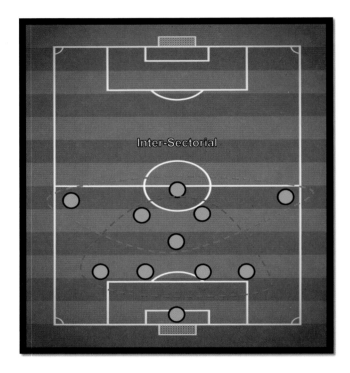

Sectorial relationships deal with the various lines of the team. An exercise focused on training the sub-principles of a sector would involve an entire line playing together. A common one used by coaches, even those that don't apply tactical periodization, is any training exercise that works on the back line defending together.

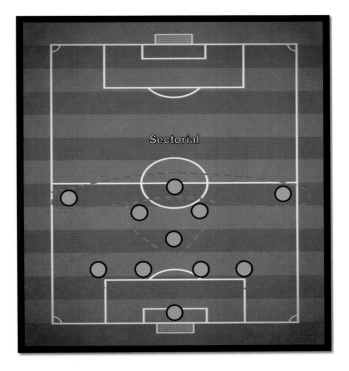

THE REAL GIANTS OF SOCCER COACHING

A group involves players from different lines of the team that often work together. An example of this would be training the goalkeeper, center backs, and holding midfield player together in order to work on building out from the back. These players play on different lines of the team—or different sectors—but work together as a group to achieve specific aims of the game model.

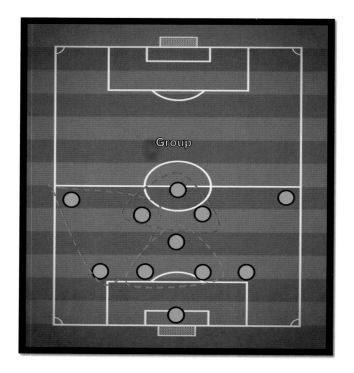

Finally, the sub-sub-principles are the micro patterns. Nick Cowell describes these as the little details of your game model that may change from day to day or week to week, depending on the opponent, results, new players, injuries, and so on. Another way to look at the sub-sub-principles are the individual tactics.

Individual principles are those moments of the game where interactions with teammates are not significant. An example of this may be working on the center back's ability to break the midfield line of opposition pressure with a firm pass played between lines. Defensively, individual tactics can be trained to work on the timing and speed of an individual's role in the pressing structure.

Understanding the dynamics of collective, sectorial, inter-sectorial, group, and individual tactics are vital to creating a game model. The goal is to define the game model by starting with the four moments of the game described earlier. A coach must determine the large principles that will govern how the collective group organizes during those four moments of the game. Within those moments are sub-principles and sub-sub-principles that serve the purpose of defining the behaviors of various lines and groupings of the team within the larger principle.

Here is an example of how a game model may look conceptually.

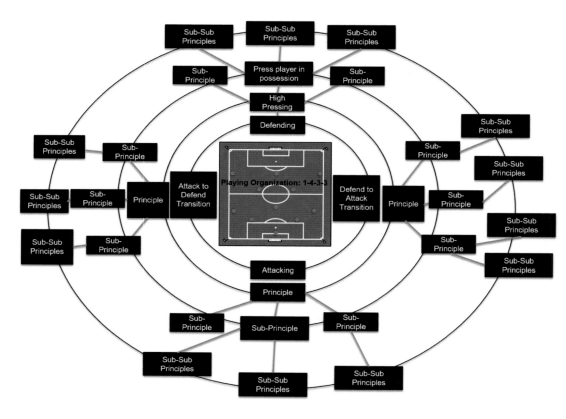

This gives you an example of how the game model would be built. After considering the identity and ability of each player on your team, the goals and structures of your team, the culture of the team and league, and other things discussed earlier in the chapter, you will want to build a game model by looking at the four moments of the game and how you want your team to behave in each moment. Creating the game model in the way above will help you see what you are asking of your players in each moment of the game. "The idea of the game model is to reduce the complexity of the game for the players. That is the entire point of breaking the game model down by principles, sub-principles, and sub-sub-principles—so that what the coach wants can be delivered in order to reduce the complexity of the game."

Once you have a clear understanding of the principles, sub-principles, and sub-sub-principles, you can begin thinking about basic formations. Formations should be chosen because they give your team the best chance to organize and execute the game model you have created.

Based on the game model that the coach and his staff create, the next task is to develop training exercises that teach the players the game model. Joao Gama Oliveira, a professor at the University of Porto, identifies the key to creating training exercises from the game model. "The aim is to improve playing quality and organization; therefore, those abilities can only be developed through training situations and drills that require that organization. Training means improving the play." Jose Mourinho sums it up even more succinctly: "The goal is to find training exercises that task the team with doing what is expected of them in the game."

Finally, we get to the periodization portion of tactical periodization. Vitor Frade created the weekly morphocycle to reflect the principles of horizontal alternation in specificity and performance stabilization. The morphocycle includes an off day, two match days, a recovery day, three acquisition days, and one pre-match activation day. During a week where your team plays two games, the weekly structure would look as follows:

Saturday	Sunday	Monday	Tuesday	Wednesday	Thursday	Friday	Saturday
Game Day	Day Off	Active Recovery	Strength	Duration	Speed	Activation	Game Day

Here is a breakdown of each phase of the morphocycle, and the relevant information regarding their planning and use.

ACQUISITION DAYS

The real key to understanding tactical periodization is to use your understanding of the game to interpret how you should create your game model. I can't tell you how your team should play. That is for you to determine and interpret, based on all of the information above.

Now we are ready to look at the planning details of tactical periodization. When we talk about tactical periodization from a planning standpoint, there is a methodological matrix that helps us apply the principles of periodization. For example, *horizontal alternation in specificity* means that we are planning our sessions in order to vary the physical systems stressed and the muscular contractions made. This brings us to the acquisition days. In simple terms, these days are the days where our players acquire knowledge about the game model, stress to their physical systems to improve their specific fitness and physical capabilities, and so on. These are our development days, in other words. However, Nick warns that the physical components should not be taken literally and trained in isolation. "The most important thing to remember is that no matter the physical component we are training under, we are still training the game model. A speed day doesn't mean we run sprints. We are still playing soccer, but we vary the muscular contraction, size of the pitch, number of players, and principles to avoid carrying fatigue over from one session to another."

The acquisition days are broken down as follows:

Acquisition Days

Strength	Duration	Speed

The aim of these acquisition days is to train different principles and sub-principles of the game model or playing style. In addition, they each emphasize a different muscle contraction that is required to execute soccer actions. The three main muscular contractions used in soccer are tension (strength), velocity (speed), and endurance (duration). The purpose of varying these muscular contractions is to ensure that we are not over-training certain muscular contractions or carrying fatigue into the next match. It also allows us to direct our exercises to promote a dominance of the specific contractions we want to feature and train.

The way you can look at these days is as follows:

Training strength involves a high density of accelerations and decelerations, and a lot of changes of direction with plenty of duels, jumping, and shooting. We are trying to overload the interaction between eccentric to concentric muscle contractions. These exercises should be performed in smaller areas, with a limited number of players. Our activities should be short in duration, and the rest periods should be long in order to ensure that the players are fully recovered and ready to make explosive actions again. The strength—or tension—day is typically the longest session of the week. It involves very demanding efforts with long recuperation periods.

In addition to the muscular contraction focus, tension days also focus on sub-principles and sub-sub-principles. Due to the use of small spaces with a low number of players, the goal would be to train various sub-principles or sub-sub-principles of the game model.

Duration days should reflect actions and effort similar to what we see in the game. On these days, we are using bigger areas, a larger number of players, and a longer duration of activities. Endurance—or duration—days also pay close attention to the large principles of the game model. The demands placed on the players should be very similar to the demands of competition. Tactical attention is predominantly paid to the large principles affecting the four moments of the game. In addition to playing for longer durations, the training activities should also have very short rest periods in order to maintain the continuity of the training to reflect the continuity of competition. The durations should be longer, but not so long that the intensity of effort is reduced. For example, it is better to play two rounds of 10 minutes than one round of 20 minutes.

Speed—or velocity—days are not necessarily related to the physical capacity of speed, but more to cognitive speed. These exercises should promote a high speed of decision making, execution, and action. Speed days should involve pitch sizes and a number of players that allow the players to achieve the intended objectives. This means that there should be fewer opponents on these days (5v3, for example). The duration of these exercises should be short, and the rest should allow for full recovery.

Velocity days also focus on the sub-principles and sub-sub-principles of the game model. The sub-principles and sub-sub-principles trained should attend to the inter-sectorial, sectorial, and especially the individual tasks relevant to the game model. Training tasks on this day should also include very little opposition. The focus is on the speed of execution of decisions.

ACTIVE RECOVERY AND ACTIVATION DAYS

Obviously, this day is aimed at helping the players recover from the match. The goal is to accelerate the recovery of the players. However, aspects of the game model should still be trained on this day as long as the periods of work are very short and the rest periods very long. Usually, teams will use small-area games with large numbers of players on these days in order to minimize the actions made by the players. For example, Dave Tenney, high-performance director for the Seattle Sounders, will have his team play 11v11 in a very tight area to maintain aspects of the game models, but with no further muscle damage. Vitor Frade believes that in order to improve the recovery processes, the energetic pathways must be stimulated in a similar fashion to how they are stimulated in the game. Therefore, recovery days should include aspects of the game model trained in a very intense way, but for very short durations, and with long recovery periods.

The goal of the activation day is to accelerate the recovery of the players following the acquisition days. These days should look to recreate moments or parts of the game that will be integral in the upcoming match. However, these should be trained for very short durations with very small volumes (only a few repetitions). These days should also utilize longer rest periods.

Activation days should not be very complex in nature either. The goal is to taper the cognitive demand of training prior to the match day. Relevant sub-principles that will be important for the next day's match should be the predominant use of training time, but trained for very short durations. The training duration for this day should be very short.

OFF DAYS

Research shows that players are typically more sore and fatigued 48 hours following a match. However, tactical periodization does not just look at the physiology in isolation. The cognitive demands of a match are considered in planning the off day. Due to the emotional and cognitive demands of the game, it is often difficult for players to fall asleep the night of a match day. When you compound that with the emotional load of the match—let's say that a team just lost in extra time—Vitor Frade recommends giving the day after the match off for players to spend with their families, and to recover physically, cognitively, and emotionally from the match the previous day. Additionally, because we want to address specific aspects of the game model, even on recovery days, it is important to consider the cognitive status of the team. If a recovery day is chosen for the day after the game, the concentration of the players may be very low, which would render the recovery session less effective.

MULTIPLE-GAME WEEKS

During multiple-game weeks, the acquisition days are the first days to be removed. If there is a midweek game, resulting in a three-game week, then acquisition days would be out of the question. The major aim of the weekly preparations would be geared toward recovering from the previous match and activating the players for the next match.

Saturday	Sunday	Monday	Tuesday	Wednesday	Thursday	Friday	Saturday
Game Day	Active Recovery	Activation	Game Day	Day Off	Active Recovery	Activation	Game Day

As a college coach, Nick Cowell deals mostly with this morphocycle. "In college, most of our season is recovery. We don't get a chance to do strength, endurance, and speed very often. One of the mistakes I made when I first started implementing tactical periodization was that I wanted more acquisition days and less recovery time. Unfortunately, that doesn't work. The priority has to be recovery. From there, you can see where acquisition days fit in."

Acquisition days are not used during this type of morphocycle, which means that recovery and activation days need to be used wisely in order to continue teaching the players aspects of the game model. It is not uncommon for players to forget principles and sub-principles of the game model during periods with a lot of recovery days, matches, and activation days. The coach needs to find ways to keep the game model and the playing philosophy of the team alive during these periods. Jose Mourinho uses video analysis to remind players of principles, and to even show sub-principles or sub-sub-principles that may be different based on the upcoming opponent. Video is a very useful tool because it helps keep the game model alive while not overloading the players from a physiological standpoint. Jose Mourinho will often use activation days to play very short 11v11 games in order to re-visit aspects of the game model as a tune-up for the match.

Here is a template that you can use to plan your weekly morphocycle's depending on the amount of time you have between matches.

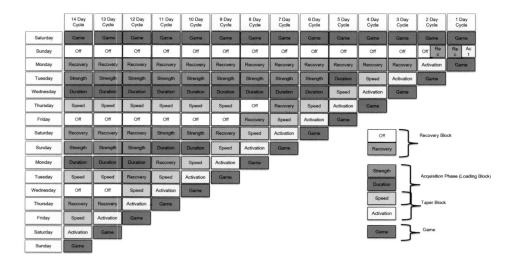

	14 Day Cycle	13 Day Cycle	12 Day Cycle	11 Day Cycle	10 Day Cycle	9 Day Cycle	8 Day Cycle	7 Day Cycle	6 Day Cycle	5 Day Cycle	4 Day Cycle	3 Day Cycle	2 Day Cycle	1 Day Cycle
Saturday	Game	Game	Game	Game	Game	Game	Game	Game	Game	Game	Game	Game	Game	Game
Sunday	Off	Off	Off	Off	Off	Off	Off	Off	Off	Off	Off	Off	Off / Rec	Rec / Act
Monday	Recovery	Recovery	Recovery	Recovery	Recovery	Recovery	Recovery	Recovery	Recovery	Recovery	Recovery	Recovery	Activation	Game
Tuesday	Strength	Strength	Strength	Strength	Strength	Strength	Strength	Strength	Strength	Duration	Speed	Activation	Game	
Wednesday	Duration	Duration	Duration	Duration	Duration	Duration	Duration	Duration	Duration	Speed	Activation	Game		
Thursday	Speed	Speed	Speed	Speed	Speed	Speed	Off	Recovery	Speed	Activation	Game			
Friday	Off	Off	Off	Off	Off	Off	Recovery	Speed	Activation	Game				
Saturday	Recovery	Recovery	Recovery	Strength	Strength	Recovery	Speed	Activation	Game					
Sunday	Strength	Strength	Strength	Duration	Duration	Speed	Activation	Game						
Monday	Duration	Duration	Duration	Recovery	Speed	Activation	Game							
Tuesday	Speed	Speed	Recovery	Speed	Activation	Game								
Wednesday	Off	Off	Speed	Activation	Game									
Thursday	Recovery	Recovery	Activation	Game										
Friday	Speed	Activation	Game											
Saturday	Activation	Game												
Sunday	Game													

Legend:
- Off, Recovery — Recovery Block
- Strength, Duration — Acquisition Phase (Loading Block)
- Speed — Taper Block
- Activation — Taper Block
- Game — Game

Jose Mourinho—by far the most popular user of tactical periodization—knows that soccer is about a team being adapted to a specific way of playing. A journalist asked Mourinho about his ideal team. His answer reflected the importance of tactical periodization as his training methodology. "It would be one where, at any given time, at any given situation, all my players think the same way." Tactical periodization is not about getting faster or stronger, or jumping higher. It is about acquiring a certain way of playing.

Nick Cowell has been using tactical periodization for nearly three seasons. The second winningest NCAA D2 coach in the country has seen the benefits. "It really forced me to specify and be clearer about what I wanted them to do, so just from an organizational standpoint we have improved so much. The players are also less fatigued at the end of the season. My original goal was met too, which is that our team's performance is much more stable. We don't have stretches anymore where we have one good game and then one bad game. Our performances are fairly stable. Finally, we are much more prepared tactically, which manifests itself in how we behave as a team in the four moments of the game. There are times when I see all eleven players on my team think as one and, as Mourinho says, that is the goal of training."

CHAPTER 21

APPLYING CHARACTERISTICS OF A PLAYGROUND TO YOUTH SOCCER

JONATHAN HENDERSON

Jonathan Henderson is the academy manager at Bristol Rovers FC. Jonny holds a MSc in coaching science as well as a BSc honors in sports coaching. He also holds both a UEFA A license and the FA Youth Award.

A performance playground — What a skate park can teach us about how kids learn — Random practice versus blocked practice — How to get your kids to play more street soccer — What would kids do if a coach wasn't there — We are doing our kids a disservice

There are very few people that can say they grew up wanting to be a coach. All of us that love the game of soccer either fell in love with the game as a player or a fan first, but never a coach. Jonathan—or Jonny—Henderson didn't need to worry about a plan B. Jonny finished his first coaching badge at the age of 16 and hasn't looked back. Jonny originally wanted to be a physical education teacher that dabbled in soccer. Although he is employed now as a full-time soccer coach, his teaching background has unquestionably influenced the way he coaches.

As a former professional player, my coaching style in the early stages of my coaching career was very coach centered. I didn't really know how I did what I did as a player, so I often resorted to just telling players what to do. Most former players that become coaches start out that way. We coach the way that we were coached. It is only through educating ourselves on various aspects of the game that some of these players-turned-coaches eventually grow out of the coach-centered approach.

Even though Jonny didn't have a very extensive playing career, his early coach education led him down a very pragmatic way of coaching in his early career. "You sort of start out teaching how you were taught. I learned how to coach in coach-education courses, so I coached that way. I was indoctrinated into the idea that the way I was being taught was the right—and only—way to do it." Fortunately for Jonny, one of his first roles tasked him with leading sports development for schools looking at after-school programs. It was during the formation of these after-school programs that Jonny began to research topics such as free play and motor learning, which had a profound influence on his coaching methodology.

THE PLAYERS ARE THE CURRICULUM

Jonny's early roles in sport development led to his focus and attention on the individual athlete. Dan Micciche, the academy manager at MK Dons, came up with the motto, "The players are the curriculum," which is something that Jonny has applied to his own methodology. "The biggest thing that Dan talks about is the needs of the individual. How do you develop the individual within the team context? It's not a one-size-fits-all model; it's about recognizing what an individual needs at any given moment." Like Michael Beale of the Liverpool U23s, youth development for Jonny is all about the individuals. Even though his philosophy focuses on the individual players within his academy, it is the creative training sessions, and the structures around that philosophy, which make Jonny one of the most successful academy managers in England.

THE PERFORMANCE PLAYGROUND

Jonny took influence from extreme sports in the development of what he calls "the performance playground." The idea is to identify the characteristics of a playground, and determine how those characteristics apply to youth soccer. Daniel Coyle, author of *The Talent Code,* believes that skateboard parks and playgrounds are the perfect example of an environment that motivates people, helps them grow, and helps them improve. "Kids love going to the skate park because they have vivid models of what they want to become. They want to be able to do *that* trick or become *that* guy. In addition, you have a built-in model of repetition and failure. Kids can try a trick, crash, and try again." Kids also have built-in feedback loops. Internally, they can try and determine what is working, what isn't working, and tinker with a trick until they get it right. Externally, they may have older kids at the park giving them tips and advice on things to improve. Also, they have people that can model for them (i.e., kids at the park that can model the successful execution of a trick). Coyle sums up the skate-park environment perfectly, "You are struggling on your own in a tough environment, but you are surrounded by people you want to be."

Jonny looked to the skateboard park and playground environments when creating his ideal soccer performance playground. "We developed a methodology that is very play based and child centered, and it turned out that kids were much more engaged when we gave them a bit of an opportunity to have a say in what was going on. It was totally the opposite of traditional coaching where kids were told what they were going to do and how to do it, but with almost no engagement."

Jonny created a mixed-age-groups league that consists of players from their under 13s and under 16s. Once a week, players from those age groups get together, they are put into teams that mix the players across all age groups, and they play. "It avoids the traditional idea that 13s play with 13s and 14s play with 14s; it's got that real peer-to-peer leadership stuff, older and younger kids mixing together. The challenges that brings are tremendous." The mixed-age-groups league allows the older players to learn to lead. One of my favorite quotes of all time about training soccer players comes from Jorge Valdano: "If we are only building obedient players, then we cannot criticize that we are lacking leaders." The mixed-age-groups league allows the older players to lead their peers and experience what it means to be a leader. This is very similar to how Thailand approaches youth volleyball. John Kessel will have more on that in his chapter, but the essence is kids coaching kids.

Another positive of the mixed-age-groups league is that it presents models to the younger players. A 13-year-old will now be able to play with, compete against, and watch a 16-year-old that they want to be like at the club. That 16-year-old may be able to do a skill that they can't, which will create an intrinsic motivation in the younger player to want to improve and be like the older player.

Bristol Rovers FC have also started a once-a-week program where the players show up in the parking lot of the stadium, the coaches supply the gear, and the players organize themselves into teams to play street soccer. "It was a way for us to include things that people my age maybe took for granted. When I was growing up, we would play soccer in the streets all the time, but the kids we coach maybe don't have an opportunity to do that as much, so this is our attempt to give them that opportunity. Our job is to try and create those necessary things that still might be missing from their environment."

Jonny earned his Master's degree in coaching science, but with an emphasis on the study of free-play environments. "I basically tried to answer the question of what did kids do when they were left to their own devices in playground settings. What we found were characteristics that made up a great training environment for soccer."

Performance playgrounds are:

- Chaotic—Free play in playground settings is chaotic. However, chaotic environments promote decision-making and problem-solving skills that are essential to developing soccer players. Chaotic environments also result in a variety of returns. Just like the kid crashing at the skate park on one attempt but nailing a trick on another, a chaotic soccer environment allows for kids to experience different returns while playing soccer.
- Structured—Chaotic environments also provide structure. Contrary to many people's interpretations of chaotic environments, there are always rules of the game that provide a framework. For example, the skate park may have a rule against multiple people using the half pipe at the same time.
- Engaging and fun—Just like the skateboard park creates the perfect environment for motivation, so too does a playground environment adapted for soccer. In child-led settings, the players are intrinsically motivated, which leads to a higher level of effort and commitment.
- Led by the players—This is another way of saying that the children have a say in how their training is delivered and progressed. The child-led approach gives opportunities for ownership and social development that are often neglected in youth development.
- Competitive—Finally, the performance playground allows players to experience both success and failure.

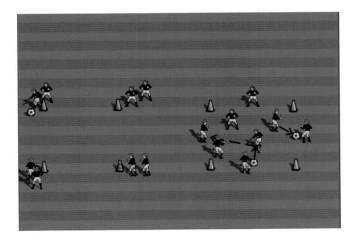

Here is an example of two different approaches to a passing warm-up. On the left is a simple box-passing exercise. The players make the same vertical pass to the player in front of them and then follow their pass around the square. "It is unopposed and the kids will get success, but it lacks real-world decision making." The exercise on the right can be done with the same number of players, in the same-sized area, but in the essence of a performance playground. There are now four players on the inside and four on the outside. The only rule is that players must receive on the inside and play to the outside. "Players are still unopposed, and receive a lot of technical repetition and movement. With the four players on the inside running around, we have created chaos and interference, which will create decision making and problem solving." Coaches that use exercises like the first one will argue that the players will get more passing repetition and so it is better. However, Jonny says that is a myth. "With the box-passing exercise, the players may get 100 repetitions in a short period of time, but it's the same experience 100 times in a row. They are making 100 of the same passes that may never happen in the actual game. The more chaotic version will allow for variability between passing experiences which creates randomness and decision making more like the game."

A common argument from youth coaches is that players in Europe or South America have better technique than players in the US, Canada, and England. This argument has convinced coaches that we need to put an emphasis on technical repetition in training. However, Jonny thinks that is one of the biggest mistakes a youth coach can make. "I don't think players in other countries are better than us technically at all. I think they have better decision making." This is something that both Rene Meulensteen and Todd Bean emphasize in this book. The problem around the world isn't technique, it is decision making.

If you wanted to create even more chaos in the second exercise, you could put the players into two teams.

Here you see the same passing exercise, but now only red can pass to red and blue can pass to blue. Again, there isn't a book of drills or activities that you can copy from Jonny to build a performance playground. The key lies in understanding what makes a playground successful in producing attention, motivation, and growth in children, and then applying that to youth soccer. Any coach can develop exercises like this; it just takes a little bit of thinking and an intention to create exercises that are chaotic, structured, fun, competitive, and child led. "I think coaches can still have learning outcomes. You can still say you want to have players learn to pass and receive. But in the more static and traditional exercise that is all you get. With a more chaotic exercise we get movement off the ball; we get agility, balance, and coordination because they aren't running in straight lines; we get problem solving because they have to figure out where to move to become a passing option; we get awareness of where your teammates and opponents are; and, of course, we get decision making. For me, you will get more returns out of a performance playground than your traditional drills."

The training methodology to create this performance playground is unique in its adaptation of the playground environment to soccer. "We have a game-based approach to training that is random and variable. It always looks something like the game." Random practice

is a research-backed approach to improving motor learning and retention of a skill in athletes. Traditional blocked training forces players into performing a particular skill over and over with repetition being the key. However, research has shown that blocked practice doesn't lead to as much improvement or retention as random practice. Random practice is when an athlete is put in a situation that tasks them with working through various skills throughout a single session that are presented in a random fashion. This forces the athlete's cognitive system to adapt, rethink, and problem solve in choosing the best motor pattern to achieve the execution of the task. John Kessel's chapter includes more specific examples of random training versus blocked training, so don't worry if you don't quite understand the difference yet.

Unfortunately, coaches still use blocked practices because they result in better performance during practice. Random practice, however, results in poor performance during practice, but improved performance during competition. Robert A. Bjork, PhD and co-author of a famous 2001 study on random practice, explains the reason why we still use blocked practices. "It's natural to think that when we're making progress, we're learning, and when we're struggling and making errors, we're not learning as well." In other words, blocked training makes practice look good, which tricks us into thinking our athletes are getting better. Random training makes our practices look chaotic and bad, and sometimes that can look like our players aren't getting better, but research has shown that they most certainly are.

Jonny has created a checklist for coaches to be able to determine if they are creating a performance playground for their players to enjoy and grow as players and children.

Playground activities should have the following things.

- Activities should create interference and make use of variable and random practice.
- Activities should reflect the modern game. "I see a lot of shooting drills where the players play the coach and he lays the ball off for players to shoot. But statistics show that 85% of goals occur inside the penalty area on one or two touches. So, does our training environment replicate that?" Activities

should replicate the skills required in the actual game so that the skills they are learning transfer into the game. We need to remember that when our kids go and play at the playground, all they do is play the game. They don't do kickball drills, they just play kickball. "They only learn the skills in the game so we have to make sure that our training replicates the game."

- Activities should be designed with the skillset of the players in mind. "We need to teach appropriate skillsets. If I have a group of 7- and 8-year-olds, I'm not going to put them in a 6v4 rondo where there is massive pressure, massive decision making, and massive opportunity for it to break down because they won't actually learn from it. Instead, I might make it unopposed, but with some interference like the passing exercise described earlier. That way they still get the decision making inside a chaotic environment, but one that is suitable for them."

- Activities should always involve all the players. Anything that includes a line should be thrown away and never used again. Some coaches may only have their kids for 90 minutes twice a week, if they are lucky. The time spent in training needs to be deliberate and the players should always be involved.

The biggest mistake coaches make in their interpretation of a game-based approach is that the game is the only teacher. It is a common expression ("Let the game be the teacher" or "The game is the best teacher"), but Jonny believes that if that is a coach's only answer to youth development, then they are doing it wrong. "If that's the only thing you use, then you are doing it wrong because your job as a coach is to provide guidance and support. You are the more knowledgeable person in the relationship between player and coach. You can have the environment set up perfectly, but if Joey doesn't know how to receive on his back foot, and he has been doing it wrong for half an hour, the coach is mistaken if he thinks Joey is going to figure it out on his own. However, our job isn't to just tell him how to do it; it's to prompt the discussion and use guided discovery, question and answer, or whatever method you want to use to help him understand how he can solve the problem. What's going wrong there, Joe? What could you have done differently? What might you try next time?"

The performance playground is about creating the best possible learning environment in a soccer context. Jonny figured out that we don't need to look very far to determine the best environment for kids to learn because it already exists. It is the playgrounds and the skate parks. But, that doesn't relegate the coach to a silent bystander. The coach needs to provide guidance and support to help kids solve problems within the game. "If a kid can't get it within the game, chances are the game isn't going to help him figure it out just by doing it wrong over and over." That doesn't mean we change the environment and use isolated passing and receiving drills because the game-based environment is correct; the thing that needs to improve is the guidance and support provided by the coach. "I like the idea of trial and error, but eventually trial and error needs to become trial and success. If the player leaves the session and it's still trial and error, then he isn't learning anything from it. Our role as coaches is to provide guidance and support within the practices to help players find the answers to different problems."

The coach has additional duties as well. Guidance and support is great when the player is having problems, but what happens if Joey receives on his back foot perfectly ten times in a row in the first 30 seconds of the practice? What does the coach do now? "Some coaches may say, 'That's good, he has nailed that, but the game will teach him something else.' But is that true? The coach may have to challenge the player to do something else and prompt his thinking to solve different problems, or the same problem in a different way."

The role of the coach goes beyond guidance and support into understanding how to challenge players to extend themselves even further. However, by far the most important role of a coach is to provide an engaging learning environment similar to the performance playground. "If we don't promote an environment where the kids want to come to train, to learn and develop, and to give their best, then we are doing it wrong, and we are doing them a disservice."

Jonny wants coaches to embrace the chaos of the playground. Practice may look ugly and chaotic, but random-practice research has shown us that practicing to look good in practice is not in the best interest of the player's actual development. Coaches should never have their practices too dissimilar from what happens in the game. If you can do something in a modified game environment, then do it. "You want to stimulate all the aspects of the environment that would be created if the players were left to their own devices. If you throw a ball into a playground, what happens? Within 30 seconds a game breaks out and the players have made the teams. Perhaps then, we have become too fixated on the coach being in control and looking smart, rather than the players learning and getting better." Creating a playground means thinking what would the kids do if you weren't there. They would just play the game. You are there to provide guidance, support, and challenges, but still maintain the child-led environment. "Give the players opportunities to challenge themselves, to come up with the rules; ask them what they would like to do in training, and come up with something based on their needs and desires. Then, as the coach, your job is to just be there to support them throughout it."

CHAPTER 22

SOCCER TACTICS AND TRAINING METHODOLOGY

ALBERT RUDE

Albert Rude is the first-team assistant coach at CF Pachuca in Liga MX. Albert is one of the co-founders of the MBP coaching methodology that offers a four-month immersive course in Barcelona called the Master of High-Performance Football. In Albert's first year, CF Pachuca finished second in La Clausura 2016 after finishing in seventh place in 2015. In 2017, CF Pachuca has advanced to the CONCACAF Champions League Final against Tigres.

The nine soccer structures — The importance of culture in building a game model — To understand the future, we must understand the past — Win one game, get two more — If you want big rewards, they come with big risks

The story of how Albert Rude ended up as the first-team assistant coach at CF Pachuca is of cinematic proportions. Honestly, if you have seen the movie *Hidden Figures*, the story of how three African-American women played integral roles in helping the US land on the moon during the 1960s, you would be hard pressed not to mistake the story line for Albert's soccer coaching journey. In the movie, NASA mathematician Katherine Johnson, played by Taraji P. Henson, takes her chances at an unsolvable math problem to determine the landing coordinates for a space launch. As Katherine begins moving the chalk at lightning speed, a crowd gathers on the NASA floor to watch. The chalk, nearly gone at this point, finally is placed on the table and silence ensues. The problem that was considered unsolvable by some of the world's brightest and most intelligent mathematicians (all of whom were white men) was solved by an African-American woman in less than ten minutes.

Albert Rude was visiting CF Pachuca to talk to some of their academy coaches about his coaching methodology called the MBP method. While being given a tour of the facility, Albert wandered into the film room where a very intense figure sat, eyes fixated on the video screen, watching a clip of a goal Pachuca conceded the week before. The intense figure cursed out loud as he watched the clip again, clearly astounded by his players' inabilities to deal with the situation. As the tour guides rushed to move Albert from the room, Albert said, "You see the problem, don't you? The center back stepped to the attacking midfielder and the striker was waiting for him to do that. Once the center back stepped, he ran into the space that he left and the player on the ball made the easy pass. The center back should have never stepped in that situation." The intense figure stared at the screen watching the goal play over and over again. Albert left the room with the tour guides who were aghast with disbelief. "I can't believe you just said that. Do you know who that was, Albert?" Albert replied calmly, "The video analyst?" "No, that was Diego Alonso, the manager of Pachuca." Less than a week later Albert was employed as Diego Alonso's assistant.

MBP METHODOLOGY

Albert is a very young coach at just 32 years old, but one of the brightest young minds in global soccer. At the age of 22, Albert was fully engrossed in soccer theory and the study of soccer tactics and training methodology. He noticed that most training methods and tactics employed by coaches around him were based on flawed thinking, subjectivity, and a lack of methodology. Albert realized that the world of soccer desperately needed people that could supply coaches with objective ways of analyzing the game. This realization led Albert to the development of the MBP methodology, which stands for *making better players*. A few years ago, Albert met Jaime Vidalp who runs the business behind Albert's brilliant methodology. Currently, MBP has a variety of programs aimed at teaching coaches the fundamentals of the game in very challenging environments. Their most advanced course is the Master of High-Performance Football that requires students to relocate to Barcelona for four months and undergo 350 hours of intense coach education.

Albert developed this methodology during his early coaching career. Albert was fortunate enough to spend time learning from coaches at FC Barcelona, Fiorentina, and Paris St.

Germain. "I was very lucky to learn a lot of things from them, so at the age of 21, I began to work as the director of soccer coaching at one of the best soccer universities in Spain, where I began to teach my methodology." The opportunity at the university allowed Albert to link the practical field work he learned from coaches at Barcelona, Fiorentina, and PSG with the academic research he was doing in the field of soccer theory. "I was able to make connections between a lot of practical information that I saw coaches at the highest levels use, and combine it with the theory and research behind those methods. From there, I began to actually organize that knowledge into digestible information that I could teach to other coaches."

Albert's methodology is built on the objective truth that soccer is a complex system. Vitor Frade and Paco Seirulo pioneered this idea, which has influenced the best coaches in modern soccer: Guardiola, Mourinho, Klopp, Conte, and so on. "Soccer is complexity and uncertainty. We play on a pitch that is 7,000 square meters of space—which is a lot of space—and then in that space there are 22 players moving around. In addition, the rules are not very restrictive, and the players are playing with their feet. The game is extremely complex so we need to consider how these components interact and form relationships, which is the foundation of my methodology." Albert's time as a researcher allowed him to really analyze the complexity of soccer from an academic perspective. Without a team to manage and coach, Albert spent a lot of his time analyzing and theorizing on the complexity of what is sometimes considered a simple game.

THE NINE SOCCER STRUCTURES

One of the academic developments that Albert created were the nine soccer structures. "If you look at the game from an ontological perspective, you find that there are nine soccer structures."

1. Meta-game—These are all of the things that are surrounding the game but not happening on the field. "An example of meta-game is if the main sponsor of the club plans to pull their sponsorship and leave the club, if the team were to lose today's game. This may not have to do with 11v11, but it is affecting the game and it is affecting the players and the coach, and, of course, if it is affecting those things, then it is affecting the soccer being played."
2. The game—This is the actual game, the 11v11 on the field.
3. The team—Inside of a game there are two teams, each with their own playing styles, management styles, and player abilities.
4. Constellations—These are the parts of the team. If you refer to Nick Cowell's chapter on tactical periodization, you will recall the concepts of collective,

sectorial, inter-sectorial, and group dynamics. Constellations may be the lines of a team (e.g., the midfield line).

5. The players—This refers to the individual players.
6. The coach—The coach is perhaps the most important structure, as he is responsible for managing all eight other structures simultaneously.
7. Infra-team—This is all of the emotional things that are linked to the team. Examples might be the position of the team in the league table, or the result of the last game.
8. Infra-player—This is all of the emotional things that are linked to the player (e.g., the player's status within the team, whether they are a starter or a reserve player, or a personal issue away from the game).
9. Infra-coach—This includes all of the emotional things that are linked to the coach (e.g., contract negotiations between the coach and the club).

The nine structures of soccer are extremely important in theory, but, especially for coaches, they are also extremely important to understand. "The structures are each linked to one another. That means that a change in one structure will impact and change the other structures. The reason is that the complexity of soccer and these structures are totally linked. An emotional problem in the infra-player will affect the player—but the player affects the constellation, the constellation affects the team, the team affects the game, the game affects the meta-game, the meta-game affects the infra-team, the infra-team affects the infra-coach, and the infra-coach will affect the coach. Therefore, everybody is going to be affected if one of the structures has some change." A coach needs to constantly be aware of these changes.

The role of the coach is to manage all nine of these structures of the game. Although the structures are logical that doesn't mean they are easy to manage. In fact, Marti Perarnau, in his book *Pep Guardiola: The Evolution*, explains that being an excellent coach isn't really about knowledge of the game. "People tend to assume that elite coaches are the experts in all things soccer, but you'll find coaches at all levels within the game with just as much understanding and knowledge. What sets top coaches apart is their ability to work under intense pressure, manage world-class soccer players, and hold their own against other first-rate competitors." In other words, Marti believes that the top coaches manage the nine soccer structures better than others.

Albert believes that the infra-team, infra-player, and infra-coach structures are the most difficult to develop and manage. The infra-coach is difficult to manage, but because the coach has complete control of his emotions—or should, at least—that one is the most manageable. The infra-team and infra-player, however, are the two most difficult structures to manage in the game of soccer. "It is so, so difficult because you cannot see these emotional things. You have to start a process in order to understand and know the emotional things linked to the players and the team." Because these are the most difficult structures to manage, they are also responsible for the biggest coaching mistakes. "We make a lot of mistakes that are not good for us, the team, or the player, and they often have a direct effect on the performance of the team."

One of the biggest mistakes a coach can make when it comes to managing the soccer structures is to not manage them or pay them any attention. "A lot of coaches may say, 'Well, I have a great game model, so, you know, I'm all set,' but that is a huge mistake. If you have a great game model but you are not connected emotionally with your players and the team, they are not going to buy your project. They are not going to say, 'Okay, that is what you want and we want the same. We are on the same page and we are going to fight for that. So if you are not connected in that way with your players and team, then you will not be successful." Managing the soccer structures is an ongoing, neverending process. The coach must constantly be aware of the soccer structures and the existence of any changes within them.

ON THE SHOULDERS OF GIANTS

Albert believes that modern coaches are successful due to the iterations and ideas created by the coaches through the early history of the game. Young coaches like to take credit for novelty or creativity, but a lot of the modern tactical ideas, systems, and formations have come from the past. A friend of mine likes to say, "There is nothing new under the sun." In fact, if you want to learn how to innovate as a coach, the answer—or at least part of the answer—exists in the past.

Coaches like Pep Guardiola, Jose Mourinho, and Jurgen Klopp are all using methods, tactics, and playing styles that were used 25-50 years ago. "A lot of these aspects that people say define modern soccer were created in the old soccer. Johan Cruyff, Arrigo Sacchi, Rinus Michels—these are all coaches that many would say fail to define the cutting edge, but of course they are on the cutting edge! Of course. A lot of the things that coaches are doing currently—like formations and various structures, tactical fundamentals for the players, ways of building the game, ways of defending in the low block, the mid-block, the high pressure—were invented a long time ago. So a lot of modern coaches are having success because of those strategies. We have to respect the things that the old coaches did for our sport."

A perfect example of this is Pep Guardiola's use of the classic W-M formation with Bayern Munich in 2014. Although Pep is credited with a lot of novelty in modern soccer, many of his ideas and concepts are minor adjustments to formations and systems used as far back as the 1930s.

Here is Guardiola's use of the W-M with his 2014 Bayern Munich team. The W-M formation was actually developed by Herbert Chapman while managing Arsenal in the 1920s and 1930s.

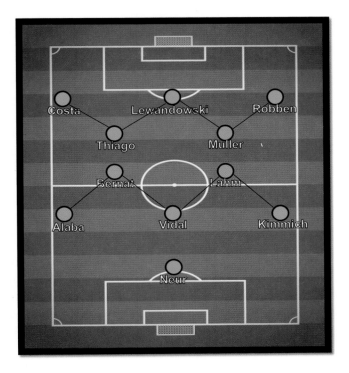

Here we can compare Guardiola's use of the W-M to the original W-M developed by Herbert Chapman.

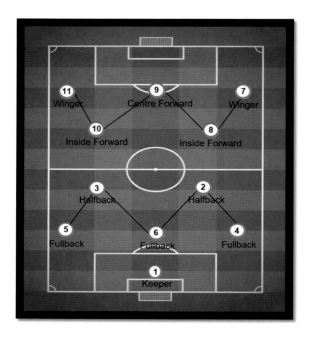

GAME MODEL

Nick Cowell explained the concept of a game model in his chapter on tactical periodization, but the game model is central to Albert's methodology as well. "The game model is the way you structure and organize your team. It is the way that you approach and manage the fundamentals (i.e., individual, line, and team). Finally, it is the way that you manage or account for the quality of your players." However, perhaps most important to the creation of any game model is the game idea of the coach. A coach needs to know how he wants his team to play soccer. "What are your ideas about soccer? What is your philosophy? How do you understand soccer and why?"

Once a coach has established his game idea, he can then start to dissect the abilities of his players. This will help the coach determine if his current players are suitable for his preferred game style. Based on the evaluation of his players' abilities, a coach may adjust his game model to accommodate the abilities of his current players. However, the opposite can happen too. A coach may have a preferred game model, but the ability of his players could allow him to accomplish more in a certain phase of the game. For example, if your team purchased Lionel Messi tomorrow, your game model would most likely change to account for Messi's unique capability.

Perhaps the most important thing to consider is the culture of the country in which you coach. Many would argue that Pep Guardiola neglected this aspect of his game model during the 2016-2017 English Premier League season, his first season in charge at Manchester City. Although there is nothing wrong with applying his possession-based philosophy, many wondered how much attention was paid to his team's defensive approach to a very direct style of play. For example, Guardiola's teams like to apply high pressure, but if the opponent is happy to go long—and organized to go long—a high-pressure system may not make sense. "There are certain philosophies in certain countries that you need to take into consideration. For example, if you are playing in Germany, you would be entering a country that has a lot of counter-attacking. So, if you are playing with just two defenders in your build-up, then you may have problems defending the counter-attack." This step in building the game model cannot be overlooked. For example, if you neglect the possession-based style of Spanish soccer, and your team is always losing possession, then your team will never truly be in balance. "In the UK, there are a lot of long balls, so if your team is not equipped or prepared to handle these long balls, then you are going to have trouble in a lot of games. All of these things are vital to understand and manage in order to create a great game model."

OPPONENT SCOUTING

Pep Guardiola revealed in Marti Perarnau's 2014 book, *Pep Confidential*, that his true key to success lies in understanding his opponent. Although renowned for his tactical adjustments and strategies, Pep doesn't come up with those adjustments on a whim. In fact, Pep watches anywhere from 10 to 15 of his opponents' matches in order to come up with the tactical adjustments necessary to defeat them. One of the common debates coaches have when it comes to opponent scouting is the amount of alterations a team should make due to the playing style of their opponent. The first step in opponent scouting for Albert at Pachuca is to analyze the patterns of his opponent. "What we are trying to scout and analyze are the patterns. Patterns in the different phases and moments in the game. For example, what are the patterns when they are in the starting game zone? What are the patterns when they are in the building game zone? What are the patterns when they are in the finishing game zone?"

It is important to mention that Albert's methodology splits the field into three zones. The three zones are the starting-game zone, the building-game zone, and the finishing-game zone. The starting-game zone is where most teams begin their attack, typically exemplified by a team building from the back. The building-game zone takes place in the middle third of the field, where the team with the ball begins to orchestrate how they are going to finish their attack. The finishing-game zone is obviously the zone where they hope to finish their attack with a goal.

Albert uses these zones to analyze the patterns and behaviors of the opponent in each zone. For example, how do they typically organize themselves to start the game? Perhaps the center backs split wide of the 18, the outside backs push very high up the pitch, and the holding midfielder comes between the center backs to start the attack. This information would help Albert orchestrate his team's high press.

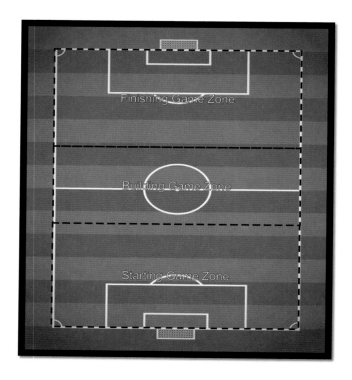

Defensively, Albert looks at how the team organizes themselves in each zone as well; however, when a team is defending, the organization of the zones changes. For example, the way you would defend a team in their starting-game zone could be considered a high press. In the building-game zone, it would be called a middle block, and in the finishing-game zone, it would be called a low block. "What are the patterns that we can analyze when they are defending in high pressing, in middle block, or in low block?"

At this point, Albert has dissected the attacking organization and defensive organization of his opponent in the three zones of the field. The next step in the scouting of an opponent is to analyze the patterns of an opponent's attacking and defending transitions. "All of these patterns are giving us some important information that is very useful for us in order to adapt our game model for that specific team in that specific game." It is at this point that Albert makes an important stance. It is important to adapt your game model to the opponent, but the identity of your team should remain unaltered. "We are not going to eliminate our essence as a team in order to play that game. It is most certainly not like that. We are going to keep our essence while adapting that essence to the things we learned in analyzing the opponent." Imagine a team that starts the game using both center backs and the holding midfielder to build up. That team is playing an opponent that only presses with one striker. So the team building up no longer needs three players to start the game, they only need two. Therefore, the team is not going to change their essence as a team that likes to build from the back, but they will change how they accomplish that by building with two players instead of three. "We are going to adapt our essence and our game model in that phase, in that moment, in order to have more success in correctly starting the game when the other team is going to press with one striker."

Albert also creates what he calls a game map for each opponent. "The game map helps us understand and know what we want to happen during the game. All the players must know these things." The game map also prepares the players for the uncertainty that defines the game of soccer. For example, the coach might anticipate the opponent pressing with one striker, but maybe they begin the match pressing with two strikers. The game map, which influences the training preparation, creates scripts to handle any situations that occur. Pep Guardiola is famous for his game maps.

Against Borussia Dortmund in 2015, Pep prepared Bayern Munich for three different possibilities in their organization for the game. Depending on how Borussia's manager, Thomas Tuchel, planned to set up his team would determine the response from Guardiola and his men. Dortmund came out in a 1-3-6-1 and every single player on Bayern knew what that meant: long balls down the outside. They had prepared endlessly for a situation where Dortmund loads the midfield to stop Bayern from playing centrally, but Pep had already coached his players to know how to exploit the areas left unmanned by Dortmund's organization (i.e., the wide areas where the fullbacks usually are). Bayern won the match 5-1. It is important that a game map prepare the players for a multitude of possibilities from the opponent. Of course, it is important to remember that the opposition is also scouting you and your team. Although they usually press with one striker, they may press with two or even three because of how your team typically starts the game. "The game map has built-in strategies to account for any possible changes. This way, we know that if there are any changes, we can adapt our style of play."

A successful game map does not only include tactical adjustments, but also emotional ones. What happens if your team goes up a goal? How about down a goal? How about down two goals? Albert's game maps have strategies and detailed explanations to account for his team's response to any goal scored.

TRAINING METHODOLOGY

Albert's training methodology is not easily identified by a specific model. In fact, he would say that his ideal training organization is a mix of a variety of different models. "For me, it's a mix of different training strategies. I believe that it should be 60% tactical periodization. The reason why we can't use 100% tactical periodization is because of the mental burnout it can cause." If you recall the chapter on tactical periodization, Albert is referring to the mental intensity that defines tactical periodization. In other words, the tactical concentration of each training session can produce a phenomenon called tactical fatigue where the players can no longer sustain the level of concentration required to execute the correct actions. I like to compare it to study fatigue and study breaks. I am sure everyone can remember an instance where you were studying for so long that you began to forget things you understood a few hours before. That is when you know it is time to take a break.

Although tactical periodization accounts for tactical fatigue by including variation in the daily intensity of concentration, Albert likes to think of it as using tactical periodization only 60% of the time. "It is very difficult to sustain that kind of training for a long time. The specificity of that kind of training is very difficult to manage for the player and the player can feel the mental effect called burnout."

At Pachuca, Albert and his staff use tactical periodization 60% of the time and what he calls integrated training 30% of the time. "Integrated training allows you to train very important things related to the game. You cannot train the principles of organization or structures of the phases and moments of the game, but you can introduce some very important things." An example of integrated training is small-sided games without game-model specificity. These are training drills that don't relate to the game model but instead focus on things like speed of play, shooting, passing and receiving, dribbling, and other skills and behaviors necessary to play soccer.

The remaining 10% of Albert's training organization is what he calls analytical training. "There are some things that we can only address with the individual. We need to optimize certain things for each player individually. So the 10% of analytical training is used to complete the profile of the player." Analytical training is mainly characterized by individual video sessions, but can also be completed on the field during 1v1 or small-group training sessions aimed at individual soccer actions. Marcelo Bielsa is famous for this type of training. An example of analytical training could be a right-sided center back working on line-breaking passes after receiving from the goalkeeper. Analytical training would put intense focus on that specific action and everything that precedes it, such as the center back dropping with an open body shape to create space. An intense focus would also be put on the action itself such as the first touch to prepare for a line-breaking pass, scanning the field to look for a vertical option, as well as the speed, weight, and direction of the pass. Finally, analytical training would also focus on the behaviors following that action like moving forward to provide support to the advanced player following the pass.

Albert looks at everything coaches and players do in training as investments. "I look at it that way because you don't know which things are going to be the details that can help you win. Some things you might not think are very important, but then it may end up deciding who wins and who loses, so you cannot neglect the importance of the training process." The details of the game are so important. Coaches need to make sure that they are investing the training time in things that could actually take place in the match, even if they aren't sure they will occur. For example, you may not want to spend five minutes going over defending set pieces from wide areas, but if the opponent earns a set piece in that area, it could be the difference between winning or losing. Look at everything you do in training as an investment, but make sure you are investing in the truly important and valuable things.

THE PRESSURES OF LIGA MX

It is no secret that managing in the top flight of professional soccer is characterized by intense pressure. If you look at the structures of the game, the meta-game has a massive influence on the other structures in professional soccer. The owners, sponsors, fans, and journalist can all affect the infra-player, infra-coach, and infra-team in negative and positive ways. Albert has been given some great advice from Diego Alonso regarding the pressures of professional soccer management: "It is said that in the highest level of soccer, if you win one game, you have two more games. If you lose those two games—in other words, you lose two in a row—then you have one more game. If you win that game, then you have two more. But if you lose that game—losing three in a row—then you can be fired."

Albert joined CF Pachuca last year and, unbeknownst to him, the team had lost two games in a row. A couple of days into his new job, his fellow staff members informed him of the win-one-get-two rule. "I thought to myself, 'Wow, I just moved from Barcelona and I may only be staying in Mexico for a few weeks!' I had left my job at the university and the comfort of home, and I was afraid I would already be on my way back to Barcelona." During Albert's first game with Pachuca, the team tied Tijuana. Albert wasn't explained the meaning of a tie by the staff, just wins and losses. "What does a tie mean? Are we getting fired?" The staff informed him that a tie meant that everything carries over and the next game is still a must win. Luckily, Pachuca won the next two games, including a massive victory over Club America at Estadio Azteca. "The thing that I have taken away from the pressure is that you have to be very sure about what you want from life because it is so risky. But if you want to challenge yourself and try to reach the highest level that you can as a coach, then it is part of the job." Albert likes to say that with high risk comes high reward. "Of course, you are risking a lot, but if the risk pays off, the rewards can be huge. Many coaches will say, 'No way! I am not taking that kind of risk' and that is perfectly fine, but then you won't have the big rewards or moments that come with coaching at the highest levels." Albert's first season at Pachuca may have started off rocky, but Pachuca beat Monterrey in the Clausura championship to claim the sixth league title in club history. "You have to bet on yourself in the game of soccer. You have to trust that you have what it takes and that requires taking a risk. But if you believe in yourself, then anything is possible in the game of soccer for you."

Albert believes that the first thing coaches need to do before beginning their coaching journey is to find out what their biggest dream is. I am reminded of a quote by Holocaust survivor and psychologist Victor Frankl in his must-read book, *Man's Search for Meaning.* "The man that has a why can endure almost any how." Although coaching can be stressful and full of pressure, if you have a clear why, then nothing can stop you from achieving your dreams and purpose. Albert's dream is ambitious, but it is so very clear. "My dream is to win the Champions League as a first-team coach. I have had that goal clear in mind for many years. I used to want to win a Champions League as a part of the technical staff, but now I want more. I want the responsibility of a head coach and all of the decisions that come with that role. I think winning as a head coach has a different feeling than being an assistant coach. That is my biggest dream and I hope to achieve it someday." Albert and Pachuca won the 2017 CONCACAF Champions League trophy, but I don't think that was the Champions League Albert was talking about. He now has his eyes set on the biggest dream he has.

CHAPTER 23

IMPROVING PLAYER COMMUNICATION IN SOCCER

GERARD JONES

Gerard Jones is Head of Coaching at Bristol Rovers Football Club. He previously served as the director of coaching for Eastside FC, a club located in Michigan, USA. Gerard has an MSc in performance coaching from the University of Stirling. Prior to his role working in the US as a director of coaching, Gerard was an assistant coach for Bradford City AFC U21s. Gerard was also the first-team manager at Eccleshill United FC. Lastly, Gerard became a published author in 2016 with his first book on communication psychology in soccer called Let's Talk Soccer: Using Game Calls to Develop Communication and Decision Making in Football.

Game calls — The biggest communication mistakes that coaches make — We want the knowledge on the field, not the sideline — How to get your players to talk more than you

Gerard is the youngest coach referenced in this book, but don't mistake his age for a lack of experience. "I first started coaching at 15 years old. I knew I wasn't going to make it as a player, but I loved the game and I wanted to learn all that I could about it." Gerard has been steadily improving his coaching for the last 10 years. Even though Gerard is only in his mid-20s, he has already coached at clubs in the UK, Italy, US, Norway, and

New Zealand. In addition, he earned his UEFA A license and is a certified teacher with a Master's degree. And let's not forget that he has already contributed to the theory of soccer by becoming an author in 2016 with his book on soccer communication.

GAME CALLS

Prior to his role as the director of coaching at Eastside FC, Gerard worked as the U21s coach at Bradford City. It was during his time at Bradford City that Gerard realized the importance of clear communication in the game of soccer. Raymond Verheijen has theorized about the importance of a common soccer language. Raymond uses the Dutch-to-English metaphor as an example. During his courses, he will start speaking in Dutch to a room of blank stares to make the point that we often do that same thing in soccer. For example, the fitness coach may tell the soccer coach about aerobic this and anaerobic that, but he might as well be speaking Dutch. A common soccer language means that when we come together for training; we all speak the language of soccer, not physiology, psychology, or physics.

Gerard believes that we can apply this same metaphor to the way we communicate with our players. "It all comes down to your preparation. A lot of coaches don't take the time to plan their vocabulary." Gerard explains that some coaches may describe a particular moment or action in the game differently than the way another coach may describe that exact same moment. Two words with the same meaning is very confusing for the players.

Coaches need to share a common vocabulary within their teams—and even their clubs—so that the language used during a player's development is consistent. In order to accomplish this, Gerard takes the time to always plan out the language he will use with his team. "Let's say we are working on playing out from our goalkeeper. There will be certain words I use that are intended to influence the decision making of my players. I call these game calls."

Gerard believes that game calls give the players a better understanding of the game and the way they communicate with their teammates. "I work to give the players a common vocabulary so that they understand the definitions and what something looks like in a particular moment. The goal is to avoid the coach having to constantly shout from the sideline to communicate what he wants. By providing a common language within your team, the players can communicate effectively to one another." Gerard believes that the key lies in getting the players to communicate, not the coach, so that the players can take ownership over the game and their learning.

An example of a game call that Gerard created for his team is *start again*. For example, if his team is building out of the back, but they fail to create superiority behind the opposition line or fail in being able to play forward, he has taught his center backs to shout, "Start again!" This call signals the player on the ball to make the decision of playing back to the center backs to restart the build. In order to be most effective, game calls need to have context within the playing style of the team. For example, if your team is really direct, then start again doesn't really fit in the context of your playing style.

Introducing the game call with a tactical concept encourages the use of a common language, but it also requires players to make the correct decisions. In other words, the only way the center back will know to say start again is if he recognizes that the team has failed to create superiority or that there are no passing options forward. The game calls help give the players ownership over the game and influence their decision making in a positive way.

Another example of a game call that Gerard has created with his team is *play around*. If the opponent is very horizontally compact and it isn't possible to penetrate them, then players on the other side of the field may shout, "Play around!" This is a signal to the ball carrier and the other players to circulate the ball to the other side quickly in order to spread the opponent out horizontally, and penetrate around them on the other side.

The key to making a successful game call is to pair the game call with a specific tactical behavior you want from your players. The game calls play around and start again are paired with an actual decision and behavior that Gerard wants to see from his team. However, instead of Gerard joysticking the game from the sideline by shouting "Start again" every 30 seconds, he has given his team ownership over the game and the recognition of when to make certain decisions. Johan Cruyff put it best, "You don't want all the knowledge on the sideline with the coaches, it has no use there. The knowledge needs to lie with the players; they are the ones that make the crucial decisions."

Gerard Jones is good friends with the former Liverpool U23s coach, Michael Beale. Michael was hired as the assistant coach at Sao Paulo in 2017 and was at the IMG Academy in Florida for the team's pre-season. At the same time, Gerard was completing his USSF B license at the same location. Gerard, ever the keen observer, noticed that Michael was using game calls with his team during the session. "He uses game calls with his team at Sao Paulo but in Portuguese. I was watching their session on pressing and he was urging the players to communicate the phrase *espara,* which is to wait, and *vá,* which is to go. You could hear the players loudly shouting, 'Espara, espara, espara, agora vá! Va!' It is important to teach your players aspects of your game model and playing style, but game calls go the extra step in giving your players ownership over the game model. Without game calls, you will continually lose your voice as a coach because you haven't given your players the tools necessary to communicate effectively to one another. Communication is so important. In fact, I think it is normal—and even helpful in some cases—for coaches to communicate from the sideline. Unfortunately, we don't have the best view of the game during the match, our players do. There are many instances in a game where the player on the ball may not see the best options available. That is why coaches are constantly yelling. They are afraid the player on the ball is going to make the wrong decision. However, that is where game calls come in. Game calls encourage awareness, decision making, reading, and communication from the other ten players on the pitch. Instead of the center back passing the ball forward and thinking, 'There we go, my job is done,' he now has to constantly read the play and communicate to the players on the ball what options are available. I think that's the key: giving players an understanding. We are talking about one or two words, not overpowering them with information. You are giving them just enough to be able to take control of the wheel, so that the coach can sit back and observe, and assess the actual decisions being made without making the decisions for the players. Game calls can paint a picture in the mind straight away, and that's what I try to establish with my teams."

It is important that there is a give and take that exists in the establishment of the game calls. The game calls can't always be the words of the coach because the players are the ones that need to communicate on the pitch. "I really like start again because it paints a very nice picture, but you have to be able to adapt. In the US, for example, a lot of my players like the word *restart*. I'm not a huge fan of restart because it implies the ball having gone out of bounds, but if there is something the players understand better—and they are willing to use it—then you have to try and adapt it."

Gerard has had a number of players identify a game call with the name of a famous player. "I like to use the game call *holding space* when tasking players with staying in their position to be able to receive the ball. Instead of them running around the pitch, that game call encourages them to hold their position. But one of my players prefers the game call Messi. For him, this paints a clearer picture of what I want him to do. The best game call is going to be the one that paints the clearest picture in a player's head of what action or decision they should make. You are creating a vocabulary that is detailed to try and help the players."

Gerard will almost never provide a game call during an actual match. "As a coach, my view of the game is horizontal and often skewed, but the players see the game vertically. The players are also the ones in the moment. So I may think a player should play the ball around to the other side, but he might see an opportunity to penetrate. I really don't like to say anything at all because the players may have the right decision based on their perspective." However, sometimes the wrong game call is verbalized. But anytime that happens it is a learning moment for the players and the team. "There have been some instances where we have the ball inside the 18 and the center backs are shouting, 'Start again!' because they want to get on the ball, but I love moments like that! Those moments give us a chance to watch the video and ask them if they would make that same game call again given the situation. It provides another way for them to learn. But by letting them express themselves during the game, they gather information about when it is right to make that game call and when it is not. We want the players to be in control of the decision making, not the coach."

One of the biggest communication mistakes that coaches make is forcing decisions upon players. For example, it is not uncommon to hear a coach shout, "Play it to Joe! Play it to Joe!" right after his team has won a set piece. In this situation, the coach might see that Joe is open, but by the time the player taking the set piece hears the information, processes it, sends the neurons to his muscles, and plays it to Joe, the opponent has moved into position to intercept the pass and they score a goal. "I feel that is one of the biggest mistakes coaches make. Whereas if we just let the player make the decision we can still coach them and influence them, but not in the moment." Maybe we educate the player during a film session about that same situation, or if we still want to influence them during the match, we could wait for a stoppage in play and say, "Hey Nick, did you recognize that you could have played Joe quickly?" Regardless of the method, forcing decisions on players almost never ends well.

An even bigger problem at the youth level is the parental influence on decision making. How common is this scenario: a player has received a through ball behind the opponent and is on a breakaway. As soon as the player receives the ball, you can hear parents from the sideline shouting, "Shoot it! Shoot it!" "You are telling the player what to do and you are also putting him under a lot of pressure. When you think about that moment in the game, the player needs to be clear. There can't be a lot going on upstairs, but how often do coaches and parents think about the influence their communication has on the players?" Parents and coaches may put the player under a lot of pressure by shouting, "Shoot!," but that's not even the primary issue. The primary issue is the fact that the parents and coaches aren't empowering the players when they choose to yell those things. For example, a lot of today's players—Messi being a prime example—are very patient on a breakaway. They may be waiting for the goalkeeper to move, or maybe they plan to dribble around the goalkeeper. But parents and coaches shouting out the decision they want to see takes away the power of the player to be the decision maker. That is as anti-development as it gets.

Gerard isn't saying that coaches need to become Zen mutes that must relegate themselves to no communication at all on game day. That is going from one extreme to the other. "It's about recognizing the moments to communicate. Guardiola is actually one of the best in the world at this. He may wait for the ball to be played deep into the far right corner before asking the left back to come see him for a quick message. Other times for coaches to communicate are when the ball is out of play for a corner or a throw-in. It's not that we *can't* communicate, it's that we need to know *when* to communicate. But I will say that communicating during the game to the player on the ball is disempowering the decision making of your players."

Another communication mistake that coaches make is the length of their communication. If we refer back to the image of Guardiola calling his left back over during the game, it is maybe a message that takes 10-15 seconds to communicate. That provides a really important lesson for coaches. "Don't talk too long. If you are going to stop the game, you better be stopping it for a reason." This doesn't just apply to the game, but to training as well. "If you are going to stop all of the players during training then it has to be a global message. If it's just applicable to one person, then why not just say it to him?" Whether you are talking to an individual player or the team, the message has to be short and sweet. "I would say maybe 15 seconds or less—or a minute at the absolute max." A mentor of mine is the infamous strength coach Vern Gambetta. He has a saying to describe the best coaches he has worked with, including the legendary John Wooden. "You have to be a Twitter coach (i.e., 140 characters or less)." In other words, your coaching points should be no longer than a tweet.

Gerard has a simple maxim to describe the role of the coach during the week at training. "The role of the coach is to design practice in a way that the players are making the decisions you want. This is accomplished through the constraints the coach places on the practice." As an example, a coach may want to influence the decisions of his players by providing a rule that if you can score in five seconds or less after winning possession, then that is worth two goals. "That is going to influence and encourage counter-attacking, but it's the players that are making the decisions."

Mistakes in training are the best thing that could happen for a coach. If no one makes any mistakes, then there isn't anything to coach. Gerard handles mistakes by waiting for them to happen a second time. For Gerard, when it happens two or three times in a row, then that is the moment a coach should step in. If you refer to Jonny Henderson's chapter, we don't want them to keep practicing the mistake! But the coach should still guide the player toward his own decision using question and answer, guided discovery, and other techniques. Questions like: "What went wrong there? What could you have done differently? Can you show me? Could you try this?" Anytime Gerard steps in to make a coaching point he has a simple rule, "I just want to talk less than the player. Can I get them to speak more than me?" That is the art of coaching.

CHAPTER 24

POSSESSION AND SCORING TACTICS

ROBIN RUSSELL

Robin Russell is the CEO and founder of SportsPath, an e-learning business focused on coaching education. He left the English FA in 2005 to work for UEFA as a soccer development consultant. He founded the LMA School of Football Management in 2010 that has involved over 3,000 coaches in 50 countries. He is an adjunct professor at Ohio University.

How data can change the way you train finishing — Why national teams are always worse than club teams — Why scoring the first goal gives your team a 95% chance of not losing — In-swingers, out-swingers, and the reasons why set plays may be more important than you think

DATA AND STATISTICS TO CHANGE THE WAY YOU TRAIN

Robin Russell spends a lot of his time analyzing the data that defines the game of soccer, and subsequently translating it into best practice. Jonny Henderson is a great example of a coach that looked at the data and said, "All right, does my training replicate what happens in the game?" So when data showed that most goals (80%) are scored from inside the 18-yard box (gold zone), Jonny began questioning why all of his finishing sessions featured shots from outside the 18-yard box. Data isn't meant to change everything we do, and there is no question that a lot of data can be flawed with human bias and errors. But good data—data that was collected without bias and with objective tools of measurement—are useful in helping move the game of soccer forward. This type of data can help coaches understand the game that we assume we know so well.

This figure shows the shot chart of James Rodriguez, a striker for Columbia, during the 2014 World Cup. Notice the amount of blocked shots outside of the 18-yard box. Inside the gold zone, James scored on five of the six shots that he took.

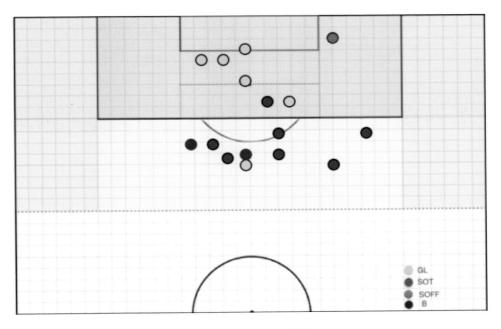

Data from the Sports Path World Cup Technical Report 2014.

This image is a depiction of Thomas Muller's shots taken during the 2014 World Cup. Again, we see that most of the goals Muller scored came from inside the gold zone. The implications for coaches is that, first and foremost, our players should be encouraged to shoot inside of the gold zone. With that said, we shouldn't ban shots from outside the 18-yard box, but sensible decision making should be coached. Many players settle for shots outside of the penalty area because they run out of ideas to break down the defensive unit in front of them. Therefore, that moment should be examined much more closely by the coach, and trained so that the players are comfortable with the ball inside the 18-yard box and prepared to score from that position.

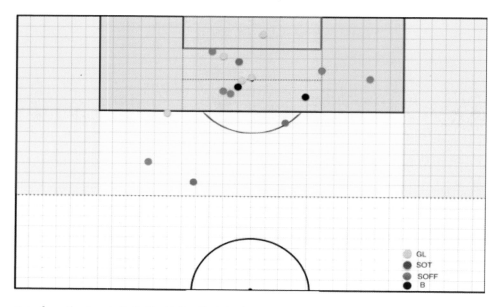

Data from the Sports Path World Cup Technical Report 2014.

How does the ball get inside the 18-yard box? Well, Robin Russell and SportsPath looked into that as well. They determined that, when trying to penetrate into the gold zone, the most effective areas to play the ball from are the central attacking zone (CAZ) and the box-pass zone (BPZ). Therefore, coaches should think about ways that their players can sustain or earn possession in these key areas (CAZ and BPZ). How can we work to influence the decision making of the players in those areas to create shots from inside the gold zone?

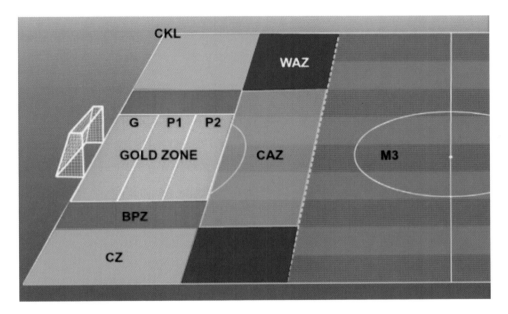

Data from the Sports Path World Cup Technical Report 2014.

WHY NATIONAL TEAMS AREN'T AS GOOD AS CLUB TEAMS

One of the most interesting pieces of analysis that Robin conducted was on the ability of national teams and club teams. "By and large, the standard of play of a national team is not as good as a club team. The reason is simple: they don't play together as much as a club team does. On average, 30 competitive national team games can span almost three seasons, whereas 30 competitive games in most leagues—depending on the number of competitions the team is in—will last only about half a season." The fact that club teams train together and play together on a nearly year-round basis is a critical aspect of their playing standard and style. This is a big reason why, historically, some of the best national teams have been comprised of players that play for the same club teams. The perfect example is Spain, the 2010 World Cup Champions. The starting line-up for the Spanish team that won the World Cup featured seven players from Barcelona and four from Real Madrid.

THE REAL GIANTS OF SOCCER COACHING

Robin's company was heavily involved in the 2014 World Cup won by Germany on Brazilian soil. Some of his findings reveal information about the game that is often hidden from the human eye. "We really had a hard look at the importance of the first goal. By and large, the team that scores the first goal has an 85% chance of winning and a 95% chance of not losing." Obviously, common sense would prevail in understanding that scoring a goal—particularly the first goal—is a good thing, but that isn't really the point. The point is more about the psychology of a goal. Statistically, teams that give up the first goal appear fragile. Imagine if there was a statistic that said 85% of boxers that land the first punch win the fight. Boxers and MMA fighters go into a fight knowing they will get punched in the mouth, but do we, as coaches, prepare our teams in the same way? Why is it that giving up the first goal leads to an almost-certain loss for the team that conceded, and an almost-certain win for the team that scored? Perhaps the data can help us, as coaches, better prepare our players to deal with how we respond to conceding the first goal. That is beyond the scope of this book, but it is something for you, the reader, to ponder. If your team gives up the first goal, how can they avoid becoming a statistic?

Here are some statistics that Robin Russell and his team have gathered in recent times:

- 33% of all goals scored in the game of soccer come from set plays.
- 50% of all first goals come from set plays: free kick, corner, throw in, etc.
- 80% of all first goals occur within 7 seconds of possession.
- 90% of all first goals occur within 10 seconds of possession.
- 10% of all first goals occur within 20 seconds of possession.

Why do nearly all first goals happen with such a small percentage of possession? Should we stop possessing the ball? If you think about the game, the above statistics make near-perfect sense. Remember that when we are analyzing first goals, we are analyzing a 0-0 game. What characteristics make up a 0-0 game? Both teams are playing extremely tight defensively so as not to give up a goal. In addition, because both teams are organized well defensively, both teams are losing possession more frequently. Another factor is the lack of fatigue that has yet to set in. Players are very fresh, which means that the gaps and spaces between defensive units is still very small. Therefore, it makes sense that half of all first goals come from set plays. The other team is very strong defensively in the run of play, which allows them to restrict the opportunities of their opponent. However, during a set play, the chances of a shot on target are very high. It doesn't matter how fresh or organized your team is, a well-struck set piece or a perfectly executed corner are near impossible to defend.

It really isn't that surprising that 90% of goals come within 10 seconds of possession. Think about it—in a 0-0 tie, both teams may begin to attack more openly as the game wears on because they may push to grab a goal. However, simultaneously, they leave themselves more exposed to a counter-attack. Most counter-attacks take 10 seconds or less to execute, which tells you that a good portion of the first goals—those with a small amount of possession—are counter-attacks. The remaining percentages of first goals come through a spell of possession defined by quick passing combinations that bypass opponents. That makes sense because if teams have tight defensive units in a 0-0 match, then the only way to bypass their defensive organization and move the ball into the key spaces of the game is through quick passing movements of the ball.

Oddly enough, the more goals there are in a game, the longer the duration of the possession that create those goals. This again makes sense. If your team is winning 3-0, the opponent will not be defending as intensively as before, which means that there are plenty of spaces and gaps to exploit and pass through. This means that teams will have an easier time keeping possession and will be less likely to have to combine quickly or counter-attack. However, sometimes a team that is trailing may sit everyone in behind the ball to avoid conceding again. This strategy reduces the amount of spaces between lines of the defensive team, but this allows the team on the ball to freely circulate the ball from side to side, which creates a longer spell of possession before a goal. Either way, the more goals in a game, the longer the spells of possession become that create those goals. Regardless of the data, these statistics shouldn't totally change the way we play the game or organize our team, but they do provide objective data that explain the unexplained phenomena of the game.

One of the more staggering findings from the 2014 World Cup, which has influenced global soccer in recent years, was the statistics regarding goalkeeper distribution. On average, World Cup teams achieved possession from the goalkeeper's distribution in the attacking third 17% of the time. However, teams that finished in the top four of the World Cup had an average of 37%. Germany's Manuel Neuer achieved a 38% success rate. This means that the goalkeeper's distribution contributed successfully to achieving possession in the attackingthird , either directly or indirectly, 38% of the time. In other words, teams that built from the back using their goalkeeper, center backs, holding midfielders, and outside backs had a greater success rate of earning possession in the attacking third than the teams that chose to go long from their goal kicks.

Nearly 70% of the top teams' goalkeeper distribution methods came from short ground passes and throws. One of the more heavily contested debates in soccer theory is whether teams should play short or long from the goalkeeper.

This figure shows that 71% of the total distribution from top-four goalkeepers were distributed into their defensive zones. Twenty percent of these distributions were to zone 10, a pass to the right-sided center back.

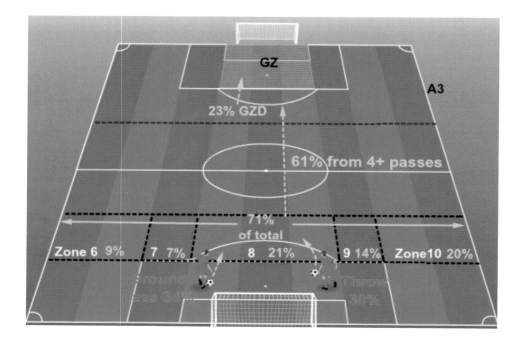

Additionally, 61% of the attacking-third possessions, initiated by goalkeeper distribution, consisted of four or more passes. Another statistic from this image shows that 23% of goalkeeper distributions contributed to gold zone deliveries (GZD) or passes into the gold zone.

These findings show that, statistically, building from the back contributes to more attacking-third possessions and chances created in the gold zone than simply having the goalkeeper kick it long. Further, the most successful teams—the teams in the top four at the 2014 World Cup—used their goalkeeper's distribution in effectively moving the ball from their defensive third to their attacking third.

From this statistical analysis we can draw a couple of conclusions. First, a goalkeeper's distribution ability is vital to achieving an attacking-third possession. Therefore, the coach must work with his team to develop a plan and prepare a coordination of how they will use the goalkeeper and defensive players to move the ball into the attacking third. Second, it is essential to develop the ability of your defensive players to receive the ball outside of the penalty area. This is a vital part of being able to build the ball from the back and into the attacking third. Things like awareness of space, receiving the ball under pressure, and making accurate forward passes become extremely important to being able to achieve an attacking-third possession.

Like I said, statistics and data are tools that we can use. Based on the data from the 2014 World Cup, it is possible to conclude that the better a team can build from the goalkeeper, the more successful they are at achieving attacking-third possessions and gold-zone chances. In other words, they win more games. As it turns out, kicking it long from the goalkeeper is a more effective way to *lose* possession in the attacking or middle thirds. Building from the back and using your goalkeeper to distribute are much more effective tactics with the aim of achieving possession in the attacking third.

THE IMPORTANCE OF SET PLAYS

Robin has shown that set plays account for nearly 33% of all goals scored in soccer. In addition, we now know that over half of all first goals scored are set pieces—and I don't need to remind you of the importance of first goals in winning matches. So why is it that coaches acknowledge the importance of set plays in theory, but not in practice? Most coaches and teams pay lip service to set plays, but how seriously do they train them? How many teams set aside 15 minutes at the end of the last training session before the match to go over them?

I am reminded of Albert Rude's advice to look at all training inputs as investments. If we know that 33% of our returns come from set plays, why is it that less than 1% of our training time is dedicated to it? Robin thinks that coaches neglect set plays for a multitude of reasons. "Players would rather do other things than practice set plays. Coaches would rather do other things than practice set plays. It's really that simple. But what I noticed in the lead-up to the EUROs, was that Iceland manager Lars Lagerback strategically set up friendlies against lesser opposition. The reason for that scheduling was because against lesser opposition there are typically a lot more set plays." Call it luck or coincidence, but Iceland did end up getting a lot of their goals during the European championships from set plays.

The real takeaway is that set plays are extremely difficult to practice in training. As Robin said, players and coaches would rather do something else, not to mention the difficulty that lies in mimicking the intensity and pressure of an actual set play that would occur in a match. Nevertheless, Lagerback knew that training set plays wasn't as realistic as training them in the match. So, he set up friendlies to produce a lot of opportunities to practice set plays, and instead of manufacturing a training environment, Iceland practiced set plays in a true competitive environment.

Let's say that we are on Robin's page. We realize we have been neglecting set plays, but now we are going to make a conscientious effort to train set plays every day. Is that enough? Will my team start scoring on set plays with no problems at all? Of course not. As in training our teams, just being out there isn't enough. Practice has to be deliberate. In other words, there needs to be clear intentions of what the players are trying to achieve. Players need to know exactly where they are supposed to run, where the ball should be played, and the speed and timing necessary to execute the set play correctly. Although there are many ways to draw up a set piece, Robin has found some key commonalities among teams that are successful in scoring from set plays.

Let's take corner kicks for example. In-swingers are balls that are served with a flight path toward the goal, making it easier to head the ball in a downward trajectory. "Balls that are easier to get down are more likely to lead to goals." Out-swingers are balls that are served away from the goal, which makes it easier to head the ball upwards. In other words, they are much more difficult to score from. In addition, in-swingers are not only easier for the attacking team to score from, but they are much more difficult for the defending team to clear.

Robin also points out that debating about which types of service lead to more goals, assumes that all corners are scored from first-time shots. Surprisingly, perhaps, that isn't the case. "It's the entire phase of play that surrounds a corner: the service, the first contact, the clearance, and the subsequent play. There are a lot more goals scored off of bad clearances than direct strikes." It is much easier to head an in-swinging ball down than up, which means that even if the defenders win the first ball, there will most certainly be a second-chance ball inside of the gold zone. "Because it is harder for the defenders to clear an in-swinger, it gives the players at the top of the box a better chance at a direct shot or moving the ball wide for another cross."

Set plays are too often viewed as a necessary evil in soccer. Players and coaches would rather do something else. But isn't it strange that we treat such an important moment of the game this way? I mean, set pieces play a massive role in the final result. They very often determine the winner and the loser. Perhaps we need statistics to remind us just how important set plays are. You can argue that working on them is just as important as working on defending, attacking, and transitioning. Perhaps the data can finally influence coaches to change the way we include set plays into the training regime. If we train our game model and playing principles every day, why don't we train set pieces every day? We have all watched thousands upon thousands of soccer matches in our lifetime, and yet we are still blind to some of the most obvious aspects of the game: the importance of set plays, the influence of the first goal, the benefit of goalkeeper distribution, and the understanding of key spaces such as the gold zone. Robin Russell and SportsPath will continue to collect data that can help illuminate hidden aspects of the game that we all strive to understand deeper. We just need to be willing to take a look ourselves.

CHAPTER 25

YOUTH DEVELOPMENT IN SOCCER

TAB RAMOS

Tab Ramos is the head coach of the U20 US Men's National Team and the US Soccer Youth technical director. Tab was also an assistant coach with the US Senior National team from 2011 to 2016 under Jurgen Klinsman. In 2017, Tab led the U20 US Men's National Team to the first U20 CONCACAF Championship in country history. The U20s subsequently qualified for the 2017 U20 World Cup in South Korea. Tab is also one of the most successful American players in the history of our country, making 81 appearances for the Senior US National Team.

Stop giving yourself so much credit — You're not a good coach just because you won — Stop talking so much — What your player's faces can tell you about your coaching ability — How to be critical of your own training sessions — Learning every single day — Why you should be optimistic about youth development in the United States

THINGS YOUTH COACHES SHOULD AVOID

As the youth technical director of US Soccer, Tab is leading the charge to improve the way we develop youth players in the United States. Tab believes that the key to this lies in developing better coaches. Tab feels that, far too often, coaches in the US prioritize winning over development. Before we start teaching our coaches some of the finer details of the game, they have to first get their priorities straight. "Coaches give themselves far too much credit for a win. I think winning games is important, but too many coaches depend on that. They think that because their team wins that automatically means they are a good coach, which just isn't the truth." Tab also believes that coaches can go to the other extreme as well. Far too often they blame themselves for a loss or take a loss too personally. In youth development, the coaches need to distance themselves from the outcome by placing their focus entirely on the process. "Because we have a pay-to-play model in the United States, that creates this underlying assumption that if you aren't winning games, then you aren't doing a good job of developing players, and that is—most of the time—not true."

In the United States, and perhaps elsewhere in the world, coaches wear the results on their sleeves—literally. It is not uncommon to see teams and coaches with shirts and jackets that boast about the number of games they have won, or the tournaments and titles they have earned. In fact, there are a number of websites in the US dedicated to tracking and totaling arbitrary points for teams around the country based on games and tournaments won or lost. "What's really most important is the development of each individual player, not the results of the team." Tab certainly practices what he preaches as well. A few years ago, Tab was in charge of a U10 boys' team at his club in New Jersey. He implemented a rule with his team to improve their decision making under pressure. The rule was: no matter what the circumstance, the players were not allowed to kick the ball out of bounds. The purpose of this constraint was to force his boys to play out of pressure, rather than just kicking it out of bounds. Tab's team took some lumps because of that rule. There were times where a player would try to get out of a tough situation, but would lose possession close to his goal that led to the opponent scoring. "We lost a few games because of it, but I think it was a good rule because it forced my players to think more about their own creative ways to get out of difficult situations." Tab prioritized development of his individual players over the result of the team, which has been echoed continuously throughout this book as the mission of youth development. As Michael Beale likes to say, "In youth development, there are 11 'I's in a team."

Tab isn't sure we could implement a rule like that nationwide. In fact, the emphasis on results in youth development is so intense that many coaches would lose their jobs. "Coaches are under way too much pressure in this country to win games at the youth level. Everybody is supposed to have winning teams and be producing players that can move on to the college or professional level, so it is very difficult for coaches to implement things like that rule where your team can't kick the ball out of bounds." Tab believes that the only way it could work is if the coach created a trust and credibility with his players and their parents. Right, wrong, or indifferent, in the United States, as long as we have a pay-to-play model, the parents will have a stake in the development of their players because they are paying customers. Imagine buying a hamburger from McDonalds, but getting a salad instead because the employee argues the benefits of the salad versus the hamburger. That is the problem with pay-to-play. Coaches will need to continue to do their best to win games and produce players for the next level, which are often opposing ideals.

Tab isn't sure if there is an objective way to evaluate the ability of a coach. Winning at the youth level doesn't tell the whole story, but what does? Tab isn't sure, but he thinks that "coaches should be able to determine the answer to that question on their own. Are you doing a serious job of trying to do the best that you can for the players, or are you just there because it's a job?"

There is no question that Tab Ramos' youth-coaching philosophy begins and ends with the individual in mind. He feels that one of the biggest wastes of time in youth development is an overabundance of playing stoppages made by the coach during training. "I think a lot of coaches spend so much time stopping the play and explaining things when it is sometimes more important to let the play continue. Yeah, every once in a while you may need to stop the play and have a teaching moment, but I have seen way too many stoppages in my experience." As the youth technical director, one of Tab's main responsibilities is to travel the country evaluating coaches and players, so he has seen his fair share of training sessions. Regardless of the area of the country, his evaluation is still unanimous. "Thirty to forty percent of the training sessions I see have the players standing around listening to the coach."

One of the most common complaints I hear from youth coaches is that they don't have enough time to train. However, the funniest thing about time is that it's something we want the most, but that we use the worst. In youth development, there isn't a lot of time dedicated to training. Unless you are coaching at an elite academy that trains six times a week, chances are you have your team for 90 minutes twice a week. Therefore, instead of begging for more time, what if we better utilized the time we did have? "There are so few hours that the players get on the ball and play, so if half of that time is spent listening to a coach, then we just aren't really getting a lot accomplished."

Tab has circled the soccer fields of this country many times over and he sees the same thing everywhere he goes. "I sometimes will walk from field to field and see kids leaving a training session without having even broke a sweat." If coaches really don't want to sacrifice their teaching or talking time as a coach, Tab recommends that they show up to their sessions 15 minutes earlier than normal to explain to the kids what they will do in training that day. In fact, Tab knows some coaches that e-mail or text their players the session plan a few hours before the session. "That way you won't have to make as many coaching points during the session, but your players will still understand and learn the things you want to teach them." There are many creative ways to still get your teaching in, but sacrificing the time spent playing during training shouldn't be one of them.

I have to refer back to Vern Gambetta's maxim: "Be a Twitter coach. 140 characters or less." In general, coaches need to keep their coaching points short and sweet. Tab has a simple method of determining if he is making a coaching point for too long. "The player's faces are my reference. Are the players having fun? Are they being active? Are they even looking at you? If you are getting the players to a point where you have more than one looking away or staring at the ground, then you are probably spending too much time talking. Chances are you have already lost them."

THE BIGGEST BANG FOR OUR BUCK IN YOUTH TRAINING

A very common question when evaluating training programs in all sports is, "What 's the biggest bang for our buck?" In other words, where should we be spending the majority of our training time. Again, time is a commodity that we want the most, but misuse the worst. Tab believes that youth coaches need to be spending the majority of their training time having their players in 1v1 situations. "In general, across the country, I think we spend far too little time putting players into 1v1 situations. And that can mean a lot of things. It could mean a 1v1 going to goal, or really young players dribbling in a circle with defenders and not letting them kick it out—you just get so much out of a 1v1 situation. There are defensive points, attacking points, body positioning, strength, balance, and so on, and I think more time should be spent in those situations."

Obviously, Tab knows that this idea depends on the age of the player. As players get older, they will need to have the context of teammates and opponents to be able to perceive situations and make decisions. But, at the younger ages, Tab doesn't believe teammates are that important. "When you are coaching the little guys, how quickly they pass the ball to someone else isn't all that important. The positioning of a pass or the timing of when they pass is not necessarily that important. What's important is their comfort on the ball." Keep in mind that Tab isn't advocating isolated skills and drills. He used the term *1v1* intentionally. Put your players into situations where they have to manipulate the ball themselves but in relation to a pressuring opponent. Then, as the players grow older, we can add in the context of teammates.

LEARNING ON THE JOB

Tab has been coaching with US Soccer for nearly a decade, which has provided him with the learning opportunities of a lifetime. Tab has spent time with Mauricio Pochettino, Thomas Tuchel, and youth academy directors at Bayern Munich, Stuttgart, Porto, and other top clubs around the world. However, Tab learns most on the actual job. The daily planning of training, coming up with tactics, scouting opponents, and conversations with his staff and players are where he learns the most.

In July 2016, the US U20s played the Dutch U20s in an exciting 3-5 loss. This game was one example of Tab learning on the job. "I like to high press the opposition, that is one of my main game ideas. For some reason, however, Holland was just getting out of our press every single time. At half-time I met with my staff to try and solve the way they were building out and we actually couldn't come up with a solution at half-time. So we made the decision to just wait for them by sitting in a lower block and trying to counter because we just couldn't press them successfully." Later that night, Tab and his staff watched video on those moments of high pressure. They worked late into the night talking about ways they could solve that problem in the future. "That is the best thing about the game: you never know what problems will be thrown at you. The fun of coaching is in trying to figure out ways to solve these problems." For Tab, that is the best way to learn. "You can spend time with clubs and listen to podcasts, but you learn the most on the job, being confronted with tactical problems and trying to solve them in the moment."

Tab has had a lot of opportunities to learn, but perhaps the most insightful thing he has learned is far removed from tactics, man management, or training methods. "I have learned that becoming a good coach doesn't come naturally. It is something that you constantly have to work on and refine. It's a never-ending process." Tab didn't pick that maxim up on a coaching course. He learned that the old fashioned way, through sheer experience. "I used to be a guy that, when I passed my A license for example, thought, 'Well, now I have my A license, so I must know everything,' and I was so far from the truth."

The biggest thing Tab wants to improve in his coaching is his ability to delegate responsibilities to his staff members. "Sometimes I will set up training or plan an exercise in a certain way, and I micro-manage my assistants to make sure it's run exactly how I want it to be run. So not being able to delegate is a real weakness of mine." Perhaps the biggest reasons Sir Alex Ferguson is considered one of the best managers of all time was his ability to delegate. Alex Ferguson would often trust Rene Meulensteen or Carlos Quieroz to run the team training sessions. That ability to delegate afforded Sir Alex the time necessary to tackle bigger picture items. Things like, "Who is performing well? Do any players appear unhappy? How is the motivation level and morale of the team?" These are the things that the best coaches always have their eye on. Tab's ability to coach and lead a training session is a strength, but it also leads to a major weakness: his inability to delegate. For Tab, the ability to delegate has become a major focus area for improvement.

In general, Tab feels that he can improve all aspects of his coaching. Being able to delegate is an area that sticks out, but he never leaves a session feeling completely satisfied. "It's such a difficult question to answer because I always leave a session thinking, 'Ah, I wish that would have been a little bit better, or that I made the space a little bit smaller, or I wish my coaching point was a little bit clearer or more succinct.' So it's just a daily tally of little things that you can improve upon."

THE CURRENT STATE OF YOUTH DEVELOPMENT IN THE US

My all-time favorite podcast is called *Philosophize This!* hosted by Stephen West. Stephen had an episode on philosopher Martin Heidegger that covered the topic of phenomenology. In that episode, Stephen covered something that I feel has so many parallels to coaching theory. "If you're somebody that's interested in making novel social commentary or even just being the person at the party that has the most interesting take on the world, here's a tip from your Uncle Steve: You don't want to focus your time studying the things that everybody's arguing about. No, don't do that. You want to focus your time studying the things that everybody pretty much agrees on because it's in those areas that people's ideas are the least challenged." I love this quote because it is so profoundly true. How many things do we assume to be correct and factual that are actually purely based on popular opinion?

Something that pretty much everyone in the US has come to believe is that we have the worst youth development in the world. We can't produce players, we don't know how to produce players, and we never will produce players like the rest of the world. Well, Tab Ramos wholly disagrees with that familiar sentiment. "I think the US soccer world has come to define itself as fairly pessimistic. Everyone is quick to criticize with no real factual information. I think we are doing a great job of developing players. That is something I truly believe, regardless of the opinion of the pessimists. This is a humongous country. It is hard enough scouting players nationwide. So, with the changes US Soccer implemented in 2008 with the development academy and the youth national teams, I think we are starting to develop players with the potential to be worldwide, legit, competitive players." Tab believes that we still have a lot of room for improvement, no question, but he feels that we are doing a better job than often acknowledged. Christian Pulisic is just one player that Tab cites as an example, but he feels that there are others being developed currently that will ascend to similar heights.

Tab's role within US Soccer has him asking the same question every single day regarding youth development in the US: "How do we take the next steps?" On August 1, 2017, US Soccer changed the way the game is played from the youngest ages to the oldest ages around the country. The youngest age groups will play nothing bigger than 4v4. As players progress in age, the field size and numbers will progress accordingly from 4v4 to

7v7 to 9v9 and finally to 11v11. "We implemented small-sided games for all players under the age of 13. We don't want players playing on a full field because we want to build players that are creative and comfortable on the ball. If the field is too big too early, then they won't get enough touches on the ball or opportunities to be creative. These are the next steps to address the long-term development of our players."

CHAPTER 26

GAME-BASED DECISION-MAKING AND PLAYER DEVELOPMENT

MIKE MUÑOZ

Mike Muñoz is the head coach of LA Galaxy 2—or Los Dos—in the USL. Prior to his role with the LA Galaxy USL team, Mike was the academy director of the LA Galaxy and the head coach of the U18 LA Galaxy academy. Mike has been involved with the LA Galaxy, the most ambitious US professional club, for the last five years. During his time with the academy, Mike has been responsible for helping 14 players reach the LA Galaxy professional teams. Mike has completed the infamous French Formation License and earned his USSF A License.

It is non-negotiable to outwork the opponent — Technical training that actually transfers — How to create an environment built on feedback from your peers to improve your coaching — Always have your windows and your doors open

Mike grew up in a Mexican-American family that was nothing short of soccer crazy. To intensify the matter, Mike's first encounter with the game came during the 1986 World Cup that was played in Mexico. "I remember watching some of the games with my dad on the couch, and I vividly remember telling my dad that I wanted to be a professional soccer player." Mike grew up playing in the US system and the progressive youth setup in southern California. After four years of college at the University of California, Mike's dream came true. "I was drafted by Chivas USA in the first year that club came into existence under Thomas Rongen."

We all know the stories and statistics regarding the difficulty of playing professional sports. It is often said that less than 1% of youth athletes will make it to the professional level. However, the difficulty of staying at the professional level once you are there is an oft-forgotten reality. "I ended up bouncing around the country playing for a variety of USL teams and eventually ended my career with the Galaxy, but I didn't have a stellar career. I was never the high-level professional that I aspired to be; I think I was always on league minimum."

As a former USL player myself, I can fully relate to Mike's experience. There are usually three types of professional players. First, there are the guys that have a high ceiling that they have yet to reach. These are the guys in the locker room that everyone is happy to share the field with. They are usually at a more humbling moment in their career before their big break. Then there is the group of guys that have no business being a professional player. But the third group may be the most interesting of them all. This group is made up of guys like Mike and me. Guys that are good enough to sustain a career as a professional but know they will never make enough money or reach the heights necessary to have what I would call a true professional career. So, every day they think about what's next. They know they have maxed out their soccer-playing potential. The end stage of my soccer career was akin to white-knuckling an orange hoping to get a few extra drops of orange juice, or squeezing a tube of toothpaste to get one last bit out. The truth, however, still lingers: eventually I am going to have to get another orange and buy a new tube of toothpaste. Mike, like me, knew what was next. "I always knew that coaching was going to be the next step for me. I was fortunate to play for a lot of top managers in the US that gave me so much insight into coaching at the professional level. My coaches were Thomas Rongen, Bruce Arena, Bob Bradley, and Hans Westerhof, and I just soaked it all in."

It was not uncommon to see Mike in the back of the film room during video sessions taking notes for a different reason than most of the other guys on the team. "I was already beginning my study of the game. I knew I wanted to be a coach and I didn't want to miss out on the opportunity to learn, in the moment, from my coaches. I was prepping myself for the next step after my playing career." Mike even completed his coaching badges while finishing his playing career, which, when combined with the things he learned from his coaches, allowed Mike to step right into his coaching career.

YOUTH-DEVELOPMENT PHILOSOPHY

Mike has been fortunate to have some of the greatest coaches in the history of US Soccer mentor him to some capacity. Bob Bradley, Bruce Arena, and Thomas Rongen have all influenced his identity as a coach. Mike also worked closely with current Toronto FC coach, Greg Vanney, in starting the Real Salt Lake Academy that has been cited as one of the most successful US academies to date. While at Real Salt Lake, Mike forged his youth-development philosophy by combining elements of every coach, experience, and conversation he had up to that point. "When it comes to a playing philosophy, the first thing that comes to mind is the ball. Everything revolves around the ball. I want to control the ball. For me, I compare the ball to the protagonist in the game. We want to own it and dominate with it." Mike understands that if his team has the ball, it is impossible for the opposition to score. Mike wants his teams to have more of the ball than the opponent. In that same light, Mike's defensive philosophy centers around limiting the amount of time the opponent has possession of the ball. "Winning it back immediately, pressing, being aggressive, not letting our opponents breath—those are staples of my playing philosophy." In order for the playing philosophy to be implemented to the level that Mike demands, it becomes non-negotiable for his team that they outwork the opponent. It is essential. "Just because we have good, technical, and tactical soccer players doesn't mean I tolerate being outworked. My players know that we are going to outwork our opponent and outrun our opponent. Of course, there are many layers to the philosophy, but at its core, that is the essence of my teams."

FRENCH FORMATION LICENSE AND OPPOSED-TECHNIQUE TRAINING

Like many of the coaches I have interviewed for this book, Mike completed the French Formation License, a grueling and intensive two-year coaching education experience that challenged some of Mike's preconceived ideas about the game. "It really opened my eyes to the principles of the game. There are a number of principles that every player has to understand in order for the team to be successful. These principles are what make it possible to build out of the back, to possess to progress, to unbalance and get behind a back four, and to press from front to back, and as a coach, I need to master those principles myself before I can transfer the knowledge to my players."

Mike looks at coaching as a game of transferring knowledge to your players. His guiding light is ensuring that it is knowledge they can actually use. In order to make sure the knowledge is applicable, he tries to understand what actually happens to his team during the games. Through analysis, Mike realized that most teams choose to sit in a low block against his Galaxy team. Most opponents anticipate not seeing a lot of the ball against Mike's teams. Plus, they know that a poorly coordinated press against a Muñoz team is bound to be broken consistently. This reality forced Mike to reconsider certain aspects of the game that they were training consistently. For example, why spend so much time working on building from the back in training, when their opponents allow them to freely bring the ball to at least half? Instead of spending a majority of their time in training bringing the ball out from the back, Mike started to train his team how to break down a low block. "We needed to learn how to break down low blocks, how to create superiority in wide areas, and how to get in behind with very little space to get in behind, so those became elements that we taught quite a bit."

Mike's analysis of his team's games also showed him that his players knew how to press—that wasn't an issue—but they were giving up a lot of chances through counter-attacks. So, instead of constantly training the pressing coordination of his team, Mike began working on ways to prevent the counter. "Because most of the teams sit in against us, we realized that we needed to spend more time training to prevent the counter-attack than pressing the opponent during their build-up from the goalkeeper." The takeaway for coaches is to never forget that the starting point is always the game of 11v11. When soccer reaches the competitive stage—whether it is the professional level or older academy ages—the reference for your team needs to be the game.

One of the ways Mike likes to develop his team's ability to break down a low block is to overload numbers in wide areas. The key to creating superiority in wide areas first lies in moving the opponent to one side. As Guardiola says, "the secret is to overload one side of the pitch so that the opponent must tilt its own defense to cope. You overload on one side and draw them in so that they leave the other side weak." The opponent will start to move more and more players to one side of the pitch the longer that the ball remains on that one side. In fact, the longer the ball stays on one side, the more the opponent feels like they can win it. "They should feel like they have an opportunity to lock us in, to trap us on that side, but right at that moment is when we switch the ball to the other side. This allows us to get our winger and outside back in a 2v1 situation." Mike trains this moment by focusing on his team's ability to recognize the exact moment that the opponent has committed themselves defensively to one side of the field. "We have the ball on one side to score from the other."

The 2v1 or 3v2 scenario that is created through the switch of play is what allows the attacking team to get in behind the opposition back four, and finally breach the frustrating low block defensive organization.

For Mike, constraint-based games are the best way to train this principle most effectively. "Usually, I will create a game where maybe the rules give the team on the ball superiority in wide areas. So it could be a flank game with wide channels where the winger is going against the outside back of the opponent, but the outside back on the attacking team is able to jump a zone and join the wide area to create a 2v1. It's a 2v1 because another rule might be that the opposition winger isn't allowed to defend in the wide area." The session would progress from this constraints-based game into what Mike calls a tactical game. "Tactical games are basically just repetition of a specific tactical principle using an offense-against-defense organization. We just go over the scenario again and again so the players understand how to execute and recognize this moment in a game."

Something that Mike picked up from the French Formation License is the use of a technical exercise at the later stages of the training session. For example, after the constraints-based game and the tactical game, Mike moves to a technical exercise aimed at replicating the same moment they have been training, but with no opposition. "It's just the players and the balls going through the movements so that we can really zoom in to the path that the ball needs to take, the pace of the pass required, the speed at which the winger needs to dribble at the opposition outside back, etc. It's all aimed at improving the execution portion of the decision that we have been training." From there, Mike finishes the session with a game that has very few constraints—if any—in order to see if the principle they have been training reveals itself. "Can the players recognize the situation now, but in a more chaotic environment resembling the real game?"

The French Formation course also opened Mike's eyes to how he constructs and implements technical exercises. The course showed him that the game of soccer is really a game of decisions. Although technical execution is a part of that, without the decision, there is nothing to execute. "Just because a kid can trap the ball, pass, receive, and dribble around cones doesn't mean that he will know when to do it in the game. The technique and the tactic have to go hand in hand; it's all about decision making." Obviously, the best way to train decision making is in the context of a game-like situation. Making decisions that have no context to the game are useless.

A lot of coaches may have passing exercises where players need to pick their head up and recognize a color or a number being held up by the coach, but that doesn't transfer to the game. Awareness of the number of fingers a coach holds up and awareness of the position of your teammates and opponents couldn't be more different. Remember, "the technique and the tactic go hand in hand." Mike does use unopposed technical exercises, but if you look at his session from start to finish, it is predominantly opposed. In addition, the unopposed technical exercise is paired directly with the tactic they are training and that is the difference. Passing in a square around specific cones doesn't relate to a tactic or a decision. But creating a 2v1 overload in the wide channel after a switch of play with position specific actions is an example of training the technique with the tactic. Don't confuse the French use of technical execution during training sessions as a sign that any old technical exercise will do. "The technical exercise needs to be related to the game-based exercises you are using in that session. The players should be in their positions, and the actions they are making need to be specific to the tactic being trained." In other words, your center backs shouldn't be crossing the ball from the wide channel.

Decision making is the true key to player development. "Exercises that incorporate the player having to make decisions with pressure on the ball are going to better challenge their technique. So, if a kid can do a one-touch pass, fantastic, but can he do a one-touch pass with a defender running at him? Can he take a touch away from pressure with a defender running at him? That, for me, is where we really take technique and tactic and put them together."

Mike understands that coaches want their players to have success, but success in practice doesn't necessarily mean success in the game. John Kessel's chapter in this book will deconstruct the science of motor learning and why practicing to be good at practice isn't the same as practicing to be good at performance. If you refer to Jonny Henderson's chapter and the reasoning behind his performance playground, it is all about embracing chaos. So if you train your players in a way that creates interference, opposition, and pressure, they may fail. Training will look chaotic and disorganized, and you may think the players aren't improving. If you train your players in a very organized way—a pass to this cone, run to that cone, sort of way—then, yes, training will look fantastic, but you will continually be disappointed on game day as nothing will transfer. "I understand coaches want their players to really understand the aspects of a technique and to have success, but that just isn't the game. The game is about making real-life, split-second decisions against real pressure. If we can start to incorporate that into the training sessions of the younger ages, then we are going to be pushing the level of development of players higher."

Mike has a simple maxim that he lives by when it comes to planning a training exercise: "As close to the game as possible." Nearly all of Mike's crossing and finishing exercises or wide-area exercises include opposition in many capacities. There will be defenders in the box to mark the forwards as they make their runs, and the wide players may have a defender tasked with chasing them down to give them a realistic game-like crossing situation. So the session may still be considered technical, but it certainly isn't unopposed. "Anybody can hit a ball into the box unopposed, but if you really want to develop high level pros, they have to be able to do it under pressure."

The technical exercises that Mike includes in his training, therefore, will always have opposition to some capacity. How do we define a technical exercise then? If it has opposition, is it not just a small-sided game? It depends. Technical training can be defined as training the execution of a decision that results in the execution of a specific soccer action repeatedly. However, we can only define soccer actions by how they are executed in the game. Our players don't cross the ball or head the ball without interference from the opposition. But if we always train these actions in a training game—let's say a 5v5 game—then the repetition will be minimal. Mike constructs these technical exercises with repetition in mind, but not repetition without the game-like decision making. An example would be the way he constructs his crossing and finishing from wide areas.

Here you can see the right midfielder and right outside back create a 2v1 in the wide channel. After a wall pass, the outside back receives the ball in behind the opposition fullback. The left fullback for red waits for this pass to be made before turning and running down the right outside back in black. Simultaneously, the two strikers in black must make runs into the box while eluding the opposition center backs in red.

This exercise allows for a lot of repetitions of the specific crossing action that Mike wants his team to execute in the game. However, it includes opposition and interferences that are realistic to that same moment in the game. Now the outside back will have to execute his crossing decision with the pressure of the opposition fullback sprinting toward him.

These technical exercises not only complement the game model of the LA Galaxy U18 team, they also help develop the individual tools of the players. Similar to Michael Beale, Mike Muñoz believes that every player needs to have a weapon to be able to make it as a professional player. "Every player that is going to have a chance has to have a weapon. It could be crossing, it could be shooting, it could be a guy that wins tackles—whatever it is, he has to be excellent at one thing to give himself a chance." The LA Galaxy make sure they talk with each player to determine what that weapon is going to be. Step 2 is to train it and train it consistently.

Had I interviewed Mike two years ago, I would have been speaking with a coach that thought he was pretty good at what he did. However, the French Formation Course opened Mike's eyes to his deficiencies and flaws. "The course kind of put me in my place and humbled me quite a bit." Not everyone reading this will have access to the French Formation License (currently available to MLS academy staff only), but the methods of improvement are available to anyone willing to get out of their comfort zone. The following are some habits you can add to your routine as a coach that candidates are subjected to during the French Formation Course.

- Be prepared to receive heavy criticism from instructors and fellow candidates on session design, coaching instruction, field set up, etc.

- Film every session with recorded audio.
- Review the entire film with your staff and a mentor following the session.

Obviously, this list doesn't include the methodology that Mike was taught, but the feedback provided by his peers was what produced the biggest change in his coaching and in the way he viewed himself. "It really exposes you for where you are at. So I would say, in terms of where I am now? Yeah, I have a long way to go, but I guess I'm a good youth soccer coach at the end of the day." Mike isn't willing to settle, which is why he went through the intensive two-year program with the French Federation, but his message is one that every coach should heed. How much feedback do you get from your environment? Does anyone challenge you on the way you set up your sessions, plan your exercises, or make your coaching points? How about the way you communicate during a session? What about the way you present yourself? Why not?

Mike went from being a self-described "good youth soccer coach" to his dream of being a professional soccer coach. Shortly after our conversation, Mike was chosen to lead the LA Galaxy 2 team in USL. Without the daily feedback he received from his peers at the LA Galaxy academy, Mike isn't sure he would have reached his goal of coaching professionals. "It's the only way, in my opinion. You have to have a mentor. You have to have someone that is an expert above you or beside you, constantly challenging you and evaluating you. Simple things like filming your training sessions, evaluating the vocabulary you use, your body language; these are things that you would have no idea about unless you see them yourself." Mike believes that video and feedback make it impossible for coaches to hide from criticism because the video won't lie. "There are a lot of times where a coach may put a training session together, but the principles they want and the topic they want just don't come out. However, because they are so into it, they just can't see that it has nothing to do with the topic they created. You can't know unless someone points it out to you." While receiving feedback can be difficult because you won't always be hearing things you want to hear, Mike has developed an appropriate mindset for welcoming criticism. "You have to be humble and you have to keep an open mind. The phrase we always use is that your windows and your doors should always be open. If they are closed, then you have no chance of becoming better."

CHAPTER 27

THE SCIENCE OF DEVELOPING BETTER PLAYERS

JOHN KESSEL

John Kessel is the director of sport development for USA Volleyball. He is an expert in motor learning and has been applying motor-learning principles to USA Volleyball for the last 25 years. USA Volleyball has won over 20 Olympic medals across indoor and beach volleyball since John began working to change the curriculum from a focus on drills to a focus on specificity and a game-based approach to skill acquisition.

Why facts don't change people's minds — You don't coach soccer, you coach people — How did you learn to ride a bike — Stop doing drills — Why your players should coach other players — What free-throw shooting can teach you about practicing set pieces more effectively — At the earliest ages of youth soccer, the worst teams win — What Stephen Curry can teach you about producing professional players

John Kessel hates to be the bearer of bad news, but the science of neuroscience has proven that what we call *drills* are not as effective in promoting skill acquisition and motor learning as game-based programs. Fortunately, since 1975 the science of motor learning has shown that game-based training programs and what we call *specificity* are what produce elite performers, not isolated drills. Unfortunately, "facts don't really change people's minds."

In 1975, a study was conducted at Stanford University that presented individuals with pairs of suicide notes. Of the two notes, a random individual had written one, while a person who had taken their own life had written the other. The subjects in the study were then asked to determine which of the pair was real and which one was fake. The subjects were also, unknowingly, split into two groups. One group was told that they correctly identified the real note 24 out of 25 times. The second group was told that they only chose the real note 10 times out of 25. However, the study was a setup. Both groups actually guessed correctly about half of the time. So what was the study really about?

The goal of the experiment was to see how the subjects responded to *thinking* they were right, or *thinking* they were wrong. In the second phase of the study, both groups of subjects were informed that they were lied to about their original success rates. The subjects were then asked to guess at how many notes they thought they *actually* guessed correctly given the new information that their original results were fictitious and random. Oddly enough, the group that originally received a high score—24 out of 25 correct—guessed that they had done much better than average, even though their original score was chosen completely at random. But the original high score allotted to them convinced them that they actually had some sort of skill or ability at picking the correct notes. The low-score group—those that were told they got 10 out of 25 correct—thought the exact opposite. They assumed that they had actually guessed well below average, even though, again, their original score was given to them completely at random. The alarming aspect of the study was that both groups had absolutely zero reason to believe they did extremely well or extremely poorly.

The study proved that once impressions or ideas are formed in a person's mind, they become extremely resolute. In other words, even though people's beliefs are totally refuted by the facts, people still fail to make appropriate and necessary revisions to their beliefs. Are you starting to see the parallels between this study and coaching? How many coaches do we know that believe in their methods despite objective and scientific evidence that points to the contrary? There are many coaches that still believe in unopposed technical-training exercises, even though the science of motor learning and skill acquisition that has been available for more than 40 years completely refutes its efficacy.

It is still unclear why facts don't change people's mind, but early research in that area points to the strength of the many brain biases that govern human behavior, such as the confirmation bias, which describes the tendency we have as humans to embrace the information that supports our beliefs and reject the information that contradicts them. Some psychologists theorize that it is a biological adaptation that has developed to support the human desire to win an argument. In the book *Denying to the Grave: Why We Ignore the Facts That Will Save Us*, author and psychiatrist Jack Gorman argues that humans feel a rush of dopamine when they process information that supports their beliefs. "It feels good to stick to our guns, even if we are wrong."

The soccer world is in desperate need of people willing to be wrong. There probably is a way to convince people that research-based protocols are essential to creating best practices, but it is well above my intellectual capacity to know how to achieve it. My hope is that John Kessel, the director of sport development for USA Volleyball and an expert in motor-learning science, can explain why it is absurd to ignore the science of how we can develop better soccer players.

WHAT DO YOU COACH?

John is a world-renowned speaker that has presented in over 50 countries regarding youth development. The first thing that John likes to do is ask a member of the audience what they coach. Like clockwork, the coach being questioned responds with their sport, but John hopes coaches never answer that question like that again. In fact, every time a coach answers with their sport, John will go and grab a soccer ball or a basketball, hand it to them, and say, "Here you go. Coach this."

John's point is that we don't coach basketballs or soccer balls or even soccer players, we coach human beings. "We coach amazing athletes that are aspiring to be great. The reason why I make that such a big point of contention is because the focus on people and relationships often gets lost in the desire to think that you are just a soccer coach." We don't just coach soccer. If that were true, then we would end up with a bunch of people that can do something on a pitch, but nothing in real life.

John likes to refer to John Wooden and Johan Cruyff as examples of coaches that didn't just coach their sport, but coached people. They coached people on leadership and life skills, and we simply don't have enough of that anymore. It is important to acknowledge that maybe 1% of the athletes we coach will end up in the Olympics or the World Cup. So the question becomes why isn't our coaching focused on preparing the 99% for real life? "The 99% are who we, as coaches, should be working on the most. Of course, we need to develop their skills on the pitch, but we must go way beyond that."

WHAT VOLLEYBALL CAN TEACH US ABOUT MOTOR LEARNING

There are 220 nations that compete for a spot in the Olympic volleyball tournament. Of those 220 teams, only 12 qualify. "Getting into the Olympics is harder than winning the Olympics." When John was playing competitive volleyball during his youth, the US failed to qualify a team for the Olympics throughout the 1970s and early 1980s. In fact, the US went 16 years without qualifying for an Olympic volleyball tournament.

Around that same time, John met and studied under Dr. Carl McGown, one of the pioneers in applying motor-learning principles to sport development. It was at that time that John made the connection that we spend far too much time drilling in practice and not enough time playing. So, USA men's volleyball began to utilize the science of motor learning in the development of their youth- and adult-level players. Since that time in the 1980s when these principles began to be applied, the US men's team has won three Olympic gold medals and two Olympic bronze medals. At the world level, the US men's team has won four additional gold medals at the World Championships and World Cup.

In that same time period, the US women's volleyball team failed to earn a gold medal at the Olympics. Now, the interesting point here is that women's volleyball in the US is the most popular sport played by female athletes. Due to that fact, colleges that fund a women's volleyball team give out a combined 15,000 scholarships every single year. Logically, you would think that the men must then have close to 20,000 scholarships, right? Not even close. Not only is volleyball one of the least popular sports played by males in the US, but there are only about 200 scholarships available for males that want to pursue college volleyball. This begs the question: how have the men been so dominant in world volleyball despite the lack of interest and support? Even more interesting, how have they been able to consistently outperform the more lucrative and popular women's teams? "The reason is that the men have been trained under the principles of motor learning for the last 30-plus years. The women, unfortunately, have just recently begun to include these principles in their training."

THE PRINCIPLES OF MOTOR LEARNING

Motor learning might seem like an esoteric topic that doesn't pertain to soccer coaches, but to think that way is to live in a world of ignorance. Motor learning is essentially the goal of any skill-related training program. "It's how we learn, in this case, a motor skill, which is a physical skill, as opposed to the other skills that we have: mathematics, reading, writing, etc. But the major area that we are talking about when we discuss motor skills is sports." The vast amount of research on motor learning can be summarized in one word: *specificity*. The simplest way to understand the concept of specificity is to ask yourself how you learned to ride a bike. John asked me that question and our resulting conversation details the purpose and benefits of specificity.

John: "So Joshua, let's see how loved you were. Did your parents hire a
 bike-riding coach to teach you how to ride a bike?"
Josh: "Nope."
John: "How about drills? Did they put you through bike-riding drills?"
Josh: "Nope."
John: "How about bike-riding summer camp?! Did they send you away for
 two weeks to bike-riding summer camp?"

Josh: "Negative."

John: "Progressions? Did they teach you to pedal right-footed 20 times and then left-footed 20 times before you finally put the two together?"

Josh: "No."

Often when John uses this example someone in the audience will shout out, "Training wheels!" But the research on training wheels supports John's position on motor learning. "The training-wheels argument comes up quite a bit, but they don't actually exist in other parts of the world. Training wheels tend to only exist in the Western world where we have lawyers and hyper-protective parents. There was a study conducted in Germany that actually showed that training wheels slowed the learning curve process down by 60% versus just riding a bike. So you actually learn faster by just riding the bike." What this tells us is that the principle of specificity comes down to this, "you learn to ride a bike by simply riding the bike."

John wants people to understand that the science of motor learning proves that "kids learn to play soccer by, God forbid, playing soccer."

THE OVEREMPHASIS ON TECHNIQUE

John has spent a lot of time teaching and coaching volleyball around the world. While in Brazil many, many years ago, before the days of his understanding of motor learning, John was coaching a volleyball team. "The ball came over the net around chest height, which would usually be bumped up using the forearms, but this guy squatted down and used his head to direct the ball perfectly to the setter. I interjected into the session, and I found myself beginning to tell this guy that he was wrong. The problem was that he wasn't wrong, *I was wrong*. It is perfectly legal to use any part of your body in volleyball, so there was nothing inherently wrong with what the player did, but I was so focused on this concept of technique that I failed to see that." This story has become far too common throughout youth sports. "Most coaches are way too concerned with technique and not skill. And the most important skill is what we call *reading*." In volleyball, much like soccer, reading is one of the most important skills a player can develop. Reading is the ability of the player to judge the flight and trajectory of the ball and the direction the ball is going to be hit—basically it is another word to describe their perception. In soccer, we often term this decision making or game insight. Reading can be thought of as a player's ability to read or perceive a situation and formulate a decision.

Decision making is of a higher importance in the game of soccer. For example, a player may be really good at dribbling the ball between two cones, but that is an isolated technique. More important—and much more difficult to develop—is the ability to read or perceive when they should dribble in the game, where they should dribble, and how fast they should dribble in relation to their positioning on the field, the positioning of their teammates, and the positioning of the opponent. "We talk technique far too much in sports when, in reality, it wasn't a technical error, it was the player not being in the right place, or the right time based on whatever situation the game presented." Now, here comes the part where science may trump our preconceived notions of what works. "You don't develop reading and soccer IQ in drills. It develops through the interactions of the whole game and how the game plays out. That part a lot of people forget."

In volleyball, for example, a lot of coaches neglect the existence and importance of the net in their sport. "Sadly we ignore the net that we play over all the time and do all this training on the same side of the net. Coaches always admire how good their team looks during these drills, but then when they go to play and perform a serve and receive, the players can't serve-receive to save their life." Can you identify the problem in this situation? The vast majority of the actions made in volleyball involve receiving and hitting the ball over the net. If a coach plans training so that a majority of the time is spent training without a net, how effective is that training program in improving the player's ability in the actual game? It's not.

The soccer world is not exempt from this mistake. How many training exercises do we see coaches use that involve mannequins, cones, and flags in an attempt to represent real opposition? The issue with training without opposition is that 100% of every soccer game involves an opponent, and yet the majority of many training programs are spent in unopposed situations. That is akin to having our players hit the ball to each other on the same side of the net when we need to be spending our time training them to be able to serve-receive over the net.

Richard Schmidt, one of the pioneers of motor-learning research and author of *Motor Learning and Performance: From Principles to Application,* has a theory as to why coaches spend so much time in drills versus actual game-based training exercises. At a conference where he was listening to a coach advocate for the use of drills, Richard Schmidt offered this game-changing thought, "It sounds to me like you're practicing for practice, and not for performance." That is clearly what is happening, but it still doesn't explain why coaches use drills and other training methods that go against what we know about motor learning. Fortunately, John knows exactly why coaches tend to use drills even though they know them to be ineffective at improving motor skills. "When we do drills, the practice looks good. It's controlled, it's organized, it's structured, but when we go out and play, the transfer doesn't occur. When this happens, the players have to start learning when they play the actual game because practice isn't game-like enough." The problem is that we want to look good in drills and we pursue that objective in spite of the fact that it ends up making us look really bad in the actual games.

This is one of the biggest arguments for the use of small-sided games. If nothing else, motor-learning principles show us that we learn by doing, not by watching. "Small-sided games result in much more repetition and more learning, and players get better faster."

THE REAL GIANTS OF SOCCER COACHING

The fact is that we learn motor skills by doing the actual thing we are trying to learn or improve. John likes to make that point by asking people how they learned to drive. "My kids watched me drive for 16 years; they sat and watched me drive, but do you think they knew how to drive? No chance. They didn't learn how to drive until they started to drive."

Small-sided games allow younger players to get a lot of repetitions at specific soccer actions, but within the context of the actual game. "The net is so important in volleyball, and yet we just blow it off. We plan training in front of it, we think it looks good, the practices are beautiful, but then the ball comes flying over the net and the players look like they have no idea what they are doing because, guess what? They don't know what they are doing! And they don't know what they are doing because they haven't *done that*."

John encourages coaches to embrace the idea of training ugly. The fascination with drills comes from the fascination with organization and training that looks good. I mean, if training looks good then we have to be getting better, right? That is the usual logic, but in reality, the answer is actually no, we aren't getting better. Again, we are so slow to admit we are wrong—in spite of contradicting evidence—because we think we are right. The biggest reason that training ugly is so effective is because it results in better retention. As John Wooden said, "You haven't taught until they have learned." The terminology we can use to describe the two training approaches—drills versus game based—is more scientifically defined by two more, perhaps unfamiliar terms: blocked training and random training.

Blocked training is best depicted by imagining a training session where the coach has the players work on passing for 15 minutes, then dribbling for 15 minutes, and then shooting for 15 minutes. Further, these training exercises are usually characterized by the coach having the athletes perform a single skill, such as passing, over and over again with repetition being the key. However, the variance within the performance of that skill is minimized or completely non-existent. The simplest example may be two players passing back and forth for 15 minutes.

The issue, however, is that we know random training is more successful in creating retention of the motor skill being learned. "The remembering is superior when you train randomly versus blocked, which is what most drills are. When you do drills that are repetitive or blocked, the remembering is not as effective and the ability to problem solve and read things is not as effective. In the end, it's all about learning and how our brain remember things more effectively." The biggest issue with drills is that they are not effective in producing a learning effect. Random training—a training environment that creates a frequent change of tasks to confront and challenge the player with different stimuli to problem solve—is much more effective in creating a learning effect.

John likes that word. *Effective*. He doesn't like to think about this discussion as right versus wrong. What he wants is for coaches, across all sports and countries, to be more *effective.* "We know that random training is more effective. We know that whole training, instead of part training, is more effective. So the sooner you can get to the whole game and the random—including your being comfortable with the ugliness that may ensue—the better the skills will be remembered."

A secondary problem that usually follows the utilization of drills and blocked training is the use of very explicit coaching (i.e., telling players what to do). Telling players what to do is "the least effective way of creating a learning effect." Explicit coaching creates soccer players that turn to the coach to get the answer to every problem they have. The result is that these youth players grow up to become adult players that never learned to problem solve on their own. In other words, we are producing players that have underdeveloped in-game decision-making abilities.

The opposite of explicit learning is implicit learning, which lets the athletes figure everything out themselves. If we refer back to the example of how you learned to ride a bike, implicit learning is the reason that you could go find a bike right now and start riding it successfully, even though you probably haven't been on a bike in a few months or years. The reason you can do that is because you learned that task implicitly, so the retention of the motor skill still exists. "Getting on a bike after a year away from riding one and being able to take off right away shows you that those motor skills are really well learned." Again, we need to ask the question: do motor-science principles relegate the role of the coach to nothing more than a passive bystander? Of course not. John compares the role of the coach to the role Socrates, the ancient philosopher. "The role of the coach is to ask questions. Not because you don't know the answer, but to *guide* the athletes' discovery so that *they* give you the answer." Helping the athlete discover the answer to a specific problem helps the neurons in the brain remember the information more effectively, and for a longer term.

This is an example of a simple misunderstanding among coaches around the world and across all sports. You see, so many coaches are out to prove to other coaches that they know a lot. They are fearful that if they don't make long-winded and esoteric coaching points, their colleagues will look at them as inadequate and lacking knowledge. However, coaches that ask questions to their players and guide their learning do not do so because they don't know what they are doing. No, they do that because they want their *players* to know what they know. As John likes to say, "I know a lot of shit, but I want the players to know what I know."

MORE ON DRILLS

There are two main reasons why coaches still utilize drills. First, by far the most substantial reason behind the use of drills is that we teach the way we were taught. Unfortunately, many of today's coaches learned to play their sport through the use of drills and not based on the research regarding motor learning. The second reason is that coaches have to work harder when they can't control the drill. A common drill in volleyball is for the coach to stand on one side of the net while the players line up on the other side of the net. The coach serves a ball over, and the player receives the ball, bumps it to himself, and hits it back over to the coach before relegating himself to the back of the line. This drill is easily managed by the coach and doesn't require a lot of effort on his part. The problem is that the coach ends up getting more repetitions than everyone on the team!

John smashed that drill to pieces by breaking kids up into pairs and having them hit the ball over the net, bump it to themselves, and hit it back over repeatedly in a 1v1 fashion. He basically created a lot of mini 1v1 games across the gymnasium. "I had to work harder because I now have to manage all these smaller groups and I am running around trying to help all of these smaller groups." Drills have become commonplace because they are easy, controllable, and make practice look good, but the comfort of the coach should not take priority over the development of young athletes across the world.

There was a study conducted that looked at the development of professional players across the youth academies of the English Premier League teams. What the study found was that nearly all of the players received very similar drill-based programs, game-based programs, and competitive games, but by far the most important variable in deciding whether kids were signed to a professional contract by age 16 was the amount of "unstructured play they had, where there was no coach." That was where the biggest difference was because all of the other variables were pretty much the same. The kids that played more street soccer—or any soccer without a coach—ended up having the best chance of becoming a professional player. This is the reason why Johnny Henderson's Bristol Rovers academy has been a lightbulb in a dark room when it comes to producing better players. The performance playground, much like unstructured play, is characterized by "uneven, ugly, and chaotic games that have specific rules made up by the kids and a wide range of ages participating."

KIDS COACHING KIDS

John has had a profound question he has been asking for many, many years. "We know that what you teach, you learn—we know that to be true. So, knowing that, why do we not have our older players coaching and teaching the game to younger players?" If our eighth-graders taught our seventh-graders, how much better would that make our eighth-graders? It is an interesting question and fortunately, this concept has been applied in other parts of the world with massive success.

There is a U11 volleyball team out of Thailand that John has had the chance to visit and spend time with. "This U11 volleyball team could beat any high school team in the US without question." How is that possible? Because they have employed a program that tasks kids with teaching kids."This is what's so cool about it. School lets out and for the first 30 minutes of practice, the fifth-graders coach the first- through fourth-graders. The head coach sits on the side and relaxes and chills and tries to observe if what he has been teaching the fifth-graders is being understood. After 30 minutes of small-sided games—never bigger than 2v2 or 3v3—the head coach comes out and coaches the fifth-grade team for the remaining 30 minutes of practice. So, for half of the practice time, the fifth-graders are coaching, not playing. They are teaching the game!" There is a video online that shows the incredible skill these 11-year-olds have. "When you watch them play, you are just absolutely blown away because they are so skilled, but it's because they are applying the principle that what you teach, you learn." John believes that soccer clubs should take notice of this idea because it is a gift to your sixth-graders and your eighth-graders. It will make your eighth-graders better because they will be teaching what they are learning and your sixth-graders will respond better to being coached by someone they view as a peer rather than some "old fart" (John's words).

WHAT FREE-THROW SHOOTING CAN TEACH US ABOUT PRACTICING CORNER KICKS

One of the things John noticed about the way basketball coaches practice free throws—which is not too dissimilar from the way soccer coaches practice corner kicks and set plays—is that the players practice free throws by taking hundreds of free throws in a row. However, is that really how free throws (and corner kicks) appear in the game? "The problem is that, in the game, free throws are completely randomized. You might take one free throw ten minutes into the game, then another twenty minutes later, but you never take more than a couple in a row." Therefore, the learning the players experience in the actual game will be more effective than the learning they experience taking 100 corner kicks or set plays in a row in practice. "The learning will be more effective because of the forgetting the player experiences between free throws." Therefore, the key to maximizing the learning of a free throw is to take those 100 free throws and randomly insert them throughout the 90-minute practice.

If you look at set plays and, specifically, corner kicks, we see the same issue. It is perfectly fine to want to practice twenty corner kicks, but taking twenty corner kicks in a row is not as effective in creating a learning effect as taking twenty corner kicks randomly distributed throughout a training session. "Maybe you take two corner kicks and then you don't do any for ten minutes. Then the coach can blow the whistle and the players can take two more, and by the end of the practice, they will still get twenty corner kicks in, but because the players' brains had to forget the other corner kicks and then come back, they are going to remember the corner kicks better and problem solve new things more effectively." Retention of a motor skill occurs when we have to forget before we have to remember.

PLAYING THE RIGHT WAY FOR DEVELOPMENT

Although I don't believe there is a right way to play the game at the highest levels, I believe that there is a right way to play the game when developing players. John coached his son's youth soccer team growing up and encouraged his team to pass the ball to one another in order to progress the ball down the field. Unfortunately, this led John to a stark realization. "In soccer, at the lowest and youngest levels, the worst teams win." In other words, John realized that the teams they were playing against were perfectly happy to kick the ball down the field as far as they could close to John's goal. More often than not, the other team would score from this tactic. On the other side of the pitch, John encouraged his team to pass the ball to one another to progress the ball down the field, which often led to a loss of possession as his young players were learning the skills of the game.

In volleyball, John experienced a similar situation. John's youth volleyball teams always hit the ball three times on their side of the net in order to maximize the skill and motor learning of each player. However, the opponents would hit the ball back over in just one hit, which will lead to fewer mistakes and more points at the youngest ages—at the expense of the learning and skill acquisition of the players on that team. "My team is trying to pass it to the setter who is in a specific area and the setter is trying to set it along the net somewhere and then the final person is trying to jump as high as they can and hit it over the net and down to the court. The other teams, however, just hit the ball over in one hit. Any way they can get it over is good, anywhere in the court is good, and any height they hit it over at is good—it doesn't matter. So, at the beginning level who is going to win? If my team is going pass, set, and hit, and the other team is just hitting it over in one, of course we will lose more often." But, the question is: who is *learning* more?

John's experience, which I am sure a lot of youth-soccer coaches will know to be true, is that once his team learned to read a ball hit over the net on the first attempt and they learned how to pass, set, and hit with their teammates, they never lost to those teams again. At the beginning stages of the game, playing to win by having your kids forego skill acquisition and the ability to read and perceive game-like situations will cost those players in the long run. John's teams may lose at the earliest ages, but while your team is kicking the ball as far up field as they can, John's team is learning to perceive, read, and make decisions on where, when, and how to pass the ball, which will lead to them beating your team as they get older and acquire the skills necessary to execute those decisions.

POSITIVE AND NEGATIVE ERRORS

When John begins coaching a group of players, he is always on the lookout for what he terms the perfect, positive, and negative executions of a decision. For example, in volleyball and soccer, every technique or execution has a positive error and a negative error. For example, in volleyball, the perfect execution would be hitting the ball into the court. However, two possibilities are the player hitting the ball into the net, or hitting the ball outside of the court. But which mistake is better? "Hitting the ball into the net is always bad. Hitting the ball into the net doesn't teach the other team what *out* looks like, for example." So hitting the ball over the net but out of the court is better than hitting the ball into the net. Hitting the ball out of the court is a positive error and hitting the ball into the net is a negative error.

In order to coach his players implicitly, John places two pieces of tape on his volleyball nets. The first piece of tape is at the top of the net with an arrow pointing up labeled, "HEAVEN." The other piece of tape is placed below it with an arrow pointing down labeled, "HELL." "When I hit over the net, I always want my players to hit into heaven and never into hell. When I serve, the same thing applies because all of these good things can happen if they hit the ball into heaven, you know? The other team may touch it, or the referee may call it in—all of these things that aren't possible if you hit into hell. Nothing good ever happens when you hit it into the net." Every skill, regardless of sport, has a grey area of errors that are better than others.

In soccer, we can use the example of shooting on goal. Hell—or the negative error—would be a player shooting at the goal, but hitting it off target, meaning they hit the ball over the goal or wide of the goal. Heaven—or the positive error—would be shooting the ball on goal, but directly at the goalkeeper. This positive error still might result in something good (e.g., the goalkeeper could not make the save, he could give up a rebound), but nothing good happens if our players shoot into hell.

GAME LIKE

One of the biggest mistakes coaches make when it comes to creating game-based or game-like exercises in training is that they forget the concept of scoring. "Game-like activities should include the concept of the score, so players get comfortable with scoring." It is not unheard of for John to make the warm-up competitive. One of his favorite ways to warm up his players is to have them play short-court games of 1v1 or 2v2, but he always makes them keep score. With that said, there are a few different ways that John likes to keep score.

First, John uses cooperative scoring. Cooperative scoring involves the players working together to see how many volleys over the net they can get in a row, in game-like fashion.

In cooperative scoring, the players are keeping score, but they are working together to achieve the highest score possible. Competitive scoring is the more familiar version of scoring that measures who earns more points. John sometimes uses cooperative and competitive scoring together. Anyone that has ever played ping-pong will be familiar with this concept. When you are trying to decide who serves in a game of ping-pong, both players participate in a cooperative rally of five hits back and forth before they make the game competitive. After the fifth volley over the net, the two players will compete and try to hit an unreturnable shot. The phrase that John came up with to define this type of scoring is called *transition scoring*. The benefit of transition scoring is that it allows the players to establish a rhythm and get repetitions in before making the game competitive. In soccer, we use this quite often and might not even know it; it is quite common for the first-pass-is-free rule to apply to many possession games and rondos. That is an example of transition scoring. The first pass is made and, after the first pass, the defenders are allowed to defend. However, without the use of transition scoring, it may be impossible for the players to get the ball moving as the defenders can easily read the direction of the first pass. All three types of scoring are important to use in order to maximize motor learning, success, and repetition all in game-like scenarios.

There isn't a secret to John's practice designs. He doesn't have a database of 300 drills because he hates drills. John keeps it simple. He plays a variety of small-sided games and may have a theme for the day that he emphasizes (e.g., shooting with your left foot) which is always challenged inside of the small-sided game. John will use the same small-sided game setups all the time, but he will change the focus point (e.g., left foot becomes right foot), or he will change the scoring. John wrote a book that is available for free called *Mini-Volley* that has over 70 different scoring variations. "You come up with these fun ways to keep score differently, but you still play the games 1v1 or 2v2. The most important concept that coaches need to understand is that we don't *drill* soccer, we *play* soccer."

John has a riddle that he likes to call soccer math. What do you call it when there are four players and a ball? The answer is 2v2 (i.e., if four kids are together and they have one ball, they will play 2v2). But what do you call it when there are four players, one ball, and one coach? A drill, or 4v0. "That should give coaches an idea of where they are going wrong." As I mentioned earlier, John has spent a lot of time in Brazil, as volleyball is one of the biggest sports in the South American country. For this reason, John has had access to a lot of conversations with Brazilian athletes of all sports. John found himself discussing some of the concepts of motor learning with a Brazilian soccer player, and the player said something that really hit home for John. "He looked at me and he said, 'My first coach was the game.' What I find is that because the drills look good, coaches and players feel that automatically translates to improvement, but we know that it doesn't. These are the teams that can drill, but they can't play."

STOP CUTTING PLAYERS

Everyone has an opinion regarding the best methodology for producing future professionals, but the truth is that the method is the least important factor in creating pros. Honestly, the coach that claims he has the secret formula for producing pro players also has a bridge for sale in Brooklyn. John has two easy steps to produce top talent in any sport:

1. Decide slowly
2. Keep kids playing

The real factor in producing top talent is how many kids continue to play the sport as they get older. "The goal is to keep as many kids playing as possible because you don't know who is going to be good, or when they will be good." John still can't believe that there are tryouts and cuts in youth sports around the world.

John worked with a local high school near his residence in Colorado Springs to test this concept. "We had 100 kids try out at the junior-high level and then they would cut 75 kids to make the seventh- and eighth-grade teams. I talked to the athletic director about creating a league for the 75 kids that were cut from the team; they only practiced one time per week, but they would get the other court in the gym to be able to play games all the time. By the time this group was eligible to try out for the varsity team, over 50% of the kids that made the varsity team were from the group of kids that were originally cut." The message is that because the kids that were originally cut were given a chance to continue playing and improving, they were able to develop their skills and many of them progressed to the point that they became the stars of the varsity team. In the past, before John Kessel came to town, those 75 kids never would have picked up a volleyball again.

Stephen Curry is probably the best example of why we need to decide slowly and keep kids playing. Many people will cite Michael Jordan, but he wasn't cut, he was just put on the junior-varsity team. Ironically enough, being put on the JV squad was probably the best thing that could have happened to Jordan because he got more repetition as opposed to sitting on the bench for the varsity team.Stephen Curry, on the other hand, was only offered one college basketball scholarship. "Look at where he is now? At 18 years old, all the expertise in the world is saying that Stephen Curry is only worth one college basketball scholarship to one school. And how wrong were they?" Stephen Curry is exactly why we need to decide slowly and keep kids playing the game.

CHAPTER 28

GAME-LIKE PRACTICE AND HOW KIDS LEARN

TODD BEANE

Todd Beane is the founder of the TOVO Soccer Academy in Barcelona. Todd moved to Barcelona in 2002 to begin working with Johan Cruyff to launch and build the Cruyff Institute and eventually Cruyff Football. Todd married Chantal Cruyff, Johan's daughter, and worked with his father-in-law for nearly 15 years before Johan's untimely death in 2016. The TOVO Academy is Todd's continuation of the legacy he set out to establish with his late father-in-law. Over the past two decades, Todd has learned from practitioners at La Masia, Barcelona's infamous youth academy, and his father-in-law, Johan Cruyff, to develop clear ideas about youth development, positional play, rondos, and all aspects related to the success of Spanish and Catalonian soccer.

Doing a start-up with Steve Jobs — How to think like Johan Cruyff — If it's not fun, then why are we doing it — Most of the training in the US is crap — Messi doesn't have 50 moves — It wasn't a move, but a solution — Quizas — How a bushel of apples can make you a better coach — What soccer coaches and doctors that used bloodletting have in common — A Montessori school for soccer — The consortium of coaches — How to coach a rondo — Cognition versus competence: missing the boat in youth development

"Who knows, Josh, you could have been Messi if you had better training growing up." That is the sentence that best depicts Todd Beane's thoughts on youth development. Although I doubt the validity of that statement, there is no question that I would have been a much better player had I not been subjected to so many drills and outdated training methods during my youth career. But if there is someone that would have an idea about how to build the next Messi, it might be the guy that ate dinner next to Johan Cruyff every day for the past 16 years.

Todd Beane moved to Barcelona in 2002 to begin working in Johan Cruyff's basement to build the Cruyff Institute. A fax, a couch, and a desk were the only pieces of equipment available in Johan's basement, which doubled as the Cruyff Institute's headquarters—humble surroundings considering Todd was about to meet one of the greatest minds our game has ever seen.

Johan had just come back from Amsterdam, but the jet-lagged #14 still had enough energy to make his way downstairs and meet the young American kid eager to learn. "It was like doing a start-up with Steve Jobs" is how Todd describes the first time he met the soccer genius. "He sat down next to me and explained to me what his vision was and what he wanted to accomplish. Then he started asking me to brainstorm and all of a sudden there I was brainstorming with one of the best minds in soccer, and I was trying to come up with something intelligent enough to keep my job."

It wasn't very long after that first encounter that Johan Cruyff the boss became Johan Cruyff the father-in-law. Todd married Chantal Cruyff and began an odyssey in Barcelona to build a legacy in the name of Johan Cruyff. One of Johan's greatest wishes prior to his untimely death in 2016 was to build something that would make great strides in educating the next generation of players. Todd has made Johan's mission his own; launching the TOVO Academy in 2016 was Todd's way of giving back everything Johan taught him in order to create the next generation of Iniestas, Xavis, and Messis.

Present-day Todd Beane is a little bit different from Todd Beane prior to meeting Johan Cruyff. A product of the US Soccer education system, Todd grew up outside of Boston, Massachusetts playing more hockey than he did soccer. Todd played college soccer at Dartmouth and played professionally in the US professional leagues. However, Todd soon discovered that his real soccer education had yet to begin.

HOW TO START THINKING LIKE JOHAN CRUYFF

If I could summarize the biggest difference between Todd Beane and Johan Cruyff when they met in early 2002, it would be that one watched soccer by looking at the ball, while the other watched for the space. "I didn't really understand the game in terms of spatial relations until I met Johan. Every comment that he would make had to do with position play." Countries like the US still look at the game very sequentially. We assume that there is a logical order and sequential structure to the flow of a match, but Johan understood that the game is consequential. Like a chess match, soccer is about asking the question "Who is capable of doing what, and in what space, to attack the opponent relative to your strengths and weaknesses?" Johan was a chess master when it came to soccer and like a chess master he saw the game fifteen moves ahead of everyone else. "Johan would always use chess as a metaphor—to describe positional play, he would say things like "If you move your pawn to the right that might be okay for now, but in ten moves that is going to problematic because of the spatial relationship that it will cause." Todd learned, during those conversations with Cruyff, that the first step to becoming a better coach was to stop looking at the ball and start focusing on the space.

I asked Todd if he ever disagreed with Johan Cruyff about certain aspects of soccer and Todd kindly reminded me that "you don't necessarily disagree with Johan Cruyff about anything related to soccer, especially when you are a kid from Westminster, Massachusetts." Fair enough. But Todd did expect there to be some secret formula or hidden ingredient missing in the US that existed in Barcelona regarding player development and soccer strategy that would give Todd an advantage over other practitioners of the game. However, Todd soon realized that this was not the case. For example, there are many soccer coaches and sport coaches that talk about character. Perhaps our problem is that we only pay those words lip service, while countries like Spain and practitioners like Johan Cruyff make that the focus of their awareness. "I can't tell you how many times Johan would talk about the character of a person first. He needed to understand the character of a person first to be able to understand where that player can play and what he can handle."

Another aspect that coaches in the US tend to overlook is the importance of fun in the act of coaching, playing, and watching soccer. That is something that Johan Cruyff talked about more frequently than positional play or spatial relations. "Johan really believed that soccer needs to be enjoyed at every level, even the highest, most pressure-filled environment that Barcelona would be at." You see, for Johan Cruyff, it was more about the spectacle than the result. Winning with style, playing for fun, and playing with passion took precedence over pressure from the media, the fans, or the board to win. Johan would always say to his fitness coaches and trainers, "We have to be fit, but we have to be laughing." Sometimes we lose sight of that sentiment; soccer is supposed to be fun. In fact, Johan would sometimes be challenged on that belief. Fellow coaches and players would look at him and say, "Yes, Johan, we can have fun, but soccer is also very serious, so we can't be laughing all the time," to which Johan always replied, "If it's not fun, then why are we doing it?"

MOST OF THE TRAINING IN THE US IS CRAP

Todd is pretty unapologetic about his views regarding the training methodology of most coaches and clubs around the US. "Most of the training I see back home is crap." Like John Kessel, Todd sees coaches continually ignore everything we know about pedagogical practices and neuroscience. "It drives me crazy that we continue to train in the way that we do under the premise that this is the way it's always been done, even though it flies in the face of modern research regarding learner-centric programming, neuroscience, and the way that kids learn applied skills (i.e., motor learning)."

Part of the problem in the US—and other countries—is that we tend to judge what happened and prejudice our own past. For example, just because a player from your club gets a college scholarship, a youth national team call-up, or signs for a professional club, that doesn't always mean that he received great training. "That's what we call a false relationship because you don't know what would have happened had there been different training." For the longest time, the US has really advocated the use of unopposed training exercises even though we know those exercises lack any scientific validity on how kids learn skills. Therefore, just because all of the best players the US have been produced using that sort of training doesn't mean that it is a good or sound training methodology.

Todd doesn't really look at it from a standpoint of unopposed versus opposed training exercises. Instead, he looks for what he calls the 3 Cs:

1. Cognition—Is it developing cognition?
2. Competency—Is it developing competencies?
3. Character—Is it developing character?

If a training exercise is able to include all three of these elements, then Todd knows he has done a good job. Isolated drills without opposition give the coach and the players a false sense of learning. "When you look at the studies on longer term retention, unopposed and isolated activities are some of the worst ways to learn an applied skill." One of the questions that Todd always asks himself and other coaches when they are planning training for the day is "Would this be something you would enjoy participating in?" Todd has put coaches through training sessions where he included lots of lines, cones, and mindless repetition, and within two minutes they all had enough and were bored to tears. The question then becomes "Why would we impose that on our players when we know there are better ways of engaging the brain and the body?"

Todd believes that the United States has dissected the game into unrecognizable parts. We have dissected the game into the idea that players need to learn 50 moves and then they will be Messi—and that's not true because Messi doesn't have 50 moves. We haven't just done this in soccer, but also in our approach to education. We want a child that is intelligent, talented, and capable, but our approach to achieving that has been severely misguided. Kids today have 45 minutes of social studies, 45 minutes of math, and 45 minutes of English, but we are just teaching kids facts. "When the kids get older and they have to problem solve on their own, they are totally lost."

Where did this dissection of the game come from? Wiel Coerver, the legendary Dutch coach, famously dissected the game into its various parts in order to understand how we could develop more creative and capable 1v1 attacking players. Public educators took a similar approach in thinking that dissecting the whole into its parts would somehow allow us to produce a better whole. "The problem with that approach is that it flies in the face of sound and natural learning processes; that is not the way children learn."

Todd's background as a teacher has helped him understand the theory of education and how kids truly learn. "It comes down to this: kids learn through play and prototyping, and then refinement." Kids learn by diving into the subject matter; they make sense of the success and failure around that, they refine it, and then they redo it. This establishes patterns and processes that become imbedded in the neural circuits of the child that help them make sense of the environment around them. "When you dissect something, it actually goes against the natural process of learning, which means that you are developing a different part of the brain than the one needed to be able to perform and play the match on the weekend."

We are doing a disservice to young soccer players across the globe when we dissect the game into these unrecognizable parts. The result is that the players become lost when they have to put all of this training together in a match that requires the understanding of the subject of soccer as a whole. "The kids can do 50 moves, but they can't decide when, where, or why to do that move." Todd visits the US quite frequently, and every time he does he has the same observational takeaway. "I see kids who are equally skilled as the ones in Spain, but who have such a poor sense of positional play and cognition." Unfortunately for the rest of the world, that is what Barcelona and Spain do so well. They teach the kids at the youngest ages how to understand the spatial relationships and how to solve problems based upon the variables the defenders present to them.

The funniest thing is that Cristiano Ronaldo doesn't have 50 moves. Lionel Messi doesn't have 50 moves. In fact, Johan Cruyff never even practiced the infamous Cruyff turn until the second that he did it in the game. Johan gave Todd some insight into that infamous move, and it turns out, it wasn't a move at all. "I will never forget this, but he looked at me and told me that he never practiced that move. It wasn't a move, but a solution." That is what Johan Cruyff instilled at Barcelona, "developing young players that are capable of thinking—in real time—about the solutions that they want to execute."

When you think about the game in terms of solutions, you realize that there are no real absolutes in the game of soccer. We, as coaches, have no idea what problems are going to arise during each moment of a specific game, but if our players are well versed in problem solving, then our worries will be lessened. One of the absolutes that Todd can't stand is when coaches say things like, "Pass and move." Todd was working with a team in Los Angeles and every single player was running all over the pitch like mad men. "I asked them why they were running everywhere and they said, 'Our coach says to "pass and move,"' and I thought to myself, but why move if you are in the perfect position. Sometimes it should be pass and stand."

Another common training error is the use of pattern play against mannequins or cones. Players are asked to repeat a standardized pattern to goal in the hopes of creating some sort of muscle memory of the pattern. The issue, however, is that this eliminates the interference of the defenders, which distorts the perception of the players. Instead of perceiving the spaces vacated by the defenders' shape, conceiving which space they should move into, deciding to move into that space, and then executing an action in that space, the players are just executing an action in a specified space. Nobody wants to acknowledge that predetermined patterns fail in transferring to the game because the only way a specific pattern works is if the defenders are positioned *exactly* as the mannequins and cones they are playing against. Oh, and if we really want there to be a transfer, we better hope that we are playing against mannequins on the weekend too. So, why do we do patterns? Like John Kessel mentioned in his chapter, it is because practice looks good. It is organized and the players will be able to successfully execute the pattern demanded of them. The issue is that the players are not tasked with recognizing the positional cues of the opponent in determining that pattern. The point is that there are no absolutes in soccer. We cannot tell our players exactly where to stand or run because without the reference of the opponent, their teammates, the ball, and the spaces available, it is impossible to know. So, sometimes a comment like "Pass and move" should really be "Pass and stand."

In Spain, they have a saying to answer questions that are dependent upon varying circumstances. "Quizas. *Quizas* means maybe or possibly. So in Spain, we may show a player that they can go into a certain space, but quizas—or maybe—if the variables change, maybe you don't. The only person that can determine that is not on the sideline; it is the player in real time with the vision in front of them. So we need to be focused on developing the type of player that can deal with those variables. Maybe you do, or maybe you don't." The goal, for the coach, is to stay away from the absolutes and teach players how to manage the variables and attempt solutions.

One of the biggest reasons why this is so hard for coaches to do is because they want control over everything. They want to control every single variable, but that just isn't how the game is played. We want the knowledge on the field, not on the sideline. Early on in his coaching career, Todd realized that he was frequently trying to control everything from the sideline. This is often termed *joystick coaching*, a reference to coaching like you would play a video game. Todd wanted to stop himself from doing this so he purchased a bushel of apples that he brought to every single game. "Anytime I felt the urge to say something stupid, I would grab an apple and take a bite and that prevented me from saying stupid things or trying to control every little detail." This wasn't just something that improved Todd's coaching, it also improved the players. "I learned that my players got better. By the end of the season, they were much more capable of coming up with their own solutions because I wasn't trying to provide them from the sidelines."

Todd's advice to coaches still dissecting the game and using isolated passing, dribbling, and shooting drills is simple. "Let's put the game back together, let's make meaningful progressions, but let's do conceptual layering rather than technical layering, and let's give the kids an opportunity to solve those problems in real time in order to hone their cognitive skills as much as we have been honing their competencies or their technical skills." Todd feels that if we can do that, then we will become capable of producing a midfielder of high credibility.

This is how Todd would break down a simple concept such as passing and receiving. Passing and receiving deals with execution, so we are talking about competence. However, there is always a cognitive element to soccer as well, but the cognitive element in an isolated passing-and-receiving drill is severely diminished. "In isolation, the coach has prescribed for them what to do—A to B, B to C, C to D—so there is no perception. There is no need to conceive because the coach has done it for them. There is no need to decide because that has been done for them, and there is no need to deceive because they are playing against cones." Even though Todd despises the use of cones to mimic opponents, he does wish they could replace actual opponents—at least during his career. "Hell, if I played against cones I would have been a national-team player." However, if the coach can take a diamond- or square-shaped passing drill and add a player in the middle, that changes the entire cognitive process of the players. The players now have to perceive relative to that defender and the space available to them. This forces them to decide whether they should move right or left before they have the opportunity to deceive because there is pressure—and they still have to execute the passing and receiving, with applied pressure this time. "Drills done in isolation rob the players of the cognitive process that is critical to becoming a talented player. That theft is an injustice to them, and that is why we don't develop players in the United States as we should."

Todd and I went back and forth discussing the repercussions, in the business world, of a company that continues to use methods to create products in the same way that they did 30 years ago. In soccer, that is exactly what we see coaches continually do. Can you imagine a company, in today's world, still making flip phones? "I don't think we should be doing things in the same way that we have been for 30 years, especially when we have yet to produce a world-class midfielder while countries like Spain have produced around 100 in that same time span. There are very few industries where what was happening 30 years ago is still happening today and being profitable."

Todd doesn't exclude himself from the criticism. "I was a guy that didn't give enough credit to my players' capacities to solve problems on the field. I used a lot of exercises that weren't as fruitful as I know now from studying the learning process, so it's important to understand that criticizing our past isn't intended as a way to beat ourselves up. It's just to progress as a profession." Could you imagine taking a visit to your doctor's office and having them put leeches on you to get rid of an illness? Obviously, that would be ridiculous, so the question we need to ask ourselves as coaches is "What are we doing today—still—that we know is not as effective as the alternative and then why are we still doing it if we know it's not justified?"

There are many clubs that are still applying outdated and ineffective methodologies, but perhaps even worse is the lack of direction that clubs apply to their methodology. Todd believes that it is essential for a club to know what kind of players they want to produce. If a club doesn't envision the end product of their player-development program, then how can they even think about a correct methodology? That would be like a soft-drink company spending time worrying about the manufacturing of their cans when they don't even have an idea of what they want the drink to taste like. "Clubs have to identify the type of player that they hope to produce."

Todd has taken inspiration from Italian educator Maria Montessori. Montessori education is a model of human development that aligns with the way that Todd believes children learn; it resonates with him, and it's the type of schooling he wants to send his children to. Todd believes that is how youth and professional clubs should determine the philosophy that will help guide the application of that philosophy. For example, Todd would want "a Montessori school to be filled with craftsmen of Maria Montessori's vision of education in order to understand it, implement it well, and be consistent in its implementation." Todd also wants the same thing from a soccer club.

The real secret to FC Barcelona's success is that they have chosen a philosophy for their club, and the coaches within the club are craftsmen of that philosophy. They refine their abilities daily to understand and implement that philosophy consistently. More specifically, the philosophy at Barcelona is based on Cruyff's understanding of the spatial relations of the game, often called positional play. Therefore, the coaches throughout FC Barcelona are craftsmen of positional play. Their jobs are to become the very best at understanding and implementing that philosophy on a daily basis.

In the United States, on the other hand, we have what Todd likes to call a "consortium of coaches." "The U7s are doing something, but the U8s are doing something else. I don't think we would stand for it in education, and I don't think we should stand for it in our own soccer-club culture either. A child could be with a club for 12 years and not one would be aligned with the next, and for me, that is incoherent and incomprehensible. I would want a coherent and cohesive plan; of course, within that plan there is flexibility based on what the players are accomplishing and what still needs to be learned." Unfortunately, established philosophies and research-based methodologies are virtually nonexistent in soccer clubs across the US and elsewhere. "Without a coherent curriculum, plan, or identity about how and why we are developing a specific type of player, I think children end up lost as to what it is they are supposed to be learning. What ends up happening is that the learning of the child becomes a variable that comes with the coach that they have." When that happens, the best thing that the child can hope for is that they have a good coach. "If they get a bad coach or a different coach next year, then the variables change once again. That is not an effective way of helping players learn a cohesive programming over the course of ten years, which makes building competent and talented soccer players very difficult."

THE REAL BARCELONA WAY

Unfortunately, there is a lot of misinformation about Barcelona and their youth-development methodology that circulates, particularly, in the United States. A lot of coaches that have never even been to Spain are telling other coaches and technical directors how Barcelona approaches youth development. Well, Todd is here to set the record straight. As someone that has lived in Barcelona for nearly the last two decades, Todd has a good idea of what La Masia, Barcelona's infamous youth-development training center, has done to build professional soccer players such as Iniesta, Messi, and Xavi.

La Masia and the Barcelona Way really began in 1989 with the arrival of Johan Cruyff and his implementation of continuity in the programming and concepts being taught across the entirety of the club. Cruyff placed a massive emphasis on the cognitive development of each player and applied novel research toward the way people learn in order to encourage the youth players to learn through mistakes. However, the real secret—if there is one—is that Barcelona established their metaphorical Montessori way. "The reason why clubs like Barcelona—and even Ajax—continue to be in the top three of the European Clubs Association regarding player development is because they have committed. They have picked their poison, so to speak; they've committed to a curriculum, a style of play, and the production of a certain style of player, and they are religious in their approach to that."

Todd is fortunate enough to be able to speak to coaches at La Masia on an almost daily basis and what he finds is that these coaches are true craftsmen. Their mission is to master the curriculum, style of play, and pedagogy necessary to continually produce the type of players that Barcelona want to produce. Unlike a lot of unsuccessful clubs, in terms of youth development, coaches at La Masia don't get to show up to training and do whatever they want. "Although they are very qualified coaches—more so than your average US coach—they don't just get some balls, some pinnies, and some cones from the club and say, 'Hey thanks, I'll see you guys in June.' They are held accountable to following the Barcelona curriculum in a cohesive fashion." The flexibility, ingenuity, and innovation come from the many conversations that the youth coaches participate in. The coaches get together constantly to talk about the efficacies of their current practices and methods, which creates a constantly evolving conversation about being craftsmen. "They stick to the curriculum, tweak it as needed, but stay faithful to the overall essence of the club." That is really the success of Barcelona. Johan Cruyff established and created a certain style of play based on his interpretation of the game and then he went through and thought about how they could create a Xavi, an Iniesta, and a Messi. The current Barcelona coaches still contribute to that vision faithfully. "It's a clear philosophy, it's just one interpretation of the game, but they are faithful to it."

HOW TO COACH A RONDO

Rondos have become YouTube and social media fodder for players and coaches around the globe. Unfortunately, this has led to a mass adoption of rondos as a training exercise, but without the conceptual understanding of what rondos are intended to teach players about the game. In fact, Major League Soccer made a video in 2016 that publicized the 5v2. Many coaches in the US probably think that is the only rondo in existence, but that is beside the point. The point is that the video showcased the global misconceptions about rondos. They aren't just a warm-up exercise or an exercise for the players to have a bit of fun. Rondos are a fractal representation of the game of soccer, full of attacking, defending, and transitioning moments that can be used to teach various concepts of a coach's game model. Rondos are a far cry from the poorly applied versions I have seen in the US and elsewhere.

Rondos are a staple of Spanish training methodology and TOVO Academy, but not the rondos that many coaches have come to acknowledge. "A rondo is more than just the YouTube download where guys are just standing in a circle and playing." For example, Todd may do a 4v1 rondo that puts a check next to all the items on his three C checklist.

1. Cognition—"Is there perception, conception, decision, deception, execution, and assessment? Those are the steps that we consider to make up the cognitive process in soccer."
2. Competencies—"Are there competencies required? Yes, passing and receiving."

3. Character—"Is there character required? Yes, because it is a competitive exercise and if you give up the ball, you are in the middle—and nobody likes to be in the middle."

However, the rondo fails in achieving these three elements if it is done in the US fashion; in other words, it has to be done *seriously*. "If it is done flippantly while the coach is setting up cones, and the players are passing, moving, and receiving poorly, then it is of no value." It is important to understand that the rondo, in and of itself, has no more value than any other exercise. Just like any training exercise, it must be done with purpose and intention in order to maximize the value taken from the exercise.

Todd views the rondos as massively important in teaching conceptual items regarding the spatial relations of the game. "For me, it is the first relationship a player will have with a system of play." In the aforementioned 4v1, the player on the ball will have width and depth—two wide players as options and a deep player as an option. Obviously, this is width and depth, but it can also be used in relation to a system of play. The player on the ball can be the center back, the two wide players can be the outside backs, and the deepest player can be the striker or attacking midfielder. "It is the first spatial understanding of width and depth that you begin to fill out in the player's understanding of the game."

Todd will build this rondo into what he calls positional games that always require a neutral player. Basically, Todd will build the 4v1 rondo by adding more players into the middle until he ends up with a 3-2-1 formation, which is what he likes to play in his seven-a-side system. That leads into a 3-2-3 system, which leads into a 4-3-3 system. "So, for us, a rondo isn't just passing and receiving and getting your legs warmed up; it is a rigorous competence, cognitive, and character-development exercise." If the rondo is taken seriously and conceptually layered into a positional-play game and finally a training game, Todd believes that the players can a lot out of a session with that structure. "Rondos, into position games, into training games is the structure we like to follow so that the players can recognize those patterns, and the patterns can become embedded into the brains of the players so that they begin to solve problems they have seen before."

This figure is an example of a positional 4v1 rondo that teaches players the concepts of width and depth.

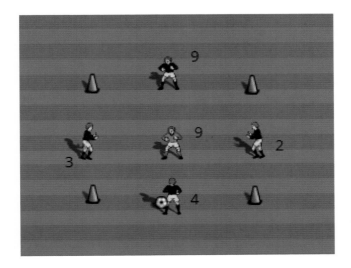

This figure shows an example of a positional game that uses a 4v4+3 to put both teams in a 3-2-1 formation when in possession of the ball. This exercise serves as a nice progression of the 4v1 into a more complex environment, while still working on the concepts of width and depth.

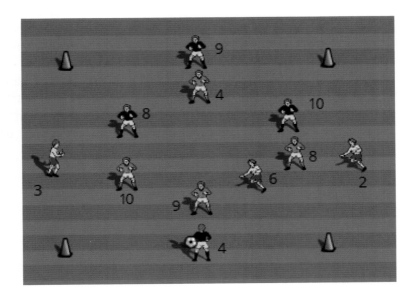

A training game would be a more traditional 3-2-1 versus 3-2-1 that resembles a game. The hope would be that the concepts of width and depth are exploited and utilized in the full complexity of the game of 7v7.

Todd had a high-level academy team come down from Portland, Oregon to train with the TOVO Academy late last year. He started them off in a 4v1 rondo inside of an 8x8 yard square that is quite large for TOVO standards. Todd noticed right away that the kids had never been taught how to do a rondo properly. "Instead of passing the ball across the body of the person receiving, they would pass to the foot closest to them, which ends up delivering a burden, instead of a blessing. They approached the rondo as 'I don't want to be in the middle no matter what kind of pass I deliver.'" Todd's TOVO teams know to receive the ball across their body and deliver a blessing of a pass, not a burden. "Passing with intent, receiving with intent, and executing impeccably—when the players do that, you get rhythm."

The Portland players excitedly told Todd that they also do rondos in Portland, but with the qualifier that they didn't do them *like this*. Todd asked them to expand further and they responded with, "We kind of just joke around, we just kind of do it, but nobody ever teaches us why. It's kind of a warm-up and we don't really take it seriously like you do here." That is the difference. In a 4v1, Todd is adamant that his players receive across their body, pass across the body, and keep their hips open to the passing options, and it is an overload on the cognitive process of perceiving the options that are available, using the best option available, and adjusting accordingly.

Todd had that team in TOVO for eight sessions. By the eighth session, they revisited the 4v1, but this time in a 3x3 yard grid. "Eight sessions prior to that final session, they were playing in an 8x8 and they could barely string together seven passes. In the 3x3 grid, they strung together more than twenty passes with ease." The players were amazed at how much they improved over the course of eight sessions and the last thing they said to Todd in reference to their improvement was, "Nobody has ever explained it to us like this." The takeaway for coaches is that there is doing a 4v1 and then there is doing a rondo.

Todd finds that more coaches need to ask *why* when they come across a training exercise that they like or want to use. It's not good enough to just print out a drill that Guardiola used because it's Guardiola. "Coaches need to ask *why*? What does the coach get out of it?" Only then can it have a chance of becoming something a coach can adopt to their arsenal. "Every time you go through that process, it makes you a better coach. It forces you to ask yourself the question 'Do you really know why you are using this drill?'"

Todd has extensive experience as an educator and likes to tell the story of an English teacher he worked with to drive home this point to coaches. Todd asked the teacher what was going to be on the final exam and she began to answer, "Well, we have twenty minutes of vocabulary..." and right away Todd said, "Stop." Todd thought for a second and asked her, "Why are you doing vocabulary?" The teacher frustratingly answered back, "I know you, Beane, now you are going to drive me crazy with all sorts of questions." They both chuckled before Todd got to his point. "This is the final exam. This is when a student is supposed to celebrate all that they have learned and show you that they have mastered something that you are proud of and that they can bring with them to the next grade level. So, my question is whether vocabulary is the most important thing that you are teaching them." The teacher responded, "No, of course not." To which Todd responded quickly, "Then what is?! What is the most important thing?" The teacher answered, "I want them to be able to, in written and verbal form, articulate a coherent argument." Todd excitedly responded, "That's a brilliant answer! But are you testing that?" The teacher acknowledged that she wasn't testing that through vocabulary, to which Todd responded with a logical idea, "Then just get rid of the vocabulary." Todd's message, in this context, can be applied to a host of different things regarding child development. "Let's hold the kids accountable for the most important things." In soccer, the most important things are the cognitive processes and impeccable execution, but it is not just execution or the amassing of 50 moves.

KNOWING WHEN TO USE TOUCH RESTRICTIONS

Raymond Verheijen likes to say that touch restrictions are for coaches that can't coach. In other words, it is better to teach your players *why* it is important to play quickly than to put everyone on two-touch limit. The learning adaptation will be much greater if you teach them why. Todd's approach is similar. As he calls it, "We change the variables and observe."

The variables that Todd changes are often termed *constraints*. Constraints are rules of a small-sided game or training exercise that encourage a specific adaptation that the coach wants the players to learn implicitly. In other words, Todd may say that the only way to score is from a cross in the widest channel, a constraint that encourages the adaptation that he wants without him explicitly telling the players to cross the ball from the wide channel. "We change the variables and observe."

Todd uses these constraints to better observe the reaction of his players to the task demanded of them. "If I change the variable in an exercise, I am immediately watching for two main things. First, is there a cognitive adaptation happening, meaning has the player thought through what this means to them? Second, is there success in execution or competence?"

Referring to our example of the wide-channel constraint, Todd first looks to see if the players recognize that using the wide channel to create scoring opportunities is an effective way of bypassing the opponent. Second, Todd looks to see if they are successfully able to execute creating crosses in wide areas and execute the crosses themselves.

Todd is keen to observe the mistakes the players make as well. "I don't just look at success in competencies as, 'Oh, they gave the ball away,' I am always looking for one of two things: Did they give the ball away because they had a great idea but poor technique? Or did they give the ball away because of a poor idea but great technique?" In other words, a player may make an overlapping run and cross the ball in, but his cross may be over everyone's head. So the cognitive element—his decision—was perfectly fine, but his execution let him down. Now, if we refer back to John Kessel's chapter, we need to look for the good mistake and the bad mistake, and correct from there. However, the player may also cross the ball with excellent technique, but he wasn't in the correct position, or crossed the ball at the wrong moment. "We are always observing to see if the player is struggling with a cognitive element or a competency."

The cognition of the players in Spain exceeds the players in other countries due to one big difference. "If you take the cognitive process—perceiving your environment, conceiving of your options, deciding on the correct option, and then adding some deception—most players that come from the United States do that *when* they get the ball. Most players in Spain, however, do that *before* they get the ball." Todd has seen players in the US with just as good—if not better—technique than players in Spain. The difference, once again, is one of cognition, not competence. "Before players in Spain even receive a ball, they have scanned where the defenders are, they have conceived of which options will be available to them when the ball does get to them, they have usually decided in advance, which allows them to add some deception to their execution, which is the final step in the process." In the United States and many other countries, the training process is intensely focused on the execution of the players. But that is the fifth step. Much more important are the four processes that occur prior to that execution and that is where Spanish culture has focused their training: on perception, conceiving, decision making, and deception. "We are so focused on execution in the States that we have isolated it, thinking it is enough when it just isn't enough. There are a lot of players that can kick a ball, pass a ball, and shoot a ball, but to do so with a capable speed of cognition? There are very few players. That is where we are missing the boat in the United States."

CHAPTER 29

POSITIONAL PLAY TRAINING

ADIN OSMANBASIC

Adin Osmanbasic is a tactical analyst for the German tactics website Spielverlagerung.com. He also served as a performance analyst for the Columbus Crew of Major League Soccer.

The essence of positional play — Finding the free man — Why do teams play a 1-4-3-3 — What happens after we find the free man — How to defend a Pep Guardiola team — The six areas of defensive organization — Why training with goals may be unnecessary — What Pep Guardiola and Antonio Conte have in common, and how they are different from Thomas Tuchel and Jurgen Klopp

It was nearly five years ago that a video posted on Metacafe.com—a website that pays homage to the early days of the internet—served as the catalyst that sparked a career in soccer analysis for Adin Osmanbasic. Since that time, Adin has become a successful analyst for the German soccer blog *Spielverlagerung* (tough to pronounce, but easily recognized as one of the best tactical analysis websites around). In addition, Adin has also written articles on Marti Perarnau's infamous blog *The Tactical Room*. Perarnau is most widely recognized as the author of two books chronicling Pep Guardiola's tenure at Bayern Munchen.

They say success breeds opportunity, and in 2016, Adin was offered a position as a performance analyst for the Columbus Crew. After one season of helping influence the playing style of one of MLS's most progressive teams, Adin took a step back to focus on his coaching while putting some of his analysis work to the side. However, he is still one of the foremost experts on tactical trends and strategies such as pressing, positional play, counter-pressing, and counter-attacking.

POSITIONAL PLAY FOR DUMMIES

Kieran Smith profoundly told me that in a four-hour presentation he could maybe cover 10% of all the conceptual nuances of positional play. Although his chapter delves deep into many of the concepts of positional play, Adin has developed a very simple way of explaining the essence of positional play. I believe it was Albert Einstein that said, "Things should be made simple, but not simpler." Adin's interpretation of positional play is simple, but not simpler. "Positional play, at its core, is about getting the ball toward the opponent's goal by passing through a free guy. The way that you make that free guy is by creating it through your positioning being better than the opponent." As mentioned in Kieran Smith's chapter, this free player is someone that has space and time to make their next action, hence why positional play is structured around finding the free man. If we are able to find the free man, then we can advance the ball closer to the opponent's goal. Eventually, as we get closer to the opponent's goal, we will find a free player that can make a shooting action and hopefully score.

The concept of the free player is one of the basic concepts of positional play, but it has its roots in the idea of creating triangles and diamonds. In fact, basic rondos serve the purpose of training positional concepts like creating the free player and achieving superiority. Let's explain the idea of finding the free player by taking two basic rondos as an example: a 3v1 and a 4v2.

The shape of the 3v1 in a rondo should create a triangle. Triangles are a preferred geometric shape in soccer because they create two passing options for the player on the ball. When playing against one defender—like a 3v1—it becomes impossible for the defender to take away both passing options, unless the attacking players have an incorrect shape. If the players can continually make triangles and passing lines between them and the ball, then in theory, they should never lose possession.

The shape of the 4v2 in a rondo should create a diamond. Diamonds are a preferred geometric shape in soccer because they create three passing options for the player on the ball. When playing against two defenders—like a 4v2—it becomes impossible for the defenders to take away all three passing options unless the attacking players fail to create the proper positioning. Again, if the team with the ball has correct positioning, they should never lose possession.

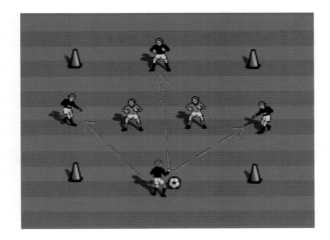

Both of these rondos are very simple and basic; however, their implications to the game and positional play are of immense importance. The basic idea of these rondos is that if a team creates the right positioning between them, they should always be able to find the free man (i.e., the player that has space and time to make their next action). So, when Adin defines positional play as finding the free guy by creating a positioning that is better than your opponents, this is exactly what he is talking about—but at the 11v11 scale. This is why many coaches that use positional play employ a 1-4-3-3 or a 1-3-4-3.

The advantage of the 1-4-3-3 or the 1-3-4-3 is that they make the creation of triangles and diamonds much easier due to the starting position of each player. These geometric shapes allow teams like Barcelona to have an easier time finding the free player.

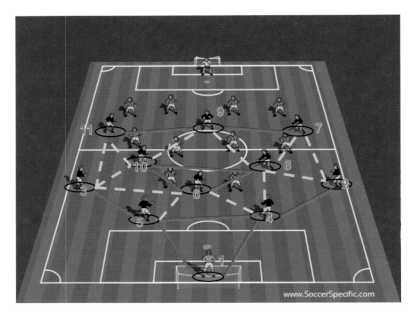

Source: www.google.com/url?sa=i&rct=j&q=&esrc=s&source=images&cd=&ved=0ahUKEwjXgNiAl cvWAhXBSyYKHQ89AfEQjhwIBQ&url=https%3A%2F%2Fwww.si.com%2Fplanet-futbol%2F2015 %2F02%2F23%2Fbarcelona-tactics-luis-enrique-lionel-messi-champions-league&psig=AFQjCNH -fPy_cx136QM_48lS4gYlgnqzzw&ust=.

Adin does pose a word of caution before coaches start adopting a specific formation and claim they are using positional play. "Developing free guys in the opponent's shape is not specifically about what formation you have. It's more about the details of how your players move and how you coach them to move. The goal is for them to move themselves into a position that creates passing lanes between them and the ball." The coaching of the movements that you want from your players is much more important in achieving free players than any specific formation. This is why coaches like Pep Guardiola have referred to formations as "nothing more than phone numbers." Although that is a little hyperbolic, the movements and positioning that you teach your players to have is much more influential in aiding their ability to achieve a free player than their starting formation.

Adin understands that there are many ways to coach your players to move. In fact, two teams that currently use a version of positional play are Antonio Conte's Chelsea and Pep Guardiola's Manchester City. However, each coach finds the free player through the use of different movements and positioning. Therefore, coaches shouldn't marry themselves to one particular way of movement or positioning, but general concepts. "The general idea is to disorganize your opponent so you can have a guy that has more space and time, and there are a ton of ways to do that." For example, the action of dribbling the ball can cause the opponent to press out of their defensive shape, which can create a free player. This movement can be coached and encouraged regardless of the team's system. Here is an example of how a dribble can create a free player from a 2017 match between Feyenoord and Excelsior.

In this game, the right winger from Feyenoord (in red) received the ball on the right sideline before dribbling centrally. This caused the left back from Excelsior (#23) and the holding midfielder from Excelsior (#8) to press the right midfielder. The attacking midfield player for Feyenoord (#10) now became the free man in the space behind the pressing players from Excelsior. As Adin puts it, "a dribble can attract more opponents than just one," which can free up a teammate.

Another movement that can be used to disorganize the opponent is the use of the false fullback that defined a lot of Guardiola's early positional movements at Manchester City. The false fullback is the movement of the fullback from a wide position into a central position to disorganize the opponent and improve the chances of creating a free player. Along these same lines, the false #9 is another movement made famous by Pep Guardiola and Lionel Messi that employs the #9 as more of an attacking midfielder that drifts off of the opposing center backs to find the ball with space and time behind the opposition's midfield. The winger's move inside to occupy the center backs creates the space and time necessary for the #9—employed here as more of a central midfielder—to be free. The principle to take away from all of these potential movements is that they are trying to accomplish the same outcome: disorganizing the opponent to find a free player. This idea is more important than any particular movement in and of itself.

One of the difficulties a coach will face in training positional play is that many players have an innate desire to constantly move to find the ball. However, this often means that they move from a position behind the opposition to a position in front of the opposition. This used to be one of the biggest questions I had as a coach—in fact, my players would often ask me, "When is it okay for us to move from behind the opponent [because they can't find the ball] to a position in front of the ball so we can get on it?" If you have a creative player that can help your team break through the opponent's defensive shape more easily, then you may allow them to do so. Therefore, instead of having to recirculate the ball in the hopes of finding a free player behind lines, a player—like a Messi—can drop out of the opponent's shape and create a free player by dribbling and drawing pressure or playing a difficult pass through the opposing lines that other players on your team can't play. Examples of coaches that allow players to drop out of the opponent's shape to get on the ball include Mourinho with Wayne Rooney and Luis Enrique—or any Barcelona coach during the Messi era—with Lionel Messi. "They allow players like Messi to get on the ball and either play long diagonal balls to bypass the opponent's defensive organization, or they may start using their dribbling ability to penetrate." The important thing to remember when deciding if you should allow certain players to drop out of the opponent's shape is that the players must be capable of actually helping your team get past lines of the opposition. "You don't want someone dropping out and then they can't actually offer your team anything in terms of helping you get through the lines because now you just lost a presence between the opponent's lines."

Some coaches—like Guardiola and Paco Jemez—hold a stricter philosophy. Players are asked to stay positioned between the lines of opposition pressure unless there is a specific cue. "Typically, you would want a player to stay between the lines unless there is too big of a space between the team, or the buildup players are under too much pressure, which would require players to drop out of the opposition's shape to give the buildup players an extra option, but it really depends on the coach."

One of the biggest questions youth coaches have is whether they can teach positional play to their young players. Adin feels that positional play can be taught in a simple fashion and he has trained his U12s to understand some of the fundamental concepts of positioning. These concepts have included things like: making the pitch big by having players occupy spaces in width and in depth, keeping your positions and not running all over, always having two players in wide positions, making connections with your teammates, always trying to get closer to the opponent's goal, and other simple instructions that build a foundation of positional play.

In a recent session with his U12 boys' team in Atlanta, Georgia, Adin had a perfect moment to coach an aspect of positional play in a really simple way. Adin's team plays 8v8 due to their age and he chooses to employ them in a 1-3-3-1 formation. "We were playing a 6v3 positioning game with five players on the outside and one player in the middle playing against three opponents. The grid was probably 15 by 20 yards and I kept seeing the same thing over and over again. A player on the outside would get the ball and then the central midfielder would be uncomfortable receiving the ball between the three opponents, so he would drop out of his position between those players and move to a corner of the grid. Now the player on the ball is unable to pass the ball to the outside player on his right because the central player dropped into the right corner, effectively blocking his own teammate. This allowed me to teach them a principle of ours which is that we should never have two players in the same passing line." This happens quite often at the highest level as well. A central defender may be on the ball and looking for passing options, but his central midfielder and striker are in the same passing line, which makes it much easier to press. In this situation, the central defender only has one passing option, but if the central midfielder can move a little to the right or left, now the player on the ball has two passing options. What Adin was trying to teach his central midfielder was a simple principle: "to try and keep the most connections that you can with your teammates without blocking them."

Adin also taught and encouraged his central midfielder to be comfortable receiving between multiple players. "It's okay to receive and look for little spaces between multiple opponents because, even though it seems compact, once you receive it they will pressure you and now you can play to an open player because you attracted defenders." This translated nicely to the game on the weekend because the player that Adin focused on was employed as the only central midfield player. During the match, when the back three received the ball, this player was now holding his positioning instead of running toward the ball, which allowed him to receive with more space and time so he could turn and play passes in behind the opposition's defensive line. As Kieran Smith says, "Positioning over possession, every time."

This notion of positioning over possession has been the genesis of the marked fields we have seen adopted by most European clubs. These marked fields include specific grids and markings that help players understand where they should be positioned based on

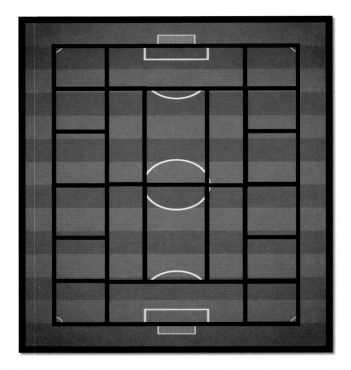

Source: spielverlagerung.com/2014/12/25/juego-de-posicion-under-pep-guardiola/.

the position of the ball. "The positional grids are generally used to teach the players how to keep their distance from one another and ensure they have adequate positioning on the field. These grids help teams understand that if they are at risk of losing possession from drawing the opponent to one side, they can trust that there are players on the other side maintaining their position."

An aspect of positional play that I still don't fully grasp is the understanding of what happens after we find the free player. For example, let's say that my team is in a 1-4-2-1-3 and we create our #10 as the free player behind the opposition's midfield but in front of the opposition back line—what happens now?

Adin believes that regardless of the structure or formation your team has, when you are able create that free player that has the ability to turn, certain things should happen. "What you want to provide for the player that can turn is as many options as you can in behind the opponent's back line.

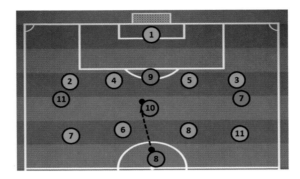

Here you see an example of the movements that could be made to give the player on the ball—the #10 in this scenario—as many options as possible in behind the opponent's back line. The wingers both sprint in between the fullbacks and center backs, which forces the fullbacks to drop back, creating more space for the player on the ball. The striker's movement—looking to receive between the center backs and behind the center backs—also forces the opponent's center backs to drop.

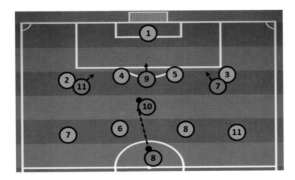

All of these movements create even more space and time for the player on the ball. However, if one of the defenders doesn't drop into a more compact structure, then that would be the pass the #10 would look to make. For example, if the right back (the #2 in this scenario) fails to drop, then the left winger (#11) is the free player that should be played.

There are priorities to this situation as well. According to Adin, you would ideally like for the player that has turned (#10) to have a shot on goal or, as a second priority, pass to someone that has a clear shot on goal. This ties in nicely with Jed Davies' analysis of the philosophy of Marcelo Bielsa. The first priority is to score, the second priority is to assist, and the third priority is to assist the assist. It is important that the coach doesn't teach his players to move according to the way he prefers. The identity of the players needs to be considered well before any ideal or preferred movements are taught. For example, if you force a player like Robben to play more inside as a winger, that would go against his identity as a dribbler who needs a lot of space by playing wider. "The strategy—and your specific positioning—depends a lot on your type of players, but also it can depend on the opponent."

HOW TO DEFEND A PEP GUARDIOLA SIDE

Throughout my conversation with Adin, I was reminded of the Einstein's quote: "Things should be made simple, but not simpler." I asked Adin how a team would combat a side like Guardiola's that is so well trained at positioning players between lines and finding free guys. His response was simply one word: compactness. Obviously, that is nothing new; compactness is a principle of defending, but it is one that is often neglected.

During an interview in his home, Johan Cruyff was asked about his defensive philosophy. He used the room they were sitting in to highlight the importance of compactness. "If I had to defend this entire room, then I would be the worst defender in the world. But if I only had to defend this little corner, then I would be the best." In other words, the smaller the pitch size when a team is defending, the easier it will be to defend. Adin has analyzed and determined the key concepts to create a compact defensive structure that would make even the best possession teams whimper. "The keys are to remain compact, have your lines shifting toward the ball, and have individual players block passing lanes into the players near the ball; the idea is to make the spaces tighter so that if the ball gets played within your shape, you have multiple teammates ready to attack the player on the ball." In other words, if a Pep Guardiola team is trying to create a free player with space and time, then the only chance a team has to successfully defend them is by eliminating space and time.

One of the biggest mistakes that compact defenses make is that they fail to create pressure on the ball carrier. If your team is compact and they shift to the ball together, but nobody puts pressure on the ball carrier, then the player on the ball will simply play into the space that your team has not occupied. Pressure on the ball is essential. "A lot of teams these days are compact and they are shifting, but when the ball gets played into their shape they fail to react and press with multiple players. That is another important concept. When the ball gets played into the player within your shape, you have to make sure multiple players close down the ball, not just one or two."

In the end, the type of the defending that a team employs really comes down to the coach's idea and what he wants to do in combination with information about the opponent and his own team. Adin has written extensively about defending and pressing in particular. All in all, there are six distinct areas that a team can defend in and each of those come with their own principles and reasons for choosing them.

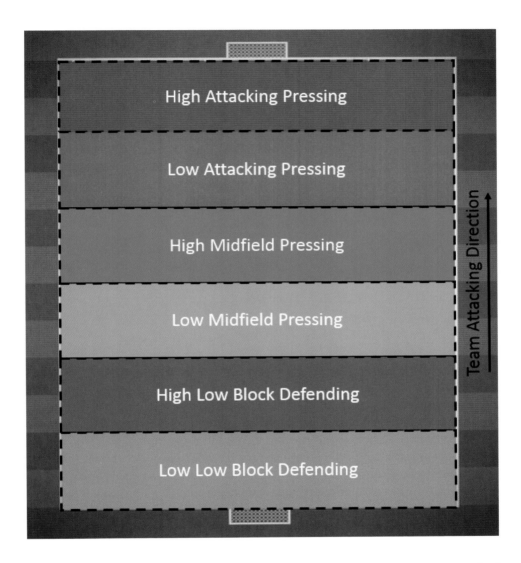

Adin breaks the field up into thirds: attacking, midfield, and defending. However, each of those thirds is then split in half to form six distinct areas of the field. A team can perform a high or low version of defending in each third, as characterized in the image to the left.

Adin has already mentioned the general principles that apply to defending in each area of the field. For a defensive organization to be successful—regardless of what area of the field they choose to defend in—they need to maintain the general concepts of defending. "General principles that apply to all of them are remaining compact, keeping a close distance between each player, shifting together toward the ball, applying pressure to the ball carrier, and pressuring anybody receiving inside your defensive shape." The reason these concepts apply to any defensive organization—regardless of the formation or chosen area of defending—is that a team that is compact has more defensive players available to make defensive actions like tackling or intercepting a pass. In addition, having your players closer to one another provides support for individual defensive actions so that if someone fails in making a tackle, there is another player available to make a subsequent action to prevent the opponent from progressing.

Typically, a coach will want his teams to embody all these defensive concepts regardless of his intended formation or chosen area of defending. So how does a coach decide if his team should high high press, or defend in a high low block? That question has multiple criteria that influence the answer ranging from things like the style of the opponent, the positioning of the team in the league, the player personnel you have available, and the fatigue level of the players. The general concept to understand is that the higher up that you choose to organize your team defensively, the greater chance you have of winning the ball closer to the goal you are attacking. However, you are also giving up a lot of space in behind your team, which can cause problems if your team cannot gain access to pressure, or if you have players not equipped to win head balls or duels on the back line. The lower you choose to organize your team defensively, the less space you will give the opponent to play into. This is why you see a lot of teams in relegation battles choose to set up in a low block. A low block forces the opponent to be really good in possession to be able to play through the shape of your team. Most teams fail to be patient enough when playing against low-block defenses which leads to them forcing passes into a low-block defensive shape. This, in turn, creates a lot of counter-attacking opportunities. The downfall of a low-block defensive organization is that upon winning possession, it can be very difficult to get your team up the field quickly to take advantage of the opponent's lack of defensive organization. A midfield-oriented defensive organization generally splits the difference between the two extremes of high attacking pressing and low block defending. A coach really needs to understand his team, player personnel, opponent, position in the league table, the way he wants to attack, and a multitude of other factors before deciding where he wants to position his team to be successful in defending.

It is also vital to consider your team's ability to gain access to pressure. Like Adin mentioned, if your team is compact but fails to gain access to pressure the ball carrier, then you are essentially clumping your team into a small area of the field, making it easy for the opponent to play over or around your team's shape. Therefore, a well-organized defensive team will constantly be aware of their ability to gain access to pressure the opponent. "When you don't have pressure on the ball—or can't get pressure on the ball—the general principle is to drop off and lessen the space in behind so that there is less space for the opponent to play in behind your defense. If a team cannot maintain compactness and pressure on the ball, then they should drop off and wait for a moment to reorganize their positioning to be better equipped to force the opponent back toward their own goal through pressure and compactness."

IS TRAINING WITH GOALS NECESSARY?

Adin's analysis has shown him that soccer really comes down to a team's ability to progress the ball through zones. Teams try to progress the ball through zones of the field using movement of the ball and the player's subsequent movement in relation to the ball. Therefore, Adin posed an interesting question: if soccer is mostly about progressing through zones, then is training with goals really necessary? If you have your team play a 5v5 small-sided game, is it realistic to have them shooting the ball from 15 yards out with five defenders still in front of them? Not to mention the fact that they are only 15 yards from their own goalkeeper... Should small-sided games be relegated to mostly end-zone games, or goals on only one end of the field?

It is an interesting thought and Adin isn't making a statement of fact as much as he is seeking to climb a philosophical ladder of soccer. "I really don't think it is absolutely necessary to train with goals all of the time." Many may argue that finishing on goal is the most difficult part of the game, so we should always train with the goals, but that argument really doesn't hold up when scrutinized. "If you look objectively at the game of soccer, you will see that 99% of the game is getting the ball through space to get close enough to the opposing goal to have the opportunity to make the final action of shooting on goal. But the actual shooting on goal is not the most important part of that entire sequence of events." Of course, in a sense, it is the most important part of that sequence because it results in a goal, but that moment doesn't occur spontaneously. In fact, the shooting action doesn't happen without the complex movements, actions, and decisions that occur before it that move the ball and the team into a position close enough to the goal with the smallest amount of interference from the opposition to be able to achieve the shot on goal. "It's not the most heavily weighted concept of the game. The majority of the game is playing through spaces to move closer to the opponent goal."

With this in mind, Adin prefers training exercises that utilize end zones or target players in order to focus on the most important aspect of the game—moving the ball through space. "You don't always need to have goals. I prefer possession games that put the players inside a certain grid in order to emphasize moving the ball through space and supporting each other through angles. Training how to support your teammates and move through space is much more influential in making them better players because those actions are happening far more frequently in the game than finishing on goal." Adin believes that training with goals can be detrimental to training certain aspects of the game, especially positioning, playing through pressure, supporting your teammates, and playing through space. "Goals can decrease the number of times these aspects actually happen in a specific exercise because the players will be shooting more often or losing the ball more often due to specific actions that are influenced by the goal." Training without goals means that the coach should be emphasizing how to actually *get to* the goal, instead of training how to finish on goal. Training with goals may be better used for sessions dedicated to finishing the play after your team has progressed the ball through specific zones.

Adin writes a lot of tactical theory articles for the popular German blog *Spielverlagerung*, and this is exactly what this is—theory. Adin isn't saying that training with goals is useless—although their relevance in specific exercises is definitely being questioned—but what is really important for the coach to understand is knowing *why* you are or aren't using goals. In fact, any simplification of the game—a small-sided game, positional game, or even a rondo—lacks some realism to the actual game. Anytime we aren't playing 11v11—or 9v9 or whatever it might be depending on the age group—there are aspects of the training exercise that lack realism: pitch size, number of players, duration, size of goals, and so on. Therefore, the bigger point that Adin is making is that coaches need to decide what they are willing to compromise between realism and the intended training effect.

If we are talking about a session dedicated to improving our team's ability to play through the midfield, then yes, it may be detrimental to the training effect to include goals because the goals will end a lot of actions quicker due to the players' increased propensity to shoot. However, if that game includes end zones or targets, the players can focus specifically on playing through zones—and the coach will have to live with the fact that training without goals is also unrealistic. "As a coach, you have to decide what aspect of the training exercise you are going to deal with in order to garner the training effect you want." So a 5v5 small-sided game with big goals may allow players to shoot in situations that they normally wouldn't—which is unrealistic—but there might be a certain purpose of that game. "The coach may want to train them from a fitness standpoint and playing with big goals may overload the players' ability to apply pressure on the ball. This would also result in a lot of actions per minute—namely an increase in passing, shooting, pressing, and dribbling—that the coach would like to overload from a fitness standpoint. It really depends what the coach wants from the exercise."

ALTERNATIVES TO POSITIONAL PLAY

Barcelona's growth under Johan Cruyff—and continued evolution under Pep Guardiola—propelled the philosophy of soccer known in Spain as *juego de posición*, or positional play to the masses. However, its growth and popularity got Adin and myself discussing what alternatives are available. There isn't a name for alternative styles of play, so what is it called when you aren't using positional play? There are clearly alternatives, but what are they?

For Adin, there are countless example of teams—Atletico, Napoli, and Red Bull Leipzig to name a few—that employ alternatives to the sacred position play. "Red Bull are less positional, in terms of occupying spaces across the entire field, and they have more of a focus on putting four or five players directly in the center of the field and using short passes and combination play to penetrate through the opponent centrally. Atletico is another one that tries to create overloads on the wings to create crosses into their strikers. It's not always about being spaced out over the entire field and passing to each point to try and get in behind the opponent. It is entirely possible to have four or five players in one specific area—like the wing or the center—where you are trying to play through it with tighter combinations and intense pressing after losing possession because you have so many players in that area." This helps us to understand that how a team chooses to organize their attack influences how they choose to organize their defense, and vice-versa. Pep Guardiola's teams—employers of a positional style of play—tend to rely on more narrow defensive structures to prevent counter-attacks and counteract the big shape of their attacking organization. However, teams that use a narrower spacing or organization in the attack can afford to have their fullbacks overlap and push higher up the field because the narrow shape of their strikers and midfielders will allow them to press more easily.

Maurizio Sarri's 2016-2017 Napoli team is an example of a team that utilized a more tight, narrow, and combinational type of attacking organization that equipped them with the ability to play through pressure with short passes, layoffs, and passes into depth. The narrow structure creates a close proximity between the players on offense, allowing them to press immediately upon losing possession of the ball because they have so many players around the ball. "It's not always about keeping everyone's position and playing to each specific position that is rationally occupied across the field. It can be mixed with things like central combinations, wing combinations, and things like that."

Adin isn't entirely sure that Pep Guardiola's style of play can even be considered an attacking style of play. "Team's like Guardiola's or Conte's are teams that have a defensive structure with the ball, and they try to play offensively through that." The purpose of this way of organizing your team is that it puts your players into positions during the offensive phase that make it nearly impossible for the other team to counter-attack once possession is lost. "That is because they have positioned themselves in a way to be safe when they lose the ball." This is why Adin argues that managers like Conte, Guardiola, and even Zidane don't truly have an offensive intent in organizing their team; in fact, they are probably thinking more about defending than they are attacking.

Conte's 2016-2017 Chelsea team played a 1-3-4-2-1 with defending in mind. The three center backs and two holding midfielders are always set to defend transitions. In attack, the two wingbacks are allowed to move up the field for crosses, which places Hazard, Willian, or Pedro in the pockets of space created by Costa. "But that isn't really committing a lot of players to attack. It is more positioning the players in specific ways and with specific distances in order to prevent transitions and, subsequently, relying on the individual quality of the players to create goal-scoring opportunities while ensuring that you are always safe from the counter-attack." The idea here is to build through the opponent's lines to be able to put them into a low block and keep them there through constant pressing. This may not be the most efficient way to organize the attack—you would be attacking with fewer players, more crossing, and longer-range shooting—but your team will never get counter-attacked because the focus is on controlling the transitions.

On the other hand, teams like Napoli and Red Bull and managers like Jurgen Klopp and Thomas Tuchel, have a much more attacking-oriented structure with the ball. "There are more players in offensive and central zones, and much more combination play through the center." This style of play makes it more difficult to defend the transitions, but it creates a much more efficient attack with more efficient and clear goal-scoring chances. These teams are characterized by an offensive formation for defensive purposes, while a Guardiola or Conte team would be a more defensive organization for offensive purposes.

A team like Red Bull will organize four or five players in the same central zone with the intent of playing very risky vertical passes. Therefore, they are organized in an offensive way, but they know there is a high chance of those passes being intercepted or not completed. So Red Bull are trying to create chances through the use of vertical combination play, but that is not their most often used method of chance creation. The defensive purpose of this structure comes into play when they lose possession. "They know they have a high chance of losing possession with these risky vertical passes, but by organizing multiple players in one small area of the field, they can easily press the ball to win it back and then create a chance off of their pressing." Hence, it is an offensive structure for defensive purposes.

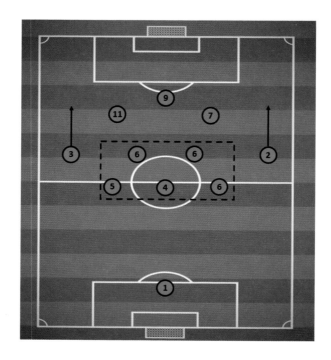

CHAPTER 30

COACHING AUTHENTICALLY

ANSON DORRANCE

Anson Dorrance is one of the most iconic coaches in the history of global soccer. He led the US Women's National Team to World Cup victory in 1991, and has won 22 national championships at the University of North Carolina-Chapel Hill.

Coaching is a thankless profession — Most people think they are competitive, but I am here to tell them that they aren't — The misapplication of the competitive cauldron — Rules were meant to be broken — Why we are all wrong about substitution

I first met Anson Dorrance at a coaching course that took place in Rotterdam, Netherlands at the Feyenoord Academy. The course was a grueling week of education, instruction, and feedback on our coaching sessions, abilities, and ideas implemented with the U19 academy team. I was one of the youngest coaches in attendance, but not the most inquisitive or curious. In fact, the person asking the most questions was a 66-year-old legend that had a World Cup and 22 national titles in his trophy room. But, as you may have already guessed, that is what makes Anson the best women's soccer coach in history and one of the best the sport has seen. Anson reads almost nonstop, and his voraciousness to learn and consume information and ideas, combined with his experience, culminate in a man filled to the brim with wisdom.

WHAT IS A COACH?

I say it almost every day, but coaching is a thankless profession. Lose, and everyone assumes you are an incompetent moron that doesn't know the first thing about your profession. Win, and everyone agrees that if it weren't for the unbelievable players you had, you would be nothing and no one. That is exactly why a common theme in this book has been the battle between process and outcome. Coaches that measure themselves by their results will certainly not be coaching for very long, but coaches that can achieve enlightenment and realize that it is about much more than winning a game—those are the coaches that become great.

You would think that a coach like Anson, with more national championships than his players have years on this planet, would define his job purely as to win games. That isn't to say that Anson isn't competitive; in fact, Anson may be the most competitive person I have ever met. He is the type of guy that might race you to the elevator without you even knowing you were in a race. But Anson has developed enough wisdom to know that coaching is about others. "A coach is someone that—through the development of some sort of environment—is able to transform someone to a higher level. We try to determine the different elements that we could add or change that might help an individual improve. So really, the coach's role is to figure out what he can say, or what he can encourage someone to do to be transformed." Defined this way, we can throw away any images or daydreams we might have of us holding a trophy above our heads as we are carried on the shoulders of our players. Coaching is all about getting the most out of someone else because it is what *they* want, not what you want. The best part about winning 22 national titles for Anson? "Watching the players celebrate that accomplishment with one another."

Jim Radcliffe has been the head strength and conditioning coach at the University of Oregon for nearly 35 years. I have had the pleasure of meeting him briefly and hearing him speak. He is the epitome of a coach. They say that a picture is worth a thousand words and this picture of him after Oregon qualified for the NCAA College Football playoffs explains everything you need to know about coaching.

The coach isn't the star—although not every coach feels that way. But rest assured that the best coaches—the ones that have fulfilling lives away from the field—are the ones like Anson and Jim that put everything into perspective. Simply put, it's all about the athletes.

Coaching hasn't always been viewed in this way, of course. Anson has been coaching long enough that he has seen the evolution of a coach from the stoic dictator to the compassionate communicator. "It used to be that the coach felt he had all this extraordinary knowledge that he wanted to impart to the athlete and the way he

Photo by Jason Quick.

accomplished that was by driving it into the athletes' skulls with a nail." However, those days are gone, or at least they should be. The coach is no longer driving information into their players forcibly, but delicately. "Today, the coach has to convince the player that this is the way to do something and they need to persuade the athlete that the coach's ideas are going to make them more effective." The days of the aggressive, authoritarian coach are long gone. Today's players need to know why you want them to do something, which is why the image of the modern coach looks a lot more like Brad Stevens, the young coach of the Boston Celtics, and Julian Nagelsman, the 29-year-old head coach of Hoffenheim—coaches that understand that telling their players *what to do* pales, in comparative importance to explaining to them *why to do it*.

Anson believes that the modern coach looks deeper than just the way they deliver information. "Perhaps the most important thing is the connection that they have with each player. Do they get to know the player away from the field? Are they involved with their actual lives? Even the classical disciplinarians like Alex Ferguson knew how important it was to connect with their players and treat them well away from the field." However, Anson is not saying that every coach should try to be like Alex Ferguson or Brad Stevens.

Finding out what kind of coach you are is the same process as finding out what kind of person you are. Are you caring, compassionate, and kind in your everyday life? Then why would you try to be someone else? "Coaches need to understand their own personality and what they value, and then build their coaching identity based on those characteristics. What are you good at doing? What are you comfortable doing?" There is no bigger fallacy in coaching education than the idea that you need to have the personality of a coach like Pep Guardiola or Jose Mourinho in order to be successful. The truth is that those guys are successful because they are wholly—and unapologetically—themselves. Their secret is that they are authentic, and they don't apologize for it.

Anson has learned that the other thing a coach needs to consider is the personality of the individual that they are coaching. Do not misinterpret his advice to be yourself as an indication that you should coach every single individual in the same fashion. "There isn't a line drawn in the sand where you say, 'Okay, this is going to be my consistent behavior with everyone from now on,' you have to understand that just like coaches are different, so too is every single athlete. Because they are different, some athletes need to be *led* differently." You still have to be yourself, but just like you may talk to your mom differently than your best friend, you apply varying masks of your personality to varying circumstances. "The evolution of a great coach is when they start to understand what button they need to push with each player, but with the understanding that all of the buttons are different. If they push a specific button and it doesn't work, then they need to be able to find a different button in order to coach effectively."

The art of coaching is the ability to keep trying different buttons until you find one that works. That creates what we like to call experience. Based on this experience, the coach is better equipped to coach that specific type of athlete. Anson has been coaching for so long and with so many different types of players that he has developed an expertise in what aspects of his coaching personality apply to the various player personalities. "Some coaches say 'I am going to be like this all the time and I am going to have a consistent idea of doing this,' but I don't think that really works. I think the coaches with a high emotional intelligence are going to sort out what will work for each individual player." There isn't any specific formula or secret alchemy, just the coach being himself and reading the personality of the player he is trying to impact.

THE MISINTERPRETATION OF THE COMPETITIVE CAULDRON

The idea that Anson is arguably most famous for is the idea of the competitive cauldron. Anson has already written about this extensively in his books, so I will not cover the cauldron in detail here. Basically, the competitive cauldron is Anson's way of making everything within his team competitive. From the warm-up, to small-sided training games, to fitness tests, and actual competition, Anson awarded points for everything and kept track of the accumulated points of each player outside of the locker room. This served two purposes. First, it taught the players about the importance of competitiveness and added motivation to everything that they did, even the little things like the warm-up. Second, it helped Anson and his coaching staff determine who was actually performing, winning, and succeeding day-in and day-out. This information made it easy to explain to players why they weren't starting or traveling.

The publication of Anson's competitive cauldron in his books timed nicely with the success and dominance of his UNC women's team and the US Women's National Team World Cup win in 1991. However, Anson says that the competitive cauldron has become one of the most misunderstood and misappropriated concepts across world sports. This misappropriation—or misapplication—of the cauldron stems from Anson's advice about coaches being their true, authentic selves and not someone else. Anson designed his program around Anson and his players—that's it. Anson didn't sit in his office one day and make up the competitive cauldron because he thought it might be a great idea; he values competition, so he designed his program around that value. The cauldron was a mnemonic afterthought.

Anson travels the world speaking to coaches, administrators, and directors across all sports, levels, and leagues, and by far the most frequent question he gets is about the cauldron. Anson is often perplexed as to why he gets asked so much about the cauldron because it is such a simple idea. "The idea is that you basically keep score in everything. You rank players as to how they have done on everything, you create a couple different competitive categories, and in the end, you are just trying to create competition in practice." However, the issue with the cauldron is that coaches across the world—and across nearly every sport—have adopted the cauldron with mixed success. The cauldron is very comfortable for Anson to coach because of who he is. "The way I have designed my own program at UNC is by designing a program that I, myself, would love to play in." The cauldron has been successful at UNC under Anson because it is an authentic manifestation of Anson himself. Anson is competitive to his core and the players can see that. It refers back to Anson's advice about coaches finding their personality. The takeaway is that if you aren't a naturally competitive person, then the competitive cauldron will not come across as authentic or natural, and eventually you will scrap it as a staple of your program. "For a coach that's not naturally as competitive as I am, the competitive cauldron is not going to be something they are going to feel comfortable with. They can't just go all in with my ideas because my ideas come right out of my personality and every coach should try to coach through their own personality." If you adopt the competitive cauldron because you heard that it worked for Anson Dorrance, then you *didn't learn* from Anson. If you really want to learn from Anson, then find values that are wholly and uniquely you, and build your program around them. "All of us have to coach through our own personalities and what we genuinely believe is the aspect of the game that we cherish and value the most. That should be the platform of their expression."

PRINCIPLES VERSUS RULES

I had the good fortune of attending a presentation where a high school coach out of California, Clay Erro, was presenting on culture. His presentation started with a simple maxim: *Rules were meant to be broken.* Clay explained that too many teams have rules, but rules were meant to be broken and they *will* be broken.

Anson hates rules, not just as a coach, but as an individual. "I don't have any rules in my program because I don't like rules myself. I am insulted when I am in an environment with a lot of rules because rules are an insult to my morality and my intelligence." For Anson, rules seem to imply that he doesn't have a sensibility or moral code to be able to make intelligent decisions. "Rules about being on time, drinking, or curfew—they absolutely drive me crazy because I would like to be treated as an adult." Anson built his program with the vision of building an environment that he would enjoy playing in. Anson doesn't enjoy rules and he would prefer to be treated like an adult, which means that is how he treats his players—like adults.

Instead of rules, Clay Erro had what he called *instructions* for his team. Clay referenced building a table from IKEA: you follow the instructions to get to the end and accomplish what you set out to. In a similar light, that is how he viewed team culture. He explained to his team that if we follow these instructions—of which there were only four—then we will build our table, metaphorically speaking. Anson uses what he calls *principles* and *core values.* "These give our players *ideas* on the correct behavior, but then I want them to make the *choice* to do the right thing." The *choice* is the key. Anson is not just developing players; he is developing people. He explained to me that he wouldn't be doing his job as a coach if he gave his players a bunch of rules to follow and handicapped their ability to make their own decisions because "in the real world, these players will have to make real decisions about going to bed early so they have energy for their meeting in the morning, about staying at the office late to finish a project, about eating healthy, or going to the gym, and if I don't set them up for that during their time with me, then I am setting them up to fail in the *real world.*" Rules don't require thought, but life does.

EPILOGUE: YOU

"If I have seen a little further, it is by standing on the shoulder of giants."

—Isaac Newton

In *Pep Guardiola: The Evolution,* Pep Guardiola pays homage to what he terms his footballing fathers. He is referring to the history of soccer and those that came before him. The history of our great sport is characterized by the mentor-apprentice relationship. The knowledge of those that come before us is passed down from mentor to apprentice and coach to player. The players are the future coaches of tomorrow, so we need to prepare them as such. Jimmy Hogan influenced Josef Blum, who worked with Karl Humenberger, who taught Michels, who taught Cruyff, who taught Guardiola, who taught Xavi Hernandez and Xabi Alonso.

As you can see, it is the generosity of those that have come before us and their willingness to share their knowledge and insights that have created a platform for soccer innovation to occur.

And now, here you are. You have just gained the wisdom and insights from over 30 coaches across the globe working in all aspects of the game. From the tops of the Premier League to the trenches of grassroots soccer and everywhere in between, you are now equipped to stand on the shoulders of these giants. That doesn't mean that you have to be just like them, or agree with everything they believe—in fact, that would be the opposite of standing on their shoulders. Don't write down or remember what they literally said. Think more about what it triggers in your thinking. What can you add to their thoughts? What can you improve in their methods? To stand on the shoulders of these great coaches means to innovate, to invent, and to initiate the next progression of this beautiful game. It is your mission to take the art and science of this great craft we call coaching to its next unknowable and uncertain frontier. My hope is that these coaches have educated you, of course, but more than anything I hope they have *inspired* you to take their ideas and make them better and more effective.

Prussian statesman Otto Von Bismarck once said, "Fools learn from experience. I prefer to learn from the experience of others." The best thing about books is that they allow you to absorb the accumulated thoughts of someone else's entire life. All of Todd Beane's experiences with Johan Cruyff are now yours. Anson Dorrance's carefully curated thoughts on winning 22 national championships are now yours. Rene Meulensteen's thoughts on player development are now yours. But the question facing you now is: *What are you going to do with them?*

> *"And in the end, the students' achievements far surpass those of their mentors for the simple fact that they've been carried upon the shoulders of giants..."*

> —*Marti Perarnau*

CREDITS

DESIGN AND LAYOUT

Cover Design: Katerina Georgieva and Annika Naas
Interior Design: Annika Naas
Layout: Amnet

EDITORIAL

Managing Editor: Elizabeth Evans
Copyeditor: Anne Rumery

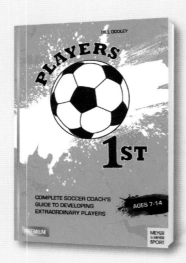

FROM MEYER & MEYER

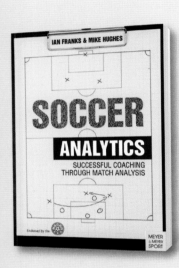

Ian Franks & Mike Hughes

SOCCER ANALYTICS

SUCCESSFUL COACHING THROUGH
MATCH ANALYSIS

Match analysis in soccer has become increasingly important. Nowadays, no professional soccer club plays a single match without having analyzed their own and their opponents' matches to find the best possible match plan and maximize their success. This book explores soccer analyses and uses the results to develop realistic, progressive practices to improve the performance of the individual players and the team. In addition, the coach's behavior during practice and matches is analyzed. This helps evaluate different coaching practices to find your ideal coaching style. Any coach reading this book will find help in developing and improving their coaching as well as gain a better understanding of the science of soccer.

344 p.,color, paperback,
199 Illustrations
6.5" x 9.25"
ISBN: 9781782550815
$22.95 US

MEYER & MEYER Sport
Von-Coels-Str. 390
52080 Aachen
Germany

Phone   +49 02 41 - 9 58 10 - 13
Fax   +49 02 41 - 9 58 10 - 10
E-Mail   sales@m-m-sports.com
Website   www.m-m-sports.com

All books available as E-books.

**MEYER
& MEYER
SPORT**

"I have approximate answers, possible beliefs, and different degrees of certainty about different things, but I'm not absolutely sure of anything, and many things I don't know anything about."

—*Richard Feynman*

To all the coaches that are reluctant in their proclamations and doubtful in their certainty. Stay curious.

The Real Giants of Soccer Coaching

WITHDRAWN